The Psychology of
Ego-Involvements

The Psychology of Ego-Involvements

SOCIAL ATTITUDES
&
IDENTIFICATIONS

by

MUZAFER SHERIF

●

HADLEY CANTRIL

Princeton University

New York: JOHN WILEY & SONS, *Inc.*
London: CHAPMAN & HALL, *Limited*

PRINTED IN THE UNITED STATES OF AMERICA

PREFACE

In this book on the psychology of ego-involvements we are attacking a problem which it seems crucial to solve if we are ever to acquire a scientifically defensible account of man's relationship to the world around him with all its natural laws, its technological developments, and its social products.

Here we are only able to sketch in bold relief what appears to be the psychology of ego-involvements. Much more must be added later to complete the account. But, as we point out in the first chapter, it seems to us that the broad outline presented here will accommodate this further work without any major alterations.

Evidence from a wide variety of sources, including studies from the experimental laboratory, investigations of everyday life behavior, public-opinion surveys, observational studies of children and adolescents, sociological data, and field material of anthropologists and ethnologists, has almost fallen into place of its own accord. Although we have cited rather extensive references, our job has been more one of selection than accumulation of data: in nearly every chapter, we have had to satisfy ourselves with the inclusion of only a few of the many reports, observations, or experiments that might have been mentioned. Those who are familiar with the various areas we have touched on will know the vast literature it is possible to tap.

The bulk of chapters 2, 3, and 4 were first published in the *Psychological Review* in November 1945 and January 1946. These articles have been slightly elaborated here. The material is republished with the permission of the American Psychological Association. The writers acknowledge the permissions granted by the various publishers and authors for the quotations used. Great care has been taken in each instance to provide bibliographical references by means of which the reader can identify the author and publisher to whom credit is thereby given.

A State Department fellowship to Princeton University for

Sherif and a contribution from the Marshall Field Foundation to Princeton University, enabling Cantril to be relieved of some teaching duties and allowing us bibliographical and secretarial assistance, combined to make it possible for us to work closely together. We acknowledge this assistance most gratefully.

Carolyn Wood Sherif has worked with us since late 1945. She has greatly aided us in selecting some of the material and in preparing certain chapters.

We gratefully acknowledge the help of Drs. Harold and Mary Cover Jones of the Institute of Child Welfare of the University of California for allowing us to go over some of their unpublished material on adolescence.

We are indebted to Donald Stauffer and Whitney J. Oates of the Princeton faculty for their apt suggestions of certain of the literary passages cited in chapter 13. Mildred Strunk also assisted us in the selection of examples for this chapter.

Elizabeth V. Deyo has ably managed many of the details connected with our work and has prepared the manuscript for publication.

Dr. Herbert S. Langfeld made a number of editorial suggestions which improved the manuscript.

M. S.
H. C.

Princeton, N. J.
June 24, 1946.

CONTENTS

CHAPTER 1

INTRODUCTION

Among other problems brought into sharp focus by the impact of momentous events and changes are the problems of human beings themselves. A growing sense of dissatisfaction and disillusionment with things as they are today is causing many people to question traditional conceptions of "human nature" which have tended to be taken for granted. Many social scientists, who perhaps feel called upon even more than psychologists to give some explanation or to find some solution for things as they are, almost inevitably put forth, concoct, or rehash verdicts concerning human problems and the role the human factor plays in our complex world. Often some account of "human nature" is vigorously advocated as a premise with which to justify the perpetuation or acceptance of an existing set of human relationships in religious, social, or economic life.

And certain aspects of these accounts of "human nature" have important bearings on ego problems. Some people argue that human beings are self-seeking. Others deny it. Some maintain that man is endowed with a craving for power. Some find primarily in man's nature the elemental seeds of a need for outstripping others. There are those who assume that "human nature" is the source of all harmony and solidarity. Problems of "human nature," as related to war and peace, to egotism and altruism, to human self-centeredness or selflessness, are among the current topics of hot debate among a good many people within and without the psychological profession. Such issues touch closely on the facts that concern us in this book. They indicate that ego problems are matters of everyday life human relationships; that they are not mere academic topics to be discussed and argued by those who can afford the luxury of such an exclusive pastime.

The word "ego" is a much-abused word. It has long suffered

1

scientifically objectionable associations in religious, philosophical, ethical, and psychological writings. Because of this, it might have been safer to refer to the mass of material we are handling in this book by a new term. But psychology today seems to be overflowing with new terms, especially among those who write on topics concerning social psychology and who create concepts to suit their personal preferences. So we reluctantly chose to retain the word *ego*. But we have taken pains to use it only in factually demonstrable connections.

For there is great need for such a concept. The differential character of a tremendous number of reactions observed both in the laboratory and in everyday life must be designated by some such concept. The ego is inferred from behavior whether verbal or nonverbal. To be more specific, reactions are modified and altered to a greater or lesser degree when they are ego-involved. The ego, as we shall repeat time and time again, is not an entity. It is not fixed and immutable even after it is formed.

In the following chapters we have preferred to use as much as possible terms like "ego-involved reactions" instead of "ego." For expressions such as "ego-involvements" or "ego-involved reactions" are less tainted with the objectionable associations which "ego" has suffered historically in the substantive form. The expression "ego-involvements" and its derivatives have come into use in psychology during the past decade, chiefly in connection with experimental investigations or theories related to empirical evidence.

An innumerable wealth of hitherto disconnected observations and facts have all converged to compel us to formulate certain conclusions concerning the formation and functioning of a constellation in the psychological make-up of the individual which may be designated as the ego. There are observations on the genetic development of the integrated person, as well as on the varieties of disintegration and breakdown. There is a great mass of data on the effects of collective behavior. There is an impressive array of experimental facts obtained during the last ten years and concerned with the differential effects of ego-involvements.

The reason these scientifically collected data lend themselves so readily to a concise formulation is that they have their concrete counterparts in everyday life. They are so general that it took almost no effort on our part to find further verifying evidence from concrete human relationships and from the colorful expressions of personal relationships found in literary works. This converging of facts from so many different sources is, in a nutshell, the hypothesis the following chapters verify. Dogmatic statements presented as hypotheses here in the introduction will acquire substance or remain as mere idle intellectual chatter on the basis of the evidence we have tried to bring together in this volume.

The ego is not innate in the sense that certain other psychological functions, such as perception, are innate. Nor is ego-striving innate in the sense of an instinct, drive, or need such as the innate striving for food, water, or a sex object. There is no instinctive ego drive, no innate need for domination or submission, for succorance or idol worship. Nor is the ego a basic personality pattern, unique and unchangeable in the person. That constellation in the psychological make-up of the *human* adult which may be designated as the ego (or by any other convenient concept) is a genetic formation. The newborn infant, even though biologically integrated, has no ego. And no ego would develop in him through maturation if it were not for two facts. First, the fact that his psychological functioning—and *his alone* in the whole animal kingdom—can take place on a conceptual (symbolic) level. This enables him to grasp reciprocal relationships and to make effective use of the accumulation of diverse concepts and symbols. Second, once man is equipped biologically with the possibility of functioning psychologically on a conceptual level, he has to live in a lawfully ordered world of nature where social relationships and their products impose on him the necessity of regulating and adapting himself to lawful nature and to the established order of human relationships. Without these impositions, these restrictions, resistances, and rewards of nature and especially of the established social order surrounding him with its material and technological products, its institutions, its accumulated symbols, values, and norms, there would be no consistent and continuous ego formation in the individual.

This is substantiated by the fact that the egos of individual members of different social orders are shaped in their major features by the image of those social orders. History and ethnology convincingly show that these images may in some cases be diametrically opposite in character. In accounting for these diametrically opposite variations, descriptions of the ego in terms of instincts or needs with long and impressive lists of ego drives utterly fail. The logical argument to which instinctive ego drive theories must resort is to posit the existence of different human species at different times and in different places.

In brief, the ego consists of many attitudes which from infancy on are related to the delimited, differentiated and accumulating "I," "me," "mine" experiences. These attitudes, which may be designated as ego-attitudes, are constituent components of the ego. Apart from the constellation of these ego-attitudes, there is no such entity as the ego. In fact many attitudes are not discrete affairs in the psychological make-up of individuals. They are attitudes that define and qualify an individual's relative standing to other persons or to institutions in some more or less lasting way. They are attitudes that determine the more or less enduring character of one's personal identity with the values or norms incorporated in him. When these attitudes are situationally called for, when they are at any time consciously or unconsciously involved in a psychological function, we become personally involved. And when we do become personally involved, then our discrimination, judgment, perception, remembering, thinking, and explicit behavior are accordingly modified or altered.

Once formed, the ego is by no means rigid and unchangeable. To a large extent, ego-involvements are situationally determined. The same words of insult that may be gracefully swallowed in one situation may lead to violent exhibitionistic reactions in another. In certain cases the threshold of sensitivity of ego-involvements may be quite low, in other cases quite high, depending on the demands of the situation and the psychological condition of the individual. These thresholds of ego-involvement may be measured in an empirical way. Since attitudes, the constituents of the ego, are subject to change and transformation, the ego is also subject to change and transformation with changing situations of a major character. Such transformation can be clearly observed in the changing ego of the adolescent boy or girl, especially in times and in societies where social transition is rapid.

The psychology of the formation and functioning of ego-attitudes is governed essentially by the same principles as the general psychology of attitudes. The psychology of attitudes is, therefore, basic to the psychology of the ego. Consequently, we have had to deal first and at some length with the psychology of attitudes and carry the conclusions reached there to the treatment of ego-involvements. Characterized in broad outlines, an attitude is an established readiness which has a subject–object relationship of highly variable content, which is learned (formed), which has affective properties with various degrees of motivational components, which may refer to whatever stimuli are encompassed in the subject–object relationship, and which determines that an individual will react to a stimulus in a selective way. Once formed, an attitude serves as an anchorage to structure or modify subsequent experience or response.

This broad characterization of attitudes also holds basically true in the case of ego-attitudes. Many attitudes and especially ego-attitudes are formed in relation to and directed towards objects or persons that satisfy basic needs. Hence the affective and emotional halo of many ego-strivings that make an individual highly selective and highly self-centered—sometimes to the point of appearing deaf and blind to cues in objective situations—spring from such relationships. Many of the attitudes revealed in everyday life contacts define an individual's status for him in relation to other people. Many embody the values a person upholds for himself and regulate his claims and aspirations in relation to others. These ego-attitudes are therefore highly charged affective anchorages.

Every individual strives to place or to anchor himself as an acceptable member in his social milieu or in some social setting, whatever the particular criteria for acceptance by his group or his aspired group may be. This is true for any individual in any culture, whether highly competitive or highly co-operative, whether primitive or advanced. There is an unmistakable striving on the part of the individual *to belong* to his group or to some aspired group. Lack of social belongingness and conflicts in belongingness (marginality) are painful. Once the ego is formed to the degree of grasping reciprocal human relationships, this striving to anchor oneself becomes more compelling because of the emotionally charged character of ego-attitudes.

Yet mere acceptance of an individual by a group in his milieu or by some group he aspires to will not do forever. The mere sense of belongingness does not bring lasting satisfaction. A young man may aspire, as an ideal, to enter a certain college. But once he gets there, he acquires new ideas and tries to be somebody as prescribed by the hierarchical arrangement of social relationships in the college. A man may reach his ideal of belonging to some club. But after admission as a member, he may set his eyes on some position at the top of the club's social pyramid. In groups everywhere social life is necessarily hierarchical.

The striving for social acceptance and approval, which at times reaches intense proportions, does not have to be attributed to the urges and stresses of some special instinct. All attitudes function in well-formed frames, in referential settings. If the situation does not produce its appropriate frame in an individual, he tends consciously or unconsciously to structure the situation, at least precariously, in a way determined by the stresses of his internal and internalized desires, deprivations, and anchorages. Experiences of ambiguity and confusion are tense and unpleasant. Relief from such experiences becomes even more imperative in connection with ego-attitudes, for these delimit and define one's sense of personal security. If ego-attitudes are experienced as relatively stable, then, psychologically, one's sense of status in relation to other persons, groups, or institutions is secure. At times, any status, any standing in a group is preferred to none, even though it may be felt as quite unsatisfactory by the individual himself. Many a person has preferred to sweat out his ego problems in a group rather than face ostracism or break away into uncertainty.

It seems plausible to us to regard individual differences of ego-striving as due to individual differences in glandular activity and other temperamental factors, to individual differences in the functioning of basic drives such as those for food and sex, and to individual differences in general physical vitality and intelligence. In addition to such basic individual differences, of course, favorable or adverse circumstances for the satisfaction of basic needs, or for the attainment of a secure position, further contribute to differential ego-strivings. There is no need to assume any differential ego instinct.

A conservative capitalist and a revolutionary communist may both defend their respective views with equal intensity. A Republican and a Democrat may fight one another tooth and nail over the Administration's foreign policy and may both be frustrated persons. The millions of people who followed Hitler were surely not all perverse psychotic creatures. The flourishing *post mortem* accounts which attribute fascist barbarism in Germany to the perverse complexes of Nazi leaders look ridiculous when one remembers the predictions and warnings made to the world in all earnestness in the early 1930's by those observers who took the situational determination of social movements seriously.

We are not arguing here that personality characteristics, individual frustrations, or elations are not important psychological facts. Far from it. We have to learn as much as we can about them. But we do maintain, on the basis of accumulating evidence in several fields, that, in dealing with the identifications, ego-involvements, and loyalties of individuals, the social psychologist (for these are social psychological problems) should start *first* by relating the individual to his reference and membership groups and then proceed to the finer details of personality problems. For an individual's identifications and ego-involvements, his more or less lasting loyalties, and the values he does so much to uphold as his own, have no meaning apart from his reference and membership groups. For the social psychologist, the fact that a person identifies himself with the Catholic Church or with a revolutionary party, or that he is a marginal man and hence has conflicting loyalties, is at least as important as a knowledge of his measurable or unique personality traits or of how his toilet habits were handled in infancy. Once a person is placed situationally in his group setting, then information concerning his personality characteristics will further help us account for the differential character of his reactions. These two approaches should not be regarded as a dichotomous antithesis but as different aspects of the work to be done if the picture of man's ego-strivings is to be complete.

In this volume we have tried to give only the broad outlines of the psychology of ego-involvements. It is, therefore, an incomplete treatment of the subject. The all important topics of motivation and personality must be considered in further work. Although incomplete, still, in our opinion, the main sketch of ego-involvements presented here will not have to be changed to any considerable degree when motivational and personality factors are brought into the picture. For the values one upholds as his personal values, the goals he sets for himself, do not function in a vacuum or in abstraction. These values and goals as well as all major ego-attitudes are formed in or in relation to social groups. Investigations of motivation, personality characteristics, or other differential qualities will more adequately account for an individual's particular reactions in interpersonal relationships and more accurately predict his ego-involvements in a given situation if he is studied first in relation to his reference and membership groups. It seems safe to say that apart from a person's reference of himself to such groups, he would not develop the consistent ego which defines his identity in a more or less continuous way from one day to the next.

CHAPTER 2

THE PROBLEM OF ATTITUDES: UNIFIED

During the past two decades the problem of attitudes has become central in social psychology. Thus, G. W. Allport writes:

> The concept of attitude is probably the most distinctive and indispensable concept in contemporary American social psychology. No other term appears more frequently in experimental and theoretical literature. [1, *798*] [1]

Murphy, Murphy, and Newcomb, in their monumental volume summarizing the state of social psychology in 1937, again emphasize the point:

> Perhaps no single concept within the whole realm of social psychology occupies a more nearly central position than that of attitudes. [19, *889*]

We need not multiply these representative statements from other sources to demonstrate the important position the concept of attitudes holds in contemporary social psychology.

The study of attitudes is by no means the concern of psychologists alone. It is significant that sociologists feel as much at home in the study of attitudes as do psychologists. Some sociologists have gone so far as to equate social psychology with the study of attitudes. [5, 11, 27] Attitudes became a focal problem in experimental psychology in the first decade of this century. As a consequence of the introspective analysis of the higher mental processes at Würzburg, descriptions were given in "attitudinal" terms such as *Einstellung* and *Bewusstseinlage*. [21, 30] With this prominent start in experimental psychology, attitudes came to stay as an important concept in that field.

In this book we are proceeding with the conviction that experi-

---

[1] Roman numbers inclosed in brackets indicate the references at the end of each chapter; italic numbers indicate page numbers in those references.

mental and social studies on attitudes have much to contribute to each other in bringing about a unified psychology of attitudes. The psychologist's task is to give an adequate account of the psychological mechanisms involved in the formation of an attitude in any individual. The formation of a *social* attitude in the individual should be essentially the same as the formation of any attitude if the explanation of this formation is to be psychology at all. We are here groping in this direction. As we shall see, attitude studies at present do not give us a unified picture. In fact the problem of attitudes is in a very confused state. Perhaps the confusion has increased in proportion to the wealth of literature: different investigators have had different interests and points of view in approaching the problem.

Attitudes in social life. When we look at any society, whether primitive or highly developed, whether simple or complicated, we observe conformities of behavior, *within the limits of variations due to individual differences,* on the part of the individual members of any society as they carry on the daily business of living— for example, in regulating instinctive activity, dress, likes or dislikes of other groups, or responses to events which have social significance. When analysis and explanation of these established conformities are carried to the psychological level, the problem becomes primarily one of the psychology of attitudes.[2]

We have used the term "established conformity" very deliberately. For these established conformities result from conformity to social standards or norms which have come into existence in a deterministic way as a consequence of the interaction of individuals in the all important business of living. Individual members within a society come to acquire these established conformities of experience and behavior within the limits of their individual differences.[3] We may, in fact, say in a summary way that the

[2] The question of whether or not the whole of social psychology consists of a psychology of attitudes is not our problem here. We may only say in passing that it is our opinion that social psychology does *not* consist only of the psychology of attitudes.

[3] Without the enormous temperamental differences between individuals being in any way ignored, a systematic awareness of the fact that temperamental differences always function within a given social context and set of norms would undercut and bring into proper perspective typologies such as those advanced by Jung, Spranger, and Sheldon, which attempt to explain social behavior by categorizing personality. [15, 22, 25]

socialization which occurs when an individual becomes a member of a group consists mainly in the achievement of conformity in experience and behavior to social values, standards, or norms already established. And the process of achieving conformity is, if we analyze it closely, nothing more nor less than the formation of appropriate attitudes in relation to these socially standardized values or norms or other criteria of conduct.

RECENT ATTITUDE STUDIES AND METHODOLOGICAL CONSIDERATIONS

The approach to the psychology of attitude has been many-sided. The early work of the Würzburg laboratory gave the historical setting to more recent work on *Aufgabe*. In 1918 Thomas and Znaniecki stimulated other sociologists to analyze the concept of attitude further as a useful tool in the explanation of the phenomena with which they dealt. The work of cultural anthropologists, such as Boas, Malinowski, and Sapir, and of many contemporary ethnologists highlights the variation in cultural norms and the consequent differences in the attitudes of individuals living under different social systems.

Investigators such as G. W. and F. H. Allport, Daniel Katz, Bain, Faris and Lasker concerned themselves with the genesis and nature of attitudes. F. H. Allport, Thurstone, Bogardus, Likert, Droba, and others worked out procedures for measuring attitudes. The attitudes of all kinds of people toward almost all conceivable subjects have by this time been measured. Quite recently, the interest in measuring attitudes has given way to the measurement of public opinion by the use of stratified samples of different populations. While the techniques for measuring attitudes and opinion can be usefully employed to gather valuable information on attitude determinants and properties, and while the data obtained from such measurement often have a high practical, strategic, or systematic value, the great bulk of quantitative research has been designed for the primary purpose of measurement alone, not systematic understanding.

Thomas and Znaniecki held that "every manifestation of conscious life, however simple or complex, general or particular, can be treated as an attitude." [27, 27] In a critical appraisal of their work, Blumer points out that this blanket use of the term attitude makes it "a kind of psychological catchall, since, as the authors state, it may refer to any psychological process, or item of consciousness. To take as a basic datum anything that includes such diverse things as appetites, conceptions, feelings, decisions, sensations, desires, ideas, and sentiments is to operate with a complicated and indefinite concept." [4, 24 f.] After an exhaustive review of the literature on the psychology of attitudes, Nelson reports his impression, shared by others, "of the wide variety of meanings which are ascribed to this term." [20] He cites 23 rather distinct characterizations given the term "attitude" by psychologists or social scientists up to 1939, ranging from "organic drives," "neural sets," or "trial responses," to "ways of conceiving objects," or sum totals of "inclinations, feelings, notions, ideas, fears, prejudices, threats, and convictions about any specific topic." In a recent paper concerned with the definition and use of "attitude" in social psychology, Strauss points out that "the concept, despite its key position, is marked by considerable confusion." [26, 329] He notes that much of the research on attitudes has little or nothing to do with attitude theory and that the use of attitude as a "common sense explanation" rather than as a "genuine causal explanation" [334] has retarded systematic understanding.

It is therefore not surprising that some strict experimentalists, dissatisfied with what they may regard as the "practical" or unsystematic nature of attitude research in social psychology, look down on it and on social psychology in general as having little to do with pure science. They may take it as an example of why the pure scientist must follow Titchener's dictum and stand "apart from the great majority of his fellow men," disavow interpretation as something entirely "foreign to him" and move "in the domain of bare existence." [28, 69 f.]

The laboratory and everyday life. Before proceeding with a discussion of the psychology of attitudes, it is necessary to clear up the relationship between pure experimental research and the systematic study of attitudes in everyday life situations. A psychological construct, if it is to prove valid and adequate, must be as valid and adequate in handling the stuff of ordinary human affairs as in handling the controlled variables of the laboratory experiment. Various writers have fallen into the error of making a distinction for one reason or another between "psychology" and "social psychology." Klineberg, for example, makes such a distinction "for purposes of convenience" [17, 4], and puts his emphasis on a demonstration of "the wealth of social patterning" rather than on the "constants of human behavior." [8]

Science consists of a set of conceptual constructs which have high predictive value. If a psychologist is to make any claims that will have scientific validity, he must obviously be as objective as possible. This does not mean, however, as Titchener believed, that a psychologist must be "disinterested and impersonal." The highbrow superciliousness of those who hold that a true "scientific" psychologist should not and cannot deal with the concrete realities of men in their social life comes from their confusion of the fact that scientific objectivity derives from its methods and not from the aloofness of its observers. [10]   William James long ago pointed out that psychology is scientific to the extent that it uses methods which make verification possible, irrespective of the theories, biases, or prejudices of the experimenter. "The most useful investigator, because the most sensitive observer," said James, "is always he whose eager interest in one side of the question is balanced by an equally keen nervousness lest he become deceived." [14, 21]

Since the scientist's objectivity derives from his methods rather than from his own interests or from the type of material with which he deals, and since the psychologist's goal is to understand the thought and behavior of men in real life situations, the scientific psychologist becomes obligated to formulate concepts that will stand up both in the laboratory and in everyday life. [7]   His task is, of course, particularly difficult since the determinants of thought and action in real life are so complicated, the context within which they function so varied and changing.

If the psychologist becomes fearful of the consequences of crossing a border line which he feels separates his scientific laboratory research from its application to real life problems, he should remember that the concepts of chemistry, physics, and biology have been developed by frequent crossing back and forth. Theoretical concepts arrived at in the laboratory have been tested for their adequacy in normal nonlaboratory contexts. In the history of the physical sciences, real life situations have forced modifications and revision and have stimulated further research which has produced more adequate constructs. Julian Huxley, for example, has pointed out the interdependence of application and theory in contributing to the advances of the physical sciences. [13] Giving examples of research on high voltage and its use in the transmission of electricity, he notes that "sometimes it is not very clear what is pure and what is applied, or in which direction the current is flowing."

Fortunately for psychology, most of those now working in the field are becoming increasingly aware of the challenge which the explanation of everyday life situations poses for them. We mention the problem here because it is essential to our argument that any final conceptualization of the nature of attitudes must make quite explicit the mutual dependence of data obtained from the laboratory and data obtained from real life situations. In other words, the nature of attitudes is not two problems—one for the laboratory and one for everyday life—but one single problem.

The concepts or variables thus formulated will eventually make it possible to construct a psychology of attitudes which can be used to study any kind of attitude, social or nonsocial, in this or any other social system. For in spite of cultural diversities, psychological laws ought to be the same for individuals in any social system. Otherwise, logically speaking, we should be arguing, even if we do not mean it, for some sort of "cultural racism," similar to biological racism. If psychological laws are not the same for all individuals, then the German *Kultur* apologists were right in arguing that the members of their unique *Kultur* could be understood, not explained, only by the peculiar logic of their *Kultur*.[4]

Evaluation of norms. We must make one more prefatory remark before discussing psychological concepts themselves: explain

---

[4] In the field of *anthropology* an adequate synthesis of the psychology of attitude should be a guide to more adequate generalizations on the anthropologist's own level. Anthropological concepts which try to fit cultures into types or which imply the uniqueness of cultures are for a psychologist quite incomprehensible. From our point of view, the derivatives of different economic and social organizations studied by the anthropologist are social norms and values which act as social stimuli and, as such, have characteristics important for the anthropologist and the social psychologist to study.

our position concerning the evaluation of standards, social values, or norms, since this position has important ideological implications. We repeat that standards, social values, and norms are the product of human interaction in the process of living. There is no finality about them. They are not absolute. In spite of their inertia after they once come into existence, and in spite of the efforts of those who for one reason or another are vitally interested in preserving the established order, we observe in the course of history that social standards, values, or norms do change as a consequence of new modes of human interaction brought about by changes in technological and economic conditions.

Any given individual is confronted with the social standards, values, or norms of his environment. In short, social norms are first external to the individual or on the stimulus side with respect to him. As such, social standards, values, or norms are first of all the data of the social sciences, not of psychology. Strictly speaking, then, the task of the psychologist is to study the formation of attitudes as a consequence of contact with these social norms through other individuals or groups or through various products of the social and economic environment. In spite of the diversity and variations of social standards, values, or norms in different societies, human beings do by and large form attitudes in conformity to their group.

The psychologist and the social scientist, however, cannot complacently stop at this point. They can go further and show the consequences of the experience and behavior which are regulated by attitudes developed and prescribed by existing social norms. On the basis of such studies, they can reach conclusions as to whether or not the attitudes formed are conducive to a harmonious and well-adjusted personality or to a contradictory and unadjusted personality, whether or not the attitudes formed bring about social solidarity or friction. In short, the psychologist and the social scientist can reach conclusions concerning the extent to which attitudes formed from prescribed social norms conform to or are contradictory to the objective conditions existing at any given period in a given social system.

Our present task. We have seen that in spite of the wealth of material in the field of attitudes, we still do not have a unified and established psychology of attitudes. The phenomena covered by the concept "attitude" vary to a large degree in their specificity and range. On the one hand we have strict experimental laboratory investigators interested in the attitude or set to a very limited and precise stimulus situation in a laboratory setup; on the other hand we find social psychologists and social scientists working on attitudes of individuals or groups to a whole nation or race, or to values and concepts which have wide extensions such as the concepts of fascism and democracy. It is no wonder, therefore, that investigators working on one level of generality often use concepts which have very little meaning or relevance for investigators working on a different level of generality.

It is our methodological conviction that attitudes in strict laboratory situations and attitudes in the most complicated social situation have, essentially, the same psychological mechanism at bottom, that the basic psychological substrata functioning in both instances are the same in nature. As a result of brilliant experiments still in progress on the relation of vision to human behavior, Adelbert Ames of the Dartmouth Eye Institute has concluded in a preliminary report that "The processes that underlie our perception of our immediate external world and those that underlie our perception of social relationships are fundamentally the same. The insights gained in the study of visual sensation can serve as indispensable leads to better understanding and more effective handling of the complexities of social relationships." [2, 7] This is, of course, not in the least a denial of the rich and complicated motivational, affective, and cognitive factors involved in social or interpersonal attitudes. But, in order to develop concepts which have scientific generality of the kind found in the natural sciences, we must give up the purely descriptive concepts used by social psychologists and sociologists and see what functional variables have been well established and verified in experimental psychology and other controlled investigation. Once equipped with these well-established variables or concepts, we can then proceed to see if we can extend these to the more complicated cases of attitudes which lead the individual to react in characteristic ways in actual social interaction.

Our specific task then becomes self-evident. We shall look for

the most essential criteria which can be detected in any attitude—
from the relatively simple case of the laboratory setup to the more
complicated situations in actual social life. We shall proceed with
a minimum of assumptions.

A Characterization of Attitudes [5]

Attitudes are among those components of the psychological
make-up of the individual which determine that he shall react,
not in a passive or neutral way, but in a selective and characteristic
way, especially in relation to certain specific stimulus situations.
Attitudes are not, of course, the only psychological components
or states that determine that an individual will react to the environment in a selective or characteristic way. When the individual
is hungry, thirsty, or sexually aroused, or in some other emotional
state, or has been recently stimulated by a functional change in
the receptor organ or in the organism at large, he reacts in selective or characteristic ways to the environment. Attitudes, then,
are *among* the various psychological factors which determine the
individual's selective reaction to his environment.

In all the representative definitions or characterizations of attitudes, one feature is common: that an attitude, whatever else it
may be, denotes a functional state of readiness which determines
the organism to react in a characteristic way to certain stimuli or
stimulus situations. A glance at some representative definitions
of attitudes, imposes on us the fact that their essential feature is a
functional state of readiness.

> The "attitude" is primarily a way of being "set" toward or against
> certain things. [Murphy and Murphy, 18]
>
> [Attitude] is readiness for attention, or action, of a definite sort.
> [Baldwin, 3]
>
> Attitude—the specific mental disposition toward an incoming (or
> arising) experience, whereby that experience is modified, or, a condi-
> tion of readiness for a certain type of activity; . . . [*Dictionary of
> Psychology,* Warren, 29]
>
> An attitude is a more or less permanently enduring state of readiness
> of mental organization which predisposes an individual to react in a

[5] This characterization follows that presented by Sherif in [23] and [24].

characteristic way to any object or situation with which it is related. [Cantril, 6]

After reviewing these and other representative characterizations of attitudes, G. W. Allport reaches the conclusion that "the essential feature of attitude" is "a preparation or *readiness* for response." Allport gives his own definition in which this functional state of readiness is essential:

> An attitude is a mental and neural state of readiness, organized through experience, exerting a directive or dynamic influence upon the individual's response to all objects and situations with which it is related. [1]

Whatever other features attitudes may have (and the features of attitudes do vary according to the degree of complexity), it is certain that all attitudes have a state of readiness in common. However, *every state of readiness of the organism is not an attitude*. There are numerous states of readiness which cannot be called attitudes. For example, a child of two or three is hardly ever neutral or passive to his environment. He is apt to be extremely partial one way or another to the things or persons surrounding him. He is constantly seeking all sorts of satisfaction. All these momentary tendencies imply states of readiness. But in spite of all this, we can hardly say that a child of three is full of attitudes. In fact he has very few (if any) established or stable attitudes. He may have developed some attitudes toward certain persons like his mother or certain objects such as types of food. But a child at this age will even react in a very negative way to his mother if she proves to be an obstacle in his effort to gain some satisfaction at the moment. We need not elaborate here other cases of readiness which cannot properly be labeled as attitudes.

We must conclude therefore that cases of readiness are not exhausted by all cases of attitudes. The state of readiness of the organism is a more general term. Attitudes constitute special cases of readiness. Therefore, we must have some concrete criteria which single out cases of readiness as attitudes. It seems to us that the following five criteria are found in cases of readiness which are labeled as attitudes.

1. *Attitudes always imply a subject–object relationship.* Attitudes are always related to definite stimuli or stimulus situations. These may be *objects* such as home, automobile, souvenir, some particular eating place; *persons* such as one's own body, mother, father, brother, some friend, rival, teacher, sweetheart, wife; or *groups* of people such as classmates, playmates, Negroes, the community; *institutions* such as the school, college, church, club; or socially established and standardized *concepts, values* or *norms* such as the flag, the Constitution, democracy. These subject–object relationships are not innate, are not biologically given. The items or objects toward which the subject–object relationship is developed are always first on the stimulus side for the individual. Only after contact with these outside stimuli, does any relationship develop between them and the individual.

In various definitions of attitude, the *content of an attitude* is often mentioned in such terms as "objects," "social stimuli," "social objects." [20] But the content of attitudes will depend upon the particular nature of the subject–object relationship established. The contents of attitudes are as numerous and as different as the stimulus situations to which attitudes are related.

2. This means that *attitudes are formed* and formed in relation to objects, persons, and values which may or may not have motivational appeal at first. Almost any food may satisfy hunger, but we may develop a special liking for a special food, even for a special restaurant, and even a special table in that restaurant. When these particular likes or dislikes are more or less fixated, we have formed attitudes in relation to these particular objects. Almost any average member of the opposite sex will satisfy sexual need, but when it is fixated, with all its affective overtones, it becomes an attitude—an attitude toward a particular person. George Bernard Shaw has aptly defined a lover as a man who exaggerates the difference between one woman and another.

Since attitudes are not innate states of readiness, inasmuch as they are formed in relation to particular objects, persons, institutions, and values or norms, the individual has first to come into contact with them. And coming into contact is a perceptual situation. This means that the primary stage in the formation of attitudes is a perceptual stage. The presence of a perceptual stage is of the utmost psychological importance. For certain basic facts about perceptual situations provide the starting point for the formation of attitudes, as we shall see in the next chapter.

The perceptual stage in the formation of attitudes is especially important in cases of attitudes which do not have a motivational (instinctual) basis.[6] As the accumulating investigations in the field of attitudes show, many social attitudes are formed through verbal judgments of adults. Indeed the most directive and important social attitudes which determine status, social distance, and the like seem to be formed through verbalized short-cut dictums or value judgments and through situations which outwardly do not have any *momentary* motivational appearance.

The fact that attitudes are not innate but are formed as a result of the individual's contact with his environment means, of course, that attitudes are learned or conditioned. Just what the psychological or physiological mechanisms of this learning may be are irrelevant to the present discussion. We are concerned here with demonstrable psychological properties and characteristics of attitudes. Obviously, the more adequate the psychology of learning or conditioning becomes, the better will we understand the processes involved in attitude formation. But it is almost inconceivable that any final adequate account of learning developed in the future would ever negate the statement that attitudes are formed.

3. *Attitudes have affective properties of varying degrees.* Established attitudes are charged with affective or value properties in varying degrees. The affective property of attitudes may be due to motivational (instinctual) origins such as hunger and sex (as exemplified in cases of attitudes toward a certain food, a certain restaurant, a sweetheart or wife) or may be due to nonmotivational sources (noninstinctual).

The affective property of attitudes with instinctual origins is self-explanatory. The affective property of attitudes with noninstinctual sources is due to the fact that these attitudes are formed in relation to social values or norms which in themselves are standardized affective fixations. They are usually verbalized short-cut value judgments such as "the home is a sacred institution."

---

[6] We are using the term "motivation" here to denote only drives, needs, or instincts, which have a definite origin in the organism of the individual.

Value judgments are always given in adjectival form. And all judgments given in terms of adjectives certainly have affective properties. The social values presented in short-cut dictums, or in other ways accompanied by praise or blame, naturally are affectively charged. The individual is forced to respect and uphold the values of the family, school, church, or other institutions he is a member or would-be member of. If he does not respect and glory in his flag, he is compelled to. The very fact of membership and participation in group activity or ceremony makes certain standardized values or practices sacred, justifiable, right, honorable, or dutiful in the individual's eyes. Consequently, the attitudes an individual forms in relation to such activities or practices become affectively charged.

Another important reason why attitudes are affectively charged is the fact that many attitudes prescribe the individual's relationship, status, or role with respect to other individuals or groups (such as teacher, worker, boss, minister, assistant). And experiences connected with status are affectively charged.[7]

4. *Attitudes are more or less enduring states of readiness.* There are states of readiness which are more or less momentary, depending on the state of the organism and the situation at the time. For example, we may be very hungry and snatch a loaf of bread. After we have eaten enough and become satisfied, the loaf may be pushed aside. At the time of sexual tension, a person toward whom there is no established attitude but who can satisfy the sexual need may be passionately seized, but, after the need is satisfied so that the tension is resolved, one may never look at the person again. In these cases the state of readiness dissolves as the satiation point is reached, at least for the time being. But not so with attitudes. They are more or less enduring states of readiness. Thus a wounded soldier tries to show his respect to his superior officer who has really shared the hardships with him. A very much preferred food may be the subject of praise after the point of satiation has been reached. A sweetheart still has the sentimental halo in the eyes of her lover even after sexual satisfaction. A dear

[7] Without making a special issue of it at this point, we may note in passing that attitudes related to role or status are ego-involved. And ego-involved experiences and responses have affective properties (see chs. 5, 6, 11).

friend is still liked even during moments of minor friction. Some people in India actually starve to death rather than eat meat which is "forbidden" by the very rigid norms established and accepted by Hindus. These examples are sufficient to illustrate the fact that attitudes, once formed, are more or less enduring states of readiness, quite independent, within limits, of the momentary states of the organism.

An attitude becomes a more or less enduring state of readiness because of the cognitive components in its formation. We have seen that attitudes are not innate entities, that they are formed as a consequence of contact with objects, persons, or situations to which they are related. We referred to these contacts as the perceptual stage in the formation of an attitude. It is this perceptual stage which begins to give an attitude its cognitive component in the process of formation. Since the first stage in the formation of an attitude is a perceptual stage, we can begin at once to utilize the concepts developed to account for perceptual situations. Here we are on relatively safe ground. The fact that attitudes are more or less enduring indicates, further, that attitudes are learned. And the more adequate the account of learning becomes, the better will we be able to understand the basis for an attitude's enduring quality, just as we will better understand the basis of its formation. And it is also almost inconceivable that any final explanation of learning would alter the statement that attitudes are more or less enduring.

We should be very clear on one point, however, so as to avoid misunderstanding. We have said that attitudes are more or less enduring states of readiness to stimuli, objects, persons, groups, values, or norms, in relation to which they are formed and which determine the individual to react in a characteristic way in relation to them. But attitudes are not absolute fixed states of readiness. Since they are formed as a consequence of contact with objects, values, or norms to which they are related, they may change or disintegrate. For example, good friends may become deadly enemies; a religious person may become an atheist; a conservative may become radical as a result of contact with new facts and events.

5. *Attitudes range in the number and variety of stimuli to which they are referred.* Since attitudes develop as a consequence of experience, and, since attitudes involve a cognitive component, the extent or range of stimuli to which an individual will relate an attitude will vary according to the nature of the source of the attitude and according to the relationship the individual makes between an attitude and the stimulus situation he confronts. Although certain attitudes, especially some of those created in laboratory situations or those of children, may only be evoked by the situation under which they originally developed, the more usual process is that an attitude, once established, will be related by the individual to a variety of objects or situations that have not necessarily been active in its original establishment.

The wide range exhibited by some attitudes is possible because of the fact that the stimulus situation toward which the attitude has developed is itself extensive, that is to say, possible of representation or expression in many different specific contexts. When we noted as our first characteristic of attitude that it always implied a subject–object relationship, we pointed out that we could label institutions, concepts, social values, or norms as "objects" in this sense. Social attitudes toward such stimulus situations are, we have said, often derived from the verbal judgments of others. For example, once an individual has accepted the value judgment of his group that "Negroes are inferior" and should occupy a lower status in society, he can and does easily relate his acquired attitude to innumerable specific situations. As we shall see, a considerable body of research in the past two decades has shown that attitudes have a directive effect in specific situations, that a very general attitude will reveal itself in a wide variety of ways.[8]

Classifications of attitudes. This approach to the problem of attitudes renders meaningless various attempts to classify them. G. W. Allport has summarized the major varieties of classification:

[8] In this connection, the experimental work on meaning and association time is significant, in view of the fact that the upshot of the controversy was that meaning is more immediate than specific association. (See the experiments of Moore, Tolman, Weld, and Cantril.) This being the case, the immediate "meaning" reaction determines the range rather than specific associations. This is illustrated in the references, for example, to Kay's study of personal and general frames [16] and Horowitz's study on the development of race attitudes. [12]

positive and negative, specific and general, public and private, common and individual attitudes. [1] Since the characteristics of any attitudes in any individual will vary according to the situation or circumstances under which the attitude has developed and the function the attitude serves for the individual, any classification of attitudes becomes almost as nebulous as any classification of stimulus situations (including objects, persons, groups, values, and norms) or of personal and societal relationships. Simple dichotomous classifications especially distort and falsify the problem. Take, for example, the distinction made by Thomas and Znaniecki, between "common" and "individual" attitudes. Their use of the word "common" refers to attitudes "common to all conscious beings," their use of "individual" refers to attitudes "peculiar to only one individual member of the group." [27, 18] Such a distinction makes no place for the attitudes of members of small or large groups, or the attitudes characteristic of a given social system, not to mention the elaborate and tenuous classification that would be necessary to place an attitude according to the subtle variations it might have for the individual with reference to the attitudes of other members of the same group or social system. And just because some attitudes are common to a large enough number of people to lend themselves to measurement does not mean that a distinction between "common" and "individual" attitudes has any more than a loose descriptive value. Classifications of attitudes, like classifications of personalities, represent a rigid structural approach which is apt to obscure or be mistaken for a truly functional analysis.

The psychology of value included in the psychology of attitudes. We have said previously that attitudes always imply a subject–object relationship and that attitudes are affectively charged. Hence the stimulus or object or group to which an attitude is related is reacted to affectively. In other words, the stimulus, object, person, group, or norm in relation to which an attitude is formed has value, either positive or negative and in different degrees for that individual. We are using the word "value" to denote these affective qualities. Therefore, the problem of value as an affective quality is part of the psychology of attitude.

We do not mean to say that all attitudes are social attitudes or that all attitudes are related to social values. An attitude may be developed toward certain woods in which a person has taken solitary walks, or an attitude may be formed in relation to almost anything peculiar to the surroundings and experiences of the individual. And we might mention in passing the abnormal fixations sometimes made by individuals on queer and unusual objects.

In spite of this fact, however, the attitudes most important in daily life are social attitudes—attitudes formed in relation to other individuals, groups, institutions, tools and technology, standardized values, or norms. These are the attitudes that really determine an individual's reaction to other people, other groups, and that map out for him the main boundaries of his experience and taste. Most of these social attitudes are transmitted by short-cut verbal value judgments. Words are the most common medium for both the formation and the expression of social attitudes. And it is probably for this reason that some psychologists have characterized attitudes as *verbalized* dispositions. Although we know the social attitudes of others largely from the words they use, most of us do have many quite personal attitudes not related to social values, which we may seldom if ever express—attitudes toward some loved one, some one we strongly dislike, some personal keepsake, some house. To be sure, if we are probed concerning these things, we will be able to express our attitude. But many attitudes we may have which we may never verbalize are just as much "attitudes" as those we do verbalize spontaneously. The point is that all attitudes, whether social or nonsocial, whether verbalized or nonverbalized, function essentially according to the same psychological principles, even though there may be differences of content, richness, compellingness, or endurance.

Although the psychology of values is involved in the psychology of attitudes, it should be borne in mind that social values, being first on the stimulus side in relation to the individual, are essentially the data of the social sciences. Social psychologists become interested in and concerned with social values simply because social values are part, and an important part, of the stimuli that surround man and, through stimulation, influence him.

Special cases of attitudes. Various terms such as "set," "stereotype," "prejudice," and "opinion" may all be regarded as attitudes with particular characteristics which have been given certain labels by common use. The psychological states described by all of these terms are developed in relation to certain stimuli in the identical way that attitudes are developed. All are affectively charged in relation to the stimuli. All are more or less lasting, all are acquired states of readiness determining the individual's characteristic reactions to the stimuli to which they are related. There are, of course, differences in the range of stimuli to which each of these forms of attitudes can be related, and there are differences in the intensity with which these different types of attitudes are displayed. There are also differences due to the conformity of these attitudes to objective conditions, as, for example, the difference between the attitude of a biologist to the facts of biological evolution and the attitude of an uneducated Baptist to the same facts. We repeat, however, that all of these forms of attitudes follow essentially the same pattern in their development.

As commonly used the term "set" is applied to a relatively restricted temporary attitude, or to momentary states of readiness; the word "stereotype" is applied to an intense and rigid attitude, while the word "prejudice" applies to an attitude still more rigid and intense and one generally based on false information. The term "opinion" is generally used to describe an attitude that is or has been expressed and that is based more on objective conditions than a "stereotype" or "prejudice."

We are mentioning the fact that these terms are special cases of attitudes for a methodological reason. For some investigators use one particular term and deal with the problems surrounding it as if they were separate problems unrelated to the characteristics of attitude or the conditions which develop attitudes. We strongly believe that we shall gain much if we unify the concepts which can be really unified and if we do not use different concepts for the same problem. Following the rule of scientific parsimony, we shall try to restrict ourselves to as few concepts as necessary.

In this chapter we have only cleared our way. We have tried to bring the problem of attitudes into clear focus. Because of the diverse and disconnected approaches made to the study of attitudes by psychologists and sociologists, some unification of the problem is called for. An understanding of attitudes, as well as an understanding of values, demands a unification of the problem which remains the same problem whether handled by psychologists, sociologists, or any other social scientists.

REFERENCES

1. ALLPORT, G. W., Attitudes, in *A Handbook of Social Psychology* (C. Murchison, ed.), Worcester: Clark Univ. Press, 1935, ch. 17.
2. AMES, A., JR., *Sensations, Their Nature and Origin,* Dartmouth Eye Institute, Hanover, N. H., October 1945.
3. BALDWIN, J. M., *Dictionary of Philosophy and Psychology,* New York: Macmillan, copyright 1901–05, 3 vols.
4. BLUMER, H., *An Appraisal of Thomas and Znaniecki's The Polish Peasant in Europe and America,* New York: Soc. Science Research Council, 1939, Bull. 44.
5. BOGARDUS, E. S., *Fundamentals of Social Psychology,* New York: Century, 1931, 2d ed.
6. CANTRIL, H., Attitudes in the making, *Understanding the Child,* 1934, **4,** 13–15.
7. —— The social psychology of everyday life, *Psychol. Bull.,* 1934, **31,** 297–330.
8. —— A psychological reason for the lag of "nonmaterial" culture traits, *Soc. Forces,* 1935, **13,** 376–9.
9. —— The effect of modern technology and organization upon social behavior, *Soc. Forces,* 1937, **15,** 493–5.
10. —— and D. KATZ, Objectivity in the social sciences, in *Industrial Conflict: A Psychological Interpretation* (G. W. Hartmann and T. Newcomb, eds.), New York: Cordon, 1939, 9–18.
11. FOLSOM, J. K., *Social Psychology,* New York: Harper, 1931.
12. HOROWITZ, E. L., The development of attitude toward the Negro, *Arch. Psychol.,* 1936, no. 194.
13. HUXLEY, J., Science and its relation to social needs, in *Scientific Progress* (Sir Halley Stewart Lecture, 1935), London: Allen & Unwin, 1935, ch. 6.
14. JAMES, W., *Will to Believe and Other Essays in Popular Philosophy,* New York: Longmans, Green, 1896.
15. JUNG, C. G., *Psychological Types,* New York: Harcourt, Brace, 1924.
16. KAY, L. W., Social norms as determinants in the interpretation of personal experiences, *J. Soc. Psychol.,* 1944, **19,** 359–67.
17. KLINEBERG, O., *Social Psychology,* New York: Holt, 1940.
18. MURPHY, G., and L. B. MURPHY, *Experimental Social Psychology,* New York: Harper, copyright 1931.
19. —— —— and T. M. NEWCOMB, *Experimental Social Psychology,* New York: Harper, copyright 1937.
20. NELSON, E., Attitudes: I. Their nature and development, *J. Gen. Psychol.,* 1939, **21,** 367–99.

21. ORTH, J., Gefühl und Bewusstseinslage, *Abhand. Geb. Padagog. Psychol. u. Physiol.*, 1903.
22. SHELDON, W. H., *The Varieties of Temperament*, New York: Harper, 1942.
23. SHERIF, M., An experimental approach to the study of attitudes, *Sociometry*, 1937, **1**, 90–8.
24. —— Some recent investigations on the psychology of attitudes (in Turkish), Univ. Ankara Publications, Psychology Series, **II**, 1944.
25. SPRANGER, E., *Lebensformen*, Halle: Niemeyer, 1927.
26. STRAUSS, A., The concept of attitude in social psychology, *J. Psychol.*, 1945, **19**, 329–39.
27. THOMAS, W. I., and F. ZNANIECKI, *The Polish Peasant in Europe and America*, Boston: Badger, 1918, vol. **1**.
28. TITCHENER, E. B., *Systematic Psychology: Prolegomena*, New York: Macmillan, 1929.
29. WARREN, H. C. (ed.), *Dictionary of Psychology*, Boston: Houghton Mifflin, copyright 1934.
30. WATT, H. J., Experimentelle Beiträge zu einer Theorie des Denkens, *Arch. f. d. ges. Psychol.*, 1904, **4**, 289–436.

CHAPTER 3

SOME EXPERIMENTAL FACTS CONCERNING THE BASIS OF ATTITUDES

Attitudes are inferred from the reactions (verbal or nonverbal) of man. When an individual reacts *repeatedly* in a characteristic way (positive or negative) in relation to a certain stimulus object, we infer that he has an established attitude toward that stimulus. When a group of individuals react *repeatedly* in a characteristic way to a stimulus situation, we infer that the members of the group have an established social attitude in relation to it. This characteristic reaction of groups of people is sometimes called "conforming behavior." These conformities are discriminatory or selective, as all attitudes are. This means that all attitudinal reactions are *judgmental* activities. It is, therefore, not a mere coincidence that social value judgments reveal themselves in the psychology of the individual as established attitudes. Whether these discriminative activities revealing attitudes are verbally expressed as short-cut judgments of opinion or value, as in logic, or are expressed only in behavior does not matter a bit psychologically.

As we said in the previous chapter, attitudes always imply a subject–object (stimulus–organism) relationship. Attitudes always are related to some object, person, group, or standardized norm. This relationship is not innate, it is formed. In order for it to be formed, the individual first has to come into contact with the object (person, institution, norm). This is a perceptual situation. Therefore, the first stage in the actual formation of an attitude is a perceptual stage, with the internal factors of the organism and external (objective) factors of the stimulus situation coming into play.

The term "attitude" (used in everyday language to denote an established state of readiness) does not express any specific psychological mechanism. It is a composite term, especially useful to denote in an empirical way an important common ground between psychologists and sociologists. When it is characterized psychologically and traced from the point of view of its formation, it becomes evident that the psychology of attitudes is intimately related to the psychology of perception and judgment. This is true, *no matter what the motivational basis or diversity of content of an attitude may be.* In the present approach towards the psychology of attitudes, we shall put our emphasis on perceptual and judgmental processes and see how far it can carry us. Here we do not need to take sides in favor of any learning theory. We have already pointed out that any final adequate psychology of attitude will someday be linked closely with the psychology of learning or conditioning, especially in accounting for the more or less enduring character and for the range of attitudes.

General selectivity of perception. The objective world around us—rivers, hills, trees, buildings, and the like—is, of course, not affected by our perception of it. These objects are there objectively, determined by physical laws, whether or not we perceive or experience them. On the other hand, what we perceive of the natural and social world around us is highly selective, determined by biological and psychological laws. Because of this deterministic selectivity, men perceive or experience different aspects of the world around them. For example, in the Dark Ages, because of the fact that men were so confined to themselves owing to the prevailing social and cultural system in which they were living, they paid little attention to nature. [8] They needed, among others, a Rousseau, the rebellious child of the bourgeois system rising against the decaying feudal aristocracy and clergy, to call attention to his fellowmen that nature was around them in all its glory. Today, in India, for example, many people are so much preoccupied with their mystic ways, that they simply are not concerned and, therefore, do not notice the beauties of nature. We do not have to resort to any typologies to account for these facts, as Jung does, for example. [25] In a discussion of the "artist's frame of reference," F. H. Allport [1] has nicely pointed out that the meaning, the unity, the beauty seen in a picture are determined by a "psychological frame" and that the psychology of "frame of reference" "goes back to the simplest principles of human perception." [3]   At the basis of this selectivity is the bipolar nature of perception: the determination of perceptions by external and internal factors following certain laws, and the formation of certain enduring states of readiness.

The selectivity of perception is a universal human phenomenon not confined to any special cases. As Woodworth puts it in developing what he terms "situation set," "the individual is not an unbiased registering instrument." [55] Anyone can easily cite numerous cases from daily experience to prove that what he observes and notices around him is a selective matter: what he sees in a strange city, what he reads in his newspaper, and so on. It would be very useful to make longitudinal studies of perception also and find out through a period of time what actual items a person does perceive in his surroundings. Such longitudinal studies would certainly reveal the highly selective nature of our daily perceptions as determined by external and internal conditions.

Experiments in the psychological laboratory require subjects, through carefully formulated "instructions," to observe precisely certain aspects of the stimulus presented and usually made focal for them in a controlled way. Already some representative laboratory studies furnish evidence of the general selectivity of perception. Here we refer to the long line of investigation started over 40 years ago by Külpe when he ventured to study the psychology of the so-called higher mental processes against the vigorous protests of his former teacher, Wundt, who argued for the completion first of the "mental chemistry" of sensory processes. In Külpe's laboratory it became increasingly evident that the "set" assumed by the observer as a result of "instructions" was playing an important role in determining response to the experimental situation. Külpe himself specifically undertook the study of this problem. [30] In his experiments he tachistoscopically presented different stimuli, such as printed syllables, about which different aspects or "dimensions" could be reported, for example, the *number* of letters involved, the *locations* of the colors, or the *total pattern* composed by them. Külpe found that more items were noted and more correct judgments made by the observer about that aspect of the stimuli which had been emphasized by the "set" produced as a consequence of the initial instructions; subjects noticed more fully and in more detail those aspects of the stimulus field they were set to observe. Two decades later Yokoyama and then Chapman verified Külpe's results. [6, 9]

In the Külpe line of experiments, the "set" is produced by the instructions of the experimenter. But the internal factors ("set" in this case) need not always be due to instructional set. In more natural settings some motivational stress, some social pressure, or some established norm in the individual may and does produce the "set" or "attitude" with which the stimulus field is observed. Take, for example, the case of the hungry man looking for bread or the case of a lover waiting in a crowd for his sweetheart. Cantril has pointed out that

> The literature of experimental psychology is filled with research which demonstrates conclusively that a frame of reference is an inevitable accompaniment of any series of judgments a person may be asked to make; and that when the situation is unique and specific, as it is frequently deliberately designed to be in the laboratory, the frame of reference is a function of the relationships discerned between the series of stimuli. No matter how hard the experimentalist, especially the psychophysicist, may try to work on the peripheral level of judgments and side-step central issues, he finds it almost impossible to avoid in the laboratory the phenomenon we are describing that occurs so constantly in judgments of everyday life. [7, 24]

In his impressive series of experiments carried out over a period of years (1913–32), Bartlett obtained a well-integrated series of results on remembering. [2] This classical work breaks down the artificial classificatory boundaries imposed between the functions of perceiving, remembering, and even imagining. Bartlett unanswerably demonstrated that the perceiving, imagining, and remembering of even relatively simple objects are selective— influenced in an important way by such factors as the interests, attitudes, temperament, of the observer. He makes his experiments on perceiving the starting point of experiments on remembering, indicating a functional continuity between perception and memory. In the experiments on perceiving [2, 14–33] he presented to his observers simple designs and patterns, and complex pictorial material. His instructions were neutral; that is, he did not try to produce a "set" or "attitude" in the observers in relation to any given aspect of the stimulus field; in fact, he was especially on his guard "against the use of suggestion other than that conveyed by the material itself." [17 f.]   His results and conclusions are clear-cut.   In his own words:

> Very rarely indeed did a subject thus differentiate clearly between a sensory image set up by the stimulating object and his interpretation of the object itself.   But, though they did not realize it, the observers were throughout *constantly utilizing an imaged setting, or background, for their perceptual reactions.* [2, 30, italics ours]

Again,

> . . . to perceive anything is one of the simplest and most immediate, as it is one of the most fundamental, of all human cognitive reactions. Yet obviously, in a psychological sense, it is exceedingly complex, and this is widely recognized.   Inextricably mingled with it are *imaging, valuing, and those beginnings of judging which are involved in the response to plan, order of arrangement and construction of presented material.   It is directed by interest and by feeling, and may be dominated by certain crucial features of the objects and scenes dealt with.* [2, 31, italics ours]

The more unstructured and vague the stimulus field is, the more important is the role of set and other factors not inherent in the stimulus itself.   In one of a series of experiments utilizing the autokinetic phenomenon, Sherif instructed his subjects that the light (which was physically stationary, of course) would move to the right or to the left as the case may be. [41]   The subjects with the "set" produced by the instructions gave results generally in harmony with the instructed direction.   Proshansky and Murphy [38] used the autokinetic condition as one of three types of unstructured stimuli (lines and weights were also used) in a test of the hypothesis that "perception develops positively in the direction of reward." [296]   Although their "experimental subjects showed . . . significant shifts in estimates of lines and weights in the direction of the percepts which had been rewarded," [305] this conclusion could not be drawn from the autokinetic data.   The authors are careful to point out, however, that "with the autokinetic effect, it was found during the course of the experiment that a major source of error was operating." [302]   "Such large and uncontrolled autokinetic effects appeared in the training series as to vitiate the post-training data." [305] More recently Haggard and Rose, utilizing the autokinetic technique with a device of reward or punishment instead of direct instruction of movement, obtained results similar to Sherif's. [18]

From the facts, of which the foregoing are typical examples, it is plausible to conclude in a general way that the selectivity of attitudes is basically imbedded in the selectivity of perception. But this gives us only our general orientation. We must proceed further and try to single out more precisely the processes involved in the formation of an attitude.

A frame of reference is involved in perceptual and judgmental activity. It is an established fact in psychology that stimuli do not have an absolute stimulating value. A stimulus is experienced, perceived, judged, and reacted to in relation to other stimuli, present or past, to which it is *functionally* related. In perception this relative character of a stimulus emerges from its relationship in the organized whole [29]; in judgments, from its relationship to other stimuli (present and past) which are operative at the moment. The concept of "member character" expresses the relative nature of the properties of any stimulus to which the organism is responding at the moment and can be conveniently used to denote the relative character of any stimulating agent with respect to simultaneous *or preceding* stimuli with which it is functionally related.

The term "frame of reference" is simply used to denote the functionally related factors (present *and* past) which operate at the moment to determine the particular properties of a psychological phenomenon (such as perception, judgment, affectivity). In 1935 and 1936 Sherif brought together a good many experimental facts from various major psychological phenomena (including perception, judgment, affectivity, memory, personality) indicating the way in which a "frame of reference" is involved in each of them. [41, 42] The scale of magnitudes against which subsequent stimuli of a similar kind are judged, the organized perceptual whole which determines the particular relative properties of its parts, the established social status in relation to which responses to other individuals and groups are shaped are all specific cases of frames of reference. Unless we have good reasons to argue that frames of reference involved in various psychological phenomena have nothing to do with one another, but express psychological tendencies quite different in nature, such a general concept is needed to denote this whole background of factors which together determine the relative nature of response. Because frames of reference are involved in all major phenomena, a more precise definition of frame of reference cannot be formulated until we know more about the frames of reference in various specific cases.

Specific cases of frames of reference are most extensively elaborated in the fields of perception and judgment. Gestalt psychologists worked out in detail the psychology of perceptual frames. In fact, the whole emphasis of frames of reference in psychology is mainly derived from them. All our time and space localizations, magnitude perceptions, form perceptions, perceptions of melody and harmony are referential affairs. When we say "up" we mean "up" in relation to something below, when we say "far" or "near" we say so in relation to a starting point we have in mind.

With the shifts of the reference frames or points, perceptual relationships are altered. Thus:

> A book is small and a man is large. But if a house is large, then a man is small. And if a book is small and a house is large, then a man is of medium size. [36, *43*]

Years ago Wertheimer demonstrated that a line is experienced as horizontal or vertical in reference to the position of other things in the field of stimulation: if the observer's visual field is slanted by means of a mirror, a similarly slanted object tends to appear vertical, indicating that the position of an object is perceived in its relation to the whole organized field. [53]

In our opinion, the psychology of these perceptual frames are basically related to the psychology of attitudes. The forms, proportions, and magnitudes of things, buildings, tools, and the like, in the village, town, or city we live in become for us in time established anchorages. When, subsequently, in some other town or country we face different proportions, forms, and magnitudes of things, we perceive them against the whole background of our established frames or anchorages. Consequently they seem to us to be too large, too small, queer, or disproportionate as the case may be.

Extensive evidence of the referential nature of judgmental activities has accumulated during the past decade. As we shall see later, the implications of this important finding can be carried on to more or less complicated social problems. Chapman and Volkmann, for example, in a significant study on "A Social Determinant of the Level of Aspiration" start with the general principle that "the conditions which govern the setting of a level of aspiration (*Anspruchsniveau*), in the sense of an estimate of one's future performance in a given task, may be regarded as a special case of the effect upon a judgment of the frame of reference within which it is executed." [10, 225] They draw attention to the "general fact that all judgmental activities take place within such referential frameworks." [225] Convenient and concise summaries and discussions of the studies on judgment are found in the reports of Long [31], Rogers [39], and McGarvey [34]. If we start with Hollingworth's work on judgment, it becomes increasingly evident that judgment to a stimulus in a series is based on the whole background of previous judgments belonging to the series and affected by them in definite ways. [21, 22] For our present problem, the important fact is that judgments of stimuli shift according to the background furnished by a related series of stimuli; the particular directions of these shifts need not concern our position in this chapter. Here it is sufficient for us to call attention briefly to certain aspects of Long's and Rogers' representative studies as they bear on our present problem.

Long studied the effect of preceding stimuli upon the judgments of succeeding stimuli, using series of auditory intensities. Among other things he found that

> Under certain conditions, stimuli oppose each other in such a way that a weak stimulus preceded by a strong one is judged weaker than it actually is, and vice versa. This is referred to as contrast and its presence has been found in experiments employing a variety of stimuli: namely, tones and weights in the usual psychophysical experiments; and colors, tones, and odors in experiments on hedonic tones. Thus the reality of the phenomenon cannot be doubted, but an explanation of *why* contrast operates or what processes (either psychological or

physiological) underlie it, must be postponed until the conditions under which it occurs, or does not occur, are better known. [31, 55]

The studies on judgment with the method of single stimuli that have accumulated during the past 15 years furnish unequivocal evidence in support of the relativity of judgment. In an increasing number of studies in different sense modalities, it has been shown that the use of a standard stimulus is not necessary for the observer to give a judgment about any stimulus in the series. After a few rounds of presentation of the series, observers spontaneously establish a scale without being instructed to do so. Any stimulus in the series is judged or placed in its relative position in the scale. These experiments in which no standard stimulus is used yield a distribution of frequencies of judgment very similar to that obtained by orthodox psychophysical methods using a formal standard. [37]

Here again we see the same referential nature of response observed in cases of perception. With the shifts of the reference frame or scale to which any stimulus is related, a corresponding shift in judging that stimulus results. Wever and Zener [54] gave an observer a "light" series of weights, and after this series had become an "established" scale for the observer they suddenly introduced a "heavy" series.

> The effect of the first series on the judgments of the second was quite evident for 20 or 25 presentations, *i.e.* for four or five rounds judgments of "heavy" *predominated* for all the stimuli; from this point on, however, the *judgments showed a redistribution* conforming to the second stimulus-series. [54, 476, italics ours]

On the basis of these facts, we may say that the members of a series of stimuli manifest "member-character" just as parts of an organized perceptual field manifest "member-character," revealing "supra-local" qualities from the functional relationship in which they are found. The member-character of the stimuli in a series is clearly shown in a keen observation of Wedell in his study of pitch discriminations.

> It has been said that no judgment is "absolute" unless a long time, say 12 hours, has intervened since the last hearing of a tone. Following this line of reasoning in the present experiment, the only absolute

judgment would be the first one each day. It must be admitted that there is some basis for this assertion, because some of the subjects seemed to compare the notes with one another deliberately. *In addition to this, a subject would sometimes correct a previous judgment by saying,* "Oh, that other one must have been [so and so]." [51, *497,* italics ours]

Psychophysical studies dispensing with the presentation of a formal standard stimulus with every variable stimulus in the series were first started by Wever and Zener. [54] Because no standard was used, and each stimulus was presented singly, the method was designated as the method of "single" or "absolute stimuli," and the series of stimulus values as "absolute series." Now it is often referred to as "absolute scale" and the judgments obtained as "absolute" judgments. It is clear that the term "absolute" refers to the *method* alone. "Absolute" does not refer to judgments or their distribution. The real psychological fact shown in all these experiments is that judgments to subsequent stimuli are *relative* to preceding stimuli of a similar nature. Referring to the generality of this psychological tendency, McGarvey states in her survey of literature in 1943 that

> The relativity of judgments of lifted weights, tonal pitches, visual inclinations, etc., is paralleled by the relativity of affective judgments. [34, *14*]

It is an unfortunate accident to have the term "absolute" connected with a whole array of facts which definitely reveal the relativity of judgment, perception, and, in a word, experience in general. As the term "absolute" is used in a contradictory way to designate the relative nature of a general psychological tendency, there is bound to appear a contradiction of terms. Thus Cohen, in a study following Beebe-Center's research showing the relativity of hedonic judgments, uses the contradictory title "The Relativity of Absolute Judgments." [12] The same contradiction of terms is found in a more recent study by Postman and Miller showing the relative nature of temporal judgments. The authors state:

> An "absolute" judgment of magnitude is, of course, not strictly absolute, but is formed in relation to other magnitudes that lie within the immediate universe of attention. [36, *43*]

Again,

> Such subjective scales have been called *absolute scales* and perhaps the term is no more contradictory than the term *absolute judgment*. *Absolute,* in these contexts, means *relative* to the comparable magnitudes that form the immediate context of the judgment. [36, *43,* the last emphasis is ours]

To designate a tendency by a contradictory term does not help to clarify but only to confuse the issues in question. It may astound people to see that psychologists designate the same thing as both "absolute" and "relative."

It seems to us that nothing is gained by stretching the term "absolute judgment" and "absolute scale" (already used in a contradictory way by the mere accident of naming a method) to study the relative nature of response in perceptual and social fields. The relative nature of response in sensory judgments is only a specific case of a more general tendency. For example, contrast and assimilation effects which necessarily appear in judgments, are not effects peculiar to judgments alone. Assimilation and contrast effects result from simultaneous stimulation (perception) as well as from successive stimulation, as can be easily found by consulting any psychology textbook. Not only are contrast and assimilation effects simultaneous as well as successive—but also they are different according to the place they occupy in the figure or ground of a perceptual relationship. [4] In view of these facts, appropriate specific terms should be used to designate specific cases of reference frames appearing in other major fields of psychology. For example, "aspiration level" and "ego level" may be used as such referential terms in cases dealing with the experiences of success, failure, and status, as Hoppe [23], Frank [16], Gould [17], and others have done.

In this connection, Rogers' significant study dealing with the anchoring effect of a preceding stimulus of constant value on a scale of stimuli is pertinent. His formulation is aptly offered "as an experimental contribution to the understanding of the frame of reference." [39] His study is based on a previous investigation reported by Volkmann in 1936. [48] Volkmann obtained judgments on a series of visual inclinations, using the method of single stimuli.   In the first experiment an "instructed" position (horizontal) was used as a reference point.   As a consequence, the scale shifted and extended considerably in the direction of the horizontal.   The second experiment demonstrated that in a similar manner any value which the observer selected and held in mind could exert an appreciable shift in the scale.

In the first part of his study Rogers discusses frame of reference and "absolute scale."   He almost characterizes the "mental formation," labeled "absolute scale" in an inconsistent way, as a special case of frame of reference.   ("Mental formation" was originally used by Wever and Zener to designate the psychological scale [frame] formed after some rounds of presentation of the stimulus series in these psychophysical experiments.)   Rogers states:

> While it might be argued that the absolute scale, in this event, constitutes a frame of reference accessible to experimental manipulation and investigation, a slightly different view is to be taken here.   The frame of reference, it would seem, may most reasonably be seen as the product of a number of influences, notably the influences of stimuli which cannot all be present at any one time. [39, 6]

This is true in a general way, but not quite, because the influence of past stimuli, not present *at the time,* may be operative on an "absolute" scale as well as on any other specific case of a reference frame.   For example, in building up a mental scale ("absolute scale") using the method of single stimuli, a previously established scale or anchorage even from daily life may come in to modify present judgments.   The operation of a frame of reference or a mental scale as a specific case of a frame of reference is detected from the observable determinations or modifications of reported judgments and perceptions.   This fact is clearly noted by Rogers:

> The frame of reference, then, is inaccessible except in terms of overt responses which it governs. [39, 6]

In the experiments which Rogers conducted, he used the method of single stimuli.   His stimulus series consisted of a scale of visual inclinations (in the first experiment) and a scale of weights (in the second experiment).   In Rogers' first sessions the usual distributions of judgments were obtained, and the usual scales (or frames) were established psychologically.   In subsequent sessions, "an anchoring stimulus" was presented just prior to each presentation of a stimulus to be judged and was designated as the top category of the series. The anchoring stimulus, at first the same as the highest stimulus of the range, "was moved progressively further above the stimulus range, remaining always the same throughout any single session." This means that the most frequently presented stimulus was the anchoring stimulus: to be precise, the anchoring stimulus was presented as many times as the total number of presentations of all the stimuli of the series. In a few cases, the values of the anchoring stimuli used were within the upper part of the stimulus range. Rogers' results obtained from both kinds of stimuli (visual inclinations and weights) are similar. The anchoring or reference point, experimentally introduced, produces changes in the scale and in the category thresholds within the scale. As the anchoring point moves further from the range, it expands the scale to a certain point, and as it is carried down into the range it causes the scale to shrink. Briefly stated, the scale (frame) expands, to a certain point, or shrinks, but in both cases it is assimilated to the shifts of the anchoring stimulus.

Rogers' investigations constitute a significant contribution to the systematic experimental study of frames and points of reference and to the nature of their mutual interdependence. Our daily perceptions, experiences, relationships with other individuals are structured or altered to an important degree by the conscious or unconscious use of intruded anchorages of a social or nonsocial nature. Thus when we say "early," "late," we say them in relation to certain reference points, for example, the time of the departure of a train, an appointment, lunch time. In social life, we shift our judgments, decisions, and human relationships by self-imposed or socially given intrusions of value judgments which serve us as anchorages. In his work on remembering, Bartlett gives vivid illustrations of how the names of things used at the moment serve as anchorages in relation to which perceptions and memories are structured or altered.

A recent study by Tresselt [45] is of special importance for us in this connection, because it provides a strict laboratory demonstration of the fact that the better an anchorage is learned (even to the extent of being overlearned), the more pronounced is the tendency for that anchorage to effect subsequent judgments. Tresselt set out "to determine the effect of experimentally produced variations in the amount of past experience (with stimulus-objects similar to the objects to be used as the new task of judgment) upon the speed of agreement with the center of the stimulus-scale." She used a series of 12 weights, ranging from 11 to 560 grams. Six groups of subjects participated in the experiment. Group I was given one practice trial on each of the four heaviest weights; group II was given 4 trials on each of the heaviest weights; group III was given 8 trials; group IV 12; group V 28; and group VI 12 practice trials on the four lightest weights.

As usual in such experiments, Tresselt found that

> By the time the subjects have lifted approximately six weights regardless of the amount of previous experience or kind of previous experience, the judgments are less widely distributed and it might be said that the subjects have come to show a greater degree of conformity about what shall be called "medium." [45]

But she continues:

> *The larger the period of practice, the more slowly does the scale of judgment shift to its new position.* [45, italics ours]

The more well-established an anchorage is, the better it is learned, then the more lasting is its influence likely to be.

The shifts and other effects brought about by the introduction of anchorages into a situation (anchorages lying within or without the structure) are demonstrated by facts accumulating almost since the beginnings of experimental psychology. Thus, Henri, working on skin localizations in 1892–97, found that shifts of localizations always "are committed in the direction of the points of reference (*points de repère*)" and corresponding shifts took place with shifts of reference points. [20] What Henri called reference points (*points de repère*) in 1895 were designated "anchoring points" by Koffka in 1922 [27], "anchoring agents" by Volkmann in 1936 [48], and "anchoring points" by Rogers in 1941 [39] in studying the same effects.

Before proceeding to our next step—the experimental formation of an attitude—we shall bring together the main points reached so far. The first stage in the formation of an attitude is a perceptual stage. Because of this and because of the discriminative nature of attitudes they are closely linked to the psychology of perception and judgment. The laboratory studies on one hand and historical and empirical facts of everyday life on the other reveal that perceptions are selective. Perceptual and judgmental activities take place in referential frameworks. As a consequence of facing repeatedly the proportions, forms, or perceptual objects, scales of magnitudes (both in a physical and a social sense), these scales and magnitudes form frames of reference in the individual which serve as bases by which subsequent situations are perceived and judged. They need not be consciously formed, deliberately instructed, or imposed by others. Once formed they act as anchorages to determine or alter an individual's reactions to subsequent situations. In this fact is imbedded the basic psychology of an attitude.

And lest we be accused of too much subjectivity, it should be mentioned in passing that experiments concerning the referential nature of judgments involving manual tasks are entirely feasible. For example, Tresselt reports that in her experiment with Volkmann involving lifted weights they gathered data which "show that one subject who worked in a steel plant held the weights to be light or medium for the first eight judgments while a college professor held all the weights to be heavy or medium, except one, the very lightest." [45] Proshansky and Murphy have pointed out that "the unity of the organism would suggest . . . that whatever principles are of value in the understanding of the laws of motor response are of some pertinence in understanding the laws of perception." [38, 295]

Frames of Reference in Relation to Structured and Unstructured Stimulus Situations

We shall first consider frames of reference in relation to structured stimulus situations, beginning with the most clear-cut cases of perception. When the stimulus field is well-structured, the grouping or organization that follows gives rise to perceptions of forms, magnitudes, melodies, rhythms, proportions, relationships,

localizations, and so on, that correspond, in general, to the properties of the objective situations: the perception of a circle, a square,
an appropriately grouped succession of tones typify these situations.
In such cases the structure of the psychological frame will correspond closely to the structure of the external field of stimulation,
the figure–ground relationship being determined by the compelling features and salient reference points of the objective situation.
The properties of the different parts are determined by their functional relationship in the structure. This is expressed as the member-character of the parts. Factors in the objective field of stimulation (such as proximity and similarity) with such compelling
features have been studied extensively since the outstanding work
of Wertheimer. [52] This member-character relationship holds
true with successive stimulation as is the case in the perception of
melody as well as with simultaneous stimulation. As we have
seen, this seems to be true in the case of judgments as well as of
perceptions.

Well-structured objects or magnitudes have similar effects in
our daily life reactions, as we have already noted. An individual,
wherever he may be, is surrounded by buildings, tools, furniture,
magnitudes, timetables, schedules, or innumerable other types of
well-structured stimulus situations of one kind or another. He is
stimulated by them repeatedly. As a consequence, the particular
structures, magnitudes, and relationships become the established
scales or frames in him. This objective determination, by existing
magnitudes, scales, relationships, of lasting scales or frames in
individuals implies the establishment of lasting norms. These
norms, verbalized or nonverbalized in explicit judgments, are fundamental in shaping the mentalities of individuals living in any
social system. They are, in fact, at least as important in shaping
the mentality of members of a society as value judgments, beliefs,
or the whole superstructure of culture. Spiritually inclined culture
apologists have tended to ignore or minimize the effects of this
basic field of determination.

Now we shall consider frames of reference in relation to unstructured stimulus situations. We have ample evidence that in
cases where the stimulus situation is not well-structured the resulting psychological experience is by no means always chaos or an

inconsistent hodgepodge of reactions. It seems that a tendency to organize and group stimuli is a primary psychological fact based, of course, on underlying properties of the nervous system which competent physiologists will no doubt someday explain. Even in cases where the stimulus field is not well-structured and does not have the properties necessary to impose objectively clear-cut non-reversible figure–ground relationships, there is usually some sort of organization. For example, campers in a forest on a dark night are apt to see or hear different things around them as determined by their individual attitudes or preoccupations. But in such cases, internal factors are important in determining the properties of the resulting organizations.

The margin of possibilities for the contribution of internal factors allowed by unstructured situations is at the basis of many studies dealing with the problem of individual peculiarities, personality differences, abnormal tendencies, and the like. We find here the basis of the projective devices currently flourishing. The use of unstructured ink blots for detecting characteristics of the individual was suggested and used by G. V. Dearborn back in the end of the 19th century. [13, 14] Others soon followed him. Bartlett used a series of ink blots in his studies on remembering. The recent extensive systematic uses of projective methods based on the Rorschach ink blots or Murray's thematic apperception test are well known. [26, 35] Voth recently studied personality differences "as expressed through various forms and amount of auto-kinetic perception" using autokinesis as an unstructured unstable stimulus. [49] In more recent studies, Voth has used the auto-kinetic phenomenon as an index to pathological tendencies and has found fairly high correlations between indices thus obtained from his patients and medical diagnosis. [50]

Gradations of structure in the stimulus field. We have considered cases of structured and unstructured stimulus situations: in the former cases the resulting psychological outcome is compellingly determined by the objective situation, in the latter cases a variety of internal or subjective factors come into play to shape response. Actually, of course, there are all kinds of gradations between these two extremes of structuration.

Recently Luchins used gradations of structure or ambiguity in a series of studies on the social influences involved in the perception of complex drawings. [33] The conclusion that can be drawn from these studies is that the effects of social influence (the various devices of suggestion used in the experiment) vary with the degree of ambiguity of stimuli presented. The greater the ambiguity of the stimulus, the greater is the effect of attempted social influence. In a previous study in which the stimulus gradations were too few and too abrupt to allow the possibility of graded comparisons, Luchins seems to reach a similar conclusion:

> Whether or not subjects were influenced by A's judgment ["A" being the influencing subject in the experiment] *seemed to depend on the obviousness of the correct answer, i.e.,* the clarity of the judgment-situation, on the truth or falsity of A's judgment, and also on the subjects' attitudes to and interpretations of their task and the experimental situation. [32, *110,* italics ours]

Coffin designed an experiment to study the relationship of suggestibility to the ambiguity of a stimulus situation. The tonal attributes of pitch, volume, and a fictitious attribute created for the experiment and labeled "orthosonority" were used as the three tonal attributes varying in ambiguity. Subjects were given a tonal stimulus and then, after each tonal dimension had been defined, were told to equate the succeeding tone heard through their headphones with the original stimulus by turning the appropriate dial which was ostentatiously labeled. Subjects were divided into experimental and controlled groups. Results showed that the least ambiguous tonal attribute, pitch, was in most cases not subject to change by suggestion. Volume, on the other hand, could be reversed by suggestion with most observers, while judgments of "orthosonority" invariably followed the experimenter's suggestion. In other words suggestibility to these attributes increases with their ambiguity. [11]

In a study dealing with social determinants of the level of aspiration Chapman and Volkmann produced changes in the standards of their subjects by introducing into the situation a hierarchy of standards the truth or falsity of which could not be objectively tested by the subjects. But in a subsequent experiment, after the subjects had considerable experience with the task at hand, the introduction of new standards did not shift the standards of the subjects. With such results in mind, Chapman and Volkmann state that "the lability of the judgment, for example, varies inversely with the determinateness of the frame of reference." [10, 225] As we shall see later, Asch and his associates got similar results. Cantril's studies of a panic situation and various social movements substantiate the implications of these results on a highly complicated level. [p. 81 f.] Although research is still scanty which deals directly with the comparative effects on perception and judgment of gradations of structuration in the stimulus field, from the meager results obtained thus far we may formulate as a working hypothesis that, *all other things being equal, the role played by internal and social factors decreases with the stability, clarity, or structuredness of the stimulus situation and with the strength of frames or points of reference already established.*

As we have remarked in the foregoing, material objects, technological and other products of human labor, have a compelling effect in producing corresponding frames in the psychology of men. If the actual truth of all man's individual and social relationships were compellingly imposed on him in daily life, then he would not have any lasting and organized false attitudes. But he actually does have false attitudes about things, especially those he has never seen for himself or closely scrutinized. He has definite attitudes about gods, about life hereafter, and imposed attitudes concerning peoples about whom he really knows nothing.

As formulations and standards have been achieved in science through the laborious and not infrequently persecuted labors of scientific workers such as Galileo, science has changed and corrected many obsolete "survival" social norms and corresponding attitudes. False norms and practices connected with natural events have been corrected and have yielded their place to scientific formulations in the modern world, although there are exceptions such as the norms of Christian Science. However, in social and economic relationships and in the whole superstructure of norms determined by them, many survivals remain. Until social systems base their premises and practices on strictly scientific grounds, "survival" norms and attitudes filtering down from different historical periods and outmoded systems will continue to function.

The social system that erects itself on a scientific basis is still the exception rather than the rule. In view of this fact, the psychologist renders a real service when he takes a realistic stand and studies human nature and social systems as they really are, rather than basing his arguments on the inherent goodness or evil of man or the will to truth as Hobbes and Rousseau did in their times and as the advocates of an unchanging "human nature" are doing today. The more various interest groups strive to perpetuate obsolete superstructures of norms, the more important it is to study social organization objectively. Many a historian and social scientist has observed that unstable, ambiguous, and critical situations are those which provide especially fertile soil for the formation and inculcation of social norms.[1]

In the following paragraphs we shall try to typify experimentally the basic psychological processes involved in the formation of frames in unstructured situations. Admittedly, the studies are carried on in artificial and miniature laboratory situations. In presenting them we claim only that they are a starting point for conceptualization, the validity of which will be tested out with more concrete social material in actual situations.

Formation of a frame in an unstructured situation.[2] In line with the previous discussion, the psychologist must find an unstable unstructured stimulus situation, present it repeatedly to the individual to see if he will structure it somehow to a framework of response—proceeding with the hypothesis that psychological organization or grouping is a primary fact in unstructured as well as in structured situations. And if stimuli are organized by the individual, then the further question is, will they be organized by the members of a group collectively, and will members of a group

---

[1] It might be pointed out here that no realistic purpose is served by conducting experiments of the type in which the attempt is made, by introducing various social influences, to have a subject perceive a perfect square as a circle, or a line two inches long as longer than a line four inches long. In such obvious cases, no problem is involved, and nothing is gained by declaring as a conclusion in the face of such a compelling stimulus determination, "Ah ha, people cannot be influenced to perceive a square as a circle; thus they reveal their inherent will to truth."

[2] When not otherwise specified, the results to be summarized here refer to Sherif. [41, 42] These references may be consulted for the detailed description of the experimental situation, procedure, subjects, instructions, and so on.

eventually form a frame peculiar to the group? This query lies at the basis of the psychology of what sociologists such as Durkheim, drawing a sharp dichotomy between individual psychology and social psychology, argue so strongly concerning the supralocal, *suis generis* character of collective values or "representations" which *emerge* only as a consequence of collective behavior. [15]

The autokinetic phenomenon is one of various experimental possibilities that conveniently lends itself to a test of frame formation when the stimulus is unstructured. In a pitch-dark space a single point of light seems to move and to move in different directions. It seems to move because there is no frame of reference to give it a stable localization. With the introduction of other visible points or objects the point gains stability relative to these points, since all psychological localizations are relative affairs. Even the introduction of sounds in the vicinity of the point seems to affect its stability.

The first experiment in the series studied the formation of a frame (or scale) in the *individual alone,* thus starting with the general psychology of frame formation. The stimulus light was presented briefly and successively one hundred times in each experimental session. The time of exposure after the perceived movement started was the same in all presentations. This was true for all sessions, individual and group. The observer was asked to report the extent of the perceived movement. The results unequivocally indicate that, even though a scale and reference points are lacking in the objective situation, in the course of the experimental session individuals spontaneously form a frame and a central tendency (standard) which may differ from individual to individual in the absence of a compelling objective range of stimuli. In other words, in the absence of an objective scale (frame) and objective standard (reference point) each individual builds up a scale of his own and a standard within that scale. The range and reference point established by each individual is peculiar to himself when he is facing the situation alone.

In the second part of this first experiment it was found that once a scale is established there is a tendency for the individual to preserve this scale in subsequent sessions (within a week in these experiments). The introspective data obtained furnish further evidence of the formation of a frame. Most typical examples of such introspection are: "Compared with previous distance"; "Judgments are all relative"; "Compared successive judgments"; "First estimate as standard." Although the subjects do form frames of reference of their own spontaneously without being instructed to do so, the lack of an objective frame of reference is experienced. The following introspections are typical: "Darkness left no guide for distance"; "Lack of visible neighboring objects"; "No fixed point from which to judge distance."

Social Factors in Laboratory Situations

We can now proceed to the consideration of attitudes in *social* situations. These situations range from laboratory experiments involving social factors (which we will consider here) to complicated social conditions of everyday life (to be taken up in the next chapter). In doing so, we should stress again our conviction that, in spite of the enormous variation in the content of attitudes, psychological principles of attitude formation are essentially the same, irrespective of what the attitude is concerned with.

The first stage of attitude formation—in the most complicated social situation as well as in a restricted laboratory experiment—is a perceptual stage. The individual must somehow come into contact with the stimulus situation before any attitude is established. In strict laboratory situations this stimulus situation is generally neutral, and the frame of reference established lacks the vital affective and motivational properties so characteristic of social attitudes: in the laboratory experiment the stimuli may be a series of magnitudes, such as lines or weights or perceptual structures; in social life the stimuli may be a person, group, an expressed attitude or prejudice, a threat, or a value judgment (norm) of any kind. Some of these stimuli in social life may be relatively neutral, may have only a mild affective property, for example, the color of a dress, the shape of a house, the characterization of a city, while some may involve intense, sometimes even traumatic, experiences, for example, a girl whom one loves at first sight, a scolding received by a child for cheating, an announcement over the radio that the Japanese have bombed Pearl Harbor.

In dealing with attitudes in social situations, then, we are dealing with stimulus situations rife with affective and motivational properties, with situations that frequently involve problems of the individual's status. It might be mentioned in passing that attitudes to situations involving affective properties seem to be more readily established (learned), just as Pavlov, Tolman, and others showed that conditioning was more effective under motivational stress. Whether the perceptual experience involves direct contact with an object, person, or group, or whether the perceptual experience involves the verbal transmission of a social norm by some short-cut value judgment makes no difference whatever as far as the basic psychological characteristics of attitude formation are concerned. Both the soldier who has had direct experience with the enemy and his sister back home who has been subjected to value judgments concerning the enemy can and often do develop various negative attitudes. It is therefore systematically useless to try to categorize attitudes according to their source or origin. This is, of course, not a denial of the specific properties of particular attitudes formed in specific situations.

Experimental formation of a frame in group situations. This series of experiments was undertaken with the methodological conviction that the principles formulated and verified in general psychology are valid principles that operate when individuals participate in group action or in collective behavior. Results produced by group interaction may be, and in fact are, different from those obtained when a person is alone. They may have all the earmarks of emergent products. Nevertheless, the psychological principles involved in the group situation are the same in operation as those when an individual is not a member of a group. The emergence of new qualities is not a unique property of group action alone—perceptions of forms, relationships, and melodies emerge as unique qualities not found in individual parts. This emergence of new qualities on different levels—individual as well as collective levels—has to be stressed constantly because of the sharp dichotomies drawn by certain schools of thought. For example, the dichotomy of psychology into experimental versus cultural made by the romantic German school represented by Spranger [44] portrays experimental (individual) psychology as atomistic and static, and cultural psychology as dynamic and meaningful with total qualities. Writers of the Durkheim school of spiritualistic sociology, for example, Blondel [5] and Halbwachs [19], and Durkheim [15] himself, argue that new qualities emerge only in collective situations, whereas findings in psychology substantiate the view of dialectical materialism that emergence takes place in all levels—physical, biological, psychological and socioeconomic. In a recent study full of implications for further research in social psychology, Tresselt and Volkmann experimentally demonstrated the "production of uniform opinion by non-social stimulation." [47] These investigators express a general psychological fact when they state that "the mechanism for judging social stimuli is the same as the mechanism for judging non-social stimuli." [242]

With this methodological concern in mind, we can turn to the results of Sherif's group experiments on autokinesis. In the group situations each subject reported his judgments *aloud* and naturally was heard by the other subjects in the group. He in turn heard their expressed judgments. No primacy effect was introduced into the situation. A special point was made in the wording of the instructions to the effect that subjects could report their judgments in any order in any presentation. A subject who gave his judgment first in a particular presentation, might be the last to report in the following presentation. The building up of a frame in group situations is a temporal affair established in the course of the experimental period—the influence of expressed judgments is not restricted to judgments given at particular presentations.

Some groups faced the autokinetic situation *without any previous individual experience.* An equal number of groups faced it *after* the members had established their individual frames alone in individual experiments. The members of the groups who *first* took part directly in the group situation were therefore naive and neutral in relation to this unstructured ambiguous situation.

The results are clear. When individuals as members of a group face the same unstable unstructured situation without any previously established personal relationship among them, a scale (frame) and a standard (reference point) within that frame are established in the course of the experimental period.[8] When a member of the group faces the same situation subsequently *alone,* after the frame is established in the group situation, he experiences the situation in terms of the frame established in the group situation as a consequence of group interactions.

This result was verified by Asch and Wright in experiments performed in 1937. We give these results here in Asch's own preferred terminology.[4]

> The outstanding feature of the investigation of Sherif is the tendency of the subjects in the given experimental situation to reach mutual agreement. S. E. Asch and B. Wright undertook in a series of experiments to examine more closely the specific reasons for this tendency.

> Before proceeding with their experimental variations, they first repeated the main experiment of Sherif with four pairs of subjects. The arrangement of the experiment was as far as possible identical with that of Sherif. The main findings of Sherif were confirmed: a new norm (level of response) developed under the given conditions. However, the convergence proceeded along different paths in the different pairs of subjects. For example, some members exercised more influence on the direction than others. This finding is entirely consistent with the results of Sherif. [Variations of these experiments by Asch and Wright will be reported in their appropriate context later.] [5]

In Sherif's experiments with autokinesis, when individuals *first* establish their frames and standards in individual sessions and are

---

[8] Here we shall not digress to indicate some interesting results which revealed the differential, relative contributions of individual members and which are important for the psychology of personality.

[4] This is a summary statement of investigations, the full account of which will be reported in a forthcoming publication by Dr. S. Asch. The results reported here were personally communicated.

[5] More recently, in a series of studies dealing with "some social factors in judgment," Schonbar investigated modifications of judgments in "situations of medium and high structure," respectively. [40]   From her results she concludes "our findings confirm and extend the conclusions arising from Sherif's work on the autokinetic phenomenon." [129]   That the convergence she found in cases of high structure is almost identical to the convergence found in cases of medium structure is puzzling, in view of the differentiated results obtained with varied degrees of structure, and other factors by Asch, Lewis and Hertzman, Coffin, Chapman and Volkmann, Luchins, and Asch and Wright.

then brought into group situations, their judgments tend to converge. But the convergence is not so close as when they first work in the group situation. When an individual comes into a group situation, with his own established frames and standards, there is a tendency to stick to them to some extent: individuals bring into the situation their own established frames and are no longer naive in relation to the situation. [41, *31, 41;* 42, *104*]

In one variation of these experiments, Asch and Wright gave contradictory instructions in the individual sessions by prescribing varying ranges of movement.

> Under these conditions of contradictory individual norms, no convergence developed in any of the pairs. Subsequent questioning revealed that fully one-half of the subjects did not realize that they were in contradiction with their partners. They interpreted the addition of the integer 3 (or the dropping of the integer 3) as introduced for the sake of identifying each of the subjects in the dark room. The remaining subjects interpreted the existing difference in terms of such factors as differences of position with regard to the light, differences in eyesight, etc.

This means that even following individual sessions, with prescribed contradictory instructions and contradictory standards and norms, half of the subjects converged. The addition or dropping of the integer "3" (which the subjects thought was introduced as an experimental device) accounts for statistical but not for psychological nonconvergence as explained by the subjects who "did not realize that they were in contradiction with their partners."

In a more decisive variation aimed at the complete destruction of convergence, Asch and Wright performed the following experiment. In Asch's words:

> The aim of the following experiment was to alter in a decisive way the cognitive character of the situation. The subjects were informed in the individual session concerning the subjective nature of the autokinetic effect (each subject was paired in the present variation with a "planted" subject whose estimates differed considerably and consistently from the experimental subject's). There were ten subjects in this experiment. Under these conditions, five subjects showed no convergence effect whatsoever; the other five did depart significantly from their previous judgments and in the direction of the "planted"

subject. To explain the two forms of reaction, the subjects were questioned at the conclusion of the investigation. According to the present results, it seems that the subjects who showed the convergence effect continued to think of the autokinetic phenomenon as objective and *forgot the preceding instructions*. Nevertheless, the change found in the first half of the group conclusively demonstrates how effective the alteration of the cognitive character of the situation can be. [italics ours]

In spite of the fact that the subjects were told *beforehand* that the light was not moving at all and in spite of their individually established norms before coming into the group situation, it is surprising that there was any degree of convergence at all. We do not know if the 50 per cent convergence attributed by Asch to forgetting is in line with current forgetting curves. The lapse of time between the individual and group sessions cannot be longer than a few days.

Nevertheless the afore-mentioned variations which introduced into the situation various degrees of familiarity or objective knowledge of the situation account for the variations in the results obtained. They are in harmony with Sherif's results which showed that, once individual frames are established, convergence or agreement in subsequent group situations is decidedly affected by them. Likewise, the findings in these variations are in harmony with the conclusions of Chapman and Volkmann that previous familiarity with a situation prevents shifts in the direction of experimentally introduced standards or norms. Likewise, they are in harmony with the finding of Luchins that social influence varies, among other factors, with variations in structural clarity. And all are in harmony with the formulation reached in the previous section that the influence of internal and social factors increases directly with the increase of the unstructuredness or ambiguity of the situation, and decreases with the degree of the structuredness or unambiguity of frames and standards already established by an individual.

Experimental inculcation of a frame. As we stressed previously, frames are formed in the individual in daily life corresponding to objects and norms around him which are compelling in their objective structure. Quite frequently attitudes are formed as a direct consequence of short-cut verdicts or value judgments of grown-ups, teachers, and others around us. These value judgments may or may not be imbedded in the truth of actual relationships. We are concerned here with the psychological process involved in their acquisition. The formation of such a frame in a social situation has been experimentally demonstrated. The experiment was carried out by Sherif in the spring of 1936 at Columbia University again utilizing the autokinetic technique. [43]

The specific problem in the experiment was to see whether "naive" subjects could be experimentally inculcated with varying ranges of prescribed frames and standards. Preliminary experimentation had shown that a partner in this situation (in this case a partner with considerable prestige) could influence the judgments of the other subject—raise and lower them in his direction. When the "naive" subject was told exactly what had happened she became very disturbed, an indication that an individual can get emotionally upset by being so fooled. [92]

In the main experiment there were seven groups of two members each. In each group, one member co-operated with the experimenter by deliberately distributing his judgments around the range (scale) and a standard point within that range prescribed beforehand by the experimenter. The second member (designated as the "naive" subject) was totally unfamiliar with the situation. In each case the naive subject was not acquainted either with the experimenter or the co-operating subject. To be sure that the conformity was to the prescribed range and standard, a different range and a different standard were prescribed for each group. In order *to avoid the factor of primacy,* the co-operating subject was instructed to let the "naive" subject express his judgment first at least half the time. The first session was the group session with both the co-operating and "naive" subjects participating. In the second session the "naive" subject was *alone.*

The results indicate considerable convergence to the prescribed range (scale) and standard in the judgments of the "naive" subjects. The varying convergence in different subjects clearly indicates personality differences. The convergence of the judgments in the "alone" session, which took place the day following the group session, was, in general, even greater than that obtained in the group sessions. Introspections reveal that the subjects became conscious of the scale and standard formed during the course of the experiments: Five subjects out of seven reported in their written introspections at the end of the experiments that they were not influenced by the judgments of their partner. This clearly indicates that a social influence which continues even when the individual is alone need not be consciously experienced. Schonbar has recently obtained results which lead to the same conclusion. [40]

It is a significant fact to find convergence greater, in the majority of cases, when the individual is acting *alone*. It is not a rare occurrence in everyday life to react negatively or hesitatingly on some topic raised by some person while in his presence, but to respond positively when he is no longer in the situation. To yield easily is not a pleasant "ego" experience.

This experiment embodies in itself the rudiments of the psychology of attitude formation: a scale (or frame) is *formed* under the influence of the verdicts of another individual *in relation* to a definite experimentally controlled stimulus situation. The scale (frame) is carried from one day to another, has to some extent an *enduring* quality which provides an individual with a state of readiness by means of which he reacts in a *characteristic* way to the same stimulus situation. Here we have the main earmarks of an attitude. We must admit at once that this formation lacks the *affective* quality of a real attitude. But we do not believe this at all invalidates our conceptualization. The investigations of Beebe-Center [3] and associates, Cohen [12], and Hunt and Volkmann [24] all indicate that the mechanisms of affective judgments are not essentially different from those of other judgments. Besides, as we shall see, there is further evidence to support the general scheme so far presented.

REFERENCES

1. ALLPORT, F. H., The psychology of the artist's frame of reference, unpublished talk to Associated Artists, Syracuse, N. Y., April 17, 1945. (Outline of talk personally communicated to the authors.)
2. BARTLETT, F. C., *Remembering: A Study in Experimental and Social Psychology*, Cambridge (England): Univ. Press, copyright 1932.

3. BEEBE-CENTER, J. G., *Pleasantness and Unpleasantness,* New York: Van Nostrand, 1932.

4. BENARY, W., The influence of form on brightness contrast, in *A Source Book of Gestalt Psychology* (W. D. Ellis, ed.), New York: Harcourt, Brace, 1938, 104–08.

5. BLONDEL, C., *Introduction à la psychologie collective,* Paris: Colin, 1928.

6. BORING, E. G., Attribute and sensation, *Am. J. Psychol.,* 1924, **35**, 301–04.

7. CANTRIL, H., *The Psychology of Social Movements,* New York: Wiley, copyright 1941.

8. CHANDLER, A. R., *Beauty and Human Nature,* New York: Appleton-Century, 1934.

9. CHAPMAN, D. W., Relative effects of determinate and indeterminate *Aufgaben,* *Am. J. Psychol.,* 1932, **44**, 163–74.

10. —— and J. VOLKMANN, A social determinant of the level of aspiration, *J. Abnorm. & Soc. Psychol.,* 1939, **34**, 225–38.

11. COFFIN, T. E., Some conditions of suggestion and suggestibility: a study of certain attitudinal and situational factors influencing the process of suggestion, *Psychol. Monogr.,* 1941, no. 241.

12. COHEN, N. E., The relativity of absolute judgments, *Am. J. Psychol.,* 1937, **49**, 93–100.

13. DEARBORN, G. V., Blots of ink in experimental psychology, *Psychol. Rev.,* 1897, **4**, 390–1.

14. —— A study of imaginations, *Am. J. Psychol.,* 1898, **9**, 183–90.

15. DURKHEIM, E., *Les Formes élémentaires de la vie religieuse,* Paris, 1912.

16. FRANK, J. D., Some psychological determinants of the level of aspiration, *Am. J. Psychol.,* 1935, **47**, 285–93.

17. GOULD, R., An experimental analysis of "level of aspiration," *Genet. Psychol. Monogr.,* 1939, **21**, 1–116.

18. HAGGARD, E., and G. J. ROSE, Some effects of mental set and active participation in the conditioning of the autokinetic phenomenon, *J. Exp. Psychol.,* 1944, **34**, 45–59.

19. HALBWACHS, M., *Les Cadres sociaux de la mémoire,* Paris, 1925.

20. HENRI, V., Recherches sur la localisation des sensations tactiles, *Année Psychol.,* 1895, **2**, 168–92.

21. HOLLINGWORTH, H. L., The inaccuracy of movement, *Arch. Psychol.,* 1909, no. 13.

22. —— The central tendency of judgment, *J. Phil.,* 1910, **7**, 461–9.

23. HOPPE, F., Erfolg und Misserfolg, *Psychol. Forsch.,* 1930, **14**, 1–62.

24. HUNT, W. A., and J. VOLKMANN, The anchoring of an affective scale, *Am. J. Psychol.,* 1937, **49**, 88–92.

25. JUNG, C. G., *Psychological types,* New York: Harcourt, Brace, 1924.

26. KLOPFER, B., and D. M. KELLY, *The Rorschach Technique,* Yonkers: World Book, 1942.

27. KOFFKA, K., Perception: an introduction to the *Gestalt-Theorie, Psychol. Bull.,* 1922, **19**, 531–85.

28. —— *Principles of Gestalt Psychology,* New York: Harcourt, Brace, 1935.

29. KÖHLER, W., *Gestalt Psychology,* New York: Liveright, 1929.

30. KÜLPE, O., Versuche über Abstraktion, *Ber. I. Kongr. Exp. Psychol.,* 1904, 58–68.

31. Long, L., A study of the effect of preceding stimuli upon the judgment of auditory intensities, *Arch. Psychol.*, 1937, no. 209.

32. Luchins, A. S., On agreement with another's judgments, *J. Abnorm. & Soc. Psychol.*, 1944, 39, 97–111.

33. —— Social influences on perception of complex drawings, *J. Soc. Psychol.*, 1945, 21, 257–73.

34. McGarvey, H. R., Anchoring effects in the absolute judgment of verbal materials, *Arch. Psychol.*, 1943, no. 281.

35. Murray, H. A., *et al.*, *Explorations in Personality,* New York: Oxford, 1938.

36. Postman, L., and G. A. Miller, Anchoring of temporal judgments, *Am. J. Psychol.*, 1945, 58, 43–53.

37. Pratt, C. C., Time-errors in the method of single stimuli, *J. Exp. Psychol.*, 1933, 16, 798–814.

38. Proshansky, H., and G. Murphy, The effects of reward and punishment on perception, *J. Psychol.*, 1942, 13, 295–305.

39. Rogers, S., The anchoring of absolute judgments, *Arch. Psychol.*, 1941, no. 261.

40. Schonbar, R. A., Some social factors in judgment: the formation of social norms in the judgment of structured stimuli and esthetic preference, Ph.D. thesis, 1945, Columbia Univ. Library.

41. Sherif, M., A study of some social factors in perception, *Arch. Psychol.*, 1935, no. 187.

42. —— *The Psychology of Social Norms,* New York: Harper, copyright 1936.

43. —— An experimental approach to the study of attitudes, *Sociometry*, 1937, 1, 90–8.

44. Spranger, E., *Lebensformen,* Halle: Niemeyer, 1927.

45. Tresselt, M. E., The influence of amount of practice upon the formation of a scale of judgment, to be published in *J. Exp. Psychol.*

46. —— The effect of the experiences of contrasted groups upon the formation of a new scale of judgment, to be published.

47. —— and J. Volkmann, The production of uniform opinion by nonsocial stimulation, *J. Abnorm. & Soc. Psychol.*, 1942, 37, 234–43.

48. Volkmann, J., The anchoring of absolute scales, *Psychol. Bull.*, 1936, 33, 742–3.

49. Voth, A., Individual differences in the autokinetic phenomenon, *J. Exp. Psychol.*, 1941, 29, 306–22.

50. —— Psychologist's report, in *33rd biennial report* (Topeka State Hospital), 1942, 16–20.

51. Wedell, C. H., The nature of the absolute judgment of pitch, *J. Exp. Psychol.*, 1934, 17, 485–503.

52. Wertheimer, M., Untersuchungen zur Lehre von der Gestalt, *Psychol. Forsch.*, 1922, 1, 47–58.

53. —— *Drei Abhandlungen zur Gestalttheorie,* Erlangen: Phil. Akad., 1925.

54. Wever, E. G., and K. E. Zener, The method of absolute judgment in psychophysics, *Psychol. Rev.*, 1928, 35, 466–93.

55. Woodworth, R. S., Situation-and-goal set, in *Am. J. Psychol., Golden Jubilee vol.* (K. M. Dallenbach, ed.), 1937, 50, 130–40.

CHAPTER 4

THE ATTITUDE FORMULATION EXTENDED TO CONCRETE SITUATIONS

The conceptual scheme offered here towards the psychology of attitudes may appear to be an "artifact" based only on the results of laboratory experiments which have no counterparts in real life situations. So we turn now to some examples of more everyday life situations which seem to us to confirm the reality of our formulations. We cite here only a few of the many studies, ranging from relatively simple demonstrations to complex reactions of daily life, that confirm the conclusions reached in the more strictly laboratory settings.[1]

Irrespective of the particular way in which an individual acquires an attitude in social life, the literature of social psychology is rife with data which support the formulations reached from our survey of general psychology: that perception and judgment are selective and occur within a referential framework, that frames or points of reference are inevitably established if an individual repeatedly faces the same stimulus situation, that these frames and points of reference are by no means always confined to consciously accepted instructions or imposed norms but can become established without the individual's realization of it, and that once established these frames and points of reference serve as anchorages for perception and judgment.

---

[1] We might incidentally call attention here to the fact that most experiments on humans in the psychological laboratory are social situations at least to the extent that they involve verbal material in the instructions given to subjects. The variety of possible meanings of stimulus situations persistently gives trouble since meanings so readily intrude themselves. [38, 76, 94] It is well known that a subject's "set" or "attitude" can profoundly affect his reactions in psychological experiments. It may also be remembered that Titchener, in trying to create the "proper" set, advocated the use of "trained observers." From our present vantage point these results obtained only from observers trained to rule out objective references seem highly artificial.

It should be pointed out that, whereas scales and frames are experimentally constructed in the laboratory, when we are dealing with concrete social material it is generally necessary to select some range of stimuli which is meaningful in the particular situation we are concerned with. If some limits were not generally established by the social organization, it would be much more difficult than it is in actual practice to isolate the particular scale we may be interested in. But by and large, because of the relativity of values or norms in a given milieu at a given time, it is feasible to construct scales that deal, for example, with attitudes toward different races, government regulations, religion, occupational prestige. Likewise, everyday life judgments such as predictions made concerning the outcome of social conflicts are generally found to be made within a limited scalable range. [83]

We have already mentioned the fact that attitudes concerned with a person's position or status in social life are ego-involved and that such ego-involved experiences have affective properties. (p. 21) Since many attitudes related to social situations are more or less enduring affective fixations, they acquire a special importance to the individual. They become major constituents of the ego. The relationship between these social attitudes and the ego structure and the bearing of this relationship to motivation are considered in the next chapter. The significant fact that most social attitudes are ego-involved should, however, be borne in mind in connection with the material reported here.

In his series of experiments (one of which was referred to in the last chapter) Coffin investigated the psychology of suggestion as it was related both to attitudinal structure and to stimulus situations. [31] In his first experiment Coffin studied the relationship between an individual's attitude and the type of propaganda to which he was particularly susceptible. He found (in the winter of 1939 and 1940) significant correlations between pro-Allied attitudes on the one hand and the acceptance of specially prepared pro-Allied propaganda on the other hand. Conversely, those with pro-German attitudes accepted pro-German propaganda to a significant degree. In a second experiment Coffin used the Rorschach ink blots as stimuli with little structuration. After his subjects had rank-ordered a list of ten occupations according to their social standing, they were divided into two groups; each group was told the characteristic response given to the Rorschach ink blots by professional men, by business men, by skilled laborers, and by those on WPA, but the various characteristics were attributed to different occupations in the two experimental groups. The results clearly showed that, when these ambiguous stimuli were used, the subjects were highly influenced by the suggestions given which served as anchorages. They actively structured the imaginative situation according to the "characteristic reaction" to the blots of occupational groups they believed had high social standing. In a third experiment, testing the relationship between suggestibility and the difficulty of problem solution, Coffin found that, when mathematical problems were arranged in order of difficulty with marginal (and usually false) hints (anchorages) beside each problem as to what procedure might be used in its solution, respondents more highly trained in mathematics followed the marginal suggestions less: those who knew the most mathematics accepted less than half as many of the suggestions as those who knew least mathematics. Those persons, therefore, least able to make successful checks for themselves were most susceptible to an imposed instruction.

We have cited Coffin's experiments here at some length, since they provide unequivocal evidence of two important conclusions: (1) If a suggested stimulus is related to and consistent with an established frame of reference, it is likely to be accepted; and, (2) if a stimulus situation is ambiguous or relatively meaningless because of its difficulty, then a frame of reference verbally imposed by the experimenter is readily accepted as the basis for judgment.

A study by Ruth and Eugene Hartley concerned with poorly defined situations is particularly significant since it shows how individuals establish "individually characteristic ranges and reference points" by means of which they judge a relatively unstructured social stimulus. [43] The Hartleys had students rate a series of pictures of completely unknown men. Among other ratings, the subjects were asked to estimate each man pictured on his "general ability" and his "likeliness to succeed." They found a constancy of ranges and central tendencies in the judgments and conclude that

In making primary evaluative social responses to people, when little information is available, individuals tend to manifest characteristic ranges and central tendencies with reference to which judgments are made. [43]

The research of McGarvey "was undertaken in order to determine whether relations similar to those which have been found to hold with the psychophysical materials would appear also in judgments of verbal materials along value-dimensions." [66, 26] In her first experiment, McGarvey had subjects rate the social prestige attached to a number of occupations. After they had rated all occupations on a graphic scale, in further experimental sessions the top or the bottom category of the scale was set by an "anchoring value." In the second experiment the items judged were short descriptions of various types of social behavior to be evaluated in terms of their desirability. Again "anchoring stimuli" were introduced at either end of the scale. On the basis of these experiments McGarvey concluded that

> . . . the effect of the anchoring value was that of bringing about an extension of the absolute scale upward or downward in the direction of the anchoring value. The extension of the absolute scale involves not only a displacement of the scale with reference to the range of values represented by the stimulus-series, but also a widening of the categories of response,—a finding in complete agreement with the results obtained with psychophysical material. [66, 78]

In other words, judgment of a given stimulus is found to be determined by the frame of reference within which that judgment occurred, and the introduction of new anchorages changed the dimensions of reference frames. This precisely parallels on a social level the results obtained by Rogers reported in the last chapter.

The close relationship between memory and an individual's frame of reference was exhaustively shown by Bartlett who concluded that "remembering is 'schematically' determined," [8, 312] "an imaginative reconstruction, or construction, built out of the relation of our attitude towards a whole active mass of organized past reactions or experience, and to a little outstanding detail which commonly appears in image or in language form." [213]

The circumstances that arouse memory orientations, whether they occur in the laboratory or in everyday life, always set up an attitude that is primarily towards a particular "schematic" organization. [8, *312*]

What a person remembers, as well as what a person observes of a given stimulus situation, was, Bartlett found, clearly influenced by the particular social origin of the individual's attitude. He showed how these attitudes, and consequently recall and observation, varied according to the cultural background of the individual, how they differed among members of various groups within a given social system, and how they differed within the same individual when he was or was not in the actual social presence of other members of his group.

Various subsequent studies have indicated that material consistent with a person's attitude is much more likely to be remembered than material not consistent with it. Seeleman, in stating the problem of her experimental study of memory, says that "these differences in standards may be expressed as differences in subjective norms or frames of reference." [77, 7] She analyzed the influence of the attitude toward the Negro on the remembrance of pictures of whites and Negroes to which were attached, in one experiment, favorable or unfavorable phrases supposedly describing the individual shown. She found that persons with extremely unfavorable attitudes toward the Negro recognized fewer individual differences between the Negroes shown in the pictures, recognized correctly fewer Negro than white pictures, assigned to Negro pictures more unfavorable phrases and remembered these unfavorable phrases attached to Negro pictures more accurately than did persons favorable to Negroes. The evidence from these experiments is, then, that the attitude toward the Negro affects perception as well as memory.

Wood [93] studied the changes occurring when subjects with favorable and unfavorable attitudes toward Negroes wrote abstracts of an article concerning differences between Negroes and whites. She found that subjects omitted and distorted statements from the article and added new statements in the direction of their own attitudes. When these somewhat biased and ambiguous abstracts were read and restated by other subjects with similar attitudes, the extent of change in the direction of the subjects' attitudes was even greater than when the original, more structured, and objective article was abstracted.

G. W. Allport and Kramer have reported a study in which they found that persons who were most anti-Semitic were the most accurate judges of Semitism from pictures. [4]   Zillig showed experimentally that women tend to remember more items favorable to women, whereas men tend to remember more items favorable to men. [95]   Watson and Hartmann demonstrated that a person's attitude toward atheism clearly determined what he would remember of material concerning atheism and theism. [90]   Edwards discovered that the political attitudes of his subjects significantly determined their recognition of items contained in a speech they had previously heard about the New Deal. [34]   In another study Edwards demonstrated the extent to which a person's attitude stimulates him to rationalize his answers to factual statements with which he disagrees. [35]   Levine and Murphy have shown experimentally that both the learning and the forgetting of passages favorable or unfavorable to the Soviet Union are significantly affected by a person's attitude toward Communism. [63]

The psychology of testimony presents many vivid illustrations of the influence of attitude on observation, judgment, and memory. Stern's early experiments on *Aussage* showed the suggestive effect of leading questions and demonstrated that the effect of such suggestions often became "stabilized" to influence later or allied judgments.   He also demonstrated how persons tended to describe occurrences from the point of view of what was to them the "customary" or "usual" way for such occurrences to take place.   The attitude a witness has toward a dispute and a witness' own attitudes toward situations were apt to have considerable influence on the testimony of the witness, even though he might be a highly educated cautious individual. [86, 87]

In an unpublished study by Lazarsfeld and associates of the reaction of individuals of various nationality and racial backgrounds to the same motion picture, the effect of attitudes in determining what will or will not be observed and remembered and what emotional reactions will be aroused in different people by the same stimulus situation is clearly demonstrated.   The film was a short

British war picture, *Naples Is a Battleground,* shown to experimental groups in the early summer of 1944. Native white Americans tended to see in the film an example of American armed might and remembered particularly the showing of General Mark Clark; Negroes in the audience paid special attention to the Negro troops pictured; while most marked of all were the reactions of first-generation Italians who were impressed, saddened, or horrified by the ruins and extent of devastation. The experimenters observed that

> There were certain aspects of this film that stood out for some but not for others because of their differing mental sets as they watched it. [61]

A study of rumors made by Knapp in 1942 showed that "rumors become harmonized with the cultural traditions of the group in which they circulate." [57, *30*] Rumors are given particular twists as they penetrate groups where characteristic norms are found, such as a high degree of anti-Semitism, anti-Negro and anti-British sentiment. He noted, for example, that in the Italian section of Boston rumors of enemy submarines outside Boston Harbor were similar to rumors in other areas of the city except that people in the Italian section believed the submarines were Italian.

An experiment by George H. Smith [82] comparing the effects of fact and rumor labels on the credibility of news items has special relevance for our problem. Smith prepared as "news items" 26 statements concerning the Soviet Union. Half the statements were favorable to the Soviet Union, half unfavorable. One third of all subjects were given the statements as "actual facts" which had been completely checked, one third received them as "unverified rumors" for which the experimenter had failed to find factual support, while the remaining third reacted to statements that had no label attached. In addition, all subjects checked a scale measuring their attitudes toward the Soviet Union.

Smith found that

> The absolute amount of belief an individual places in the "news" items, under any condition of labeling, almost certainly depends in part on the initial attitude with which he approaches the items . . .

the plausibility of statements seems to be judged on the basis of some established scale. [82]

When a statement was labeled a "fact," judgment was considerably more altered than when it was labeled a "rumor," although the "rumor" label did have some effect.

> The fact label swings the subjects in the direction of greater belief and . . . the rumor label edges them toward lesser belief, as compared with no label at all. [82]

Smith's interpretation is that

> The "fact" label provides a tenuous standard of judgment which helps people to interpret a relatively ambiguous situation; but its effectiveness varies with its consistency to objective criteria or to established standards of judgment. . . . It [the "fact" label] probably served as a point of reference in "critical moments" when other factors were not adequate to lead to a decision. [82]

On the other hand,

> The rumor label is similar to no label at all in that it constitutes an ambiguous stimulus which forces people to interpret, or structure, the situation for themselves. [82]

Numerous experiments on the level of aspiration have shown how the same performance can be regarded either as a success or a failure, depending on the frame of reference in which the performance occurs. (pp. 120 ff.)   In the work of Chapman and Volkmann previously mentioned, the setting of a level of aspiration was studied under two sets of conditions. [30]   In one experiment involving familiarity with the authors of various literary passages, each of the different experimental groups was given in advance of their direct acquaintance with the task involved the score supposedly made by another group.   The score attributed to each group was the same but the groups varied in their prestige: authors and literary critics, students similar to the subjects, and WPA workers.   Results here show a clear-cut tendency for those comparing themselves to a superior group to lower their aspiration level, those comparing themselves to an inferior group to raise their aspiration level.   In their second experiment, involving a test of mental ability, all subjects were given a test in two sessions before any attempt was made to change their aspiration level by comparing their performance to inferior or superior groups. Under these conditions, no significant change in the level of aspiration was produced; "the subjects' own previous scores provided the most effective anchoring." [235] In the conditions of the first experiment, the stimulus situation is unstructured, and an imposed norm is accepted as a frame of reference; in the conditions of the second experiment, the stimulus situation has become structured through experience, and imposed norms are ineffectual.

Asch, Block, and Hertzman showed that judgments concerning the characteristics of different professional groups tend to be considerably modified when an evaluation from an authoritative source is introduced. [6] A close relationship was found between judgments on different characteristics of various professions, indicating that most of the judgments seemed to derive from underlying attitudes. They conclude that "the judgments of a single situation are related to each other by a person in accordance with an underlying attitude of acceptance or rejection" [248], that "a standard having an authoritative source tends to alter an individual's judgments in its direction" [249], that relationship in judgment becomes most clearly established "for situations which are not well-defined objectively" [251], and that "the observer, in the absence of objective criteria, and in the face of the necessity of reaching some conclusions, proceeds to arrange a scale of preference in terms of some generally favorable or unfavorable impression." [229]

Kay's study of the relationship between personal frames of reference and social judgments indicates that an individual's evaluation of various occupations is considerably more affected by accepted social norms relating to those occupations than by an individual's own preference for an occupation or his experience with it. [54] In other words, the social norms concerning the value and characteristics of common occupations are rather uncritically taken over by individuals as personal frames of reference by means of which specific judgments are made. Analyzing her data further according to the source of information concerning the various occupations rated, Kay found that for a third of the occupations "cultural" sources were mentioned most frequently, whereas the "personal" sources uncovered in the interviews were interpreted or reacted to on the basis of "personal frames of reference" and "in the light of existing social norms" rather than on the basis of the "objective quality of the experiences themselves." [55, 363] This interpretation confirms Davis' study on the attitudes of children in Soviet Russia with its finding that Russian children rated laboring people high and lawyers and bankers low. [32] In their examination of the basis of prestige judgments of various occupational groups, Osgood and Stagner demonstrated that the "decisions about characteristics of occupational stereotypes tend to conform closely to a framework which is based on the relative prestige of occupations." [75, 287] They conclude that

> . . . the mere presentation of a set of occupational stereotypes for a series of judgments caused our subjects spontaneously to establish a prestige framework which then determined in a highly reliable manner judgments on the specific traits listed. [75, 289]

Asch found that an individual's judgment of relatively ill-defined and unclear situations could be changed when the imputed judgment of congenial groups was introduced as a reference. [7] On the other hand, subjects tended to reject the judgment of antagonistic groups. Here we have evidence that an individual tends to accept an imposed norm as his own frame of reference for judging a situation when that situation is itself unclear or when he has no pre-existing, sure, or ego-involved frame of reference of his own. An analysis of radio listeners who followed a particular commentator indicated that the chief function of a news commentator is to provide frames of reference by means of which listeners can judge the plethora of events going on around them. [22] The less people know about objective conditions, the more they depend on a commentator to tell them what these events mean and to help them select items to read in their newspapers.

One of the most penetrating studies of the development of prevalent attitudes in our social system is that of Horowitz on the genesis of attitudes toward the Negro. [45] He demonstrated unequivocally that this attitude is imposed bodily and uncritically without any basis in experience or knowledge. He concludes "that attitudes toward Negroes are now chiefly determined not by contact with Negroes, but by contact with the prevalent attitude toward Negroes." [35] Horowitz developed a series of ingenious tests to measure attitudes toward the Negro objectively. These tests were administered to children and adolescents in a variety of social groups—children in the rural and urban South, all white groups in New York City, mixed groups in New York City, and a group of New York Communist children. His tests showed that children in New York City were just as prejudiced as the children in the South, that children in mixed schools were as prejudiced as those in all white schools, that contact with popular Negro children had no effect on attitudes, and that the only group of children tested who had no prejudice against the Negro were children of Communist parents—people devoid of racial prejudices which they would pass on to their children. Furthermore, Horowitz found that Negro boys in mixed schools tended to accept some of the racial attitudes of the white majority of their group.[2] His findings confirm the earlier conclusions of Lasker's well-known study that race attitudes in children are due chiefly to "the absorption of adult attitudes," [60, 371] and that contacts between children of different races are almost invariably influenced by the "adult-made environment." [371] G. W. Allport and Kramer found that if this adult environment contains institutionalized religious training a young person is more likely to be prejudiced against minority groups than if such institutionalized religious training is absent. [4] Such findings as these indicate once more that, when rigidly established norms are accepted by an individual, his thinking on and reaction to related situations is highly inflexible. [65]

In a significant study concerned with the development of stereotypes toward the Negro, Blake and Dennis [12] had students from grades 4 through 11 in a southern school compare whites and Negroes on 60 characteristics. Their results showed that there was less agreement among the younger children who had a "relatively undifferentiated" attitude unfavorable to the Negro. They conclude that

[2] This is reminiscent of the fact that in the days of slavery in the United States there was a sizable number of freed Negro slaves who, when they acquired land of their own, retained Negro slaves to work it. [39]

... the young white child acquires first of all a generally unfavorable attitude toward the Negro, which makes him unwilling to attribute to the Negro any "good" traits. With increased age and experience, the child gradually learns to apply the adult stereotypes, a few of which are complimentary. [12, *531*]

The extent to which the accepted attitude toward the Negro affects judgment and goes against all evidence has been illustrated by a public opinion survey made in 1944 on a nationwide sample of the adult white population in the United States. A majority of those with opinions believe that Negroes are not as intelligent as white people and cannot learn as well if they are given the same education. And a third of our white population believes that Negro blood somehow differs from white blood, a third of the people believe it is the same, and a third say they don't know. [72] Murphy and Likert concluded from their study of attitudes toward minority groups that

... the individual usually acquires his prejudices against a minority group not primarily from contact with this minority group but chiefly from contact with the prevailing attitude toward this minority group. [70, *136*]

The acceptance of attitudes is further confirmed by studies which have shown the ease with which people characterize various nationality groups, irrespective of their lack of knowledge about or experience with these groups. Katz and Braly found that the preferential ranking of students for various nationality and racial groups closely followed a weighted ranking of the judgment of a comparable group of students on the stereotype of these same groups. [52] Public opinion surveys have shown that less than 10 per cent of the American population feel unable to select from a list of adjectives those that best describe various nationality groups and that people in our culture have generally similar stereotypes concerning the characteristics of major nationality and racial groups. [15]

Particularly significant as an indication of the way in which even minority groups accept the values of the larger macrocosm is the comparison that can be made between the characterizations of various racial groups by white and Negro Americans. For example, Meenes's results [68] on the Katz-Braly list of racial characteristics when used with Negro students are by and large consistent with those obtained on white students in 1933. [51] White students at Princeton and Negro students at Howard had essentially similar stereotypes concerning such peoples as the Jews, English, Irish, Turks. This is quite in keeping with Horowitz' finding previously mentioned concerning the acceptance of white attitudes by Negro children in mixed schools. The single notable exception in Meenes's study is the tendency of the Negro students to judge their own racial group on the basis of a different frame and hence to assign to it fewer uncomplimentary adjectives, such as "lazy" or "ignorant."

The extent to which stereotypes influence judgment has been clearly demonstrated experimentally. Sherif, for example, showed that college students both in the United States and in Turkey were significantly affected in their rating of a literary passage by the name of the author attributed to that passage. [80] The passages used in the United States were all by one author, those used in Turkey were all by another author. The judgments of these passages, then, were made largely in terms of established values. These results are similar to earlier demonstrations of everyday stereotypes shown by Zillig [95] among others and were confirmed later on still another type of material. [19]

It is obvious that the whole psychology of fads and fashions is to be explained largely in terms of accepted norms and values that provide standards of judgment for style, correctness, and certain criteria for status, beauty, significance, and the like (pp. 348 ff.). In a note "concerning scientific progress" at the end of his *Sensation and Perception in the History of Experimental Psychology,* Boring shows that even scientists, including psychologists, tend to conform to the *Zeitgeist* and are retarded by habits of thought currently fashionable or by "laboratory atmosphere." [13] It should be pointed out in this connection, however, that atmospheres of psychological laboratories, as well as more common fads and fashions, sooner or later change with new factors imposed by objective conditions or by the accumulation of evidence. The dresses women have for everyday wear in the western world can no longer be styled without reference to the demands of the machine age in which they live; the Titchenerian influence could not remain unaffected by the results of Würzburg. As facts pile up in psychology or any other science, laboratory atmospheres and "schools of thought" become increasingly tenuous.

Newcomb measured the change of attitudes of students in a small college community where nonconservative attitudes were considered to be more "proper" and to carry more prestige than conservative attitudes. [71] He found that this "community frame of reference" [151] significantly influenced the attitudes of students in the liberal direction during their four years, irrespective of the courses studied in college. Newcomb describes this shift of attitude as general rather than as a shift of a series of specific attitudes toward specific issues. When events or new proposals were reacted to, the more advanced students more consistently reacted to them in a liberal way.

The way in which an individual's own present income provides a reference point for judging financial needs and aspiration has been demonstrated by Centers and Cantril. [29] In a nationwide survey concerned with the relationship of present income to satisfaction and wants, they found that, among those people dissatisfied with their present income, the larger the income is, the more additional money is wanted. An analysis of judgments made by persons in different income groups of the income tax people in various income brackets should pay shows that those in the low income groups have such inadequate standards for judging the incomes of people in high income brackets that they tend to find such judgments difficult or impossible to make. Furthermore, when judgments are made by persons in the lower income groups of the tax which those in the highest brackets should pay, the figure given is significantly less than the tax upper income groups think should be paid by the rich, illustrating again the way in which judgment is anchored in individual frames of reference. [40]

From his investigation of the effect of the monetary value of objects on the perception of number, Ansbacher [5] whose research follows Brunswik's [17] concluded that "monetary value through familiarity does influence perception under certain circumstances." [86] Ansbacher used stamps of different denominations in his experiment. To study the variable of familiarity, both Canadian and American stamps were shown to Canadian and American observers. Subjects were asked to compare the number of stamps of one denomination in one group of stamps with the number of another denomination in another group. Under other instructions comparisons were made of the value represented by the two groups of stamps. A controlled psychophysical series, using stamps of the same denomination, was introduced in the experimental sessions.

Ansbacher found that the judgment of the number of stamps of different denominations "is more variable than a comparable psychophysical judgment, viz., where both standard and variable groups consist of the same stamps." [83] A constant error appeared, similar to that found on judgments of size.

> In familiar stamps we find after psychophysical judgments a slight tendency to under-estimate the more valuable group with respect to number [83] . . . value through familiarity does affect perception. [84]

Especially significant for us is Ansbacher's finding that the greater variability in the number judgments disappears "if the number judgment is preceded by a psychophysical judgment . . . preceding psychophysical judgments seem to strengthen the number aspect at the expense of all incidental objects." [83] In other words, if the subjects are able to establish a scale by repeated exposure to the series of stimuli, that scale, rather than one influenced by an imposed norm is used for reference.

In a series of interesting experiments where coins were used as stimuli, Bruner and associates [1, 42] have recently studied "the influence of social value and social need upon the perception of objects under ambiguous and unambiguous conditions." [16, 241] They investigated the hypotheses that

> . . . (a) the greater the social value of an object, the more will it undergo perceptual distortion away from "objective" size, color, weight, etc., (b) the stronger the individual need for such valued objects, the greater will be the distorting effect of value, (c) ambiguity in the perceptual field will either facilitate or reduce value distortion depending upon whether it favors or opposes the prominence of value cues. [241]

In the first experiment, children from two groups with widely differing economic status (from a private school and a settlement house) were asked to judge the size of coins from a penny to a half dollar.

> For both groups, the greater the value of the coin, the greater the constant error of overestimation. Pennies were seen as 10 per cent larger than actual size, half dollars 35 per cent larger. The tendency of overestimation is significantly more marked among poor than among rich children. [*241*]

When the same experiment was repeated with adults, judgments continued to show a distortion but one that was more discriminative. The adults judged pennies, nickels, and dimes as smaller than their actual size; quarters and half-dollars as larger. Further experiments with adults using "made" money, showed that symbols with the highest value (dollars) produced greatest overestimation, that a meaningful but not highly valued symbol (swastika) produced less overestimation, while a meaningless symbol produced still less.[3] As the investigators point out, these results "suggest principles going beyond Weber's Law and Hollingworth's central tendency effect." [*241*] And they are entirely consistent with the findings of Bartlett, Coffin, and others already reported.

Kornhauser's investigations of the class attitudes of various socioeconomic groups have shown that in our American social system "logically opposed interests" do not by any means lead to uniformly opposed class attitudes. [58, 59] Kornhauser did find, however, that those persons within each economic group who were most dissatisfied in terms of their present status and opportunity did accept less frequently than others the traditional *status quo* as measured by attitudes concerning labor, government control, and the like. And although the attitudes of income and occupational groups were not diametrically opposed, still significant differences appeared between the attitudes of these groups on a number of social and political issues. In other words, objective conditions did not fit currently accepted economic and social norms. Particularly significant for our purposes are Kornhauser's reports of the in-

---

[3] The results of this second experiment were personally communicated to the writers by J. S. Bruner in May 1946.

stances where no significant differences are found between the attitudes of different economic groups. These attitudes, accepted rather uniformly, were those which reflected the traditional American ideology concerning individual opportunity either for the person himself or for his children. In chapter 6 we consider in more detail the current relationship among class identifications, status, and attitudes in the United States.

That the attitudes toward labels describing different political systems are by and large uncritically accepted without any real knowledge of the principles or implications of those political systems has been established in a number of different studies. Stagner demonstrated, for example, that people will have a distinctly unfavorable attitude toward Fascism but at the same time will accept certain fascist doctrines. [84] Menefee comes to the same conclusion in his studies which reveal that if the statement of a political or economic principle is labeled as "fascist" it will call forth a much more negative reaction than it will without the label. [69] Edwards concludes from his investigations that

> Some college students have a far greater degree of sympathy for certain fascist principles than might be expected from their otherwise antagonistic reaction to the fascist label. [36, 580]

Significantly enough, Edwards found that those persons who labeled themselves politically as "independents" were considerably more critical of statements of fascist principles than those who called themselves Democrats or Republicans. Katz and Cantril found that the attitude toward Fascism or Communism bore little relationship to the knowledge of Fascism or Communism among college students in 1939. [53] Their study also shows that, although there was an overwhelming rejection of the terms "Fascism" and "Communism," the majority of students felt at the time (before World War II had brought the implications of Fascism into clearer focus) that Fascism was a good thing for Germany and Italy but would be a bad thing for the United States, whereas Communism was a good thing for Russia but would be a bad thing for Germany and Italy and especially for the United States.

In testing the effect of the labels "Communism," "Fascism," "liberal," and "reactionary," on passages that very obviously stated a point of view, Birch found that "even a well-structured attitude is affected to some degree by the application of a socially disapproved label." [11, *310*] The fact that Birch was able to shift the *degree* of support given a statement when different labels were applied to it but was unsuccessful in shifting support from one statement to another, only emphasizes our contention that if a stimulus situation is in sharp contrast to a well-established frame to which it is easily related, no reversals in judgment should be expected. "Prestige" labeling is effective in determining a frame in proportion to the ambiguity of the stimulus situation. As we have said before, no realistic purpose is served by trying to have a person see a square as a circle. The investigations already cited show that broad symbols do tend to be accepted in social life without objective reference since objective reference is often not compellingly introduced in the stimulus situation. Those who use prestige labeling for propaganda purposes are, of course, eager to shift attention from any objective references that might contradict the frame they are attempting to build up.

Analyses of political attitudes have indicated clearly that for the vast majority of modern Americans the way in which they vote is determined chiefly by the political attitude they have accepted rather than by any analysis of different party platforms or candidates. Hartmann has shown that individuals frequently accept the stated principles of political parties they strongly disapprove of so long as they are unaware that these principles have the endorsement of those parties. [44] Cantril and Harding discovered that over half of the voting population in the United States were completely unable to tell what the differences were between the major political parties even though the overwhelming majority of these same people voted consistently for one or the other of the major political parties. [25] Their analysis of the U. S. Congressional election of 1942 shows that the overwhelming proportion of the major issues of the day which might logically be thought to have some relationship to the way a person voted and which were discussed during the election campaign as partisan issues actually had little or no importance in determining vote. They also showed how people rationalize their accepted attitude by claiming that they usually vote for the candidate rather than for the party that candidate represents. At least two thirds of the people who vote a straight party ticket claim that they vote for the man rather than the party. Even the minority of voters who classify themselves as "independents" appear, on closer scrutiny, to be considerably less independent than they claim. At least half of the "independents" vote a straight party ticket and well over half of the "independents" vote according to their father's political affiliation.

Lazarsfeld, Berelson, and Gaudet have shown that a fairly reliable index of "political predisposition" can be constructed for an individual from a knowledge of three social factors: religious affiliation, economic status, and place of residence. [62] They found that cross pressures of these three social factors tended to delay a person's decision as to how he would vote. Relatively few voters were sufficiently affected by political propaganda to change their political predisposition. Persons tend to expose themselves mainly to the political propaganda of their own party, but those whose predisposition is toward one of the major parties and who expose themselves more than others of their persuasion to opposition propaganda do tend to vote more than others for the opposition party. The less structured a person's political attitude is, because of either lack of interest or social pressures, the greater is the variability of voting behavior and the greater is the influence of propaganda from various media or the effect of personal contact.

Breslaw concluded from his detailed interviews concerned with the development of political attitudes that political attitudes can more appropriately be described as an "orientation" or "bias" than a "point of view" logically arrived at. [14]

> Attitudes emerge from the particular social life which happens to surround the individual. [14, 65]

An attitude

> . . . is an end product with no necessary relationship to the particular components of that stimulation. An attitude is something that becomes implanted—as fear of the dark becomes implanted—in many different ways. [14, 66]

The consistency with which an individual's attitude determines his reactions to situations to which he relates the attitude has been shown in a number of different studies. Vetter found that a person who was radical or conservative tended to be radical or conservative in his reaction to a wide variety of social, political, and ethical situations. [88] Katz and F. H. Allport noted the "consistency with which different attitudes seem to fit together in their respective patterns." [50, 48] Cantril demonstrated that an attitude has a directive influence on numerous specific reactions to which it is related, that an attitude tends to be enduring and constant even though the situations which evoke it may fluctuate, and that an attitude can be quite independent of the particular experiences which may have established it. [18] Stagner found that persons who are intensely chauvinistic tend to react consistently and unfavorably to a wide variety of issues such as tariff reduction, labor unions, or government ownership. [85]

In a study of the reaction of the American people to World War II, we find that, while the religious frame of Catholics previous to Pearl Harbor affected their attitude toward U. S. intervention in the European war, it did not affect their attitude toward U. S. intervention in the Pacific war—in the latter case there was no conflict between religious and nationalistic attitudes influencing the judgments of a stimulus situation. [27] The conflict of attitudes in German–American and Italian–American citizens resulting from U. S. intervention in World War II and the effect of this conflict in voting behavior is revealed by the findings of Bean, Mosteller, and Williams that these two groups significantly shifted their vote away from Roosevelt in the 1940 election. [9]

Analysis of data obtained from public opinion polls shows that major events are judged in terms of frames of reference which enable people to relate these events to their own self-interest. Hence public opinion on specific issues is highly sensitive to events. [26] Polls further show that, once the vast majority of individuals become aware that a social, economic, or political problem exists, they do develop attitudes toward that problem: the proportion of people who remain neutral or who have no opinion about an issue they are aware of is very small indeed.

Studies on the prediction of social events have indicated the enormous extent to which attitudes direct the way in which the future is projected. [21, 67, 83]   A person's attitude toward social-ism, for example, largely determines his picture of future economic trends.   But the more highly structured and clear-cut the forces determining the resolution of an issue appear to be, the less is an individual's prediction determined by his own attitude.   Predic-tions are especially influenced by frames or points of reference when the issue judged is ambiguous or unstructured because of the variety and apparent inconsistency of direction of the variables concerned.

Although the bulk of our attitudes do seem to be derived from the norms that surround us, the fact remains that—*all other things being equal*—individuals do acquire attitudes based on knowledge and reasoned analysis.   Murphy and Likert found, for example, that, next to parental influence, a student's reading habits and scholarship tended more than other factors to affect his atti-tudes. [70]   It has been shown that there was a tremendous differ-ence between enlightened and unenlightened Americans in their pre-Pearl Harbor attitudes toward U. S. intervention in the war— with enlightenment being based on general knowledge and a feeling of a clear idea of what the war is all about. [27]   Differ-ences of opinion according to the degree of "enlightenment" were found within all income groups and were considerably greater than differences of opinion between income groups themselves. Evidence from public opinion polls shows that well-informed people accept less readily than uninformed persons many of the common stereotypes of the day, the facts they know serving as reference points for discrimination. [91]   For example, Walsh [89] analyzed the relationship between the amount of information the American people had about the Soviet Union and their con-fidence in Russian postwar co-operation.   Information appeared as a much more decisive determinant of opinion than did eco-nomic status or religion.   He found that, in the fall of 1944, 73 per cent of those who were best informed trusted Russia to co-operate with the United States, whereas only 30 per cent of those least informed trusted Russia.   More highly educated people appear better able to see the implications of a point of view they

hold and are more consistent in their attitudes than are less educated persons. A study of American attitudes toward freedom of
speech, made during the critical summer of 1940, indicated that,
although well-educated people were somewhat more opposed to
free speech at that time than less well-educated persons, among all
those who did favor free speech the well-educated were more
willing

> . . . to extend their tolerance to the logical conclusion of allowing
> Fascists and Communists to speak. Such a finding seems to indicate
> that these people are more burdened by the intellectual demand for
> consistency than are persons who have had less educational oppor-
> tunity. [27, 183 f.]

Informed people are better able than uninformed to see the
implications to their own self-interest of events and proposals.
They show considerably more concern, for example, with international affairs as contrasted to relatively uninformed persons whose
predominant concern is with strictly domestic problems. [28]
The uninformed group generally has a comparatively higher "no
opinion" reaction to most public questions. Differences of opinion
according to the amount of information a person has do *not*
appear, however, with respect to issues where wish fulfillment is
clearly involved. For example, a study of the relative importance
of education and economic status in determining opinion showed
that education was more important than income only in situations
where greater knowledge gives an insight into the effect of certain
events or proposals that do not deal with an individual's financial
return in any clear-cut way. [92]   Diven's analysis of aesthetic
appreciation indicates that—all other things being equal—if a well-
informed and an uninformed person hold the same attitude with
equal intensity the essential difference between them is that the
informed man will be better able to rationalize his point of view,
supporting it with what seems to him sound evidence. [33]
A study of the nationwide panic in the United States resulting
from Orson Welles's broadcast, "War of the Worlds," showed that
when individuals are faced with a critical and apparently dangerous situation they readily accept any interpretation offered them
as a basis for judgment if they have no appropriate and sure

standards by means of which to evaluate the situation. [23] Those frightened by the broadcast were highly suggestible, believing what they heard to be true and being unable themselves to make any external or internal checks of the reports. Furthermore, for most of those who became panicked, the story was credible since it fitted into pre-existing attitudes such as the belief that God would someday destroy our planet, or an attack by a foreign power, or fanciful notions concerning the possibilities of science. People who lacked appropriate standards to interpret the broadcast properly were found particularly among those who had neither the opportunity nor the ability to acquire information or training that would have protected them with relevant points of reference. This broadcast occurred in the fall of 1938 when vast numbers of the population were unusually bewildered by the prolonged economic insecurity they had experienced and by the precarious and delicate state of world affairs following the Munich settlement. In commenting on the panic, Heywood Broun tersely and aptly summarized this effect of general, social, and political unrest by saying that "jitters have come to roost." Current norms were somehow proving inadequate to account for objective conditions; the whole course of recent history created a relatively ambiguous and unstructured situation conducive to high suggestibility.

And just as critical conditions provide fertile soil for panics, so too do they provide the optimum conditions for rumor or for individual reorientation by means of slogans or simple appeals. Knapp concludes, for example, from his study of rumors that "in proportion as the cognitive world is ambiguous or ill defined and the motivation intense, rumors will find life." [57, *31*] F. H. Allport and Lepkin in their study of rumors point out that

> The more "outer" facts, or true reports of facts, the individual has within his grasp, and the more he is stimulated to weigh this evidence objectively, the more nearly the picture he forms "in his mind" will conform to the true reality, and the less altered it will be through the effect of emotion and impulse. [3, *14*]

And Sherif points out, from his analysis of slogans,

> . . . that slogans are short-cut expressions arising in confused and critical situations . . . the more correctly and the more objectively a

set of slogans expresses the underlying forces in a critical situation, the more vital and lasting they will prove to be. [81, *461*]

In a more recent study of slogans, Bellak reaches the same conclusion with special emphasis on the role of motivational factors. [10] Since slogans can only be expected to take hold in critical times when they give meaning to or point a way out of confused situations, it is not surprising that the judgments of slogans in the laboratory are unaffected by conflicting standards, as in the experiment of Asch, Block, and Hertzman [6], or Block's later study where only restricted shifts were found in the ratings of slogans when authoritative standards were imposed under laboratory conditions. [64] The leaders of any mass movement or revolution show sound psychology when, during a critical situation where old norms have lost their hold, they try first of all to get control of the mass media of communication so they can issue new instructions, spread slogans, and otherwise try to restructure people's thinking.

Analysis of the rise of various social movements shows how persons dissatisfied with their status or the fulfillment of their needs tend to accept new frames of reference provided by a leader or nuclear group which seem to them to "explain" their situation more appropriately and to offer an apparently more effective course of action than did adherence to the more commonly accepted norms of the social system. [24] The suggestibility of a person to new norms was found to be proportional to the inadequacy of existing standards for the interpretation of particular situations, to his desire for a more adequate interpretation, or to the ease with which the norms of a new movement could be related to established frames.

FRAME OF REFERENCE IN SOME RECENT ECONOMIC WORKS

Since the 1930's, economists in capitalistic countries have been introducing psychological concepts into their construction of a "dynamic" economic theory, as contrasted to the more "timeless" classical economics. They are bringing out into the open for close scrutiny what had only been implicit assumptions of more static theories: assumptions centering around the concept of "expectations." And the expectations discussed by modern economists are frames of reference that determine or may in some way affect response to economic conditions.

The English economist, Shackle, in his *Expectations, Investment, and Income* [78] writes that

> The task of dynamic economics is to describe the inherent character of an economy in such a way that, given the particular situation existing at one moment, as to the conceptions of the future held by different individuals and the composition of the material equipment, it is possible to deduce the situation which will ensue, if there are no abnormal extra-economic impacts, after some arbitrary interval. At any one moment the expectations of a business man, which determine the decision he makes at this moment as to his action in the immediate future, are given. The totality of action by all business men in a short interval depends, if we take this interval short enough, on new decisions taken or old decisions left in force at the beginning of this interval. The totality of action in such an interval thus depends on the sets of expectations held by different business men at the beginning of the interval, and these are given. [78, 1]

Keynes made the concept of expectations central in his *The General Theory of Employment, Interest, and Money* which had such a profound influence on contemporary economic thinking.

> All production is for the purpose of ultimately satisfying a consumer. Time usually elapses, however—and sometimes much time—between the incurring of costs by the producer (with the consumer in view) and the purchase of the output by the ultimate consumer. Meanwhile the entrepreneur (including both the producer and the investor in this description) *has to form the best expectations he can* as to what the consumers will be prepared to pay when he is ready to supply them (directly or indirectly) after the lapse of what may be a lengthy period; and *he has no choice but to be guided by these expectations,* if he is to produce at all by processes which occupy time. [56, 46, italics ours]

After distinguishing between two groups of expectations, short-term and long-term, Keynes points out that "express reference to long-term expectations can seldom be avoided." [50] These long-term expectations are based on whatever data are available as well as on the confidence with which any forecast is made.[4]

The referential nature of these expectations is clearly recognized. Shackle [78], for example, writes that

> Before we can use Mr. Keynes' system to explain the economic pattern which emerges with the passage of time, we must release expectations from their status as a datum, and make them depend, at any moment, on the comparison which we may suppose business men to make between their expectations of a slightly earlier moment and what has actually happened in the interval. [78, 2]

And Shackle points out in a later article that it is necessary to "study the psychology of expectations as a process of the individual mind." [79, 99]

This concept of expectation is not confined merely to economic theory. It finds its place in concrete affairs of everyday life as is illustrated in the report of a Presidential fact-finding board set up to review the General Motors' strike in the United States in 1946. [73] The report contains such phrases as these:

> On balance, *we think it reasonable to expect* that in the early months of the new period productivity will be somewhat less than in 1941. ... *We think it reasonable to suppose* that in the year 1946, once this strike is settled and production begins again ... [73]

And the President of General Motors, commenting on the report of the fact-finding board, said that the wage recommendation made *"is based on certain assumptions* which in the opinion of General Motors are unsound." [74]

The Federal Government of the United States in trying to formulate some of its policies is relying more and more on controlled investigations of expectations so policy makers will have some idea of what the future behavior of certain segments of the popu-

---

[4] Keynes's clear awareness of the fact that the economic behavior of men in bourgeois society occurs within a limited frame of reference they may be quite unaware of is reflected in a closing passage of his "General Theory": "Practical men, who believe themselves to be quite exempt from any intellectual influences, are usually the slaves of some defunct economist. Madmen in authority, who hear voices in the air, are distilling their frenzy from some academic scribbler of a few years back. I am sure that the power of vested interests is vastly exaggerated compared with the gradual encroachment of ideas." [56, 383]

lation may be. For example, in 1942 and 1943, public expectations concerning price control were studied for the Office of Price Administration [48]; the Board of Governors of the Federal Reserve System used public opinion surveys because, as they say,

> It is particularly important to know something about the attitudes taken by liquid asset holders toward their liquid assets. [37]

And the U. S. Department of Agriculture makes periodic checks on farmers' expectations, because

> It is evident that the planning of postwar farm programs must depend greatly on what farmers themselves want and feel they must have. [2, *i*]

Thus government officials concerned with predictions explicitly recognize the fact that behavior can be predicted only if the frame of reference within which it occurs is understood.

This relationship between the concept of expectations as used by economists and the psychological concept of frame of reference has been made explicit by George Katona. [46, 47, 49] He has pointed out that "the frame of reference of important economic groups" plays a large part "in determining economic decisions and actions." [47, *340*] He notes the importance of determining whether expectations are based on rumors or on facts and emphasizes that the understanding and prediction of economic behavior can be precise only if the frame of reference used is sufficiently encompassing to take into account new problems and situations brought about by events.

In 1938, in a study of a specific social movement prominent at the time (the kingdom of Father Divine), we indicated how this cult could be regarded as a microcosm within the larger world macrocosm, how conflicts between the values of the two were inevitable and how either microcosms must "be patterned to fit the needs of an individual living in our modern world, or the conditions in the larger macrocosm must be changed to provide the satisfactions and meanings now artificially derived in the microcosms." [20, *166*] It is significant to see the same distinction made by modern economists and to read that if economic analysis is to be "truly dynamic," the relationship of a "section of the huge economic mechanism" must be related to "fluctuations of the whole economic system taken in its entirety." Frisch wrote in 1933:

> When we approach the study of a business cycle with the intention of carrying through an analysis that is truly dynamic . . . we are naturally led to distinguish between two types of analyses: the micro-dynamic and the macro-dynamic types. The micro-dynamic analysis is an analysis by which we try to explain in some detail the behaviour of a certain section of the huge economic mechanism, taking for granted that certain general parameters are given. Obviously it may well be that we obtain more or less cyclical fluctuations in such sub-systems, even though the general parameters are given. The essence of this type of analysis is to show the details of the evolution of a given specific market, the behaviour of a given type of consumers, and so on.
>
> The macro-dynamic analysis, on the other hand, tries to give an account of the fluctuations of the whole economic system taken in its entirety. Obviously in this case it is impossible to carry through the analysis in great detail. [41, *172*]

All of the representative studies cited indicate that only by means of some frame or anchorage can and does the individual judge and react to social stimuli. Individuals in social life cannot long remain normally adjusted if they are in a state of indecision. Sooner or later they must and do make some appropriate judgment or reaction to a stimulus, place it in some way meaningful to them. The psychological process they use to make such judgments and give meaning to their social environment is to refer the stimuli around them to some frame of reference or anchorage they acquire and which is a readiness for reaction. These frames or anchorages which regulate everyday social judgments to an important degree, like frames or anchorages discovered in laboratory experiments, inevitably develop with repeated exposure to the same stimuli (objects, persons, groups, values, or norms) and individuals are by no means always aware that frames or anchorages have become established. Furthermore, as we indicate in later chapters, social attitudes are among the major components of the ego. Hence the psychology of ego-involvement and its relation to motivation can only be clearly understood with reference to the basic properties of frame formation and the implications this has for ·udgment and action.

REFERENCES

1. ABROMSON, F., *Perception: Further Evidence for a Trifactorial Theory,* Honor's Thesis, Harvard Univ., Dept. Psychol., 1946.
2. AGRICULTURE, U. S. DEPARTMENT OF, *Farmers View the Postwar World,* Bur. Agricultural Economics, September 25, 1944.
3. ALLPORT, F. H., and M. LEPKIN, Wartime rumors of waste and special privilege, *J. Abnorm. and Soc. Psychol.,* 1945, **40,** 3–36.
4. ALLPORT, G. W., and B. M. KRAMER, Some roots of prejudices, *J. Psychol.,* 1946, **22,** 9–39.
5. ANSBACHER, H., Perception of number as affected by the monetary value of the objects: a critical study of the method used in the extended constancy phenomenon, *Arch. Psychol.,* 1937, **30,** no. 215.
6. ASCH, S. E., H. BLOCK, and M. HERTZMAN, Studies in the principles of judgments and attitudes: I. Two basic principles of judgment, *J. Psychol.,* 1938, **5,** 219–51.
7. ASCH, S. E., Studies in the principles of judgments and attitudes: II. Determination of judgments by group and by ego standards, *J. Soc. Psychol.,* 1940, **12,** 433–65.
8. BARTLETT, F. C., *Remembering: a study in experimental and social psychology,* Cambridge (England): Univ. Press, copyright 1932.
9. BEAN, L. H., F. MOSTELLER, and F. WILLIAMS, Nationalities and 1944, *Publ. Opin. Quart.,* 1944, **8,** 368–75.
10. BELLAK, L., The nature of slogans, *J. Abnorm. & Soc. Psychol.,* 1942, **37,** 496–510.
11. BIRCH, H. G., The effect of socially disapproved labeling upon a well-structured attitude, *J. Abnorm. & Soc. Psychol.,* 1945, **40,** 301–10.
12. BLAKE, R., and W. DENNIS, The development of stereotypes concerning the Negro, *J. Abnorm. & Soc. Psychol.,* 1943, **38,** 525–31.
13. BORING, E. G., *Sensation and Perception in the History of Experimental Psychology,* New York: Appleton-Century, 1942.
14. BRESLAW, B. J., The development of a socio-economic attitude, *Arch. Psychol.,* 1938, no. 226.
15. BRUNER, J. S., *Mandate from the People,* New York: Duell, Sloan & Pearce, 1944.
16. —— Social value and need as organizing factors in perception, *Amer. Psychologist,* 1946, **1,** 241.
17. BRUNSWIK, E., *Wahrnehmung und Gegenstandswelt,* Leipzig: Deuticke, 1934.
18. CANTRIL, H., General and specific attitudes, *Psychol. Monogr.,* 1932, no. 192.
19. —— Experimental studies of prestige suggestion, *Psychol. Bull.,* 1937, **34,** 528.
20. —— and M. SHERIF, The kingdom of Father Divine, *J. Abnorm. & Soc. Psychol.,* 1938, **33,** 147–67.
21. —— The prediction of social events, *J. Abnorm. & Soc. Psychol.,* 1938, **33,** 364–89.

22. CANTRIL, H., The role of the radio commentator, *Publ. Opin. Quart.*, 1939, **3**, 654–62.

23. —— *The Invasion from Mars*, Princeton: Univ. Press, 1940.

24. —— *The Psychology of Social Movements*, New York: Wiley, 1941.

25. —— and J. HARDING, The 1942 elections: a case study in political psychology, *Publ. Opin. Quart.*, 1943, **7**, 222–41.

26. —— The use of trends, in *Gauging Public Opinion* (H. Cantril, ed.), Princeton: Univ. Press, 1944, ch. 16.

27. —— The use of breakdowns, in *Gauging Public Opinion* (H. Cantril, ed.), Princeton: Univ. Press, 1944, ch. 13.

28. —— The issues—as seen by the American people, *Publ. Opin. Quart.*, 1944, **8**, 331–47.

29. CENTERS, R., and H. CANTRIL, Income satisfaction and income aspiration, *J. Abnorm. & Soc. Psychol.*, 1946, **41**, 64–9.

30. CHAPMAN, D. W., and J. VOLKMANN, A social determinant of the level of aspiration, *J. Abnorm. & Soc. Psychol.*, 1939, **34**, 225–38.

31. COFFIN, T. E., Some conditions of suggestion and suggestibility: a study of some attitudinal and situational factors influencing the process of suggestion, *Psychol. Monogr.*, 1941, no. 241.

32. DAVIS, J., Testing the social attitudes of children in the government schools in Russia, *Am. J. Sociol.*, 1927, **32**, 947–52.

33. DIVEN, K., Aesthetic appreciation test, in *Explorations in Personality* (H. A. Murray *et al.*), New York: Oxford, 1938, 447–53.

34. EDWARDS, A. L., Political frames of reference as a factor influencing recognition, *J. Abnorm. & Soc. Psychol.*, 1941, **36**, 34–50.

35. —— Rationalization in recognition as a result of a political frame of reference, *J. Abnorm. & Soc. Psychol.*, 1941, **36**, 224–35.

36. —— Unlabeled fascist attitudes, *J. Abnorm. & Soc. Psychol.*, 1941, **36**, 575–82.

37. FEDERAL RESERVE SYSTEM, *Surveys of Liquid Asset Holdings*, Board of Governors, September 1945.

38. FERNBERGER, S. W., Instructions and the psychophysical limen, *Am. J. Psychol.*, 1931, **43**, 361–76.

39. FRANKLIN, J. H., *The Free Negro in North Carolina, 1790–1860*, Chapel Hill: Univ. N. Carolina Press, copyright 1943.

40. FRIED, E., and H. CANTRIL, The meaning of questions, in *Gauging Publ. Opin.* (H. Cantril, ed.), Princeton: Univ. Press, 1944, ch. 1.

41. FRISCH, R., Propagation problems and impulse problems in dynamic economics, in *Economic Essays in Honour of Gustav Cassel*, London: Allen and Unwin, copyright 1933.

42. GOODMAN, C. C., *Perception: Evidence for a Trifactorial Theory*, Honor's Thesis, Harvard Univ., Dept. Psychol., 1946.

43. HARTLEY, R., and E. HARTLEY, Analysis of the judgment of pictures of people in a poorly defined situation, to be published.

44. HARTMANN, G. W., The contradiction between the feeling-tone of political party names and public response to their platforms, *J. Soc. Psychol.*, 1936, **7**, 336–57.

45. HOROWITZ, E. L., The development of attitude toward the Negro, *Arch. Psychol.*, 1936, no. 194.

46. KATONA, G., *War Without Inflation*, New York: Columbia Univ., 1942.

47. KATONA, G., The role of the frame of reference in war and post-war economy, *Am. J. Sociol.*, 1944, **49**, 340–7.

48. —— *Price Control and Business,* Bloomington, Ind.: Principia Press, 1945.

49. —— Psychological analysis of business decisions and expectations, *Am. Econ. Rev.,* 1946, **36**, 44–62.

50. KATZ, D., and F. H. ALLPORT, *Students' Attitudes,* Syracuse: Craftsman, 1931.

51. —— and K. BRALY, Racial stereotypes of one hundred college students, *J. Abnorm. & Soc. Psychol.,* 1933, **28**, 280–90.

52. —— —— Racial prejudice and racial stereotypes, *J. Abnorm. & Soc. Psychol.,* 1935, **30**, 175–93.

53. —— and H. CANTRIL, An analysis of attitudes toward fascism and communism, *J. Abnorm. & Soc. Psychol.,* 1940, **35**, 356–66.

54. KAY, L. W., The relation of personal frames of reference to social judgments, *Arch. Psychol.,* 1943, no. 283.

55. —— Social norms as determinants in the interpretation of personal experiences, *J. Soc. Psychol.,* 1944, **19**, 359–67.

56. KEYNES, J. M., *The General Theory of Employment, Interest, and Money,* New York: Harcourt, Brace, copyright 1936.

57. KNAPP, R., A psychology of rumor, *Publ. Opin. Quart.,* 1944, **8**, 22–37.

58. KORNHAUSER, A. W., Attitudes of economic groups, *Publ. Opin. Quart.,* 1938, **2**, 260–8.

59. —— Analysis of "class" structure of contemporary American society—psychological bases of class divisions, in *Industrial Conflict: A Psychological Interpretation* (G. W. Hartmann and T. Newcomb, eds.), New York: Cordon, 1939, 199–264.

60. LASKER, B., *Race Attitudes in Children,* New York: Holt, 1929.

61. LAZARSFELD, P. F., Report on "Naples is a battleground," unpublished, June 1944.

62. —— B. BERELSON, and H. GAUDET, *The People's Choice: How the Voter Makes Up His Mind in a Presidential Campaign,* New York: Duell, Sloan & Pearce, 1944.

63. LEVINE, J. M., and G. MURPHY, The learning and forgetting of controversial material, *J. Abnorm. & Soc. Psychol.,* 1943, **38**, 507–17.

64. LEWIS, H. B., Studies in the principles of judgments and attitudes: II. The influence of political attitude on the organization and stability of judgments, *J. Soc. Psychol.,* 1940, **11**, 121–46.

65. LIPPMANN, W., *Public Opinion,* New York: Harcourt, Brace, 1922.

66. McGARVEY, H. R., Anchoring effects in the absolute judgment of verbal materials, *Arch. Psychol.,* 1943, no. 281.

67. McGREGOR, D., The major determinants of the prediction of social events, *J. Abnorm. & Soc. Psychol.,* 1938, **33**, 179–204.

68. MEENES, M., A comparison of racial stereotypes of 1935 and 1942, *J. Soc. Psychol.,* 1943, **17**, 327–36.

69. MENEFEE, S. C., The effect of stereotyped words on political judgments, *Am. Sociol. Rev.,* 1936, **1**, 614–21.

70. MURPHY, G., and R. LIKERT, *Public Opinion and the Individual,* New York: Harper, 1938.

71. NEWCOMB, T. M., *Personality and Social Change,* New York: Dryden, 1943.

72. NATIONAL OPINION RESEARCH CENTER, Survey, May 1944.

73. *New York Times,* January 11, 1946.

74. *New York Times,* January 13, 1946.

75. Osgood, C. E., and R. Stagner, Analysis of a prestige frame of reference by a gradient technique, *J. Appl. Psychol.,* 1941, **25,** 275–90.

76. Rogers, S., The anchoring of absolute judgments, *Arch. Psychol.,* 1941, no. 261.

77. Seeleman, V., The influence of attitude upon the remembering of pictorial material, *Arch. Psychol.,* 1940, no. 258.

78. Shackle, G. L., *Expectations, Investment, and Income,* London: Oxford Univ. Press, copyright 1938.

79. ——— The expectational dynamics of the individual, *Economica,* 1943, **10,** 99.

80. Sherif, M., A study of some social factors in perception, *Arch. Psychol.,* 1935, no. 187.

81. ——— The psychology of slogans, *J. Abnorm. & Soc. Psychol.,* 1937, **32,** 450–61.

82. Smith, G. H., The effects of fact and rumor labels on the belief in unverified "news" statements, to be published in *J. Abnorm. & Soc. Psychol.,* 1947.

83. ——— An analysis of panel predictions, to be published.

84. Stagner, R., Fascist attitudes: an exploratory study, *J. Soc. Psychol.,* 1936, **7,** 309–19.

85. ——— A correlational analysis of nationalistic opinions, *J. Soc. Psychol.,* 1940, **12,** 197–212.

86. Stern, W., *Zur Psychologie der Aussage,* Berlin, 1902.

87. ——— The psychology of testimony, *J. Abnorm. & Soc. Psychol.,* 1939, **34,** 3–20.

88. Vetter, G. B., Measurement of social and political attitudes and the related personality factors, *J. Abnorm. & Soc. Psychol.,* 1930, **25,** 149–89.

89. Walsh, W. B., What the American people think of Russia, *Publ. Opin. Quart.,* 1944, **8,** 513–22.

90. Watson, W. S., and G. W. Hartmann, Rigidity of a basic attitudinal frame, *J. Abnorm. & Soc. Psychol.,* 1939, **34,** 314–36.

91. Williams, F. W., Information as a determinant of opinion, in *Gauging Public Opinion* (H. Cantril, ed.), Princeton: Univ. Press, 1944, ch. 15.

92. ——— and F. Mosteller, Education and economic status as determinants of opinion, in *Gauging Public Opinion* (H. Cantril, ed.), Princeton: Univ. Press, 1944, ch. 14.

93. Wood, C., An analysis of changes occurring in successive stages of verbal abstracting, Master's thesis on file in the library of the State Univ., Iowa, 1944.

94. Woodworth, R. S., Situation-and-goal set, in *Am. J. Psychol., Golden Jubilee vol.* (K. M. Dallenbach, ed.), 1937, **50,** 130–40.

95. Zillig, M., Einstellung und Aussage, *Z. Psychol.,* 1928, **106,** 58–106.

CHAPTER 5

THE PROBLEM AND A GENERAL CHARACTERIZATION
OF EGO-INVOLVEMENTS

In this chapter we briefly sketch the problem and give a general characterization of ego-involvements. Our characterization here necessarily consists of rather arbitrary statements. These will stand or fall in the light of evidence presented in succeeding chapters.

As we said in the introduction, we are using the word "ego" reluctantly. For the term has acquired many scientifically objectionable connotations, especially in the hands of certain philosophers and mystically inclined writers. The "pure ego" posited by William James, for example, is one of these connotations which has no psychological meaning for us, even though James did in other respects discuss the problem of the ego in naturalistic terms. Nor is the word "self" devoid of these objectionable associations. And inasmuch as some religiously inclined psychologists are currently grasping the term "ego" as a substitute for "soul," there might be some advantage for scientific psychology if the concept were designated by Greek symbols. But we have preferred not to do this and have contented ourselves by using "ego" in a strictly demonstrable way on the basis of the observed facts of experience and behavior.

As will become evident in the chapters to follow, what is called the "ego" consists, in the last analysis, of a constellation of attitudes which can be designated as ego-attitudes. Since scientific studies on ego-involvements are still in their initial stages, we are not yet ready in this book on ego-involvements to give a clear-cut definition of the ego. But as we go along we shall give concrete and specific cases of constellations of ego-attitudes. And in passing we may point again to the fact, elaborated later, that the ego is not a fixed and immutable entity. It is formed during the genetic development of the individual (ch. 7); it is subject to transformation (see especially ch. 9) and to disintegration under the stress of diverse factors (ch. 12).

We can perhaps take as a matter of everyday experience the fact that most of the affective fixations (attitudes) which determine, delimit, focus, and shape the selectivity of experience and response to various stimulus situations are connected with the individuals, situations, or institutions to which a person is in some way related. Attitudes are toward *my* parents, *my* school, *my* gang, *my* church, *my* nation, *my* boss, *my* friend; toward *my* friend's rival, *my* father's competitor, *my* country's enemy, and so on. Most attitudes have the characteristic of belonging to *me,* as being part of *me,* as psychologically experienced. In short, they are, to repeat Koffka's term, "Ego-attitudes." [1] [6, 562]

The personal world of every individual thus becomes centered around himself, as William Stern has pointed out. [19] Without in any way subscribing to the implications of Stern's personalistic psychology, we should call attention to his observations that in making judgments of "space" and "time" the individual inevitably uses himself as a central point of reference. This holds for what we regard as "inside" and "outside" of ourselves, what we regard

[1] In his *Principles of Gestalt Psychology* [6] published in 1935, Koffka introduced the ego as "the hero of the play." [319] Following the line of general *Gestalt* psychology, Koffka conceived of the ego "as a field object." [319] In his phenomenological analysis of the sensory experiences that segregate the ego from the rest of the environment, Koffka made out his case for "the reality of the ego." In this and in later chapters (6 and 12) we refer to some of Koffka's keen observations and to some of his fresh interpretations of the experimental psychology he knew so well. However, Koffka's formulation of the ego seems to us quite inadequate for systematic psychology and especially for social psychology, largely because of his neglect of the characteristics of attitudes, especially those concerned with social behavior, and the functional relationship of attitudes to the ego. He regarded attitudes as "forces which *have their origin* not in the surrounding field at all, but in the ego of the observer" [149, italics ours]; an "attitude is a force *which starts* in the ego." [206, italics ours] This tendency to reify the ego and to conceive of it as an entity which somehow generates and propels attitudes is incompatible with our own position and seems to us to make for unnecessary obscurity and confusion. And Koffka did not stress either the fact or the implications of the fact that the ego is a genetic development.

In chapter 14 we indicate why we cannot accept the psychoanalytic interpretation of the ego. We also indicate there why Adler's conception of the ego as an end result of the universal "feeling of inferiority" and the compensating "longing for superiority" seems to us invalid.

as "above" and "below," as "before" and "behind," as "left" or "right," as "future" or "past." [*91–97*] What Stern calls a person's "introceptible world" is for him "the cosmos of individualized carriers of significance and value, and of claims that become related to the person's center." [*88*]

We have considered the psychology of attitudes in some detail in the three previous chapters because attitudes are the main constituents of the ego. Most attitudes are not discrete and isolated entities in the psychological make-up of the individual. Once formed, they provide the major components of which the ego is built. And so before considering the problem of the ego itself and the characteristics of ego functioning, we have tried to make sure that our conception of these ego components rested on a solid basis of fact. For this reason we examined experimental evidence from the psychological laboratory and evidence from more concrete situations. The basic psychology of ego formation is essentially the psychology of the formation of attitudes. But we must wait for the accumulation of more factual evidence before we are in a position to delineate and define adequately the constellation of ego-attitudes in the psychological make-up of the individual. For the constellation of ego-attitudes is not coextensive with the whole field of psychology.

The characteristics of attitudes have already been indicated in previous chapters. Here we can give only a rough indication of the implications of these characteristics for the psychology of ego-involvement. More elaborate treatments of these implications as based on factual data are contained in later chapters. In chapter 2 we pointed out that attitudes have a more or less enduring quality. The first stage in the actual formation of an attitude, being a perceptual stage and involving both internal and external factors, implies that attitude formation is a cognitive process, that attitudes are learned. This fact takes on special significance as we consider the relationship between attitudes and the ego. For it means that the characteristic feeling of continuity and permanence the individual has about himself as revealed by the constellation of ego-attitudes is derived in large part from the enduring quality of the many social and personal attitudes which become ego components.

This does not imply, as we have noted before, that attitudes are fixed and unchangeable and, as a consequence, that the ego is fixed and unchangeable. The ego is definitely *not* a solidified structure, permanent once it is formed. Henri Wallon, in his excellent study *Les Origines du caractère chez l'enfant* [20], points out with abundant evidence the changing nature of the small child's ego relationships as he becomes involved in different situations. "Personality remains as it were connected with the situation." (La personnalité reste comme adhérente à la situation. [*247*]) He cites, for example, the case of a three-year-old girl who had spent several weeks in the country with her mother. When her father arrived from Vienna and asked if she recognized him, she said that her other father was in Vienna. When the father told her he was her daddy from Vienna, she asked if he came on the train. Wallon indicates that the child needed to recall her own trip, the change it had brought about in her own situation, before she could bring the two fathers into focus and "resolve in this way the incompatibility of the situations in which they appeared to her in the present and in the past" (résoudre par ce moyen l'incompatibilité des situations où ils lui apparaissaient actuellement et dans le passé [*247*]).

We shall also see that ego-attitudes manifested in different situations can be quite contradictory. As Healy and Bronner have indicated on the basis of their studies of delinquent children, what we call "conscience," though universally found, "plays various and partial roles in determining or motivating behavior." [3, *12*]

> Conscience may cover only certain areas in the field of conduct. In one case of our series a young boy evidently had a strong conscience about being mannerly and doing his school work well, while stealing seemed really to mean nothing to him except as he might be caught for it. And we have noted in some instances that lying was quite condoned by conscience while stealing was a sin, and that in other cases this was exactly reversed. [3, *12*]

Later we find ample evidence that the constellation of ego-attitudes can and does change in a given individual under the impact of compelling situations (chs. 9–11). When we consider the problem of ego-breakdowns, we shall see that an individual's characteristic ego structure may become completely dissociated, may entirely collapse under cases of extreme stress or pathological conditions (ch. 12). Other attitudes may be only momentary affairs, but may still involve the ego. The accumulating experiments related to ego-involvements show that even under artificial laboratory conditions judgment and reaction are temporarily altered in situations to which the ego is linked experimentally (ch. 6).

Ego-attitudes may be formed (learned) in relation to objects, persons, situations, or groups that somehow satisfy or frustrate those basic tensions, needs, drives, or instincts that do have a definitely assignable locus in the organism. As we pointed out in chapter 2, the need for food or the sexual drive as such might be satisfied by an individual in any culture by almost any kind of food or any person of the opposite sex. But in everyday life this is by no means the usual state of affairs. We acquire tastes for special foods, and we are selective in our choice of a mate. Under ordinary circumstances, the satisfaction of our instinctual urges takes place within an acquired frame of reference which is built up through experience and carries definite affective overtones as our needs are satisfied or thwarted. It is these ego-involved attitudes that, to a large extent under usual conditions, determine and direct the particular way in which the individual goes about releasing his instinctual tendencies and drives.

And since the particular manner in which an individual satisfies his instinctual urges becomes in most societies an indicator of status, behavior which has its roots in biological and localizable functions of the organism becomes inextricably interwoven with complex ego-attitudes learned from society. A particular food— its variety, quality, fashionableness, where and how it is eaten— can be and is used as a mark of a person's position in life. We see later that clothing, in addition to the function it serves in protecting the body, also assumes in most cultures a status-distinguishing role (ch. 11). We will indicate the enormous consequences for behavior when the ego-attitudes that normally direct and determine the way in which an individual will satisfy instinctual urges break down in conditions of extreme stress or deprivation (ch. 12).

All attitudes that define a person's status or that give him some relative role with respect to other individuals, groups, or institutions are ego-involved. Whether these attitudes stem from some biological drive or whether they are derived from some non-instinctual source (from some social value or norm), any attitude is ego linked which functions to shape, delimit, or point to our relative position. In the United States, for example, the individual derives and experiences a general status from such reference groups as white or Negro; native or foreign born; upper, middle, or working class; worker, employer, or independent; Catholic or Protestant. And one derives and experiences a more specific status from his relative position in membership groups, that is, as the father of a family, a newcomer in a gang, an active member of his union, a key skilled worker in a factory. Directories such as *Who's Who,* compiled for the purpose of making it possible "to place" a person, describe individuals entirely in terms of their reference and membership characters.[2] And these attitudes, which define our relative position and status, determine and regulate experience and action in a major way in all those situations we relate to them.

In addition to the evidence already presented, we will see in nearly all of the succeeding chapters how these ego-involved attitudes—in youth and maturity, in everyday life and in the laboratory—guide our thoughts and actions as we try to maintain or improve our status or as we may try to shift it with changing conditions. Our satisfaction with ourselves, our aspirations and ambitions, our failures and disappointments, our fears and anxieties are all relative affairs, relative in the sense that we inevitably use ourselves, *our* position, *our* accomplishments, as reference points against the scale of values of our reference and membership groups.

Since the ego is a genetic formation, the particular attitudes that become its major components will vary according to the situations to which an individual is exposed, the particular constellation of social values or norms which have served as stimulus situations. As a result, then, the ego will have different components for indi-

---

[2] We are not ignoring the fact that we also think of ourselves in terms of certain temperamental characteristics or abilities we may possess or wish we possessed. A discussion of these personality characteristics and their place in social psychology is much too complicated to be treated here and must be reserved for a later volume.

viduals living in different social systems or cultures. Observations
of anthropologists reveal the enormous variety of established values
or norms that become major ego constituents for individuals
brought up in different cultures. As a result of these different ego
identifications, very diverse loyalties and allegiances exist. Furthermore, individuals or groups or classes of individuals within the
same society may have quite conflicting or opposing values. The
ego components of some individuals may conflict because of basic
conflicts they reflect in objective social conditions (chs. 10, 11).
For example, those who find themselves members of a minority
group in a larger macrocosm, those who occupy marginal positions
in a society, are likely to form contrasting and conflicting ego
identifications. Ego components for other individuals may be
more overlapping and integrated, owing to the more harmonious
consistent relationship of the norms of a society.

By no means all of the values incorporated are *social* values in
the sense that they are widely accepted norms. Relatively or entirely unique personal values derived from our own distinctive
experience may and often do become important components of
the ego. In stressing the fact that major ego-attitudes for most
individuals seem to be acquired by the direct acquisition of social
values or norms, we do not mean to ignore or in any way to
minimize the fact that for some people or groups of people ego-
attitudes can be and are derived from the analysis of objective
situations, from facts, and from other direct experiences which
they have with the objects, persons, institutions, and such, which
become the content of attitudes. If this were not the case, it would
be more difficult than it is to account for the political radical, the
creative musician, artist, or scientist. These two facts—namely
that the content of ego-attitudes need not be always derived from
widely held values or norms and that they may be built up through
the direct observation, experience, and synthesis of specific facts,
specific objective relationships—help us further to account for the
enormous individual differences we see in man's ego-strivings, for
the different definitions people give to "self-interest."

Group allegiances can and do direct a person into behavior
which appears to be deviant from that of society at large. We
shall see how the complete consistency of that behavior can only

be understood in terms of the individual's group identifications (ch. 10). There is unequivocal evidence that the adolescent strives to anchor himself with some reference group that will give him general status or with some particular membership group in which the ego can be anchored more specifically (ch. 9).

We will also show in later chapters what variety, change, and shifting about there may be in the ego components of the same individuals under different situations, particularly those situations which have the elements of crisis or conflict. As Koffka has pointed out, and as becomes increasingly clear, the ego is complex [6, 333], not a unidimensional structure. Koffka noted that under varying conditions the ego will "shrink," "contract," "expand," and so on. Illustrations of this variability are found in concrete social situations (ch. 11). This constellation of ego components, shifting under different situations, has been recognized by novelists and playwrights (ch. 13).

A characteristic fact that holds for any individual in any culture is that experiences related to ego-attitudes, ego experiences, are felt by the individual with a peculiar warmth and familiarity. This was pointed out by Katzaroff in 1911 [5]:

> One may therefore assume that the feeling of familiarity (*sentiment de familier*), *déjà vu,* which accompanies a repeated sensation results from the fact that this sensation, when it passed through our consciousness for the first time became associated with the very feeling of our "Ego" (*s'est associée au sentiment lui-même de notre "moi"*) and was, so to speak, enveloped by it.[3] [5, 78]

In a passage referring to Freud's concept of narcissism, Murphy, Murphy, and Newcomb have indicated their own belief that an individual's perception of continuous stimuli contributes to the emergence of a new value, the self:

> As the primitive, vague, ill-defined awareness of personal identity gives place to a more well-defined experience, as the individual learns where his own existence stops and the rest of the world begins, the self in the accepted narrow sense is born and becomes an empirical object toward which the attitudes of the organism are built up, just as

[3] The reference to this observation and the English translation are given by Koffka. [6, 594]

attitudes are built up toward anything else . . . the thing known as the self is a selection and organization of its experiences involving the visceral tensions, muscular strains, the sound of one's name, one's mirror image, and so on; and the thing which knows this pattern is simply the organism as a whole. If this is correct, it is easy to see that the self, being a primary source of many satisfactions, must inevitably become a value. The self is something which we like and from which we expect much. [13, *209 f.*]

It is also the constant ego reference of so much of our experience that gives us our sense of continuous individuality. We are constantly reacting to stimuli on the basis of *our* attitudes. We are continually enjoying or suffering the consequences of *our* judgments and actions. And it is by means of the constellation of *our* attitudes that we experience and react to the welter of external stimulation in a more or less consistent way, unlike children lacking stable ego-attitudes. The consistency thus established defines our role in a more or less lasting way in relation to the persons, situations, and institutions we face. It sets the boundaries of our personal psychological world, a world in which our egos act as a major reference point. The physicist, Schrödinger, after his brilliant review of modern developments in physics and biology and the implications they have for the answer to the question he poses in his little book, *What Is Life?*, comes to the conclusion: "Yet each of us has the undisputable impression that the sum total of his own experience and memory forms a unit, quite distinct from that of any other person. He refers to it as 'I.' " [16, *90*]

The particular glow of individuality, the sense of "me-ness" consciously or unconsciously accompanying experience with an ego reference, assumes for the individual a special and unique value. In one way or another we all try to feel good about ourselves. In our various personal and social relationships, we try to place ourselves (our egos) securely and appropriately in our own eyes. We try somehow to orient ourselves in the concrete world we live in until the "place" we think we occupy is satisfactory to us. In this process we do what we can to protect our egos against any onslaughts from the external world which we feel might hurt *us.* If our ego is injured we resort to all kinds of rationalizations, to protective adjustments, to selective modes of reasoning and behavior in which we manipulate things, persons, memories, or ideas, in a highly selective way.

These strivings related to our ego assume very different directions, proportions, and intensities for different individuals, not only in different cultures, but in the same culture or the same small group. And, furthermore, the ego-striving of any given person can and does assume very different intensities and proportions at different times, depending upon the nature of the situation in which the individual finds himself and upon internal physiological or psychological processes.

Ego-striving Is Not Instinctive: No Innate Ego Drives

The constellation of ego-attitudes which may be referred to as the ego of the individual is a genetic formation (ch. 7). But this fact does not mean that ego-attitudes are mere cognitive formations devoid of strong affective or purposive properties prompting the individual to diverse strivings. As we shall see in the relevant studies on child and adolescent behavior, on group and gang formations, in the experimental laboratory as well as in concrete situations of everyday life, the individual strives in one way or another to maintain or to enhance his ego. And in order to learn something about these unmistakable signs of striving related to the ego and to take them into account (as we must) in any adequate and scientific formulation of psychology we cannot resort to the easy solution of positing some innate ego drive, ego instincts, or ego needs. We have already pointed out that what we regard as primary drives (instincts or needs) are those which have some definite and localizable anatomical or physiological place in the organism. Such instincts or drives, which, like hunger, appear at birth or, like sex, appear at a later stage of organic development, are innate. In this sense, therefore, any position which implies that there is an ego drive comparable to other primary drives is quite untenable. [17, *184 f.*] Since it is so important that the psychology of ego-involvements be clearly divorced from any metaphysical or spiritualistic interpretation, we shall list here a few of the reasons for our conclusion that there is no primary ego drive.

1. Ego-striving in what seems to us the only justifiable use of

the term is possible only after an individual has acquired (learned) the complex and variously differentiated patterns of human (social) relationships that surround him. The process involved in grasping these relationships is essentially coincident with that of ego development. Prior to the delineation of the baby's body from his surroundings and the formation of other ego-attitudes, ego-involvements cannot occur. For example, social distances (which can be expressed in terms of psychological variables as ego distances), social prejudices toward human groups and their individual members are found to operate only after a certain degree of ego development, that is, the degree that makes it possible for the child to experience established reciprocal group relationships such as "we" and "they."

Evidence that complex social relationships, along with appropriate values and norms of experience and behavior, are not innately experienced but are learned is seen from the fact that these relationships vary greatly from society to society and from time to time within a society. Even that important range of intimate personal relationships prescribed by kinship constellations does not always fit into the biological proximity of consanguinity. It even varies widely within the ranges of consanguineous relationships. In fact, the relative proximity of the ego links represented in kinship relationships, in spite of their biologically workable lineage based on consanguinity, can serve as a crucial piece of evidence that ego links are not innately experienced ties.

Kinship, family ties, the relative proximity of relatives, the affective components, loyalties, and responsibilities attached to them change with variations in the social organizations of different societies as determined by the character of their socioeconomic level of development and functioning. Here we can cite only a few examples. The thesis is well developed by such substantial authorities as Morgan [12], Engels [2], Rivers [15] and others. A person who cannot conceive of any other kinship relationships than the ones he is brought up to experience may be surprised to find such diverse types of kinship systems and to learn from a brief general discussion such as Lowie's that in some societies kindred may be "grouped, for example, according to generation or age level as well as to differences between direct and collateral lines of descent." [9, 568]

For the last 80 years anthropologists have piled up many examples of variations in kinship relationships. In different cultures and at different periods in the same cultures, kinship relationships present such a diverse and complex picture that many an anthropologist has attempted to formulate intricate classificatory schemes with the aim of presenting them in some sort of order. Such attempts were found necessary, for, as Radcliffe-Brown [14] points out,

> If you will take time to study two or three hundred kinship systems from all parts of the world you will be impressed, I think, by the great diversity that they exhibit. [14, 17]

A few concluding statements illustrated by examples from an anthropologist will clarify our point. Radcliffe-Brown notes the various ranges of kinship relationships and their psychological implications in terms of rights and duties:

> A most important character of a kinship system is its range. In a narrow range system, such as the English system of the present days, only a limited number of relatives are recognized as such in any way that entails any special behaviour or any specific rights and duties. In ancient times in England the range was wider, since a fifth cousin had a claim to a share of wergild when a man was killed. In systems of very wide range, such as are found in some non-European societies, a man may recognize many hundreds of relatives, toward each of whom his behaviour is qualified by the existence of the relationship. [14, 2]

And again:

> A kinship system also includes the existence of definite social groups. The first of these is the domestic family, which is a group of persons who at a particular time are living together in one dwelling, or collection of dwellings, with some sort of economic arrangement that we may call joint housekeeping. There are many varieties of the domestic family, varying in their form, their size, and the manner of their common life. A domestic family may consist of a single elementary family, or it may be a group including a hundred or more persons, such as the *zadruga* of the Southern Slavs, or the *taravad* of the Nayar.

Important in some societies is what may be called a local cluster of domestic families. In many kinship systems unilinear groups of kindred-lineage groups, clans and moieties play an important part. By a kinship system, then, I mean a network of social relations of the kind just defined, which thus constitute part of that total network of social relations that I call social structure. The rights and duties of relatives to one another and the social usages that they observe in their social contacts, since it is by these that the relations are described, are part of the system. [14, 2]

Such variations in kinship systems and family relationships are not peculiarities of geographically distant cultures alone. Changes in kinship and family relationships have come with socioeconomic changes and changes reached in the level of development. As we have seen previously, Radcliffe-Brown cites a concrete case of the changes brought about historically in the British kinship system. From the same European area, he gives the case of a kinship system which is contrary to that of the British system:

In Montenegro, on the contrary, to take another European system, the father's brothers constitute one category and the mother's brothers another. These relatives are distinguished by different terms, and so are their respective wives, and the social relations in which a man stands to his two kinds of uncles show marked differences. [14, 7]

Stern [18] has recently made a concise and intensive review of the changes of the status of women which took place in the family and in life in general as a consequence of modern technological and social changes. For example, the 17th century wife's conception of herself as given in the following quotation is quite different from a modern New York wife's conception of herself:

The dutie of the husband is to travel abroad to seeke living: and the wives dutie is to keepe the house. The dutie of the husband is to get money and provision; and the wives, not vainly to spend it. The dutie of the husband is to deale with many men: and of the wives, to talke with few. The dutie of the husband is, to be entermedling: and of the wife, to be solitairie and withdrawne. The dutie of the man is, to be skilfull in talke: and of the wife, to boast of silence. The dutie of the husband is, to be a giver: and of the wife, to be a saver . . .

Now where the husband and wife performeth the duties in their house we may call it College of Qyietness: the house wherein they are neglected we may term it a hell.[4]

2. Analysis of different cultures and different social systems, or, in some social systems, the analysis of different groups within that social system, reveals that the ego-striving of individuals may be directed to diametrically opposite ends and goals. Some Christian saints strove to satisfy their egos by dispensing with all material things, a sharp contrast to the behavior of some "acquisitively minded" individuals in most contemporary bourgeois societies. People in some cultures seek ego-gratifications through co-operative, relatively submissive behavior, whereas people in other societies obtain their gratifications through competitive relatively ascendant behavior. The ego-satisfaction obtained by a Stahkanovite in socialist competition is of a far different sort in its significance to the individual from the type of satisfaction it is possible for a skilled worker to obtain under capitalist competition (ch. 11).

Likewise, statuses aspired to by individuals change according to different hierarchical status organizations in societies. As Linton [7] puts it:

> In all societies certain things are selected as reference points for the ascription of status. [7, *115*]

Consequently, with shifts of reference points of status in different societies and with major changes in the same society at different times, the directions of strivings for status shift. The fact that reference points of status do shift is particularly important for the psychology of ego-attitudes which are the psychological counterpart of social status.

Similarly, the co-operative and competitive behavior shown by different personalities are indications of nothing other than the inculcation of appropriate ego-attitudes. These contrasting forms of behavior are culturally determined and are not the marks of innate ego drives of assertiveness or submissiveness. For example, in a series of studies representing different cultures from widely scattered geographical areas, it has been impressively demonstrated that individuals show predominately competitive, or co-operative,

---

[4] Stern quotes this passage from [10, *xiv f.*].

or individualistic behavior which is in harmony with the behavior characteristics commended in their respective cultures. [11] Thus, individuals in Manus, Kwakiutl, Ifugao societies tend to exhibit rather competitive behavior; whereas individuals of Iroquois, Samoa, Zuni, Bathonga, Dakota, and Maori societies tend to show rather co-operative behavior—all following the characteristics on which the prevailing norms of their respective societies put a premium.

3. Certainly there are individual differences in the degree and intensity of ego-strivings. These individual differences, in our opinion, can be accounted for by a complex of factors such as primary drives for food, sex, and the like; individual bodily conditions; individual differences in glandular functioning; temperament; ability; and other variations that may be largely hereditary; *together with* the direction these factors will take and the significance they will have for the individual *within the framework* of the attitudes acquired from his particular constellation of social relationships. This fact is clearly brought out by the biologist Julian Huxley who writes:

> Let us remind ourselves that superposed upon this purely biological or genetic variability is the *even greater amount of variability due to differences of upbringing, profession, and personal tastes.* The final result is a degree of variation that would be staggering if it were not so familiar. It would be fair to say that, in respect to mind and outlook, individual human beings are separated by differences as profound as those which distinguish the major groups of the animal kingdom. [4, 8, italics ours]

It should be noted again in passing that the constellation of these factors may be and usually is quite different for different individuals and that it will vary within the same individual with biological changes (for example, those that come about with increasing age), with the relative satisfaction of his basic needs, and with the opportunity afforded by the situation or the environment for the maintenance or enhancement of his position. Sudden and apparently inconsistent shifts in the direction a person's efforts will take can become meaningful only when these pursuits, these derived drives, are related to learned ego-involved values. [1, *41–52*] Chapter 10, dealing with ego-involvements in group situations, is filled with data that point to this conclusion.

4. Subnormal individuals, such as imbeciles, have ego structures that can be demonstrated to be extremely narrow and confined. To borrow a phrase used by Huxley in another connection, the difference between such a subnormal person as might be found in almost any state institution for the feeble-minded and an intelligent adult vigorously trying to achieve certain desired ends, is "comparable in extent with that between a sponge and a higher mammal." [4, *8*] However, both the subnormal individual we might select at random and an intelligent individual displaying a continuous and complex ego-striving would more than likely be found to have similar good appetites for food, similar needs for sexual satisfactions, and so on.

5. Under certain conditions, either physiological, pathological, or situational, the ego may break down, dissolve, apparently disappear for either a shorter or a longer time. This is not true of innate or biologically given instincts or drives which, by almost any definition, are constantly, and recurrently, or periodically manifested. We discuss later in some detail instances of ego-breakdown, ranging from the ungentlemanly behavior of individuals when they are drunk, the unladylike behavior of socially refined women when they are desperate for food, the resort to prostitutes of men in love when their sex needs become extreme, to more complicated and enduring dissociations brought about by extreme prolonged situations or by pathological conditions (ch. 12). In all these cases established ego-attitudes become separated from judgment and behavior. A person does not act like "his normal self."

6. We should include in our list the point previously emphasized that there is no evidence for the existence of an ego drive in the sense that this drive, like primary drives for food and sex, has a definitely assignable locus in the individual organism. We are, of course, not at all denying the fact that psychological phenomena and experiences, such as ego-involvements, are due to complex chemical or physical reactions within the organism. As Schrödinger says:

My body functions as a pure mechanism according to the Laws of Nature. [16, 87]

It is not at all impossible or improbable that in the unforeseeable future the physical scientist may work out some intricate and valid formulas to describe those processes in the organism that are experienced as ego-involvements. But if and when this is accomplished, the qualitative differences between such formulations and our current relatively precise knowledge concerning the physical basis of primary drives such as hunger and sex will almost surely be so vast that they cannot possibly be classified together.

7. There is no ego formation, no ego-involvement, in animals in the sense of reciprocal interpersonal relationships and group relationships on a conceptual level. There is no animal culture comparable to that of man. Ego formation and ego-involvement require that the organism shall be capable of functioning on a conceptual or symbolic level. The values, standards, or norms of social relationship to which the human being relates and identifies himself are possible only because he is able to grasp these values, standards, or norms conceptually. There can obviously be no involvement or identification with let us say, class, nationality, or occupational groups, unless the meaning and significance of a "class," a "nation," or an "occupation" can be conceived on a conceptual level. And in turn, of course, social groupings, organizations and institutions characteristic of human society would be impossible without the interconnections, loyalties, and traditions that are based on conceptual thinking.

This fact is of the utmost importance. For it means that findings concerned with social behavior on the subhuman level may by no means be applicable to the human level when reciprocal human relationships or the conceptual level of human interaction is in question. It means that in the psychology of ego-involvements we are dealing with a unique human characteristic, an emergent that is qualitatively different from other evolutionary products, an emergent that follows the dialectic process. What we observe as animal aggressiveness and animal affective fixations are determined by momentary situations, by relative physical strength, by brute force, or by fixations built up through the process of conditioning which does not involve reciprocal relationships on the conceptual level.

The uniqueness of human culture and its dependence upon language (concept) formation are nicely brought out and well-documented by Warden, an outstanding comparative psychologist, in his *The Emergence of Human Culture.* [21]   He writes that

> . . . the simple truth seems to be that man's primary claim to distinction rests upon the fact that he alone possesses a genuine culture. [21, *3*]
>
> The transition from the humanoid level to the first human type was coincident with the emergence of the cultural order. [21, *99*]

After surveying the social life of insects, birds, and mammals, he states bluntly that "even the rudiments of culture do not exist among sub-human organisms." [*68*]

Our human culture, then, is "an emergent," [*23*] and

> An emergent system has new properties and new modes of organization that seem to bear no definite relation to the old order from which it arose. [21, *24*]

In describing this emergent, human culture, Warden points out that

> This new type of social integration was unique in that it reached above the purely biosocial level. For the first time, invention, effective communication within the group, and the social habituation of the young became possible. The activities of the individual were no longer limited to the instinctive repertory of the species. New skills could be invented by the superior individual and passed along to the other members of the group by means of language. Simple folkways could now develop out of the greater variety and intimacy of social contacts. These new ways of doing and acting, as accepted by the group, could be impressed upon the young through language and imitation. Such of the skills and folkways as survived from generation to generation comprised a rude tradition. This new mode of social integration was cultural rather than biosocial. [21, *105 f.*]

Throughout his book, Warden emphasizes the fact that

> The cultural order was unique because the presence of language made possible a new and most important type of social integration. [*108*]

Communication, invention, and social habituation he regards as the three "basic mechanisms" that make the human cultural order possible. [21] Concerning communication he states that

> It seems altogether unlikely that a culture could emerge and main-tain itself without the support of a well-developed capacity for vocal language. [22] . . . Language becomes an important instrument for the broadening of cultural contacts. The child now learns to express its own desires effectively and to understand and heed those of others. It learns to recognize such social distinctions as attach to age, rank, and other tribal relationships. It comes to play games according to rule and custom. The channels of thought are marked out by the folklore and ideas of current conversation. The attitudes and beliefs of the group gradually become those of the child. [7 f.] . . . Moral sentiments are inculcated and many additional duties and obligations are imposed. Conformity with group norms of conduct takes on a new importance because of its relation to personal success and pres-tige. [21, 8]

The point has also been fully recognized by outstanding biolo-gists of our day. For example, Julian Huxley, in a chapter, "The Uniqueness of Man," in his *Man Stands Alone* [4] writes:

> . . . let us remind ourselves that the gap between human and animal thought is much greater than is usually supposed. The tendency to project familiar human qualities into animals is very strong, and col-ours the ideas of nearly all people who have not special familiarity both with animal behavior and scientific method. [19] . . . *In point of fact, the great majority of man's activities and characteristics are by-products of his primary distinctive characteristics, and therefore, like them, biologically unique.* On the one hand, conversation, or-ganized games, education, sport, paid work, gardening, the theatre; on the other, conscience, duty, sin, humiliation, vice, penitence—these are all such unique by-products. *The trouble, indeed, is to find any human activities which are not unique. Even the fundamental bio-logical attributes such as eating, sleeping, and mating have been tricked out by man with all kinds of unique frills and peculiarities.* [29, italics ours]
>
> *The first and most obviously unique characteristic of man is his capacity for conceptual thought;* if you prefer objective terms, you will say his employment of true speech, but that is only another way of saying the same thing. True speech involves the use of verbal signs

for objects, not merely for feelings. Plenty of animals can express the fact that they are hungry; but none except man can ask for an egg or a banana. [*3, italics ours*]

Words are tools which automatically carve concepts out of experience. The faculty of recognizing objects as members of a class provides the potential basis for the concept; the use of words at once actualizes the potentiality. This basic human property has had many consequences. The most important was the development of a cumulative tradition. The beginnings of tradition, by which experience is transmitted from one generation to the next, are to be seen in many higher animals. But in no case is the tradition cumulative. Offspring learn from parents, but they learn the same kind and quantity of lessons as they, in turn, impart: the transmission of experience never bridges more than one generation. In man, however, tradition is an independent and potentially permanent activity, capable of indefinite improvement in quality and increase in quantity. It constitutes a new accessory process of heredity in evolution, running side by side with the biological process, a heredity of experience to supplement the universal heredity of living substance. The existence of a cumulative tradition has as its chief consequence—or if you prefer, its chief objective manifestation—the progressive improvement of human tools and machinery. Many animals employ tools; but they are always crude tools employed in a crude way. Elaborate tools and skilled technique can develop only with the aid of speech and tradition. [*3 f.*] . . . Speech, tradition, and tools have led to many other unique properties of man. These are, for the most part, obvious and well known, and I propose to leave them aside until I have dealt with some less familiar human characteristics. [*5*]

The essential character of man as a dominant organism is conceptual thought. And conceptual thought could have arisen only in a multicellular animal, an animal with bilateral symmetry, head and blood system, a vertebrate as against a mollusc or an arthropod, a land vertebrate among vertebrates, a mammal among land vertebrates. Finally, it could have arisen only in a mammalian line which was gregarious, which produced one young at birth instead of several, and which had recently become terrestrial after a long period of arboreal life. There is only one group of animals which fulfils these conditions —a terrestrial offshoot of the higher Primates. Thus not merely has conceptual thought been evolved only in man: it could not have been evolved except in man. There is but one path of unlimited progress through the evolutionary maze. The course of human evolution is as unique as its result. It is unique not in the trivial sense of being a different course from that of any other organism, but in the profounder sense of being the only path that could have achieved the essential characters of man. Conceptual thought on this planet is inevitably associated with a particular type of Primate body and Primate brain. [4, *15 f.,* italics ours]

Another biologist, Leo Loeb, writing in 1945 on the *Biological Basis of Individuality* [8] shows the necessity of concept formation for man's unique individuality. He uses this fact as a stepping stone for his own formulation, in his own terminology, of the way in which the ego (the "I") emerges in man as a distinctive characteristic. And he goes still further in his book to indicate the implications this emergence has for man's identifications and social relationships.

According to Loeb, the ability to form concepts, to think abstractly and synthetically, has come about suddenly and appears only with the development of man.

There has . . . taken place an evolution of two types of individuality. The first is connected with the differentiation of the organ differentials and with the evolution of the individuality differential and its manifestations, from a very primitive character to the state of great refinement reached in mammals. The second is connected with the evolution of the psychical–social factors, leading to the gradual creation and refinement of the individual in the psychical–social sense. This second evolutionary process is related only indirectly to the development of the individuality differentials; it depends directly upon the increasing complexity and refinement of certain organ differentials, especially of the nervous system. There is, therefore, no perfect parallelism between these two evolutionary processes. While in the first process a gradual, step-by-step development of the individuality differential occurs, *in the second process the most important, far-reaching change has taken place suddenly in the transition from anthropoid apes to man.* [8, *654,* italics ours]

He finds no evidence of these higher thought processes even in anthropoid apes.

Proceeding now from the other higher mammals to man, very pronounced complications in the modes of reactions are observed. Not only does the environment, which acts on us through our sense organs, induce changes which have a much more varied and also more lasting effect on our behavior than in other mammals, but abstraction and synthesis, in which the elements in the environment are separated and then re-arranged in new combinations, become very prominent. Thoughts develop, in which the constituents of the environment may appear in combinations different from those in which they occur under natural conditions; through shifting of these constituents new concepts are formed. [8, *619*]

As a consequence of man's unique mental capacities and his interaction with both the natural and social environment, the "I" concept is developed.

As a result partly of rational thought, but largely also because of the friction, antagonism and pain developing in the social and natural struggle, the concept of the "I," as contrasted with the concept of others and of the surrounding world, develops. The "I" is the individuality in the psychical–social sense. [8, *620*, italics ours]

8. The changes in ego relationships that result from lobotomy and lobectomy demonstrate in a crucial way the close functional relationship between ego formation and ego functioning on the one hand, and, on the other hand, psychological functioning on a conceptual level. Further evidence of the dependence of ego formation on psychological functioning at the conceptual level is found in observations of persons who have lost both their ego relationships and their abstract (conceptual) functioning following certain injuries to the frontal lobes whose tremendous development in the human species gives man his unique ability to function psychologically on an abstract conceptual level. Evidence concerning these two points is found later in Chapter 12 on pages 425 *ff.* and 431 *ff.*

How to account for ego-striving. If ego-strivings do not have an instinctive basis in the sense of hunger and sex needs or drives, how are psychologists to account for these ego-strivings with all their rich affective halo, their emotional warmth, and their varying intensity? As we indicated in the introduction, a detailed account of motivation as it relates to social psychology cannot be treated here. And the more precise role of ego-striving in the whole network of instinctive behavior, reflexes, habits, primary and derived drives, personality traits, frustrations, and the like, is being deliberately reserved for later discussion. In this book we are concerned chiefly with the place of the ego in systematic social psychology.

We have already indicated the main outline of our position. We can summarize it briefly again here. The evidence we have already presented, together with that to follow, gives us somewhat the following picture: our major psychological activities —our perception, judgment, remembering, and so on—take place in referential frameworks. The ego is no exception to this general rule. We learn (or sometimes determine) what values, goals, standards, or norms are desirable for us. These become incorporated as *our* values, *our* goals. The referential framework of the ego is therefore these values, goals, standards, or norms which have become our major attitudes, which have become so large a part of what we refer to as *me*. These values, goals, standards, or norms which become our attitudes are represented by, set by, or created by group activities and social situations that form the constellation of social relationships with which we come in contact. Major attitudes are thus derived from groups to which we learn to relate ourselves or which we regard ourselves as members of: reference groups, membership groups. *My* identification and allegiances, *my* status and position are determined with respect to these reference and membership groups. If I can relate myself securely to these reference groups, *I* feel secure in my general status, insofar as the values of the reference groups themselves are compatible. If I can anchor myself securely in a membership group, *I* feel secure in my more specific membership position. Although we may have a very clear knowledge of what the norms of the larger society or of more specific groups are, mere knowledge of these norms does not necessarily in itself induce identifications. When we discuss the "deviant" behavior of gang members we shall find clear evidence that norms must serve the function of helping us place ourselves in social relationships, must offer us the possibility (consciously or unconsciously) of acquiring, maintaining, or enhancing our status before they become ours (ch. 10).

These reference and membership groups not only set for us the values or norms that become our attitudes: they further make constant demands on our loyalties as time goes on. Some of these loyalties change with age as we shift our identifications. This will be most strikingly brought out when we discuss ego formation and re-formation in adolescents (ch. 9). Other loyalties change under the impact of new situations (chs. 10, 11). But whoever a person may be and whatever social milieu surrounds him, what he learns to regard as *his* loyalty, *his* purpose, *his* ambition, *his* striving to gratify basic needs or drives is affected, regulated, or directed in a major way by the referential framework that has become so large a part of him in the course of his social development. Ego-striving, then, is the individual's effort to place himself securely in those constellations of human relationships that represent *for him* desirable values, that will make *his* status or position secure.

Owing to individual differences in characteristics such as temperament, ability, or energy there are enormous and important differences in the manner, persistence, and intensity in which ego-striving proceeds. And the relative position which will be regarded as personally satisfying to an individual is determined by such individual differences, *as well as* by the specific values he has learned. However, the important fact for social psychologists to remember is that these individual differences all function *within* the framework of norms prescribed by the reference or membership groups. Equally healthy, energetic, intelligent, resourceful people, endowed with similar temperamental characteristics and with similar glandular structure would inevitably manifest different, perhaps quite opposite, ego-strivings according to the differing or contrasting referential frameworks in which their strivings took place.

REFERENCES

1. CANTRIL, H., *The Psychology of Social Movements,* New York: Wiley, 1941.
2. ENGELS, F., *The Origin of the Family, Private Property and the State,* New York: International, 1942, first published 1884.
3. HEALY, W., and A. F. BRONNER, *New Light on Delinquency and Its Treatment,* New Haven: Yale Univ. Press, copyright 1936.
4. HUXLEY, J., *Man Stands Alone,* New York: Harper, copyright 1927.
5. KATZAROFF, D., Contribution à l'étude de la récognition, *Arch. de Psych.,* **11**, 1911, 1–78.
6. KOFFKA, K., *Principles of Gestalt Psychology,* New York: Harcourt, Brace, 1935.

7. LINTON, R., *The Study of Man: An Introduction,* New York: Appleton-Century, copyright 1936, student's ed.

8. LOEB, L., *The Biological Basis of Individuality,* Springfield: Thomas, copyright 1945.

9. LOWIE, R. H., Kinship, in *Encyclopaedia of the Social Sciences,* New York: Macmillan, 1932, 8, 568–72.

10. LUMPKIN, K. DuP., *The Family: A Study of Member Roles,* Chapel Hill: Univ. N. Carolina Press, copyright 1933.

11. MEAD, M. (ed.), *Cooperation and Competition among Primitive Peoples,* New York: McGraw-Hill, 1937.

12. MORGAN, L. H., *Ancient Society or Researches in the Lines of Human Progress from Savagery through Barbarism to Civilization,* New York: Holt, 1877.

13. MURPHY, G., L. B. MURPHY, and T. NEWCOMB, *Experimental Social Psychology,* New York, Harper, copyright 1937.

14. RADCLIFFE-BROWN, A. R., The study of kinship systems, Presidential Address, *J. Roy. Anthropol. Inst. of Great Britain and Ireland,* 1941, 71, parts I and II.

15. RIVERS, W. H. R., *History of Melanesian Society,* Cambridge, England: Univ. Press, 1914, vols. I and II.

16. SCHRÖDINGER, E., *What Is Life?,* New York: Macmillan, copyright 1945.

17. SHERIF, M., *The Psychology of Social Norms,* New York: Harper, 1936.

18. STERN, B. J., The family and cultural change, *Am. Sociol. Rev.,* copyright 1939, 4, 199–208.

19. STERN, W., *General Psychology, From the Personalistic Standpoint,* trans. by H. D. Spoerl, New York: Macmillan, 1938.

20. WALLON, H., *Les Origines du caractère chez l'enfant,* Paris: Presses Universitaires de France, 1933.

21. WARDEN, C. J., *The Emergence of Human Culture,* New York: Macmillan, copyright 1936.

CHAPTER 6

EXPERIMENTS ON EGO-INVOLVEMENTS

We have said that what an individual comes to regard as himself is a genetic development, a product of learning. In the normal course of affairs, the components of the ego include the individual's body and physical characteristics; the things he learns belong to *him,* such as *his* clothes, *his* toys, *his* keepsakes, *his* room, *his* hut, *his* house, *his* mother, *his* sweetheart, *his* children; together with a whole host of social values he also learns and with which he identifies himself—*his* country, *his* politics, *his* language, *his* manner of dressing, the characteristics of *his* particular society.

In spite of the relative similarity of the norms to which an individual in a given society or a group may be exposed, the content of any single individual's ego, what he regards as himself, is a rather distinct constellation of social and personal values that vary not only in their number and nature but also in the intensity with which they are held. Within the range of individual differences due to variations in instinctual drive, ability, and temperament, the similarity of the content of individual egos will increase, of course, with the uniformity of the situations, experiences, or norms to which an individual is exposed.

These contents of the ego, these things, persons, ways of conducting oneself, social norms of various kinds, provide for the individual the standards of judgment or frames of reference which determine to such an important degree his social behavior and reactions. And when any stimulus or situation is consciously or unconsciously related to them by the individual, we can say there is "ego-involvement." Thus, the ego in its various capacities enters in as an important determinant which may color, modify, or alter our experiences and behavior in almost any situation. For *our* standards, *our* values, *our* goals and ambitions, *our* ways of doing things have become involved. *We* feel elated, restricted, gratified, supported, disturbed, or insecure, in these ego-involving situations.

This ego-involvement can and does range from what may be a temporary moderate involvement in a laboratory experiment with some task to be performed where we feel that somehow *our* capacities or abilities are at stake, to complex social situations in which we feel involved, because of some threat to, or enhancement of, *our* position as a member of some gang, group, or class we identify ourselves with.

In recent years the fact of ego-involvements has been demonstrated experimentally in the laboratory and in other controlled investigations concerned with more everyday life situations. We are citing some of these studies here to show that the concept of ego-involvement can be and has been successfully verified under the rigorous controls imposed by scientific method.[1]

Ego-involvements in Laboratory Tasks

In one of his characteristic insights as a psychologist, James pointed out in his *Principles* (1890) that our "self-feeling" is determined by the "ratio of our actualities to our supposed potentialities." [35]

I, who for the time have staked my all on being a psychologist, am mortified if others know much more psychology than I. But I am contented to wallow in the grossest ignorance of Greek. My deficiencies there give me no sense of personal humiliation at all. Had I "pretensions" to be a linguist, it would have been just the reverse. So we have the paradox of a man shamed to death because he is only the second pugilist or the second oarsman in the world. That he is able to beat the whole population of the globe minus one is nothing; he has "pitted" himself to beat that one; and as long as he doesn't do that nothing else counts. He is to his own regard as if he were not, indeed he *is* not.

Yonder puny fellow, however, whom every one can beat, suffers no chagrin about it, for he has long ago abandoned the attempt to "carry that line," as the merchants say, of self at all. With no attempt there can be no failure; with no failure no humiliation. So our self-feeling

[1] A comparatively early and important recognition of the fact of ego-involvement was made by Murphy, Murphy, and Newcomb when in 1937 they grouped a number of different experiments together in their discussion of the ego. [50]

in this world depends entirely on what we *back* ourselves to be and do. It is determined by the ratio of our actualities to our supposed potentialities; a fraction of which our pretensions are the denominator and the numerator our success: thus, Self-esteem $= \dfrac{\text{Success}}{\text{Pretensions}}$. Such a fraction may be increased as well by diminishing the denominator as by increasing the numerator. To give up pretensions is as blessed a relief as to get them gratified. . . . [35, *310 f.*]

Baldwin, writing in 1897, noted that a man's "opinion of others must be referred to the same standards by which he judges himself" [5, *79*], whereas Cooley, in 1902, acknowledging his debt to James and Baldwin, wrote that

> The thing that moves us to pride or shame is not the mere mechanical reflection of ourselves, but an imputed sentiment, the imagined effect of this reflection upon another's mind. This is evident from the fact that the character and weight of that other, in whose mind we see ourselves, makes all the difference with our feeling. We are ashamed to seem evasive in the presence of a straightforward man, cowardly in the presence of a brave one, gross in the eyes of a refined one, and so on. [15, *184*]

In other words, James, Baldwin, and Cooley, in the comparatively early days of psychology, saw the referential nature of judgments, recognized that these were anchored in the ego.

These early observations are of more than mere historical interest. Contemporary psychoanalysts explicitly relate their modern formulations of neuroses to James's descriptions of the "social self." For example, Karen Horney, writing in 1939, states that

> To some extent everyone living in an organized community must keep up appearances. To some extent every one of us has imbibed the standards of the environment. To some extent we are all dependent on the regard others have for us. [32, *216 f.*]

And she notes that

> William James has said that to give up pretensions is as blessed a relief as to have them gratified; judging from observations in analysis the relief resulting from giving them up seems to be the greater of the two. [32, *231*]

And the considerable experimentation conducted in the past 15 years on what has become known as the *level of aspiration* is given a theoretical framework by these earlier writers.

In Hoppe's [31] experiment on the level of aspiration (1930) we have a demonstration that levels of aspiration are essentially ego-involving frames of reference or anchoring points. Success and failure are determined with respect to subjectively established scales: subjects adjust their level of aspiration according to the degree of success on previous performances; if the level of performance is outside the range of the level of aspiration (either above or below it), there is no experience of success or failure. The systematic implication that the level of aspiration can and must be regarded as an instance of a frame of reference within which ego levels are set was not made in Hoppe's original formulation, but further evidence for such an interpretation has accumulated with subsequent work.

Frank has demonstrated that when the level of aspiration is set within a frame of reference clearly involving the ego it is likely to differ from non-ego-involving levels of aspiration by being consistently higher than the level of past performance.

> Changes in the level of performance in one task affect the first level of aspiration in another even when the level of aspiration is solely an objective estimate, but can affect the remaining levels of aspiration only when the ego–level is involved in both tasks. [19, *170*]

Frank suggests that

> The size of the difference between the average level of aspiration and the median level of past performance is due to the involvement of the ego-level of the individual in the task, as shown by self-competition or social pressure. [20, *293*]

He notes, too, in his 1941 summary, that, for some people,

> The level of aspiration may be used to help protect the ego from the effects of failure by being kept resolutely high despite poor performance. [21, *224*]

He further states:

> The level of aspiration situation is usually a threat to the subject's self-esteem in that he must not only exhibit his ability for some one

else, but must openly commit himself as to his expectation of future achievement. . . . Involvement of the subject's self-esteem may often be inferred from tension, obvious effort to do well, acute awareness of the experimenter, and other signs that he regards his own "worth" as involved. [21, 223]

A notable contribution to the conceptualization of the meaning of the term "level of aspiration" was made by Chapman and Volkmann when they pointed out, as we mentioned earlier, that

> The conditions which govern the setting of a level of aspiration (*Anspruchsniveau*), in the sense of an estimate of one's future performance in a given task, may be regarded as a special case of the effect upon a judgment of the frame of reference within which it is executed. [13, 225]

In chapter 4 we described their experiment in another connection. It may be recalled that some of their experimental groups were given in advance of the task (recognition of various authors of literary passages) the score supposedly made by other groups which varied in their prestige such as literary critics and WPA workers. The result here was that those who compared themselves to a superior group lowered their aspiration level, while those who compared themselves to an inferior group raised their aspiration level. In the second experiment the subjects were allowed two performances on a mental test before any attempt was made to change their level of aspiration by comparison of their results with those of various other groups. Under these conditions, there was no significant change in the level of aspiration.

> The subject's own previous scores provided the most effective anchoring. [13, 235]

In addition to the information these experiments provide concerning the relative acceptance of imposed norms when the stimulus situation is variously structured, they demonstrate that whether a level of aspiration is socially imposed as it was in their first experiment, or whether it is based on some definite anchoring from past experience, it must be regarded as an ego-involving frame of reference. In the first experiment, a subject compares himself with others of a superior or inferior position, using his own status as an anchoring point. In the second experiment, where judgments of future performance were based on past experience, the individual identifies himself with his own past performance and, as the authors point out:

> What the subject has himself accomplished with labor is likely to have "ego value"; it means more to him than does the verbally reported accomplishment of someone else. The subject accepts his own work with satisfaction if it seems to be of high grade; he may still accept it, under the protection of some rationalization, if it seems to be of low grade. In the second place, the subject's previous scores provide the most objective basis for predicting his future ones, and the subject will use this basis if he values objectivity. [13, 235]

Since the subjects were college graduates and students in extension courses in psychology, the authors' assumption that objective estimates will have some ego value seems entirely plausible.

In 1940 Sears went farther than anyone had to date in making explicit what lay beyond the "level of aspiration" and why it involved the ego. After noting Frank's observations that ego-involvement may be either a matter of "self-competition" where the individual attempts to maintain his status or due to "an awareness of social pressure," and after calling attention to Gould's investigations [23] which pointed out the importance of knowing an individual's attitudes and the different meanings tasks might have for different individuals or for the same individual in different situations, Sears formulates her problem in such a way as to bring these variables together systematically and to relate them to social norms which can and do become interiorized as ego-involving frames of reference.

> Such differences in the individual's perception of the task in relation to himself may be considered to have been built up in somewhat the following fashion: the child is informed, by example and precept of prestigeful persons, as to what are the valued activities in the particular culture or subculture of which he is a member. These values, incorporated in the ego, become reference points for self-judgments of success or failure; that is, the child cannot succeed or fail in an activity which has for him no ego value. In those activities in which he has ego-involvement, he can, and does, succeed and fail. [57, 499]

Sears set out to test the "reasonable assumption" that "differences in success will influence the individual's anticipation of future gratification in the further performance" of tasks possessing ego value.

She chose as her subjects children of fourth, fifth, and sixth grade standing where "cultural pressures toward achievement are exerted on the child from all sides in this field." [500] Or, as Sears puts it, a child in the age range of 9 to 12 has "had sufficient experience in school to form definite attitudes with respect to his excellence of performance in the academic work." Her experimental group consisted of a "success" group of children who had had uniformly high academic standing, a "failure" group, and a "differential" group composed of children who had been successful in reading and unsuccessful in arithmetic. Reading and arithmetic tasks were assigned and were given as speed tests. There were three experimental conditions: the first a neutral one, the second a "success-conditioned" where children were highly praised for their work no matter what it was objectively, and the third a "failure-conditioned" where children, irrespective of their performances, were told they had made many mistakes and gone very slowly with respect to other members of the group.

She found that

> Self-confident, successful children react to the level of aspiration situation in a similar way, whereas unsuccessful children, lacking in confidence, may adopt one of a number of different behavior techniques in this situation. Furthermore, experimentally induced success brings the reactions of all subjects in regard to level of aspiration into a more homogeneous distribution than do the neutral conditions of stimulation. [57, 526]

> Experimentally induced success provides social norms for the individual which induce him to believe that he has been and is performing much better than the average . . . similarly, experimentally induced failure provides a condition of insecurity for the subjects of all groups. [57, 532 f.]

Sears points out the link made by Chapman and Volkmann between the level of aspiration and the effect of a frame of reference on judgment and goes on to show that the level of aspiration is set with respect to "the perceived social norms." [529] She concludes that

> The cultural pressure to excel and to keep the performance improving, plus the cognizance of the position of the self relative to social norms, seem to account for most of the results obtained in the present investigation. [57, 528]

The earlier studies of Greenberg in 1932 [25] and Rosenzweig in 1933 [55] furnish experimental evidence that the level of aspiration with its involvement of the ego does not appear genetically until the child has formed some conception of his "self," has developed a sense of "pride," or of status which he feels he must maintain within a group. "Success" and "failure" in the accomplishment of various assigned tasks are meaningless until the ego is sufficiently developed to serve as a basic anchorage. Anderson and Brandt [3] studied the levels of aspiration of fifth grade children for performances when each child knew his own previous score, his standing in the group, and the group norm. Since no child knew the scores made by any other specific child, direct "social pressure" and "competition" were minimal. In this situation, the explicit norm of the group served as an anchorage for judgments of future performances. The investigators report that "the goals or levels of aspiration of these children tended to converge on what for the group was mediocrity." [231] Other results were contrary to Frank's definition of failure as a level of performance below the level of aspiration "regardless of its absolute goodness." The children in this study who won scores in the lower quartile tended to set their goals "considerably above their achievement, whereas in the upper ranks of performance the tendency is just the reverse." [220] As the authors concluded: "The goals of these children *are related* to the 'goodness' of past achievement." [228] And, as we have seen, they are also related to the past achievement of the group. The average performance of this group of children improved significantly more during a series of trials than did those of a control group who knew neither their own score nor their ranking in the group.

In their study of the effect of relative standing in an experimental social group to the level of aspiration, Hilgard, Sait, and Magaret [28] found a tendency for those whose performance was above the group norm to estimate their future performance too low, whereas those whose performances were lower than the group norm tended to overestimate their future performance. Since the estimates of future performances of one subject were not known to the other subject, the experimenters conclude that "group pressure can be used to explain the tendency to estimate towards the mean of the group only if the desire for social conformity is somehow internalized." [421]

Several studies have been reported which show that unless and until there is some ego-involvement no level of aspiration is set and the individual has no concern about his own status. Only when an individual judges his own performance in terms of a standard he wants to maintain or achieve, does any generality in levels of aspiration appear with respect to various tasks. Klein and Schoenfeld [41] found that, when their subjects were in a neutral non-ego-involving atmosphere, the confidence they had in their ability to perform various tasks depended almost entirely on the nature and difficulty of the tasks themselves, whereas in definitely ego-involving situations (where subjects were told their scores would be sent to the personnel bureau of the college) a "generality of confidence" appeared. That the subjects did actually feel personally involved in the second part of the experiment is indicated by the report that in the second situation they exerted greater effort and experienced considerable anxiety. In this experiment the person obviously becomes involved because performance of the task is believed to have relevance to a value already interiorized as part of the ego, namely, attendance and graduation from college and a respectable standing with college authorities.

Holt [30] found that, if his subjects had any ego-involvement in the abilities needed to perform his experimental task, the estimates thus made of their performances were determined significantly less by the objective situational variables than when there was little ego-involvement. If there is less ego-involvement, "a level of aspiration is of a piece with the total response to the situation of the experiment; in that sense it is more specific, more peripheral and responsive to outer environmental forces." [*314*] Heathers' [26] study of generality in the level of aspiration points to the same conclusion. In a study of saturation with tasks after repeated performance, Karsten discovered in 1928 [37] that her subjects became more rapidly saturated (annoyed, impatient, emotionally upset) with tasks judged to be very pleasant or very unpleasant than with indifferent tasks or those only mildly pleasant or unpleasant. As Koffka concludes from this experiment "the relation of the task to the Ego is the decisive factor. In the indifferent task the Ego is not 'engaged,' with the result that Ego tensions are less easily produced." [42, *412*]

In an ingenious experiment where pairs of subjects worked together, one performing a task and estimating his performance ahead of time, the other estimating what his partner would do, McGehee [49] found considerably less variability among the levels of aspiration of those actually involved in the task than in the estimates of the observers. McGehee concludes that this difference "seems to lie in the fact that the ego-levels of the subjects are more involved in the erection of levels of aspiration than in making a judgment." [*14*] This distinction between level of aspiration and judgment obscures the relationship between them and violates what we know of the process of judgment itself, namely, that all judgments take place within some frame of reference. The estimates of McGehee's subjects who were actually engaged in the tasks are obviously just as much judgments as the estimates of the observers. But, whereas one set of judgments is based upon frames or anchorages that are ego-involved, the other set of judgments is based on non-ego-involved frames or anchorages and is therefore more determined by immediate past performance of the participating partner or other variables in the situation itself.

EGO-INVOLVEMENTS AS A SET FOR LEARNING

In chapter 4 we cited some of the studies that show the close relationship between memory and frame of reference. In all these studies dealing with everyday life material, it is clear that the investigators were concerned with ego-involving attitudes—attitudes that have been learned, largely as social values; that the individual identifies himself with, and makes a part of himself; and that have affective properties of varying degrees of intensity. Thus, the effect Seeleman [58] found of the attitude toward the Negro on the memory of pictures of whites and Negroes clearly provokes a value judgment with which most Americans at the present time identify themselves in one way or another and in different degrees of intensity. Zillig's well known study [66] of the differential ability of men and women to recall items favorable to their own sex implicitly involves or reflects sex differences in ego composition as learned. Edwards [17, 18] showed the superior recognition of items favorable to a political point of view which the individual espouses and the extent to which an individual rationalizes answers to factual statements not in harmony with his attitude, implicitly demonstrating what is common knowledge, namely, that in the contemporary United States, an individual regards the party he votes for as *his* party, party platforms as *his* expressed point of view, and party candidates as *his* candidates. Similarly, the results of Levine and Murphy [43] showed that both the learning and forgetting of material favorable to or against the Soviet Union is affected by one's attitude toward Communism, is most definitely concerned with ego-involved attitudes, as anyone can testify who observes the identification an individual Communist makes with Marxism or the Communist Party, or who has seen the emotional involvement of those who oppose Communism as something which threatens "all that they hold dear." Birch [6] also noted the definite tendency for his subjects who approved a statement labeled "communist" to write more comments than usual, dissociating themselves from Communism as such or otherwise qualifying their answers.

Wallen's experiments in 1941 [63, 64] yielded clear-cut evidence that the selective forgetting of ego-involved material differs significantly from the selective forgetting of material unrelated to the ego. Subjects were given a list of adjectives on which they made self-evaluations. They were then divided into two groups: one group was later given orally a list of bogus ratings on the same adjectives supposedly made by some acquaintance on the subject; the other group was later given bogus ratings but were told these were ratings on unidentified people. His results showed that the recall of the former group was significantly higher than the latter. In the former group bogus ratings which agreed with the subject's own evaluation were considerably better remembered than others, whereas in the second group no such tendency occurred: those who had bogus ratings on themselves recalled desirable ratings more accurately than those they regarded as undesirable, so much so that the final recall was actually much more like the original list of self-evaluations than the material actually presented for recall. Wallen believed that "the difference in instructions for the two groups can be cogently interpreted only in ego terms" [64, 36] and that "some assumption regarding an ego is needed in interpreting our results." [36] A later experiment by Shaw and Spooner [59], again involving a list of adjectives on which a specified person was to be rated, bogus ratings, and delayed recall, found superior recall of the adjectives in line with the subject's own initial characterization or judgments.

These results are comparable in their implications to the conclusions reached by Wolff [65] and Huntley [33] in their studies of judgments of expressive behavior (voice recording, handwriting, profiles, and the like). They found their subjects generally made much more favorable judgments of samples of their own expressive behavior and that in nearly all cases judgments of one's own behavior or features took on the characteristics of an extreme reaction, even though few of the subjects consciously recognized which behavior or feature presented was their own. Such experiments demonstrate in a significant way that an individual's body and his physical personal characteristics constitute an integral part of his ego.

In a study of repression, Rosenzweig [56] set up his experiment so that one group would be "aroused in a personal way" whereas the other group was in a relatively neutral situation. Both groups were asked to recall tasks they had been assigned, only half of which they had been allowed to complete. Differences in recall were clear-cut: those who had become personally involved remembering more finished tasks, those not involved more unfinished. Similar findings were later reported by Lewis and Franklin. [45] Alper's results [2] show very neatly that retention and recall are considerably different for subjects who are or are not ego-involved (she uses the terms "ego-oriented" and "task-oriented") and that the three "classical" laws of learning she analyzed can be said to hold only when there is no ego-involvement.[2]

In his study of recognition, published in 1911, Claparède pointed out that "One must distinguish between two sorts of connections: those which establish themselves *eventually between ideas,* and those which establish themselves *between the ideas and that which constitutes the Ego,* the personality. In the case of purely passive or reflex association of ideas the first kind of connections will function alone; in the case of voluntary recall or of recognition, where the Ego is involved, the second kind would play its part." [3] [14, *86*] Koffka relates how he refused to take Claparède's formulations seriously in his own early thinking because the problem of the Ego was not prominent in psychology. After praising Claparède's insight and reviewing Claparède's theory as it related to his own conception of trace systems and the Ego, Koffka concludes that

> . . . in the structure of the behavioural environment there are things close to and remote from the Ego and even some that have practically no Ego-connection. According to the theory, and to all appearances in conformity with the facts, the former are better recognized than the latter. In many cases the Ego–object relationship will be, at least partly, due to the interests and attitudes of the Ego. Thus whatever has interested us, attracted our attention, is relatively easily recognized. [42, *595 f.*]

And Koffka goes on to quote Maccurdy's contention that "The things we deny ever having done, in the face of ample testimony

---

[2] Alper concludes that ego-involved performances go beyond Ebbinghaus' three laws, whereas Bruner states that his results go beyond Weber's law (p. 75). Variations in other psychological functions (such as "social perception") are being obtained which go beyond classical laws in those fields. All these "going beyonds" can be accounted for in a conceptual scheme if they are taken as special cases of referential frameworks with different factors (anchorages) coming into play to modify experiences one way or another. Likewise, the apparently contradictory variations sometimes obtained in level of aspiration experiments done under different conditions can be easily explained if they are seen as so many special cases of referential frames and different anchorages coming into play to produce the results. This point has been nicely formulated by Chapman and Volkmann (p. 121) and Pauline Sears (p. 122).

[3] This translated quotation is taken from Koffka. [42, *595*]

from honest observers, are acts performed 'absent-mindedly,' automatically. Automatic behavior has no me-ness attached to it." [46, *124*]

Those who try to account for learning on the basis of some relatively static conception may object that the differential learning found in ego- versus non-ego-involved situations represents nothing more than the operation of different conditions of learning, and that the introduction of "ego-involved" situations is therefore quite unnecessary. We have emphasized that we regard the ego as a product of learning. And when the psychology of learning is fully understood, we shall have much more precise knowledge of the ego's development than we do now. What the experiments on ego-involvement and memory show is the necessity of recognizing the fact that the learning situation is differently organized for the individual when he feels that *he* is somehow involved and that this organization, this interest determination or interest setting as Bartlett calls it, affects *what* will be learned and *how* learning will take place.

Ego-involvements Shown in the Intensity of Attitudes

In previous chapters we established the fact that attitudes are learned either as the result of direct contact with a person or a group or by means of transmission of social norms through short-cut verbal value judgments. We also pointed out that most attitudes of everyday life concerned with concrete social situations have affective and motivational properties of varying degrees. And we cited numerous studies which showed the effect of these attitudes on perception, judgment, and behavior. We pointed out that the affective properties of attitudes derived from noninstinctual sources is due to the fact that these attitudes were formed in relation to social values or norms which in themselves are standardized affective fixations. (p. 20 *f.*)

We were careful throughout our earlier discussion of the properties of attitudes to state that affect or emotional involvement was of varying degrees. It is obvious that a sophisticated Negro who has suffered job discrimination will follow the course of fair employment legislation much more anxiously than a white person or another Negro who has only a mild hope that something can be done to improve the status of Negroes. We know that, by and large, a big employer or major stockholder is more likely to take some overt action to counter union demands for higher wages than some relatively disinterested person whose attitude toward the union may, however, be just as unfavorable when judged from conversation or measured by an ordinary attitude scale. We have seen since the end of World War II how the Jews in the United States have taken the initiative in forming committees or groups of one kind or another to seek some kind of government or intergovernmental help for the tortured and displaced Jews of Europe, while many other Americans whose attitudes toward the European Jews may have been just as favorable as that of some of their Jewish countrymen did nothing more than read with a sigh accounts about these efforts of assistance. In such cases we say that "self-interest" is involved. And we mean by this that individuals identify themselves with different degrees of intensity to various social causes, principles, ideals. In other words, the intensity with which we hold those attitudes formed in relation to social values or those personal attitudes formed in relation to particular surroundings or experiences depends on the degree to which those attitudes are ego-involved. Bruner's finding that poor children overestimated the size of coins more than rich children (p. 75) points to the fact that the value of coins as perceptual objects was clearly determined by ego-involving attitudes which varied in their intensity for the two groups of children.

Studies concerned with the intensity of attitude and the relation of intensity to the content or direction of attitude can, it seems to us, only be interpreted by regarding the reference scale by means of which a person judges the relative importance *to him* of the attitudes he holds as ego-involved. This degree of ego-involvement, this intensity of attitudes, will determine in large part which attitudes he will cling to, how annoyed or frustrated he will feel when his attitudes are opposed, what action (within the range of his individual temperament and ability) he will take to further his point of view.

In an attempt to draw a distinction between the intensity of an attitude and its direction and to determine the relationship of these two variables, Cantril [11] constructed two simple attitude scales, involving several alternatives which were rated by judges as to the place each alternative statement should occupy on an attitude continuum which ranged from most favorable to most unfavorable attitude. Two scales, one dealing with the attitude toward the Negro and the other with government regulation of business, were included in separate nationwide samples of 1200 adult white people in the United States. After an individual had indicated the statement that best expressed his own point of view, he was asked how strongly he held this opinion—very strongly, fairly strongly, or not caring much one way or the other.

The results, shown in Charts 1 and 2, indicate that, the more extreme an attitude is in its direction, the more intensely it is likely to be held.

Comparable results have been reported by Stouffer and his associates in their work with the Information and Education Division of the Army Service Forces [61]. These investigators used a battery of different questions to construct a scale on the "content" of an attitude and then measured the intensity (or certainty) of opinion. These scales were administered to Army populations. Their results, too, show that intensity is highly correlated with the extremity of an attitude. "A series of questions which form both a content and an intensity scale, will produce an invariant U-shaped curve." [4] This U-shaped curve, seen in the charts, may tend to err on the conservative side, in view of the fact that the results were obtained by the usual interviewing method where the interviewer asks the respondent his opinion. From comparisons of opinions obtained with comparable samples when "secret," as opposed to "nonsecret," ballots are used, we know that there is a tendency for people to answer in the direction of what they regard as the socially approved norm when asked their opinion on nonsecret ballots dealing with controversial issues. This tendency to conformity on the nonsecret ballot is itself obviously a further demonstration of the fact that individuals feel themselves personally involved in expressions of *their* opinions and seek to raise *their* status in the eyes of the interviewer. This tendency was significantly revealed, for example, in the finding that 13 per cent

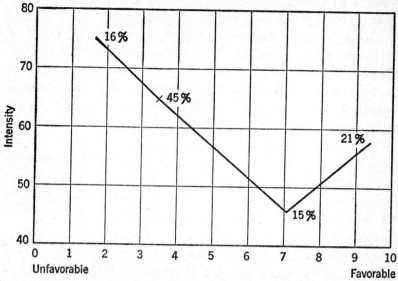

CHART 1. Direction and intensity of opinion toward the Negro.

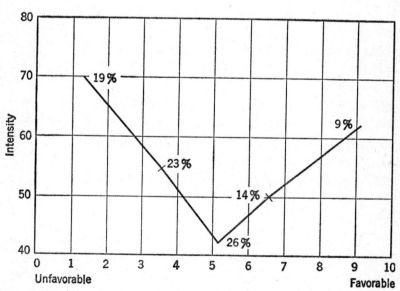

CHART 2. Direction and intensity of opinion toward Government ownership.

more of the secret ballot group than of the interviewed group stated that they had no schooling. [62]

It is the intensity with which an attitude is held, the degree of ego-involvement it has for the individual, that in large part determines the consistency of opinion, the tendency to discern the relationship of a variety of specific issues to some basic frame of reference. Katz' analysis [39] of public opinion poll results obtained before Pearl Harbor shows that those Americans who strongly believed we should help England even at the risk of getting into the war ourselves were more consistent in other related attitudes than those who shared this opinion but did not hold it so intensely. A scale constructed to measure the intensity of political interest rather sharply distinguished voters from non-voters and aided in the prediction of the political behavior of various groups. [10, *191 f.*] Postman and Zimmerman [53] have shown that, the more intensely an attitude is held, the shorter is the decision time of judgments based on that attitude.

STATUS AND CLASS IDENTIFICATION AS EGO-INVOLVEMENTS

We have stated that one important reason why attitudes are affectively charged is the fact that many attitudes prescribe the individual's relationship, status, or role with respect to other individuals or groups (such as teacher, worker, boss, minister, assistant). And experiences connected with status are affectively charged (p. 21). We pointed out further that attitudes related to role or status are ego-involved.

In his discussion of the "social" self, James made it quite clear that status identification often determines behavior in everyday life. It is a man's

> . . . image in the eyes of his own "set," which exalts or condemns him as he conforms or not to certain requirements that may not be made of one in another walk of life. Thus a layman may abandon a city infected with cholera; but a priest or doctor would think such an act incompatible with his honor. A soldier's honor requires him to fight or to die under circumstances where another man can apologize

or run away with no stain upon his social self. . . . The thief must not steal from other thieves; the gambler must pay his gambling debts, though he pay no other debts in the world. [35, 294 f.]

In later chapters we will see how an individual identifies himself with and regards as a part of himself the particular constellation of values he learns from his environment. On the basis of this learning the individual defines his own role or status: he learns what group or groups *he* belongs to; what other groups are regarded as "higher" or "lower" than his own; what groups are to be regarded as enemies, antagonists, or competitors; what as allies, helpers, or friends. For example, the behavior of the American G.I. abroad during and after World War II often emphasized in striking fashion to people in foreign countries the status roles defined by their own norms. Hilgard has reported some of his observations made during the spring of 1946, of the effect of G.I. behavior on the Japanese:

> Japanese etiquette requires courtesy to those above you in status, and does not demand much consideration between equals. . . . The lack of regard for status, foreign to the Japanese, is admired. G.I.'s like to ride in rickshaws, for the novelty of the experience, but they are just as likely to have a little fun pulling one. This sort of behavior would be unheard of among Japanese, but it is not found repugnant. [29, 347]

The same American G.I.'s would, of course, probably find their ideas of status violated by any behavior on their own home ground that deviated from discrimination concerning race, class, or sex prescribed by norms of their own.

We have already mentioned a number of experiments concerned with the effect an individual's place in a group has on his level of aspiration. A considerable body of data has by now accumulated from other controlled studies which further emphasize the fact that a person defines his role, his status, his class, on the basis of the anchorage provided him by values which he has made part of himself. By means of these anchorages he makes relevant judgments both of his own place in society and the place of others.

An especially revealing demonstration of such an anchorage is the study of Marks [48] on Negro judgments of skin color and personal attractiveness. Following up by controlled experimentation Johnson's field observations [36] that the judgments of Negro youth on the skin colors of other Negroes tended to depend upon the rater's own skin color and his observation that more favorable characteristics tended to be associated with lighter colors, Marks had each student in his class (all Negroes) rate every other student on certain characteristics including skin color, personal charm, desire to know the person well, on an eight-point scale. He found a high correlation between ratings on lightness of skin color and ratings on personal charm and "a tendency to displace the ratings of subjects considered attractive in the direction of the preferred color." [48, 376] Particularly important for our purposes here is the finding that the reference scale by means of which each subject judged skin color was relatively

> . . . independent of the subjects rated but not of the rater's own past experience. It appears further that each judge's rating scale tends to be egocentric, *i.e., a subject is seen as darker or lighter than the rater and judgments are made accordingly.* In such a scale the *relative* position of each subject will be the same for the different raters but the *absolute* position of a given subject will vary from rater to rater. [48, 374, italics ours]

Marks further points out that

> The relation between the judge's own skin color and his rating of others seems to have particular importance for the theory of social perception. The "egocentricity" of the reference scale of skin color judgments may well apply to judgments of any characteristic to which social value is attached. [375]
> The goal of neutral emotional content frequently involves a restructuring of our social perceptual field. The individual minimizes his own deviation (slight or great) from the "normal" by displacing his perception of other individuals so that they are seen as above or below average in terms of their difference from himself, [48, 375]

The subjects in these groups, Marks believed, were in large part striving to conform to an average or group norm in an attempt to regard themselves as inconspicuous, to achieve a "neutral emotional content" as discovered from their own past experience in the process of socialization.

This investigation confirms in a particularly clear-cut way two points we should again emphasize: (1) in the process of genetic development the individual's physical body and its characteristics constitute an early and important part of the ego. Judgments of the physical characteristics of others (such as their height, their stoutness, their strength, their beauty) become, therefore, ego-involving judgments in which an individual uses himself or his own characteristics as a central point of reference (ch. 7). (2) If the stimulus field is relatively well-structured, has certain discernible and compelling objective properties, an individual's frame or scale is almost bound to be determined in part by them. Thus, as Marks indicates:

> The very dark individual cannot conceive himself as "neutral" in color because his social environment insists upon the "objective" facts. A compromise results, in which the deviation may be minimized (perceived as less extreme by the individual than it is by others) but is not ignored. [48, *375 f.*]

A significant study on the psychology of status is that of Hyman. [34]   After learning from an intensive interview of each of his subjects something of the meaning, genesis, criteria of, and satisfaction with status, he constructed scales to measure subjective status along several dimensions: general status, economic, intellectual, cultural, social, and physical attractiveness. Subjects were also asked to indicate their subjective status with reference to different groups: the total adult population in the United States, friends and acquaintances, and their occupational group. He found that "within each status dimension an individual's judgment of his status shifts when reference groups are changed." [49] Among other results reported, the following are particularly significant for our purposes here: individuals strive for status with respect to those accomplishments or characteristics which they most highly value; when an individual's status is approximately similar to the status of the group he is using as a basis for comparison, then he shows no particular concern for his own status, no great drive to achieve a higher status; persons who regard the difference between their own status and a reference group as being determined by a social system they disapprove of also show little dissatisfaction with their own status.

Hyman emphasizes the contrast between subjective and objective status:

> The variables of status are mediated through an individual who acts selectively in his choice of reference group, who strives selectively for status, whose personal values affect the composition of status and the emotional concomitants of a given status, whose conceptualization of a reference group may be different from its actual character, who is not affected by all aspects of the culture nor by all references in the environment. This essentially personal aspect of status cannot be ignored. We cannot deal with these variables independent of their meaning to individuals. [34, *80*]

This study clearly indicates that an individual's conception of his own status or the status of his group invariably depends upon the other groups to which he compares himself or his own group. In other words, he uses *himself* or *his* group as the anchoring point, and his own subjective status varies according to the scale provided.

In chapter 4 we learned from several independent investigations [4, 40, 52] that individuals easily characterize various occupational groups and rank them according to a hierarchy based on the accepted social norms established in our social organization. We saw from Davis' study [16] how children in Soviet Russia ranked occupations in quite a different way from the manner they are usually ranked in the United States: lawyers and bankers were rated low in Russia and skilled workers high.

Gould and Lewis [24] found that an individual defines success differently when comparing himself to the supposed performance of college professors than when comparing himself with the supposed performance of WPA workers. Similar results were obtained by Hertzman and Festinger [27]. The experiment of Preston and Bayton [54] revealed that, although there was no difference in the level of aspiration of Negro college men when the experimental group was told it was competing with white men and the control group told it was competing with Negroes in other colleges, there was a clear indication that those who thought they were being compared with whites had considerably less confidence in themselves with respect either to the maintenance of past performance or the attainment of higher scores in the future. The ego-disturbance or ego-insecurity found here among those Negroes who believed their past performance was equal to that of a group generally regarded as "superior" is comparable to the feeling of inferiority so commonly found in everyday life among those who, objectively, are as able, as good-looking, or as successful as certain other individuals with whom they compare themselves but who, in their eyes, seem superior because of various status affiliations. In a complementary study, MacIntosh [47] found that when white subjects compared themselves with the hypothetical scores of Negroes they tended to raise their own estimates and showed greater confidence in their own abilities.

Psychologists have only recently begun to study the problem of class identification in contemporary America. We have already referred to Kornhauser's pioneering attempt to compare the attitudes of individuals whose class placement might be inferred from the amount and source of their income or from their occupation (p. 75). Certain differences between the attitudes of members of the upper, middle, or lower class, as defined by objective criteria, did appear with respect to some social and political issues. But differences did not show up with reference to those attitudes which reflected in the 1930's the traditional American ideology of individual opportunity.

In Cantril's study [9], based on a nationwide survey made in 1941, a sample of the American adult population was asked the following two direct questions: "Which income group in our country do you feel that you are a member of—the middle income group, the upper income group, or the lower income group?" and "To what social class in this country do you feel you belong— middle class, or upper, or lower?" Only 3 per cent of over 3,000 people interviewed were unable to place themselves in some social class, and only 1 per cent could not fit themselves into an economic class. That these questions were meaningful is further indicated by the reports of the interviewers who stated that they had no difficulty at all in getting the answers to the questions.

The results showed that at that time, and with only these three alternatives provided for answers, almost nine tenths of the American people identified themselves with the great middle class. This middle class tradition and ideology has its roots in frontier individualism and in the relatively high standard of living provided in this country by natural resources and technological developments and regarded as a middle class standard. Even 70 per cent of those who feel they are members of the lower *income* group still call themselves members of the middle *social* group. There is a strict correspondence between the two class identifications— social and economic—among only 54 per cent of the representative population. As Veblen pointed out so strikingly in his *Theory of the Leisure Class,* there is a definite tendency for individuals to regard their social class within a frame of reference provided by the norms of their social system and frequently unsupported by the income necessary to solidify their own positions objectively in the social level they accept as their own. The greatest disparity between income and social identification is found among the low income groups, while those who placed themselves higher in the social scale tended to base their identification less on strictly economic criteria, using in addition to income such commonly accepted values as family background, education, and professional accomplishments. It is clear from this preliminary study that nearly every adult American easily thinks of himself as a member of a class, that the great majority of Americans at that time rather uncritically identified themselves with the middle class which has for so long been the traditional bulwark of American ideology. Because of this middle class identification it is not surprising that Kornhauser found many inconsistencies in the attitudes people "logically" should have as members of different economic or occupational groups and the attitudes they actually do have.

The most thorough psychological analysis to date of class structure in America is that of Centers [12]. He carefully designed a questionnaire which would reveal subjective class identification, attitudes toward major economic and social issues, adherence to certain traditional conceptions of American ideology (for example, that this is a land of freedom and opportunity), occupation, religious affiliation, nationality background, and the like. The questionnaire was used in a public opinion survey in the summer of 1945. Approximately 1,100 representative adult white men in the United States were personally interviewed. It should be remembered that Centers' survey was made before the end of World War II, that is, while both labor and management were still by and large submerging their differences in the interests of the war effort.

The question used by Centers to reveal subjective class identification included the additional category of "working" class. This wording makes possible a more accurate and objective class differentiation (and one apparently understandable by the population) in terms of relationship to the processes of production and exchange in contemporary society.[4] Centers' over-all national results on class identification are as follows, to the question: "If you were asked to use one of these four names for your social class, which would you say you belonged in: the middle class, lower class, working class, or upper class?"

Upper	3%
Middle	43
Working	51
Lower	1
Don't know	1
Don't believe in classes	1

This subjective identification with one of the four classes described correlates highly with an individual's economic status as judged by the interviewer (see Table 1). It is possible, then, to make a prediction of some reliability concerning class identification from an individual's income or standard of living. That those who identify themselves with the working class realize the

---

[4] The difference between Centers' findings and those already reported by Cantril, as well as other results of the same type found in surveys of the American Institute of Public Opinion and the *Fortune* poll provide an excellent example of the effect of the wording of questions on results obtained in public opinion surveys and the consequent need for caution in interpretation until issues or groupings have been variously sliced. In Centers' survey for example (had sufficient funds been available) it would have been revealing to substitute on a comparable sample of the population the word "laboring" for "working" class. Other obvious possibilities also come to mind—the use of categories such as "management," "white collar," "professional."

relative uncertainty and precariousness of their jobs is revealed by Centers' finding that when asked which kind of job they would choose, those who put themselves in the working class gave as their most frequent reply "a job which you were absolutely sure of keeping," whereas those who put themselves in the middle class gave as their most frequent reply "a job where you could express your feelings, ideas, talent, or skill."

TABLE 1

CLASS IDENTIFICATION BY ECONOMIC STATUS

Economic Status	Upper	Middle	Working	Lower	Don't Know	Don't Believe in Class	Total
Above average	9%	75%	14%	0.5%	1%	0.5%	100%
Average	2	58	38	.....	1	1	100
Below average	1	23	72	2	2	.....	100

Particularly striking is the relationship found by Centers between subjective class identification and objective status as defined by occupation. As Chart 3 shows, approximately three quarters of all manual workers, whether skilled, semiskilled, or unskilled, feel they belong to the *working* class.[5] On the other hand approximately the same proportion of business owners and managers and of professional people put themselves in the *middle* class. White collar workers, farm owners, and managers appear to have a somewhat more ambivalent position. The chart shows beyond any shadow of doubt that the American people do identify themselves with a social class and that this identification is highly correlated with the particular role they play in our highly industrialized society.

A special study of foremen in American factories made by the Opinion Research Corporation in 1945 [51] shows that the majority of them identify themselves with management rather than with the workers. Furthermore, of particular significance is the fact that, the longer the foremanship tenure, the greater is the tendency to identify with management rather than with labor. The study also shows that foremen who were former union members identify themselves with management almost as much as

[5] These charts were designed by Richard Centers.

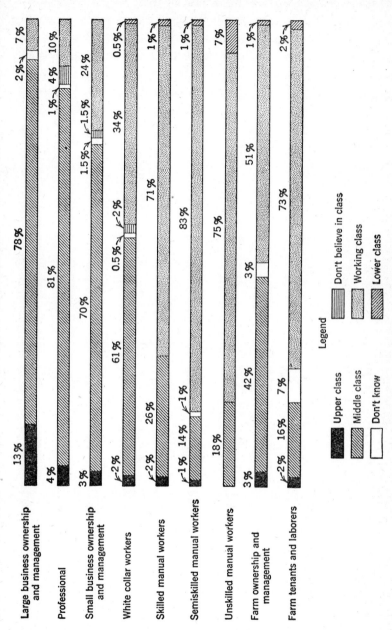

CHART 3. Class identification by occupation.

those who had not been union members (57 per cent compared to 62 per cent). Foremen clearly occupy an ambivalent membership position in our social organization. What identification they may once have had with workers tends to disappear; their loyalties become relatively mixed; they are not part of management, yet they tend to identify themselves with those in the "top" positions of authority and control.[6] Table 2 shows the answers given by 764 foremen to the question: "There are several views as to the place that foremen occupy in relation to management and the

TABLE 2

FOREMAN IDENTIFICATION BY LENGTH OF FOREMANSHIP TENURE

Foremanship Tenure	Cases	Management	Workers	Neither, in Between	Don't Know
Under 2 years	227	49%	22%	26%	3%
2–5 years	169	61	18	20	1
Over 5 years	365	64	19	16	1
No answer	3				
Total	764	59%	20%	20%	1%

workers. Would you say that foremen are a part of management, or that they are more like workers?"

The various occupational groups that members of the working and middle classes assign to their own class in Centers' study are shown in Charts 4 and 5. Charts 6 and 7 indicate some very significant aspects of class identification. Here there is a comparison of the definitions given to the two major classes, middle and working, by each of two objectively different occupational strata. A striking fact is that though people may differ greatly in their objective status they define the class with which they identify themselves in essentially similar fashion. Middle class and working class apparently means about the same thing to one stratum as to another. Yet it is noteworthy that the discrepancies that do occur in the contrasting conceptions of a given class are systematically biased in favor of inclusion in the class of "members" of the individual's own occupational group.

[6] For a more detailed discussion of the status of foremen see [22].

As would be expected, reliable differences appear between the attitudes of working class and middle class members with respect to attitudes concerned with basic socioeconomic issues. Centers constructed a scale of radicalism–conservatism from six separate questions (such as giving the working people more power and influence in government, government ownership of industry, sympathy with workers versus employers in strikes). As Table 3 indicates, those who are middle class are considerably more conservative than the working class. Differences of opinion between

TABLE 3

CLASS IDENTIFICATION BY RADICALISM–CONSERVATISM

| | Class Identification | | | |
| | Middle | | Working | |
Attitude Position	Per cent	Cases	Per cent	Cases
Radical	12	55	31	177
Conservative	67	314	36	201
Indeterminate	21	98	33	186
	100	467	100	564

the working and middle class found by Centers are probably conservative, in view of the facts that most public opinion interviewers are themselves members of the middle class, and we know from Katz' study [38] opinions reported by working class interviewers tended to be definitely more radical than those reported by middle class interviewers on working people.

It is significant that, although the percentage of working class people who are defined in Centers' scale as conservatives is only about half as great as those defined as conservative in the middle class, there are still more working class people in the conservative than in the radical group. This demonstrates that class consciousness does not rapidly and spontaneously arise. It requires leadership and organization to transform a loose numerical class into a compact psychological class. It is therefore important to bear in mind the distinction between objective and subjective class differentiation. As of 1945, although a plurality of American men identified themselves with the working class, they can by no means

be regarded as highly "class-conscious." A breakdown of radicalism–conservatism by occupational groups shows, however, a
clear tendency for conservatism to decrease and radicalism to increase as one goes "down" the occupational ladder (Chart 8). It

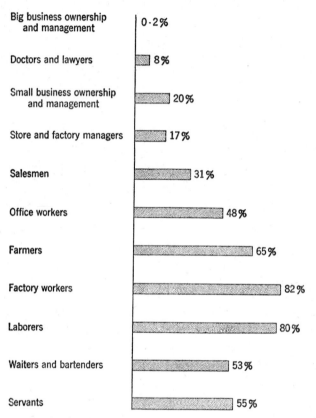

CHART 4. Occupational composition of the working class based on working-class
specifications of the occupational membership.

is also noteworthy that the size of the undecided category increases
as occupational status is lowered. Centers' data further show that
within each occupational category, those who call themselves
members of the working class are less conservative than those who
identify themselves with the middle class.

In brief, we have in Centers' study a demonstration of the fact
that individuals in contemporary America do identify themselves

with a social class, that this identification is largely determined by
the objective relation or status they have with respect to the means
of production and exchange in an industrial society, and that this
identification tends to be accompanied by characteristic attitudes

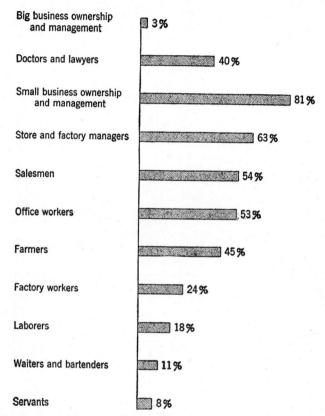

CHART 5. Occupational composition of the middle class according to the specifications of the middle class.

related to the social organization which has imposed on people
the particular role they have within it.

SOME RECENT REVIEWS OF EXPERIMENTAL LITERATURE

In order to make our position quite clear, we cite some examples
of the conclusions drawn by others who have recently reviewed
the experimental literature on ego-involvement.

In his discussion of *The Ego in Contemporary Psychology* (1943), G. W. Allport [1] brought together much of the recent

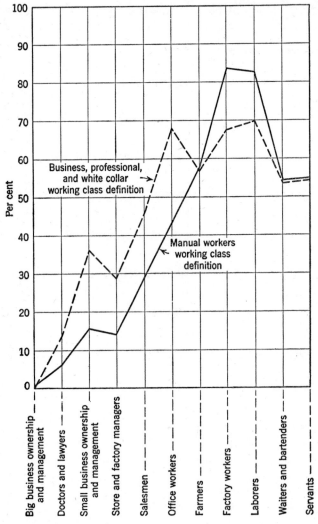

CHART 6. Comparison of two definitions of working class.

experimental work and reaffirmed the validity of the concept of ego for modern psychology. But Allport's eclectic approach seems to us to have somewhat obscured the systematic psychological meaning the term should have. He distinguished eight different conceptions of the ego as held by psychologists and believes

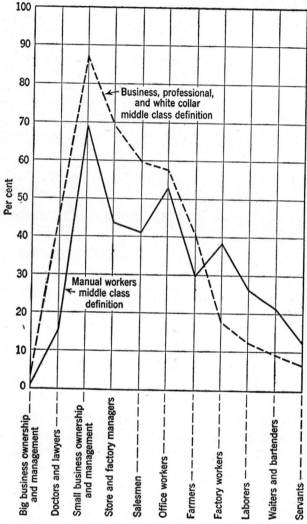

CHART 7. Comparison of two definitions of middle class.

that there is experimental support for all eight of the capacities of the ego he reviewed, even though among the eight are such divergent and conflicting characterizations as "the ego as primitive selfishness," "the ego as dominance-drive," "the ego as a passive organization of mental processes," and "the ego as the subjective organization of culture." In criticizing our earlier discussion of the ego, he contended that the ego for us is "nothing but 'the social in man.'" [458] Although we have always maintained and

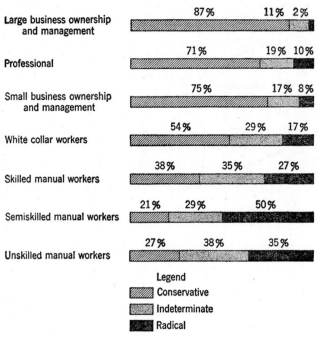

CHART 8. Radicalism–conservatism by occupation.

still do maintain that social values constitute the major portion of the normal individual's ego, we have not equated the ego with *nothing but* social values. We have pointed out in previous publications that what can be described as "personal" values, as contrasted with "social" values can and often do constitute an important part of the egos of different individuals.

For example, Sherif, in 1936, described *personal* fixations and evaluations. [60, *120 ff.*] In his summary discussion of the ego he stated:

Values are the chief constituents of the ego. *Among these,* social values, which are socially established affective fixations, form the major (directive) part. These values are the social in man. [60, *185,* italics not in original]

Cantril [7] wrote in 1940 that the "ego of an individual is essentially composed of the many social *and personal* values he has accepted." [*197 f.*]   And again, in 1941 [8], that

> Although we do conform in large measure to the common values of society and do desire a certain amount of social recognition, *in addition to this—and often much more important in terms of felt significance*—we cherish certain values which may be shared by our family circle, a few professional colleagues, a local community group, or a political party. *And sometimes we cherish, as most important of all, those values which we have worked out for ourselves and think of as our own.* . . . In such instances, we care about recognition only from a very few people, or the status we may want is status only in our own eyes. [8, *45,* italics not in original statements]

Although Allport is critical of the interpretation of the "ego as the subjective organization of culture," still, in the last analysis, the weight of evidence brings him close to our position.   He writes, for example, that "what an individual regards as himself is undeniably, in large part, socially determined." [1, *458*]   He states further that for the normal individual the "ego-system is made up of the ordinary values which spell out the significance of life to the individual." [*470*]

Allport states further that values which cannot be characterized as "social" must be called "egoistic."

> If the ego is nothing but the "social in man," one wonders what to call all the anti-social impulses and the solitary strivings that are normally called egoistic? [1, *458*]

This is more an ethical than a psychological characterization.   And a mixture of ethics and psychology makes it difficult for psychologists who want to use the term "ego" in a precise *psychological* way to show their colleagues they are not trying once more to bring into the discipline some modern version of the soul.   The tendency to mix psychology and ethics, to relate the "self" in some way to "selfish" interests, was criticized by Baldwin and Cooley around the turn of the century. Baldwin felt that any attempted equation was "quite beside the mark." [5]   Cooley pointed out in 1902 that

> Self and other do not exist as mutually exclusive social facts, and phraseology which implies that they do, like the antithesis egoism versus altruism, is open to the objection of vagueness, if not of falsity. It seems to me that the classification of impulses as altruistic and egoistic, with or without a third class called, perhaps, ego-altruistic, is empty; and I do not see how any other conclusion can result from a concrete study of the matter. [15, *126 f.*]

Lewis also defines "ego" needs as "selfish" needs [44]. But she found from her own experiments on co-operative effort that such a definition was too limited, that subjects working together identified themselves with one another so that each got satisfaction if the job at hand was satisfactorily completed, whether by one's self or one's partner. To interpret this finding, as Lewis has, as "task orientation" rather than "ego orientation" overlooks and contradicts her own statements that in these co-operative situations " 'ego-boundaries' may include the needs of other selves or 'egos,' of groups, of ideals." [45, *214*]   Her experiment demonstrates nicely that there can be and is ego-involvement in co-operative effort as well as in restricted individualistic pursuits.

A somewhat more recent review of experimental literature by Holt (1945) [30] shows the confusion that results from the attempt to get away from a formulation merely by creating a new terminology. Holt maintains that the common denominator of most meanings of ego-involvements is "self-esteem." But he goes on to say that he cannot use the term "self-esteem involvement" because it is too narrow to define all the functions that "comprise the ego."

In summary, the experiments and controlled investigations reported all add up to substantiate further the position that the ego is a genetic formation made up of a host of personal and social values and that these values serve the individual as frames of reference by means of which he makes those judgments that affect *him;* that define *for him* success and failure; that determine his loyalties and allegiances; that spell out what he conceives to be *his* role, *his* status, *his* class. Judgments and behavior resulting from this identification of oneself with a certain constellation of values we can properly term "ego-involved." "Ego-involvement" is a general descriptive term that can have many specific and more precise meanings (such as "ego-enhancement," "ego-gratification," "ego-frustration," "ego-support," "ego-misplacement," "ego-expansion," "ego-breakdown"), depending on the particular set of circumstances in which the ego is involved.

REFERENCES

1. ALLPORT, G. W., The ego in contemporary psychology, *Psychol. Rev.,* 1943, **50**, 451–78.
2. ALPER, T. G., Task-orientation vs. ego-orientation in learning and retention, *Am. J. Psychol.,* 1946, **59**, 236–48.
3. ANDERSON, H. H., and H. F. BRANDT, A study of motivation involving self-announced goals of fifth grade children and the concept of level of aspiration, *J. Soc. Psychol.,* 1939, **10**, 209–32.
4. ASCH, S. E., H. BLOCK, and M. HERTZMAN, Studies in the principles of judgments and attitudes: I. Two basic principles of judgment, *J. Psychol.,* 1938, **5**, 219–51.
5. BALDWIN, J. M., *Social and Ethical Interpretations in Mental Development,* New York: Macmillan, copyright 1897.
6. BIRCH, H. G., The effect of socially disapproved labeling upon a well-structured attitude, *J. Abnorm. & Soc. Psychol.,* 1945, **40**, 301–10.
7. CANTRIL, H., *The Invasion from Mars,* Princeton: Univ. Press, 1940.
8. —— *The Psychology of Social Movements,* New York: Wiley, copyright 1941.
9. —— Identification with social and economic class, *J. Abnorm. & Soc. Psychol.,* 1943, **38**, 74–80.
10. —— The use of breakdowns, in *Gauging Public Opinion* (H. Cantril, ed.), Princeton: Univ. Press, 1944, ch. 13.
11. —— The intensity of an attitude, *J Abnorm. & Soc. Psychol.,* 1946, **41**, 129–35.
12. CENTERS, R., *Psychological Aspects of Socio-economic Stratification: an Enquiry into the Nature of Class,* Princeton Univ., to be published.
13. CHAPMAN, D. W., and J. VOLKMANN, A social determinant of the level of aspiration, *J. Abnorm. & Soc. Psychol.,* 1939, **34**, 225–38.
14. CLAPARÈDE, E., Récognition et Moïité, *Arch. de Psych.,* 1911, **11**.
15. COOLEY, C. H., *Human Nature and the Social Order,* New York: Scribner's, copyright 1902.
16. DAVIS, J., Testing the social attitudes of children in the government schools in Russia, *Am. J. Sociol.,* 1927, **32**, 947–52.
17. EDWARDS, A. L., Political frames of reference as a factor influencing recognition, *J. Abnorm. & Soc. Psychol.,* 1941, **36**, 34–50.
18. —— Rationalization in recognition as a result of a political frame of reference, *J. Abnorm. & Soc. Psychol.,* 1941, **36**, 224–35.

19. FRANK, J. D., The influence of the level of performance in one task on the level of aspiration in another, *J. Exp. Psychol.*, 1935, **18**, 159–71.

20. —— Some psychological determinants of the level of aspiration, *Am. J. Psychol.*, 1935, **47**, 285–93.

21. —— Recent studies of the level of aspiration, *Psychol. Bull.*, 1941, **38**, 218–26.

22. GOLDEN, C. S., and H. J. RUTTENBERG, *The Dynamics of Industrial Democracy*, New York: Harper, 1942.

23. GOULD, R., An experimental analysis of "level of aspiration," *Genet. Psychol. Monogr.*, 1939, **21**, 1–116.

24. —— and H. B. LEWIS, An experimental investigation of changes in the meaning of level of aspiration, *J. Exp. Psychol.*, 1940, **27**, 422–38.

25. GREENBERG, P. J., Competition in children, *Am. J. Psychol.*, 1932, **44**, 221–48.

26. HEATHERS, L. B., Factors producing generality in the level of aspiration, *J. Exp. Psychol.*, 1942, **30**, 392–406.

27. HERTZMAN, M., and L. FESTINGER, Shifts in explicit goals in a level of aspiration experiment, *J. Exp. Psychol.*, 1940, **27**, 439–52.

28. HILGARD, E. R., E. M. SAIT, and G. A. MAGARET, Level of aspiration as affected by relative standing in an experimental social group, *J. Exp. Psychol.*, 1940, **27**, 411–21.

29. —— The enigma of Japanese friendliness, *Publ. Opin. Quart.*, 1946, **10**, 343–8.

30. HOLT, R. R., Effects of ego-involvement upon levels of aspiration, *Psychiatry: J. Biol. & Path. Interpers. Relations*, 1945, **3**, 299–317.

31. HOPPE, F., Erfolg und Misserfolg, *Psychol. Forsch.*, 1930, **14**, 1–62.

32. HORNEY, K., *New Ways in Psychoanalysis*, New York: Norton, copyright 1939.

33. HUNTLEY, C. W., Judgments of self based upon records of expressive behavior, *J. Abnorm. & Soc. Psychol.*, 1940, **35**, 398–427.

34. HYMAN, H. H., The psychology of status, *Arch. Psychol.*, 1942, no. 269.

35. JAMES, W., *The Principles of Psychology*, New York: Holt, copyright 1890.

36. JOHNSON, C. S., *Growing Up in the Black Belt*, Washington: Am. Council on Education, 1941.

37. KARSTEN, A., Psychische Sättigung, *Psych. Forsch.*, 1928, **10**, 142–254.

38. KATZ, D., Do interviewers bias poll results?, *Publ. Opin. Quart.*, 1942, **6**, 248–68.

39. —— The measurement of intensity, in *Gauging Public Opinion* (H. Cantril, ed.), Princeton: Univ. Press, 1944, ch. 3.

40. KAY, L. W., The relation of personal frames of reference to social judgments, *Arch. Psychol.*, 1943, no. 283.

41. KLEIN, G. S., and N. SCHOENFELD, The influence of ego-involvement on confidence, *J. Abnorm. & Soc. Psychol.*, 1941, **36**, 249–58.

42. KOFFKA, K., *Principles of Gestalt Psychology*, New York: Harcourt, Brace, copyright 1935.

43. LEVINE, J. M., and G. MURPHY, The learning and forgetting of controversial material, *J. Abnorm. & Soc. Psychol.*, 1943, **38**, 507–17.

44. LEWIS, H. B., An experimental study of the role of the ego in work: I. The role of the ego in coöperative work, *J. Exp. Psychol.*, 1944, **34**, 113–26.

45. —— and M. FRANKLIN, An experimental study of the role of the ego in work: II. The significance of task-orientation in work, *J. Exp. Psychol.*, 1944, **34**, 195–215.

46. MACCURDY, J. T., *Common Principles in Psychology and Physiology,* Cambridge (England): Univ. Press, 1928.

47. MACINTOSH, A., Differential effect of the status of the competing group upon the levels of aspiration, *Am. J. Psychol.,* 1942, **55,** 546–54.

48. MARKS, E., Skin color judgments of Negro college students, *J. Abnorm. & Soc. Psychol.,* 1943, **38,** 370–6.

49. McGEHEE, W., Judgment and the level of aspiration, *J. Gen. Psychol.,* 1940, **22,** 3–15.

50. MURPHY, G., L. B. MURPHY, and T. M. NEWCOMB, *Experimental Social Psychology,* New York: Harper, 1937.

51. OPINION RESEARCH CORPORATION, *Foremen Thinking Today,* a survey made by the Public Opinion Index for Industry, March 1946.

52. OSGOOD, C. E., and R. STAGNER, Analysis of a prestige frame of reference by a gradient technique, *J. Appl. Psychol.,* 1941, **25,** 275–90.

53. POSTMAN, L., and C. ZIMMERMAN, Intensity of attitude as a determinant of decision time, *Am. J. Psychol.,* 1945, **58,** 510–18.

54. PRESTON, M. G., and J. A. BAYTON, Differential effect of a social variable upon three levels of aspiration, *J. Exp. Psychol.,* 1941, **29,** 351–69.

55. ROSENZWEIG, S., Preferences in the repetition of successful and unsuccessful activities as a function of age and personality, *J. Genet. Psychol.,* 1933, **42,** 423–41.

56. —— An experimental study of "Repression" with special reference to need-persistent and ego-defensive reactions to frustration, *J. Exp. Psychol.,* 1943, **32,** 64–74.

57. SEARS, P. S., Levels of aspiration in academically successful and unsuccessful children, *J. Abnorm. & Soc. Psychol.,* 1940, **35,** 498–536.

58. SEELEMAN, V., The influence of attitude upon the remembering of pictorial material, *Arch. Psychol.,* 1940, no. 258.

59. SHAW, F. J., and A. SPOONER, Selective forgetting when the subject is not "ego-involved," *J. Exp. Psychol.,* 1945, **35,** 242–7.

60. SHERIF, M., *The Psychology of Social Norms,* New York: Harper, copyright 1936.

61. STOUFFER, S., and associates, Experiments on the measurement of intensity function and zero-point in attitude analysis, *Headquarters, Army Service Forces, Information and Education Division, Report No. D-1.*

62. TURNBULL, W., Secret *vs.* nonsecret ballots, in *Gauging Public Opinion* (H. Cantril, ed.), Princeton: Univ. Press, 1944, ch. 5.

63. WALLEN, R. W., The selective forgetting of material related to subjects' estimates of their own personality traits, *Abstracts of Doctoral Dissertations,* 1941, no. 35.

64. —— Ego-involvement as a determinant of selective forgetting, *J. Abnorm. & Soc. Psychol.,* 1942, **37,** 20–39.

65. WOLFF, W., Selbstbeurteilung und Fremdbeurteilung im wissentlichen und un-wissentlichen Versuch, *Psychol. Forsch.,* 1932, **16,** 251–328.

66. ZILLIG, M., Einstellung und Aussage, *Z. Psychol.,* 1928, **106,** 58–106.

CHAPTER 7

THE GENETIC FORMATION OF THE EGO

We pointed out in chapter 5 that an individual's major attitudes are not discrete items in his psychological make-up. Attitudes define a person's identifications and status; determine to an important degree his conformities and loyalties to his surroundings, to social groups and institutions. To a great extent, therefore, a person's experience of himself is related to these attitudinal experiences. In other words, the most important attitudes formed in relation to one's body, to surrounding objects, persons, institutions, and groups, are ego-attitudes. Inevitably one becomes somehow ego-involved when his intimate friends, his superior, his inferior, his family, his school, his church, or his flag are in question. Gratifications and frustrations connected with such persons, groups, or institutions are felt as ego-gratifications and ego-frustrations. Attitudes which direct a person to try to outdo others in everything (competitiveness) or to live and work in harmony as a group member (co-operativeness) are ego-attitudes, developed by the norms of the social system in which he lives.[1] Whatever we can learn about these ego-attitudes should contribute to a real understanding of the "human nature" about which social scientists and politicians make hasty assumptions in an effort to justify their theories and practices.

The more we study, the more we find that the ego (the self) consists mainly of those attitudes formed during the course of genetic development: attitudes related to one's body, parents, family, school, church, profession, property, class, and the like. As attitudes are formed (learned) in the course of genetic development, the ego is formed. Starting with the delimitation of one's

---

[1] We are not ignoring the fact that the intensity and expression of attitudes are, within limits, subject to individual variations.

own body from surrounding objects, ego formation rapidly expands by the learning of attitudes related to it (ego-attitudes), particularly after the acquisition of communicable language. This is repeatedly verified by empirical observations of child development, from the earliest to the most recent studies. Ego formation is not a mystic process. It can be readily detected in the behavior of the growing child. The social development a child has attained by the time he reaches school age is not the result of an automatic blossoming forth of some inherent natural endowment. In view of the persistence of philosophical speculations concerning the ego, it is gratifying to find this verification in fact. Indeed the psychology of the early period of ego formation seems to be one of the firmly established principles in the whole field of psychology. This is especially significant when we remember that the relevant observations were collected over a period of many years by observers who were geographically separated and who had different theoretical inclinations.

If this fact of ego formation, so well verified in almost every study on ego development, were given its due place in general books on child psychology and if its important implications for the process of socialization of the child were pointed out, it would be unnecessary for us to review here the ever-accumulating evidence concerning ego formation in a book on social psychology. But since the implications have not been systematically brought together, we shall summarize here some representative studies, from Tiedemann, Preyer, and Shinn to those of present-day psychologists. In reviewing these representative observations with a specific purpose in mind, we shall not ignore variations of the particular components of a child's developing ego or the factors which function in such a way as to accelerate or retard development. Briefly, it will be seen that both the components of the developing ego and the speed of its development will vary in terms of the limitations of the physical surroundings: the kind of treatment (care, resistances, and encouragements) received from adults, opportunities for language development, contact with cultural products, symbols, norms, associations with age mates, and so on. We are interested in the fundamental observations which show that a trend in development *does* occur. And we shall see that, in spite of variations, the general trend of ego development revealed in these investigations is essentially similar.

A Review of Some Studies on Ego Development

As early as 1787, long before the appearance of experimental psychology, Dietrich Tiedemann [46] published his observations on his son from birth through the third year.[2] Many of his reports are relevant to the problem of ego formation. When the child was slightly over a month old, Tiedemann wrote that

> . . . the boy did not beat or scratch himself with his hands as frequently as before; so it seemed that painful, oft repeated experience had taught him to draw some distinction between himself and foreign bodies. [46, *210*]

One year and four months later:

> His power of judgment was even more clearly evident on January 11, 1783, when he recognized his own image in the mirror. . . . Children are often held up to the mirror from earliest infancy, and thus they learn by repeated experience that the image is their own. [46, *222*]

When the child was 20 months old, we find a picture far different from that of the baby beating his own body:

> On the 27th of March he could already pronounce words of two syllables, and knew almost all the external parts of his body, which he pointed out correctly when their names were mentioned to him; . . . [46, *225*]

In the same year, Tiedemann observed:

> The boy did not approve of seeing his sister sitting in his chair or wearing his clothes; he called these things *his* things. [46, *227*]

Here, the italicized pronoun is evidence of the widening ego for mation with language development.

[2] The records were translated into French a few years later and into English in 1927.

A new impetus was given to genetic studies with the theory of evolution and with modern experimental psychology. Charles Darwin [14] published *A Biographical Sketch of an Infant* in 1877. His influence is clearly reflected a few years later in the work of Preyer, who, as we shall see, actually repeated some of Darwin's methods in observing his own child. At the turn of the century, genetic studies were made in every country where the new evolutionary theories spread.[3]

Early in this period, Preyer observed the growth of his son in Germany. He wrote:

> Before the child is in a condition to recognize as belonging to him the parts of his body that he can feel and see, he must have had a great number of experiences, which are for the most part associated with *painful feelings*. How little is gained for the development of the notion of the "I" by means of the first movements of the hands, which the infant early carries to the mouth, and which must give him, when he sucks them, a different feeling from that given by sucking the finger of another person, or other suitable objects, appears from the fact that, e.g., my child for months tugged at his fingers as if he wanted to pull them off, and struck his own head with his hand by way of experiment. At the close of the first year he had a fancy for striking hard substances against his teeth, and made a regular play of gnashing the teeth. When on the four hundred and ninth day he stood up straight in bed, holding on to the railing of it with his hands, *he bit himself on his bare arm,* and that the upper arm, so that he immediately cried out with pain. The marks of the incisors were to be seen long afterward. The child did not a second time bite himself in the arm, but only bit his fingers, and inadvertently his tongue. [*57, 189*]

Thus, at a time when the attention to what is around is already very far developed, one's own person may not be distinguished from the environment. . . . Nay, even in the nineteenth month it is not yet clear how much belongs to one's own body. The child had lost a shoe. I said, "Give the shoe." He stooped, seized it, and gave it to me. Then, when I said to the child, as he was standing upright on the floor, "Give the foot," . . . he grasped at it with both hands, and labored hard to get it and hand it to me. [*190*]

[3] For summaries of the work of this period see [42].

Another important factor is the *perception of a change produced by one's own activity* in all sorts of familiar objects that can be taken hold of in the neighborhood; and the most remarkable day, from a psycho-genetic point of view, in any case an extremely significant day in the life of the infant, is the one in which he first experiences the *connection of a movement executed by himself with a sense-impression following upon it.* [*191 f.*]

The child that at first merely played like a cat, being amused with color, form, and movement, has become a *causative being.* Herewith the development of the *"I"-feeling* enters upon a new phase. [*57, 193*]

As noted earlier, Preyer was inspired by Darwin's work. He included the following comments and quotations from Darwin:

Darwin recorded of one of his sons, that in the fifth month he repeatedly smiled at his father's image and his own in a mirror and took them for real objects; but he was surprised that his father's voice sounded from behind him (the child). "Like all infants, he much enjoyed thus looking at himself, and in less than two months perfectly understood that it was an image, for if I made quite silently any odd grimace, he would suddenly turn around to look at me. . . . The higher apes which I tried with a small looking-glass behaved differently. They placed their hands behind the glass, and in doing so showed their sense; but, far from taking pleasure in looking at themselves, they got angry and would look no more." [*57, 196*]

Preyer found that his child also failed to recognize his own image at first:

In the fifty-seventh week, however, I held a small-hand mirror close to the face of the child. He looked at his image and then passed his hand behind the glass. . . . Then he took the mirror himself and looked at it and felt of it on both sides. [*57, 198*]

Thus, Preyer's child initially behaved similarly to Darwin's apes, only later learning that the image was a reflection of himself. Preyer further recognized the emergence of the ego at the human level as a result of learning when he wrote:

More important for the development of the child's ego than are the observation of the shadow and of the image in the glass is the learning of speech. . . . By means of speech the *conceptual* distinction of the

"I," the self, the mine, is first made exact; the development, not the origin, of the "I"-feeling is simply favored. [57, *201 f.*]

A few years after Preyer's work (1895), J. M. Baldwin [2] came to similar conclusions concerning ego formation. His observations were casual and principally of his own children. Without subscribing to certain theoretical extensions of Baldwin's basic position (for example, the recapitulation theory), we include some of his generalizations which later investigations have substantiated.[4] Baldwin notes that

> . . . for a long time the child's sense of self includes too much. . . . It includes the infant's mother, and little brother, and nurse, in a literal sense; . . . To be separated from his mother is to lose a part of himself, as much so as to be separated from a hand or foot. [2, *338 f.*]

However, through the infant's interaction with objects and persons in the environment, his "sense of self" becomes more clearly defined:

> The *ego* and the *alter* are thus born together. Both are crude and unreflective, largely organic, an aggregate of sensations, prime among which are efforts, pushes, strains, physical pleasures and pains. . . . My sense of myself grows by imitation of you, and my sense of yourself grows in terms of my sense of myself. Both *ego* and *alter* are thus essentially social. [2, *338*]

Baldwin also touched upon the problem of the moral behavior of the young child, later systematically developed by Piaget. At first, the child's moral behavior is a copy of the adult's, followed with some confusion and without understanding, but finally learned.

> It is its aim—so may the child say to himself [of this code] . . . to have me obey it, act like it, think like it, be like it in all respects. It is not I, but I am to become it. [2, *345*]

The fact that Baldwin early related the problem of ego formation to that of moral development is especially significant as we shall see later on.

---

[4] The theoretical work of Baldwin in 1895 has been elaborated by C. H. Cooley [12] and George Mead [44] who were probably also influenced by James.

Shinn's studies [59] are among the classics in the child psychology of this period. Beginning in 1893, she carefully recorded the daily behavior of a child for three years. Her faithful records were published in 1899. More interested in empirical discovery than in the grand theorizing of her time, such as that of James and Baldwin, Shinn did not publish a theoretical formulation of her work until eight years later. She conceived of ego development as a constant process proceeding from undifferentiated awareness of bodily movements to increasing differentiation and localization of bodily experiences, which emerge as "the large and complex consciousness of the somatic self." [vol. 2, *133*] Shinn cites many examples of experiences which were important for the separation of the child's "self" from its external surroundings. For example, on the 132d day she wrote:

> She was sitting in a horse collar on the floor, and bent herself over the back of it till the back of her head touched the floor. She righted herself and tried again, with her head turned sidewise as if to see what touched her. In this position, she failed to reach the floor; she . . . tried again a full dozen times. . . . Finally . . . her mother took her up. She kept up the same experiment for some days. [59, vol. 1, *143*]

In a similar way, the "double sensations" involved in touching parts of her own body lead to delineation of what is "me" and "not-me."

> The 181st day her hand came into contact with her ear; she became at once very serious, and felt it and pulled it hard; losing it, she felt around her cheek for it, but when her mother put her hand back, she became interested in the cheek and wished to keep on feeling that. . . . To the end of the year, she would . . . feel over her head, neck, hair, and ears; the hair she discovered in the eighth month, 222d day, while feeling for her ear, and felt it over and pulled it with great curiosity. [59, vol. 1, *143*]

The child makes other "experiments," as Shinn calls them, after accidental contact with twigs and household objects. [vol. 1, *144*] Still, a clear notion of "self" develops slowly.

> It is possible that even pain is late in clear reference to the bodily self. Mrs. Beatly's boy, at 10 months old, crying over a bump, called

attention to it by pointing his finger to the wall where he had struck his head, not at the injured spot. [vol. 2, *115*]

In using sign language, in the second year, babies always indicate the mouth, I think, not the stomach region to express hunger. My niece at 18 months seems hardly to understand the word "eat" as distinguished from putting into the mouth, and even confused it with "kiss." [59, vol. 2, *140*]

However, a particularly severe pain was located and remembered.

In the middle of the fourteenth month, 408th day, she burned her tongue, seizing too hastily upon her potato . . . three days later when conditions were repeated, the potato before her again . . . I asked, "Doesn't Ruth remember where the potato burned her?" and she nodded and put her finger to her mouth to indicate the spot. As late as the 446th day, hearing someone speak of burns, she put her finger to her mouth with a rueful sound. [59, vol. 1, *151*]

We see one of the many ways adult behavior figured in the early development of this child's ego when "in the fourteenth week, I kissed her hand suddenly and it flew up as if by reflex, while her face showed surprise." [vol. 1, *139*]

As Preyer noted, the development of language greatly "favors" the process of ego formation. In the following incident reported by Shinn, the baby's development of a particular attitude toward her own body is indicated. This attitude clearly depends upon the segregation of the physical self from the environment. The infant's use of her own name is particularly interesting in view of later work on the use of personal pronouns.

The first instance I note of her finding kisses annoying is in the nineteenth month, when twice she cried, "Way!" (Go away) as I was about to kiss her; but during the twenty-second month, she often showed annoyance at them, and I have noted sundry protests as, "Don't kiss Ruth,—hurts!" [59, vol. 1, *139*]

Moore [45] studied her child at the same time as Shinn with the intent of substantiating the psychological theories of Wundt. She carefully noted the child's development week by week. For example:

Twenty-fourth week:—He did not notice, nor did he appear to see, a baby, but he smiled at the woman who held her. [*47*]

> *Fiftieth week:*—He stood before a mirror and made grimaces at his own reflection. He stopped the performance upon perceiving in the mirror that he was observed. [48]
> *Fifty-first week:*—He observed another baby with interest. [50]
> *Fifty-eighth week:*— . . . He observed other children closely. [50]
> *Seventy-seventh week:*— . . . he at once recognized his own reflection as that of a "baby." [45, 62]

So this child, by a variety of experience, not all of which are recorded or included here, not only learned to identify himself, but learned in addition that others in his world, occupying a similar status, were somehow like himself.

Moore also contributed observations which show how the development of communicable language aids in the conceptual delineations of the ego.

> As early as the eighteenth week, he was able to distinguish between *mine* and *yours,* and *you* and *I.* It was not until the ninety-sixth week that he began to use them. In the ninety-seventh week he substituted *I* for *Warren* and later learned to speak of himself as *he* probably because he heard himself thus spoken of. [45, 129]

As we shall see, this general picture has been found later by those who have investigated the development of language.

In England during this same period, James Sully [62] was concerned with the development of the "self." His theorizing was based on a father's diary written two years before Preyer's, on records made by mothers, as well as on autobiographical material. His conclusions agree essentially with those of Preyer, Baldwin, and Shinn. Sully pointed out that the child functions as an organism before he has any psychological experience of "self," a fact emphasized much later by Piaget and Susan Isaacs:

> The most distant acquaintance with the first years of human life tells us that young children have much in common with the lower animals. Their characteristic passions and impulses are centred in self and the satisfaction of its wants. [62, 231]

Resistances from physical objects help the child experience "this consciousness of self in its antagonism to a not-self." [235]

The child's entrance into social life through a growing consciousness of the existence of others is marked by much fierce opposition to their wishes. [231]

The acquisition of clearer ideas about self and others has been touched on in connexion with the growth of the boy's language. The first use of "I" and the contemporaneous first use of "you" (end of third month) [of second year of life] seem to point to a new awakening of the intelligence to the mystery of self, and of its unique position in relation to other things. [444]

By the end of the fourth month [of the second year] we read that "I" was growing less shy, not merely coming on the scene in familiar and safe verbal companionship, as in expressions like "I can," but boldly pushing its way alone or in new combinations. By the sixth month (two and a half) the name Ningi may be said to have disappeared from his [child's] vocabulary. His rejection of it was formally announced at the age of two years seven and a half months. On being asked at this date whether he was Ningi he answered, "No, my name Kiffie [Cliffie]." He then added, "Ningi name of another little boy." [62, 445]

All these observations are important for our theme. We see that the child's behavior is first governed by biological needs. By encountering resistances of various sorts, this "consciousness of self, in its antagonism to a not-self" begins to form. During this period, the "corporeal reference" of self is clearly manifested. [426] But with the growth of language, the ego formation becomes at the same time more precise and complex, for the conceptualization of "self" thus afforded is accompanied by notions (attitudes) of self in relation to others, as we saw in Sully's illustrations when Cliffie renounced his baby name.

Still during this elaboration of the ego, confusion as to the limitations of "I" does occur, particularly when the child encounters new experiences. Sully reports from George Sand's account of her childhood an incident that occurred when she was four years old:

It was at Madrid that she first made acquaintance with one of Nature's most fascinating mysteries, the echo.

"I studied this phenomenon with an extreme pleasure. What struck me as most strange was to hear my own name repeated by my own voice. Then there occurred to me an odd explanation. I thought that I was double, and that there was round about me another 'I' whom I could not see, but who always saw me, since he always answered me."

She spent days in trying to get sight of her double. Her mother . . . told her it was echo, "the voice in the air!" [62, *496*]

The observations relevant to the development of the ego were sufficiently well-known and in agreement to be summarized in 1909 by Tracy and Stimpfl [63] in their text. In a section entitled "The Idea of Self," the authors speak of

The phenomena which accompany and indicate the gradual emergence into clear consciousness, of what Taine calls the "unextended centre," the "mathematical point," by relation to which all the "other" is defined and which each of us calls "I," or "me." [63, *70*]

As we have pointed out in chapter 5, ego components do indeed function as reference points or anchorages in terms of which the individual relates himself to his immediate environment and to the social milieu.

It should be mentioned in passing that some sociologists of the early 1900's were also concerned with ego genesis. In 1908, Cooley [13] studied the use of "self words" by a child to see "how far and in what sense the self-idea is a social conception." [*339*] He found the use of personal pronouns, as of all communicable language, inextricably bound with social interaction. He concluded:

"I" is a differentiation in a vague body of personal ideas which is either self-consciousness or social consciousness, as you please to look at it. [13, *342*, italics ours]

William Stern [60] referred to the process of ego formation when he wrote:

At first, however, there is no ego-consciousness, no objective consciousness, but only the very first germs, entirely undifferentiated of both. [60, *76*]

These "very first germs" Stern calls "sense emotional states." [*75*] It is not our purpose here to speculate upon the "consciousness" of an infant. However, it is significant that Stern too concluded from his own study and those of early investigators (for example, Preyer and Shinn) that differentiation between the ego and the outside world ("objective consciousness") occurs in the course of development and is not present at birth. Stern also wrote that the child's

> . . . life-circle, of which his ego is the very centre, extends at first only by slow degrees; at first he has to get a sure and firm footing before he is capable of entering into living relations with his environment and the strange aims it presents to him. Hence the desires and impulses that first develop are above all of an egoistic nature. [60, 493]

Stern's material concerning play and fantasy in early childhood is also revealing:

> When we see the child's absolute absorption as he listens to a fairy-tale and tells an imaginary tale of his own, how earnestly he carries on his games, and his despair at any interruption, then we recognize that the illusion of reality is here complete indeed, or very nearly so. . . . And yet the child begins fairly early to feel dimly that other stern idea of reality possessed by us adults. He notices that many of his conscious experiences cannot be ended or changed in accordance with his fancy, but that they force themselves upon him and make their consequences felt; in short, he begins to realize his dependence on *things outside himself and to endeavour to adapt himself to them.* [60, 283 f., italics ours]

The classic work of Piaget and his collaborators gives invaluable information on the development of the ego. In fact, Piaget [52–56] systematically links the major psychological functions of infant mentality with the initial lack of and the progressive development of the ego. On the basis of actual material collected over a period of years, Piaget concludes that "the younger the child, the less sense he has of his own ego." [55, 86] In early infancy, "the child does not distinguish between external and internal, subjective and objective." [86] [5]

The infant psychologically first floats "about in an undifferentiated absolute." [54, 128] In this undifferentiated absolute there are no psychological boundaries between one's own body and other objects, between reality and phantasy. Thus a distinct ego experi-

[5] See also [53, 197] and [54, 130].

ence is the "result of a gradual and progressive dissociation, and not a primitive intuition." [128] The dominant principle regulating the orientation of this initial "undifferentiated absolute" is the satisfaction of the momentary needs or wishes as they arise. Because child mentality and behavior are governed by the "pleasure principle," to use the term Piaget borrowed from psychoanalysis, the child reacts differently to the same objects when his needs or wishes change. The infant may react positively toward a person or object at one instant, negatively a little later. He has as yet established no consistent role and status relationships with other individuals because consistent ego links are lacking. From the point of view of adult logic, such behavior is characterized by contradictions. However, this so-called inconsistency is consistent in that it follows (or is regulated by) the variations in needs or wishes as they momentarily arise. This is the stage of pure autism, and autism "knows of no adaptation to reality, because pleasure is its only spring of action." [53, 244] As we shall see later, this undifferentiated state is important in understanding the systematic extensions of Piaget's theory to ethical and social fields.

Because of the resistances met in the external world, the child adapts to reality. But in order to adapt, he must begin to make distinctions between what is himself and what is not. In this process, logical consistency dawns and gradually develops through the stages of "egocentrism" and logical thinking. In this "egocentric" period, the child talks and acts as if he were the center of reference of the whole world. There is not much logical consistency, for this can be achieved only when some well-established premise is followed step by step. In the process of ego development, differentiation takes place. Realization of the reciprocal relations between oneself and other people evolves as one learns that there are other points of view besides one's own absolutism. In order to grasp this, the child must be able to separate himself from the external world.

Although the age locations of these stages, the situations in which the highest and lowest coefficients of "egocentrism" may be obtained, the factors influencing the duration or overlapping of "egocentric" and "logical" stages are important problems for child and developmental psychology, they are not our present concern.

As we shall see, social, material (economic), and physical conditions in different social systems and classes in which the child grows may accelerate or retard the appearance of various stages. Even the particular peculiarities, economic and personal, of a specific family might produce differential timing. The value of Piaget's work for us lies chiefly in the demonstration of the general trend of a child's developing mentality, starting from an undifferentiated absolute dominated by autism, governed chiefly by the satisfaction of momentary needs or wishes, through the gradual adaptation to reality as the child meets external resistances. *During this process the ego develops.*

In the impressive work of Henri Wallon, *Les Origines du caractère chez l'enfant* [64], which consists chiefly of lectures delivered at the Sorbonne from 1929 to 1931, we find descriptions of the affective reactions of the newborn child as well as a detailed account of the progressive development of the experience and differentiation of one's own body [*155–210*] and a consciousness of the ego. [*210–265*] This latter section of Wallon's work is particularly important for our present problem. For he brings together here the diverse factors in genetic development which contribute to the formation of the ego. Starting with the conception that the ego is not innately given as a unitary experience at birth, he shows step by step how the experience of the self is achieved as something distinct from the surrounding objects and persons as the child encounters them in the course of his development. This distinction is achieved only after a progressive and laborious process of assimilation and identification.[6]

Moral character appears only as a consequence of the child's differentiation of himself from other individuals and his aware-

[6] "La conscience de soi n'est pas essentielle et primitive, comme le postulent ceux qui en font l'instrument de la psychologie. Elle est un produit déjà très différencié de l'activité psychique. C'est seulement à partir de trois ans que l'enfant commence à se conduire et à se connaître en sujet distinct d'autrui. Et pour qu'il arrive à s'analyser, à chercher les formules à l'aide desquelles il tentera d'exprimer son individualité subjective, il lui faut subir une évolution qui le mène jusqu'à l'adolescence ou à l'âge adulte et dont les degrés et les formes varient considérablement d'une personne à l'autre." [*209*] "Petit à petit cependant, par un long travail d'identification et d'assimilation, il apprend simultanément à déchiffrer, dans ses impressions, le monde qui s'oppose à lui et à s'attribuer comme sien ce qui va le rendre capable d'opposer à autrui les exigences de sa personne." [*210*]

ness of the reciprocal relationship he has with others. [*205, 221 ff.*] Wallon notes clearly that the notions and values attached to the developing ego and personality will vary according to the particular material and social circumstances that surround the particular child in question.[7]

Susan Isaacs [31, 32], with her psychoanalytic approach, places less emphasis on the social factors in development and criticizes Piaget's systematic presentation on several counts. Without entering into controversies, we see that Isaacs' results nevertheless substantiate the general conclusions reached by other investigators reviewed, including Piaget. Her work again shows that the ego is not a primitive perception but appears in the course of contacts with the external world. She remarks that

> The first value which the physical world has for the child is as a canvas upon which to project his personal wishes and anxieties, and his first form of interest in it is one of dramatic representation. [31, *101*]
>
> To him, his wishes, desires or urges, call them what we will, together with their outcome in emotions, are the one reality. [32, *286*]

There is as yet no differentiated ego. Isaacs gives a vivid picture of early child mentality in which the ego is not yet formed:

> In the same way, things "inside" himself literally mean to the child inside *his body*. And when the child takes the parents as a controlling agent, it seems to him that they are thereafter inside his actual body. They become identified with internal body processes such as intestinal movements, stomach pains, breathing, and so on; and even with actual body substances, for example, faeces and urine. [32, *295*]

With frustrations of the child's instincts (resistances from his environment, including that of parents and other persons) starts the "appreciation of the external world." [*288*]

---

[7] "En particulier, dans la période qui suit, elle va s'intégrer plus ou moins étroitement à la notion qui développera chez l'enfant la conscience de sa personnalité morale vis-à-vis d'autrui. Elle ne peut manquer aussi d'être plus ou moins à l'image des représentations suivant lesquelles il apprend de l'adulte à définir ses rapports avec le milieu physique et social. Et elle se trouve ainsi modelée par les conditions de vie et de pensée où le placent les techniques de l'existence, les formes du language, les usages, croyances, connaissances, etc., propre à son époque. Ces variations ne semblent pas avoir d'autre limite que la diversité possible des civilisations." [*205 f.*]

Lewin [39, 40] portrays the developing ego in line with the Gestalt understanding of the problem.[8] The ego is referred to as a "system or complex of systems, a functional part region within (the) psychological totality." [40, 56] The development of the ego is traced from the "undifferentiated absolute." When the child meets the resistances of inanimate objects, and the oppositions offered by other people, such as parents or nurses, he has to distinguish between himself and external things. [175]

> Analogous to this relatively slight delimitation among the various inner psychological systems, the functional firmness of the boundary between his own person and the psychological environment is also in general less with the child than with the adult. This is expressed, for example, by the fact, that "I" or self is only gradually formed, perhaps in the second or third year. [39, 121]

And the slighter "firmness of the boundary" between self and environment has a direct bearing upon the slighter separation of real from unreal strata.

As we have seen and shall consider in more detail later, segregation of the ego from the persons and objects in the child's environment, language development, and the formation of attitudes towards himself and others are necessary for the child's grasp of reciprocal relationships. As Charlotte Bühler [7, 8] wrote:

> The child is a part of his mother before he becomes an individual for himself and is part of a definite group for a long time before he can enter and join any group actively. [7, 380]

Although some of Buhler's observations would seem to throw light on the problem of ego formation, she refers to it only in passing:

> Unfortunately, we know as yet very little about the entire genesis of the sense of ego in the child. [8, 74]

Horowitz' study [27] on "localization" of the ego is very much to the point in our review of investigations indicating that the ego is a genetic formation. The problem in this study was to find at

---

[8] See Köhler's *Gestalt Psychology* [38] and Koffka's *Principles of Gestalt Psychology* [37].

what point in the body each individual subject located the "self." Horowitz varied the procedure to suit the ages of the subjects, small children and college students. The results show that different subjects located themselves in different parts of the body, for example, head, face, brain, heart, genitals, chest. Horowitz concluded from the results that

> The localization of the self as is reported in the literature quoted, in the responses on our questionnaire, in informal discussion, in the investigation of children, is not the basic phenomenon one might hope for to ease an analysis of the structure of the self and personality. The more or less stable and constant association of the self-concept with the particular body regions, functions, or external objects or conditions serves chiefly as a reference point for the individual as a whole in the situation. [27, 386]

No adequate survey of representative observations relevant to the problem of ego formation could be written without use of the vast data accumulated over many years by Gesell and his associates. [19–22]   In their 1943 publication, Gesell and Ilg summarize these observations as "behavior norms."   However, as early as 1934, Gesell and Thompson included observations of ego formation.   For example, the babies' behavior before a mirror was noted:

> At 40 weeks . . . the responses tend to be somewhat delayed and even restrained and sober. [21, 242]
> At 56 weeks, on the contrary, social, outgoing response to the image is characteristically prompt and prominent. The infant seems to be completely deceived and he acts as though he were in full social commerce with another child. [241]
> It is doubtful whether the infant identifies himself in any way with the image. Even at the age of 5 years a pair of twin girls made misinterpretations of their mirror images. Each considered the image not a self-image, but called it by the name of the cotwin. [21, 241]

In the latter example, the peculiar situation of having a live "self-image" caused confusion in one aspect of delineating the ego from what was outside the ego. In 1938, "mirror behavior" was included among other "behavior norms."

In 1940, the description of the first five years of life is rich with observations such as these:

The 1-year-old infant is not very articulate. . . . Much of his emotional expression is highly egocentric. He makes very meager distinction between himself and others. His vocalizations are only beginning to have a social reference. [19, *31 f.*]

[At eighteen months:] His social insights are not much more brilliant than his perception of eliminative functions. *He is self-engrossed (not selfish) because he does not perceive other persons as individuals like himself.* [*33*, italics ours]

[At two years of age:] Pronouns, *mine, me, you,* and *I* are coming into use approximately in the order just given. While his sense of self is not as totalitarian as it was at eighteen months, it is by no means sufficiently defined for conceptual verbalization. He is much more prone to call himself by his given name: "Peter slide down," instead of "I slide down." [*37*]

You can bargain with Three. He knows with a clarity that was quite wanting at Two that he is a person and that you are a person, and he negotiates reciprocal trade agreements. [*44*]

He must have a sense of self and of status because he somewhat disdains such a simple, babyish commission as, "Show me, where is your nose!" [*44*]

[The four-year-old] is even beginning to sense himself as one among many. He is less circumscribed than Three. He has a definite consciousness of kind, of his own kind. Once during a psychological examination he asked, "Do you spank children who don't finish?" A revealing question, which discloses that the 4-year-old realizes his equivalence with other children who come to the Clinic under similar circumstances. [19, *48*]

These generalizations based on observations conducted under conditions similar to strict laboratory controls elaborate the general picture given by earlier investigators. With the realization that particular behavior at particular times is affected in a major way by the circumstances of development and learning, both large and small, we can review the summary of Gesell and Ilg [20] on ego development "in the culture of today."

The newborn infant has no "clear sense of self-identity."

But as he grows up he must disengage himself from this universality, and become a well-defined individual. By the time he is five or six years old he must see himself for what he is. [20, *334*]

As he grows, he must separate himself from his environment by "experience which sometimes is bitter." Step by step, he undergoes

> . . . a progressive differentiation which disengages him more fully from the culture in which he is so deeply involved. Paradoxically this very disengagement also identifies him more fully with his culture; he transforms from a mere ward to a working member. [*334 f.*]

> At *4 weeks* of age, the baby's face is generally impassive. By *8 weeks* it breaks into a spontaneous social smile at the sight of another person's face . . . this double reference is at the basis of the child's socialization and personalization. At *16 weeks* the social smile is spontaneous or self-induced. . . . By *28 weeks* he already reacts differently to a stranger's face. [*335*]

> By *40 weeks* or a year he has made significant advances in self-discovery. Whether sitting up or lying down, his arms and hands now have more freedom of movement, and he uses them to explore his own physical self. At 16 weeks they were at his mouth; at 20 weeks they engaged above his chest. Following the head to foot trend which is characteristic of development, the hands at 40 weeks (and later) come down to the thighs. Just as he used to indulge in mutual fingering, he now makes contact with his genitals when not clothed. [*336*]

> In the period from *1 to 2 years* there is an increasing amount of social reference. Although the infant-child is capable of long stretches of self-absorbed activity, he is also given to numerous social advances. . . . He extends a toy to a person; he holds out his arm for the sleeve; he says "ta-ta"; he hands the empty cereal dish to his mother; . . . By all these tokens and devices, he builds up a vast body of specific perceptual experience which ultimately enables him to draw the momentous conclusion that there are other persons in the world more or less like himself. [*336*]

> *Two years* is a transitional period when the child both clings to moorings and cuts from them. *Johnny* is his name, and in his inarticulate psychology, the spoken word Johnny which he hears is nothing more or less than he himself! His name is Johnny as a person. He will soon use the pronouns *you, me,* and *I,—a further indication of a fundamental change in the psychology of his self.* [*337*, italics ours]

> "Even by the age of *3 years,* the child has attained a well-balanced sense of self. . . . He knows his own sex with assurance. His inter-

est in human anatomy remains strong; he talks freely and naturally about differences which he has observed. [20, *338 f.*]

At four years, Gesell notes: "On occasion, with bravado, he would like to be a man of the world; but he really is still closely bound to his mother. He cites her as authority in cases of dispute. My mommie says so!" [*339*] Here, and in the following quotation from Gesell, we see how the child reifies the dictums of grownups:

> Between *5 and 6 years* the child . . . has lost some of the sophomoric traits of 4 year oldness, and has more sense of status and propriety. He has a better appreciation of the folkways of culture. He shows the conservatism of youth in deferring to them, and citing them to his parents for their consideration. He does not want to be different from humanity. [20, *340*]

Another observation, valuable for our discussion, is, that at about 72 months the child begins "setting up standards for himself," forming value judgments about his own behavior.

We have not tried in this review to discover all the details of the progressive development of the ego. The variety of experiences, objects, and persons important for different children in different situations is impressive. From the observations of both early and more recent investigators, it has become evident, however, that the ego is not given at birth but is a genetic formation. The infant at first makes no differentiation between his body and its surroundings. When resistances (especially unpleasant ones) are met from the surroundings (objects and persons), the gradual process of segregating "self" from "not self" is furthered. As the child matures and as communicable language is learned, the ego becomes more precisely defined and is extended by the child with his own conceptions (attitudes) about the body and other objects, persons, and situations. This general trend has been repeatedly observed even though the process of ego formation does show variable aspects when different children are viewed under different conditions. As we noted previously, these facts and their important implications for the socialization of the child have not been systematically brought out in general books on child psychology. However, the facts have contributed to the formulations of some developmental psychologists and are almost taken for granted. For example, in her recent book (1945), Goodenough notes that goals and values can be established and plans for the future can be made only after a certain development of the ego. [24]

> Nothing is more important for the child's future than the level and type of the goals he sets for himself. And because these goals are not clearly realized until after the crystallizing effect of verbal formulation has taken place and *the distinction between the self and the not-self has become sufficiently advanced to give form and pattern to the child's social attitudes,* the period of middle childhood takes on special importance, for it is then that the child for the first time faces his future. [24, *423,* italics ours]

Such considerations should be paramount in dealing with the problems of attitude formation in general and ego differentiation in particular.

Language development and ego formation. Several investigators (for example, Preyer, Moore, Cooley and Gesell) have stressed the fact that ego formation is accelerated and expanded as the child acquires a more effective use of language. Since language development looms so important in the genetic formation of the ego, at least a few paragraphs emphasizing its role are necessary.

A number of investigations of language development have accumulated in recent years. We can refer here to only a few of them to show what valuable information they furnish concerning the conceptualization of the self. Since, as we shall see later, the results of most child study are, to a greater or lesser degree, dependent upon the particular situations under which observation is made, it is not our problem here to consider the exact percentages of any language behavior in question found at different age levels and under different conditions. The relevance of all these results to the present discussion is the consistent trend reported.

McCarthy [43] observed children when they were in familiar situations. Her analysis revealed that pronouns "represent about 10 per cent of the total number of words used by the eighteen-month-old children, and they increase to approximately 20 per cent of the words used by the fifty-four-month-old children." [*125*] Pronouns, of course, serve as conceptualizations of the self and others. Fisher's observations [17] of children from 18 to 60 months of age in nursery school situations also show a progressive increase in the use of pronouns in relation to one's self and others with age. She found "a significant positive relationship between use of *we, our,* and *us* and chronological age." [*74*]   No child used these pronouns before the first half of the third year. In Fisher's words, this increase with age suggests "a gradually increasing awareness of membership in a larger group." [*86*]

The almost traditional interest of some sociologists in the process of ego formation is shown again by Bain's observations on his child. [1]   Noting that his study agreed with those of Preyer, Shinn, and Cooley, he wrote "that infants learn the names of others before they learn their own."   The following excerpts from his records give some idea of the development of the conceptual "I" in Bain's child. Referring to herself first as "baby," then as "See" (Sheila), the child used "I" only after some confusion.

Months and Days	
14–8.	S distinguishes "daddy's ear" from "your ear."
16–0.	When told to say "Sheila Bain" she says "Baby!"
16–12.	S says "baby" when told to say her own name and also whenever she sees another baby, doll, child, or picture of any of them.
17–18.	Possessives are quite well established: "See's Dadda, See's Mama"
	. . .
20–17.	Used "my" for "I"—"My see you."
26–18.	Tonight S said "*I* want to! *I* want to!" R [her mother] said, "Who is I?" S said "I is *me!*" [1]

Thus we find, four decades later, substantiation of Moore's observation that the child refers to himself with his own name before he uses "I" or "me," a fact by now familiar to all students of child psychology. When the "I" emerges clearly, a step forward is taken in the complex process of forming attitudes toward the self and others.

Using the careful techniques of modern child study, Goodenough [23] observed children in two situations, one free play and one alone with the experimenter, and recorded their use of pronouns. She also found gradual increases in the use of pronouns with age. However, Goodenough further observed that

> Pronouns of the first person singular occur with far greater fre-
> quency during free play with other children than in the controlled
> situation where the child presumably feels less need to assert himself.
> The same trend is shown in the use of the possessives, *my* and *mine.*
> [23, 337]

Here we see the striking influence of factors coming from specific
situations upon behavior regulated by the ego. Although we shall
consider this topic in greater detail later in this chapter, it should
be noted here that the results of functional analyses of behavior
such as those suggested by Piaget (for example, coefficients of
"egocentric" behavior) will surely vary, within limits, according
to the situation in which the child is behaving.

The Effects of Certain Social Factors on Ego Formation

In this section, we shall call attention to some representative
studies which deal specifically with the effects of age-mate groups.
This subject has been badly neglected by some sociologists who
maintain that all ego-values are handed down only by the well-
established order of the adult generation at any given period.
Without attempting to give a comprehensive summary of work in
this field, we cite these studies to illustrate the influence of age-
mate contacts on the process of ego formation. In some of the
studies on the early collective behavior and play group activities
of children, there are indications that the situation often can and
does determine such interpersonal characteristics as aggressive or
co-operative behavior, referred to by some psychologists as "personality traits." In the studies of Lois Murphy [47] and Jersild
[34], to be summarized, we find, for example, evidence that these
"personality traits" are neither absolute and unchanging properties
of the individual, nor fixed characteristics formed in early infancy.
Any theory of personality will gain much breadth, in our opinion,
if the situational determinations and fluctuations, within certain
limits, of course, are given the consideration they deserve. Contemporary child psychologists have stressed the importance of
situational factors. Thus Stoddard and Wellman [61], summarizing certain considerations involved in observing the social behavior
of children, comment that one is forced "to accept the conclusion

that the amount of behavior exhibited may be so contingent upon particularized conditions that consistency from day to day or from week to week is unusual." [257] Of course, some situations, such as games continuing from day to day, perhaps for weeks, or relative roles taken by adolescent boys or girls in clique situations, may leave their imprint on the individual members to a greater or lesser degree.

We shall also refer here briefly to the effect of values or norms of the established social order usually handed down in the form of short-cut dictums. Investigators like Wallon, Salusky, and Davis have called attention with accumulating evidence to the effect of material and technological surroundings on the developing identity of the individual. The general technological level of the milieu, the amount and kind of toys and games, the size of living space, the kind and amount of nourishment, the kinds of material opportunities, and the like, as well as particular values or norms are all important parts of the child's outside world. In the next three chapters we shall consider further the effect of such factors in determining or influencing group identifications and loyalties.

Some effects of age-mate groups. Especially since the classical work of Piaget on children's play, many studies have been concerned with the implications of the child's participation in collective activities. These activities, of course, require the observance of certain rules and the conformity to specific roles relative to other individuals. From these studies we see that there is a progressive development in the social participation of the child with other children. This progressive development is observed in the child's increased capacity to take part in play and to join as a member of an age-mate group. The development is also revealed by the increasing duration of collective activity, the increasing size of the group (that is, the number of participants), and the increasing complexity of the rules to be observed in particular group situations. All of these reciprocal relationships imply that the growing child has to learn that *he* has definite relationships to other children and persons.

It is only after a child learns his own position relative to other individuals around him that he can successfully participate in group activities. And only after such a realization can the child carry on the more or less consistent behavior demanded by lasting social relationships which involve definite status, values, loyalties, responsibilities. Important implications for ego development can be derived from investigations of age-mate groups. With the increased interest in the development of the social behavior of children, significant formulations concerned with the implications of studies of group participation are beginning to appear in general textbooks on child psychology.

For example, Goodenough [24], in her *Developmental Psychology* (1945), traces the social development of the child from the rather solitary play activities of early childhood to the stage when he is absorbed in group games with age mates with whom he identifies himself:

> The four-year-old still says, "I want someone to play *with me*." But a year or so later comes the dawn of a new social concept. Now we more often hear, "I want to go and play *with the other children*." The child no longer sees himself purely as an individual but is *beginning to identify himself with the group*. [24, *394 f.,* italics in last sentence ours]

Again, Hurlock [30], in *Child Development* (1942), gives a similar picture:

> After the child has entered school and has come in contact with other children, he loses interest in playing around the house, alone, or with one or two companions. He likewise now considers it a bore and not a treat to accompany his parents on picnics, parties, or family gatherings. At the same time, interest in individual games gives way to group games, and play without companions loses its charm. The child has entered the "gang age," an age when social consciousness develops very rapidly.
>
> The child's gang is a result of a spontaneous effort on the part of the child to create a society adequate to meet his needs. . . . Through gang influences, the child receives important training in social behavior that could not be obtained with comparable success under conditions imposed by adult society. There is an awakening of social consciousness at this time which is fundamental to all social behavior. [30, *233*]

Without taking sides as to whether or not there is a "gang age," a brief investigation of the formation of age-mate groups and the frequently reported absorption of children in such groups may lead us to a better understanding of the function of values merely imposed from above and those generated in situations of active participation. During the years 1926 and 1927, Parten [49–51] conducted extensive studies on the development of social behavior in children from two to five years of age in free play situations. Classifying children's play behavior into the categories "unoccupied behavior," "onlooker behavior," "solitary play," "parallel play," "associative group play," and "cooperative group play," she found that only 25 per cent of the behavior fell into unsocial categories (the first three); all the other observations were of social behavior (the last three types). Even more important for our present consideration is the close relationship between the type of play activity and age of the children. She found that

All the correlations between age and the unsocial play types are high and negative, and all those between age and socially organized play are high and positive. . . . Only the youngest children, those from two to three years, were found unoccupied during the sixty observations. Solitary play was most common at two and one-half years but there is a decided decline in the importance of solitary play at three and again at four years. Onlookers were most prevalent among the two-and-one-half to three-year-olds. . . . The oldest children do not engage in onlooking behavior frequently. If an activity interests them they want to participate in it. They know all the techniques of securing entrance into a group, so do not remain observers for any noticeable length of time. Parallel play groups were observed most often among the two-year-olds, and least often among the children from three to four. As children became older, they invariably conversed with one another about their activities, and became interested in their associates. Associative group play increased in popularity as the children became older, and was most frequent in the oldest group. There is a marked increase in organized supplementary play beginning with the third year. This sudden interest in cooperative play is perhaps accounted for by the *popularity of the activity of "play house" among the three-year-olds. Since the young children lack the power of expressing themselves with language, they have difficulty in playing in cooperative groups.* [49, 263 f., italics ours]

Because co-operative group play is found so predominantly among older children, and because its appearance is so closely associated with the development of leaders, it is important that we examine Parten's description of these groups more closely. Such groups are organized for the purpose of making something, dramatizing situations, playing formal games, and so on.

> There is a marked sense of *belonging* or of *not belonging to the group*. The control of the group situation is in the hands of one or two of the members who direct the activity of the others. [49, *251*, italics ours]

Different roles are taken by the various group members, and the activity is organized "so that the efforts of one child are supplemented by those of another." [*251*] Before a child can participate in such a group, a certain degree of ego development must take place so that the child can see himself in some definite relationship to the other children as required by the group situation. Parten [50] found that, although in the older age groups some children had a more or less lasting leadership role even with "gang" organization, most of the children engaged in both directing and following activity. *Leadership, then, was seen to be a function of the group and its activities as well as a function of the individual child.* She also found that as the year in nursery school went on, more leadership behavior occurred. During the last two thirds of the year, individual differences in leadership became more outstanding.

> Apparently the middle period was one in which *the children found their places, and cumulative experience in these positions enabled each child to hold his place as a leader or follower thereafter with a minimum of effort and resistance from others.* [50, *440*, italics ours]

Consistent with the foregoing results was the finding that the size of the groups in which children participated tended to increase with age. Older children had learned definite ways of gaining entrance to a group, with remarks such as "Can I play too?" or "Shall I be the little brother?", while the group members also sometimes invited a child to join them. [51, *137*]

As notions of the child's self in relation to other children develop progressively with age, a corresponding change is seen in his manipulation of and interest in toys and other play material. The favorite activities and toys of older children tended to be ones involving the interaction of several children. Also, "younger and older children differ in the manner in which they play with toys and hence in the social values the toy has for them." [147]   For example, a young child's play in the sandpile seldom involved social intercourse, however, whereas the older children more often played in the sand together constructing houses, roads, and such.

Bridges' investigations [6] also show the necessity of ego development for the understanding of the reciprocal relationships required for participation in age-mate groups. She concluded that qualitative differences between the social development of young and older preschool children were best explained in terms of their consideration of themselves in relation to the other children.

> Two-year-olds usually play or work by themselves with little reference to others except to claim their toys or otherwise interfere with them. [82]

> Older children engage more often in group play than younger ones and seldom play alone. . . . They usually wait their turn for little treats and duties in contrast to the two-year-olds who always want to be first. . . . In short, between the ages of two and five years children in nursery school progress from being socially indifferent infants, through the stages of self-assertiveness and interference with the liberties of others, to a stage in which they show consideration, sympathy and kindness for others. [6, 85]

In Lois Murphy's observations of child behavior, we have one more index of the development of the experiences of one's self in relation to others. From the developmental point of view, Murphy summarizes her findings as follows:

> Statistical analysis clothes in more definite terms the impression we recorded earlier, that among children from two to four years of age in a nursery-school situation, sympathetic behavior increases with chronological age, with mental age, and with intelligence measured in terms of I.Q. Bridges' descriptions of the behavior of children in a Toronto nursery school anticipated this, and there are no data from any other investigation which could lead us to question this conclusion. [47, 171]

It should be noted that correlations of sympathetic behavior with mental age were substantially lower than those with chronological age. As Murphy observes, the investigations of Bridges, Parten, and Beaver clearly indicated that

> The beginning of social response in groups like these frequently takes the form of merely watching, then later of playing alongside another child. Neither of these stages involves overt give and take; this begins sometimes with physical contact and sometimes with verbal contact, depending on the resources of the child. [47, 51]

In other words, in the early entrance into situations with other children, reciprocal relationships are infrequently observed. In terms of sympathetic behavior, the focal point of Murphy's investigation, she finds that the

> . . . sequence of responses, appearing from one age to another, seems to be: (1) staring (paying attention to the distress of another child); (2) asking about, commenting on, and so forth (except in the case of markedly nonverbal children); (3) active responses of comfort, help, defense, and the like. [47, 152]

Clearly, the child recognizes another child to be a person like himself before the latter type of response occurs.

In this connection, Murphy points out that a very young child will respond emotionally to attacks on his mother or other persons who are close to him, but that at this early stage such behavior is not chiefly due to identification with that other person but to "lack of discrimination between self and others, or between self and the rest of the world." [296] This is confirmation 40 years later of Baldwin's observation that the small child's ego "includes too much."

After differentiation "between self and others" is clear, sympathetic behavior occurs "in varying degree in response to different individuals and is affected by variations in threshold due to differences in identifications with different individuals." [303] For example:

> In Group P we have commented upon episodes of response within a small gang, of which Louis was the leader and Stephen, the youngest, was the most gang-conscious member. Stephen's concern for

Louis and Henry was dependable, although he seldom shared concern for any other child. George was usually more sympathetic with his twin brother than with anyone at issue with the brother. [47, *314*]

Further indication that sympathetic responses occur in terms of the child's relation to other children in the group is found, for example, in Murphy's comment that

> Friends, younger children, *favorites of the group,* are most likely to receive a relatively large number of sympathetic responses. [47, *159*, italics ours]

Sympathetic behavior was also seen to be dependent upon the relative stability and the character of reciprocal relationships within the group.

> One of the most interesting illustrations of the possibility of a quick shift of attitude and expression in reaction *to a shift in ego-status, appeared in a sad drama of hurt egos, where Janet's usual consistent friendliness and sympathy turned to aggressive retaliation, after she felt she had been intentionally injured by Heidi, one of her closest friends.* [47, *180*, italics ours]

In the subsequent protocol, it is clear that restoration of the usual group activity was achieved not merely by the two children involved, but through the intervention and comfort of other group members. This is just one example in which "sympathetic responses, which ordinarily appear in certain situations, are inhibited when the ego of the potentially responsive child is threatened." [*181*] The investigation also indicated that a child might not react positively to a situation quite amusing to others when he (or his things) were highly involved in the "joke." [*87*]

We would not be doing justice to Murphy's results if we overlooked her emphasis on the influence of material and social factors from the grown-up world on the development and frequency of sympathetic and co-operative behavior. For example, conflict was found to be greater if less play space and fewer toys were available; somewhat more sympathetic responses were found for children of lower socioeconomic status; and adult values and norms were seen as potent influences on the children's social behavior.

Murphy's report of the influence on behavior of relationships within a group leads to a further inquiry into the relationships of children to their age mates. Generally speaking, investigations of factors related to friendship or companionship among young children have been relatively unprofitable, since they have usually attempted only to correlate characteristics, abilities, and similar traits of young friends and have overlooked group factors. Little relationship between the intelligence, physical development, and similar traits of childhood friends has been found. However, Furfey's study [18] indicates that proximity, that is, being in the same neighborhood or the same classroom, is an important factor in the friendship of young children. Similarly, Hagman [26] found that preschool children who associated outside of as well as in school tended to be close companions. As a criterion of friendship among preschool children, Challman [9] used the number of times a child was in a group containing another given child. With this criterion, higher relationships than usual were found between the chronological ages and ratings of sociality of friends.

Studies of the "popularity" of young children in the eyes of their age mates are somewhat more revealing as indications of the relationship of one child to others. Some of the significant findings of such studies are: one's ideas of one's self seem to be more closely related to the opinions of age mates than to those of adults (teachers in this case) [41]; less "popular" children tend to be less sure of their relationships to others in the group [36]; and relative status (popularity), once established, tends to be more or less lasting while the group is together. [5]

Returning now to studies of the social behavior of young children in general, we find several which illustrate the progressive development of children's social relationships with age mates. Berne [4] found significant differences between older children (three- and four-year-olds) and younger children (two-year-olds) on a "social behavior rating scale" for such items as "interested in the group," "socially conformant," "sociable," "irresponsible for self," "irresponsible for others." In the latter items the older children were rated more responsible than the younger. These differences were also observed in experimental situations. For example, Berne measured co-operation by placing two children in a room with one group of toys. Co-operation was scored in terms of the amount of time spent playing with the other child. Co-operative behavior, as so measured, tended to increase with age. Evidence that children's social relationships become increasingly complex with age is found also in studies of social contacts, such as those of Beaver [3] who observed that the number of social contacts in play situations tends to increase with age. Green [25] found that the time spent in group play and the size of the group involved tended to increase with age.

To stress the fact that children's participation in group games increases progressively with age in terms of the duration of the play activity and the size of the group may seem to be stressing a truism of common sense. However, in view of the emphasis sometimes placed on "sociability," extraversion, and intraversion, as inherent personality traits, the implications of the progressive development of participation in group activities are important. These participations may serve as an index of developing sociability to which situational factors contribute so significantly. And such facts as these must be emphasized if we are to get an accurate picture of the way a person acquires his sense of social identity. For example, reversals in the characteristics of social behavior have been experimentally demonstrated. Jack [33] investigated "ascendant" behavior in preschool children, ascendant behavior being defined in terms of the pursuit of a certain activity even against the interference and directing behavior of others and attempts to control the behavior of others. Finding that "self-confidence" or lack of it seemed to be the most outstanding difference between the most ascendant and nonascendant children, Jack trained the five most nonascendant children by giving them information about and chances to use the play materials. When again placed in the experimental situation, these subjects showed large and significant gains in the amount of ascendant behavior. A similar study was made by Page [48] using Jack's methods. Page summarizes her principal findings as follows:

> The data which have been presented offer proof of the modifiability of ascendant behavior in nonascendant and moderately ascendant three- and four-year-old children. This was accomplished by training

designed to increase feelings of self-confidence. Tentative, but strongly suggestive, evidence is given that the effects of these training procedures are transferred to ordinary preschool situations. [48, 50]

The investigations reviewed indicate further that the development of social behavior seems also to be dependent upon the amount and kind of contact with age mates. The results of Jersild and Fite [35] show that "children who have had previous nursery school experience enter into a decidedly larger average number of social contacts than do children who have not previously attended nursery school." [100] This was found even when contacts made by children in the "old" group with their special companions were discounted. However, during the year, the "new" children increased their social contacts from only 54 per cent as many as those of the "old" to 80 per cent as many contacts as made by the "old" group. "The opportunities for social participation afforded by the nursery school do not, according to the present findings, have the effect of submerging the child's own individuality." [108] Pointing to the necessity of appraising such data "in terms of its context" or situation, the authors describe the behavior of several children. These examples indicate that an increase or decrease in social contact is closely related to ego experiences coming from the stimulation of the group.

One of the children in question made a very low score on social contacts in the fall. About half of these contacts were aggressive: the child "went after" other children, and conflicts ensued. His spring records showed a threefold increase in social contacts, evidences of greater security and enjoyment of the company of other children and of the nursery school situation, and a decided drop in the frequency of his conflicts. Another child likewise made a low score in social contacts in the fall, and was involved in scarcely any conflicts at all. She was withdrawn and yielding. In the spring, she showed a sixfold increase in social contacts, greater security and enjoyment of the company of other children, and, with this, an increase in frequency of conflicts. Her conflicts took the form of protecting her own interests and play activities, and of warding off the attentions of a child who previously had sought to dominate her. The child's improved sociability, in this case, was accompanied by, and to some extent facilitated by, her readiness to rise to her own defense in carrying out her interests and in joining in the play of several children. In the third case, a boy who entered into a large number of social contacts in the fall exhibited a decrease in social contacts in the spring, and with this decrease there was an increase in relative frequency of fighting. This boy . . . had lost his hold on a child whom he had dominated in the fall; his records reveal that this loss was followed by signs of insecurity and loss of self-confidence. . . . [35, *103*]

A study carried out in the Soviet Union by Salusky [58] reveals the same general trend of social development through increased group contacts and participations. This study typifies the application of dialectical method and is particularly important because of the clue it gives for the study of any grouping (or collective) on the human level as contrasted to the study of interactions on inorganic or organic levels. Defining the collective as "a group of persons between whom is observed an interaction, a group which reacts as a whole to a given situation" [*368*], Salusky comments that interactions "of a social order have their own specific qualities, distinguishing them both from the interaction of unorganic particles and from the interaction of organic systems and organic elements." [*375*]

> In human associations we observe the interaction of the highest type. The best way of observing their genesis is in observation of children's collectives. [58, *368*]

Collectives may be spontaneous as in associations for play when the games originate with the children, or they may be organized, as in the case of daily meetings of homeless children. In either case, they may be of longer or shorter duration. Salusky believes that all types of such associations must be studied with a single systematic plan.

For our present discussion and that to follow, Salusky's classification of stimuli is particularly important. Behavior in the collectives is determined by exogenous as well as endogenous stimuli, the former coming from the environment, the latter from the children and within the group itself. Mentioning first some important endogenous stimuli, Salusky reports results of studies made in three districts of Ukrania. He finds a "basic tendency" that *"associations of older children are of longer life than associations of younger children.* It is only a tendency, not a general law." [*371*] The duration of collectives depends

> . . . largely upon the character of the game. The latter is determined by the child's stock of experience and by the degree of formation of his anatomic and physiological development. [58, *370*]

These factors are dependent to a large extent upon his age, but are also influenced by the milieu. Salusky noted a tendency for the number of children associated in collectives to increase with age. [*371*] However, as American studies have also shown, association in larger groups does occur, for a time at least, in the younger years.

Finally, Salusky shows the influence of the milieu upon children's collectives. Two kindergartens in Kiev were observed. One group of children came chiefly from homes of qualified workers who lived a modern mode of life in an industrial area, were socially active, read newspapers and books. The second group came chiefly from parents who were "unskilled workers, small tradesmen, and in general, the proletariat" where the old mode of life prevailed. Salusky shows the difference in the kind of games played by children from these two environments. Whereas nearly half of the children in the second group participated in games representing the old mode of life, only about six per cent of the children in the first group participated in such games. A good share of the children coming from modern homes played games dramatizing the new way of life and modern technological developments, whereas children who lived the old way of life did not participate at all in such games.

This study illustrates, in Salusky's words, that

> The behavior of the collective is determined by the children's environment and by the source of their experience. The stimuli of a situation act as the exciters. [58, *376*]

This point will help us in understanding the character and direction of the activities of spontaneously formed boys' gangs to be discussed in chapter 10.

Ego constituents derived from established society. As a result of participation in age-mate groups, children incorporate into themselves certain values which form their appropriate attitudes. We have previously pointed out the special importance of those attitudes produced by the inculcation of values by grown-ups, usually in the form of short-cut dictums. For these eventually form attitudes that define in a more or less lasting way the status and position of the individual in his community, in his class, in a "race" or nationality group, or, in short, in society at large. Such values pertaining to interfamily and class relationships, handed down by parents and other grown-ups in the immediate surroundings of the child, result in attitudes which are certainly not discrete unrelated items in the psychological make-up of the individual, but which become important constituents of the ego.

Further experimental evidence can be mentioned here to substantiate this point. For example, the studies of Ruth Horowitz [28, 29] and M. K. and K. B. Clark [10, 11] show that racial identifications and values, developing into lasting attitudes, are handed down by adults; and, further, that, if the child is to grasp the realistic grim meaning of these values to be incorporated as lasting attitudes, an appropriate degree of ego development is required. Such development must *precede* the child's grasp of the realistic (as contrasted to the earlier autistic) scheme of social relationships, whatever this scheme may be in a particular society. In this connection, we add, with larger society in view, that the grown-ups involved in this process are usually transmitting the values or norms which prevail in society at large, or in their particular section of society.

Horowitz investigated 24 children in a public nursery school, ranging in age from two to five years. [28] Some of the children were white, some Negro. In Horowitz' words, the study

. . . is limited to children's emergent awareness of themselves, with reference to a specific social grouping. It deals with the beginnings of race-consciousness conceived as a function of ego-development. [28, *91*]

Various pictures of white and Negro children were shown, and the child was then asked to tell which child in the picture was himself. Horowitz found that, on the average, over 60 per cent of the Negro children and about 40 per cent of the white children made color divisions in their choices. Commenting on this difference, she says that, for the Negro children,

> It is as if the contrast there presented is a lesson well learned and perceived immediately in terms of its pertinent elements. [28]

She traces this "lesson well learned" to the "constriction of the adult environment" in the homes of the Negro children.

In this same study, the girls were asked to identify both themselves and their brothers or playmates. Finding that the girls adhered to color divisions considerably less in the latter case, the investigator suggests:

> One is evidently clearer about one's own role and distinguishing characteristics than about those of another person. [28, 98]

Her conclusion is that

> These data seem to point to the concept of group consciousness and group identification as an intrinsic aspect of ego-development and basic to the understanding of the dynamics of attitude function in the adult personality. Before the ego has been completely formed, in the very process of becoming, we find it subtly appropriating a visible symbol that has been socially institutionalized to aid it in its work of marking itself off from all the not-self of which until such demarcation has been established it partakes. This may mean, however, that the self is defined in terms that make successive demarcations necessary, since in the perception of a difference an assertion of identification is involved. The individual's attitude toward his group evidently is an integral part of himself, in terms of which he is fashioned, under some circumstances of life. [28, 99]

Horowitz [29] has also attempted by the picture technique to study other identifications of preschool children, for example, age, size, sex, familial position or status, economic status. The most correct identifications were found in terms of sex and familial position. Other referents produced some confusion, for interesting reasons. For example, in using the pictures of children of different sizes, Horowitz found that the choice depended greatly on whom the child related to himself. If he related himself to "little brother," he, of course, chose the larger of the children as himself, while, if to a "big boy," he chose the smaller. The other pictures proved to be somewhat ambiguous for the children in one way or another.

Before leaving these studies, we should report an observation which illustrates the relative value self-identifications may have for a young child. A little girl who had beautiful curly hair made color distinctions in her choices rather consistently until she saw a picture in which the Negro child had curly hair. Although she had given clear evidence of recognizing the skin differences previously, this child, whose hair had undoubtedly often been admired, would not admit any skin difference in this case and clung to her choice of the curly haired child.

Continuing along the lines of Horowitz' provocative study, K. B. and M. K. Clark [10] studied 150 Negro children in segregated nursery schools. Fifty children were in each of the three-, four-, and five-year age groups. The technique used was essentially the same as Horowitz'. Some of the pictures included animals. These investigators also found that boys adhered to color divisions more consistently in choosing their own picture than did girls who were asked to choose their brothers or playmates. The resulting choices for boys showed an increase in the percentage of choices of Negro children from 31.5 per cent at age three to 63 per cent at age five. In the three-year-old group, 17.6 per cent of the choices were of animals. Such choices did not occur after three years of age. Some five-year-olds refused to make choices, remarking, "I'm not in that picture," or "This is a white boy; this is a colored boy; this is a lion," and so on.

Later, these same investigators conducted an ingenious study [11] using as subjects children of the same age groups, 33 of whom were of light coloring, 66 of medium coloring, and 54 of dark coloring. As they stated:

> An investigation of the factors inherent in the genesis of racial identification would obviously lead to an understanding of the dynamics of self-consciousness and its social determinants. [11, 159]

The picture technique was employed again. The results showed that the light children chose a Negro child in the pictures in 36.5

per cent of their total choices, the medium children in 52.6 per cent, and the dark children in 56.4 per cent. The percentage of choices of Negro children increased for the color groups with age. In the case of the light group, the increase was only 34.6 per cent at three years to 38.8 per cent at five years. The dark group, on the other hand, increased from 52.3 per cent at three years to 70.1 per cent at five. These results are comparable to those obtained by Marks in his study of the judgments of adult Negroes of varying complexions. (pp. 136 f.) On the basis of these results, the Clarks concluded:

> It may be stated that consciousness of self as different from others on the basis of observed skin color precedes any consciousness of self in terms of *socially defined* group differences in these Negro children. [11, *161*]
>
> At this stage it appears that concepts of self gleaned from the concrete physical characteristics of perceived self become modified by social factors, taking on a new definition in the light of these social factors. [11, *168*]

We have already pointed out that prejudices are not so much the outcome of direct personal contacts with the groups toward which the prejudice is directed, but generally are, rather, the result of contacts with the attitudes others have toward these groups. The fact has been recently confirmed by Jersild [34] who emphasizes the influence of in-group *identifications* on the formation of these attitudes which become so important in defining personal identity. Jersild believes that everyday experiences are not so important in the acceptance of certain attitudes toward various groups as "the influences that come at second hand, the prejudices passed on to the child by his elders, the attitudes that he comes to adopt through precept and example in the culture that surrounds him." [424]

> Frequently, prejudice thus has its inception in the home, even though neither of the two parents openly displays any antipathy for another group. The child may acquire an attitude of distrust simply by being exposed to family and cultural traditions which set the child and his people off from others. The very fact that a child is made aware of the national origin of his parents means that *he is being influenced to identify himself with one group rather than another.* [34, *425*, italics ours]

Extensive studies by Davis [15, 16] furnish ample evidence that children's attitudes are derived from the material conditions and social environments in which they develop. These attitudes include their relative standing and distance with regard to other children of different classes, their lasting likes and dislikes, and their views on major issues that confront them; all of which contribute to the formation of their egos. Davis' generalizations, based on the rich material at his command, neatly summarize the influence of established society upon the developing ego:

> The number of class controls and dogmas which a child must learn and struggle continually to maintain, in order to meet his family's status demands as a class unit, is great. Class training of the child ranges all the way from the control of the manner and ritual by which he eats his food to the control of his choice of playmates and of his educational and occupational goals. The times and places for his recreation, the chores required of him by his family, the rooms and articles in the house which he may use, the wearing of certain clothes at certain times, the amount of studying required of him, the economic controls to which he is subjected by his parents, indeed his very conceptions of right and wrong, all vary according to the social class of the child in question. Our knowledge of social–class training and of the biological and psychological differentials in child development as between class environments is now sufficient to enable us to say that no studies can henceforth generalize about "*the* child." We shall always have to ask, "A child of what class, in what environment?" [15, *609 f.*]

In this chapter we have reviewed some of the evidence which so firmly establishes the fact that the ego is formed in the course of genetic development. In the next chapters, dealing with adolescence, we shall see how the ego can and does become re-formed during the individual's crucial transition from child to adult. And in a later chapter we review some of the evidence which establishes the further fact that the ego can be de-formed, can and does break down and disintegrate under the stress of situational and pathological conditions (ch. 12). This formation, re-formation, and possible de-formation of the ego completely belie any notion that the ego is an innate entity.

References

1. BAIN, R., The self-and-other words of a child, *Am. J. Sociol.*, 1936, **41**, 767–75.
2. BALDWIN, J. M., *Mental Development in the Child and the Race*, New York: Macmillan, copyright 1895.
3. BEAVER, A. P., The initiation of social contacts by preschool children: A study of technique in recording social behavior, *Child. Develop. Monogr.*, Columbia Univ.: Teachers College, 1932, **7**.
4. BERNE, E. V. C., An experimental investigation of social behavior patterns in young children, Univ. Iowa Stud.: Stud. in Child Welfare, 1930, **4**, no. 3.
5. BONNEY, M. E., A study of social status on the second grade level, *J. Genet. Psychol.*, 1942, **60**, 271–305.
6. BRIDGES, K. M. B., *The Social and Emotional Development of the Pre-School Child*, London: Kegan Paul, copyright 1931.
7. BÜHLER, C., The social behavior of the child, in *The Handbook of Child Psychology* (C. Murchison, ed.), Worcester: Clark Univ., copyright 1933, ch. 9.
8. —— *From Birth to Maturity*, London: Kegan Paul, Trench, Trubner, copyright 1935.
9. CHALLMAN, R. C., Factors influencing friendships among preschool children, *Child Develop.*, 1932, **3**, 146–58.
10. CLARK, K. B., and M. K. CLARK, The development of consciousness of self and the emergence of racial identification in Negro preschool children, *J. Soc. Psychol.*, 1939, **10**, 591–9.
11. —— —— Skin color as a factor in racial identification of Negro preschool children, *J. Soc. Psychol.*, 1940, **11**, 159–69.
12. COOLEY, C. H., *Human Nature and the Social Order*, New York: Scribner's, 1902.
13. —— A study of the early use of self-words by a child, *Psychol. Rev.*, 1908, **15**, 339–57.
14. DARWIN, C., Biographical sketch of an infant, *Mind*, 1877, **2**, 285–94.
15. DAVIS, A., Child training and social class, in *Child Behavior and Development* (R. G. Barker, J. S. Kounin, H. F. Wright, eds.), New York: McGraw-Hill, copyright 1943, ch. 34.
16. —— and J. DOLLARD, *Children of Bondage*, Washington: Am. Council on Education, 1940.
17. FISHER, M. S., *Language Patterns of Preschool Children*, New York: Columbia Univ., Teachers College, Bur. Publications, 1934.
18. FURFEY, P. H., Some factors influencing the selection of boys' chums, *J. Appl. Psychol.*, 1927, **11**, 47–51.
19. GESELL, A., *et al.*, *The First Five Years of Life*, New York: Harper, copyright 1940.
20. —— and F. L. ILG, *Infant and Child in the Culture of Today*, New York: Harper, copyright 1943.
21. —— and H. THOMPSON, *Infant Behavior*, New York: McGraw-Hill, copyright 1934.
22. —— —— *The Psychology of Early Growth*, New York: Macmillan, 1938.
23. GOODENOUGH, F. L., The use of pronouns by young children: A note on the development of self-awareness, *J. Genet. Psychol.*, 1938, **52**, 333–46.

24. Goodenough, F. L., *Developmental Psychology: An Introduction to the Study of Human Behavior,* New York: Appleton-Century, copyright 1945.

25. Green, E. H., Group play and quarreling among preschool children, *Child Develop.,* 1933, **4,** 302–07.

26. Hagman, E. P., The companionships of preschool children, Univ. Iowa Stud.: Stud. in Child Welfare, 1933, **7,** no. 4.

27. Horowitz, E. L., Spatial localization of the self, *J. Soc. Psychol.,* 1935, **6,** 379–87.

28. Horowitz, R. E., Racial aspects of self-identification in nursery school children, *J. Psychol.,* 1939, **7,** 91–9.

29. ——— A pictorial method for study of self-identification in preschool children, *J. Genet. Psychol.,* 1943, **62,** 135–48.

30. Hurlock, E. B., *Child Development,* New York: McGraw-Hill, copyright 1942.

31. Isaacs, S., *Intellectual Growth in Young Children,* London: Routledge, copyright 1930.

32. ——— *Social Development in Young Children,* London: Routledge, copyright 1933.

33. Jack, L. M., An experimental study of ascendant behavior in preschool children, Univ. Iowa Stud.: Stud. in Child Welfare, 1934, **9,** no. 3.

34. Jersild, A. T., *Child Psychology,* New York: Prentice-Hall, copyright 1940.

35. ——— and M. D. Fite, *The Influence of Nursery School Experience on Children's Social Adjustments,* New York: Columbia Univ., Teachers College, Bur. Publications, 1939.

36. Koch, H. L., Popularity in preschool children: Some related factors and a technique for its measurement, *Child Develop.,* 1933, **4,** 164–75.

37. Koffka, K., *Principles of Gestalt Psychology,* New York: Harcourt, Brace, 1935.

38. Köhler, W., *Gestalt Psychology,* New York: Liveright, copyright 1929.

39. Lewin, K., Environmental forces in child behavior and development, in *The Handbook of Child Psychology* (C. Murchison, ed.), Worcester: Clark Univ., 1931, 94–127.

40. ——— *Dynamic Theory of Personality,* New York: McGraw-Hill, 1935.

41. MacFarlane, J. W., M. P. Honzik, M. H. Davis, Reputation differences among young school children, *J. Educ. Psychol.,* 1937, **28,** 161–75.

42. Mateer, F., *Child Behavior,* Boston: Gorham Press, 1918.

43. McCarthy, D., Language development of the preschool child, in *Child Behavior and Development* (R. G. Barker, J. S. Kounin, H. F. Wright, eds.), New York: McGraw-Hill, 1943, ch. 7.

44. Mead, G. H., *Mind, Self and Society,* Chicago: Univ. Chicago Press, 1934.

45. Moore, K. C., The mental development of a child, *Psychol. Rev. Monogr. Suppl.,* 1896, October, 1, no. 3.

46. Murchison, C., and S. Langer, Tiedemann's observations on the development of the mental faculties of children, *J. Genet. Psychol.,* 1927, **34,** 205–30.

47. Murphy, L. B., *Social Behavior and Child Personality,* New York: Columbia Univ., copyright 1937.

48. Page, M. L., The modification of ascendant behavior in preschool children, Univ. Iowa Stud.: Stud. in Child Welfare, 1936, **12,** no. 3.

49. PARTEN, M. B., Social participation among preschool children, *J. Abnorm. & Soc. Psychol.*, 1932, **27**, 243–69.

50. —— Leadership among preschool children, *J. Abnorm. & Soc. Psychol.*, 1933, **28**, 430–40.

51. —— Social play among pre-school children, *J. Abnorm. & Soc. Psychol.*, 1933, **28**, 136–47.

52. PIAGET, J., *Language and Thought of the Child*, London: Kegan Paul, 1926.

53. —— *Judgment and Reasoning in the Child*, New York: Harcourt, Brace, 1928.

54. —— *Child's Conception of Physical Causality*, New York: Harcourt, Brace, 1930.

55. —— *Moral Judgment of the Child*, London: Kegan Paul, 1932.

56. —— Children's philosophies, in *The Handbook of Child Psychology* (C. Murchison, ed.), Worcester: Clark Univ., 1933, ch. 12.

57. PREYER, W., *The Mind of the Child, Part II: The Development of the Intellect*, New York: Appleton, copyright 1890.

58. SALUSKY, A. S., Collective behavior of children at a preschool age, *J. Soc. Psychol.*, 1930, **1**, 367–78.

59. SHINN, M. W., *Notes on the Development of a Child*, Berkeley: Univ. Press, Univ. Calif., Publications in Education, vol. **1**, 1898; vol. **2**, 1907.

60. STERN, W., *Psychology of Early Childhood*, New York: Holt, copyright 1924.

61. STODDARD, G. D., and B. L. WELLMAN, *Child Psychology*, New York: Macmillan, 1934.

62. SULLY, J., *Studies of Childhood*, New York: Appleton, copyright 1895.

63. TRACY, F., and J. STIMPFL, *The Psychology of Childhood*, Boston: Heath, copyright 1909.

64. WALLON, H., *Les Origines du caractère chez l'enfant*, Paris: Presses Universitaires de France, 1933.

CHAPTER 8

RE-FORMATION OF THE EGO IN ADOLESCENCE

In the last chapter we found that an impressive array of studies, accumulated over several decades, all point to the fact that the ego is a genetic formation, developing from the child's contact with his physical and social surroundings. We saw what diverse factors and conditions contribute to ego formation. The infant learns, for example, to delineate his own body as his; he learns that he has a name and around this name or personal pronouns he gathers many characteristics that define his psychological identity. With the acquisition of language, ego-expansion evolves at a more rapid pace, encompassing the surrounding standardized human relationships and social norms. When a child is able to grasp reciprocal relationships extending beyond momentary needs and immediate perceptual reactions, ego development is affected in an important way by his absorbed participation in age-mate groups.

Yet no matter how important these factors may be, even throughout the whole life of an individual, any account of ego development as it functions on the adult level will suffer major deficiencies if the ego problems encountered during adolescence are neglected. For there are certain facts, almost truisms, which make the period of genetic development from early to late adolescence crucial for the psychology of ego formation.

The Problem of Adolescence in a Sociological and Psychological Setting

By the time the child reaches puberty, he has become a member of a family, a social class, a nation; he is part of the constellations formed by his school, by his neighborhood friends, or by discriminations based on sex. All of these situations carry their prevailing values which determine subsequent attitudes. But the youngster still has to acquire or be ascribed a full-fledged adult male or female status with its particular adult rights, privileges, and responsibilities. After maturing sexually as a full-fledged male or female, ready to function physiologically, almost over-flowing, he thus faces norms and serious regulations in his sur-roundings which postpone, deny, or regulate his sex activities.

Whatever the effects of infantile sexuality may be up to puberty (a point orthodox psychoanalysts have been so concerned about—see chapter 14) a whole host of norms, expectations, and regula-tions relating to femininity and masculinity now have to be faced.

In some societies, the individual is initiated into economic life during the adolescent period. In other societies, he at least seri-ously starts to look forward or to prepare for some trade or pro-fession. He may have to enter into the economic work of the adult world before he is fully matured physiologically, as is still the case in countries at the feudal economic level, and as was strik-ingly seen during the period of ruthless child labor in the last few centuries. Or the adolescent may have to assume economic re-sponsibilities owing to the poverty of his family. Situations such as these will contribute to the early development and sharpening of the ego, while in other respects the youngster may lag behind. This is likely to result in an out-of-phase development which pro-duces its own problems. In various societies, adolescents may be ascribed a definite adult *status* in earlier or later adolescence. And the status is, of course, circumscribed in a major way by the eco-nomic class and the social position of his family.

In short, the years covered by adolescence are usually a period of transition from childhood to adult status with all its economic, social, and sexual aspects. From the point of view of ego develop-ment, a period during which status changes in so many important aspects of life should be of crucial significance. For shifts in objective status are reflected as ego-shifts in the psychology of the individual. Psychologically speaking, it is especially in the ego of the individual that any status problem finds its echo.

When societies are in a period of rapid transition, the resulting confusions in status create added problems for adolescents who are themselves in a stage of transition as they strive for adult status.

Today almost all the countries of the world are in such a state of transition. Even the patterns of culture of less developed peoples are no exception, for to some degree they are affected by the inescapable impact of the technology and imperialisms of advanced Western societies. In addition, the contradictory economic and social norms which antagonistic groups attempt to perpetuate contribute their share in making status problems (ego problems) more complicated, even conflicting, especially for adolescents. The adolescent's plight is still further complicated by the alternating treatment he receives from adults: at times he is treated as a grown-up, at other times as a child.

The flux and crisis situations adolescents have to go through, at times unsuccessfully, in their strivings for a secure social status, provide excellent opportunity for the study of many problems concerned with the psychology of the ego and ego-involvements. Changes brought about by sexual maturity, by significant bodily developments with their accompanying serious effects on attitudes of masculinity and femininity, shifts (or preparation for shifts) in economic roles, and actual or more seriously anticipated shifts in social status, all make the period of adolescence a crucial stage of psychological transition involving ego problems. We have deliberately referred to this further development of the ego as a period of re-formation. In view of the complexity, many-sidedness, and interrelatedness of the problems encountered at this stage, they should be considered from many angles: physiological, economic, sociological, and others. In this and the following chapter, we can consider only those features of adolescence directly related to the main conceptual scheme of this book.

Adolescence in Different Cultures and Times

In dealing with problems of social psychology, there is almost always the danger of generalizing on the basis of behavior seen in one particular culture. Many social psychologists, as well as other social scientists, have fallen into the pitfalls of their diverse community centrisms. The comparative studies of different cultures and different times made by ethnologists and sociologists help us to acquire the distance necessary to relate events with a realistic

perspective. For example, G. Stanley Hall's [8] colorful drama-
tizations of adolescence as a universal period of "storm and stress"
and characterizations of primitive societies as "adolescent" are
challenged on the basis of comparative observations. The prevailing romanticism in Europe during the last century which
made for the immense popularity among youth of books like
Werther with their pessimistic sentimentalism is almost a dead
issue today for the descendants of these very youngsters. The
Wagnerian heroics and ruthless arrogance displayed in no uncertain terms by many German adolescents who under the well-
organized tutelage of Hitler-Jugend even spied on their own parents, seems to have faded. German youth today presents a "picture of inconsistency and confusion." [18, 4]

Observations found in diverse studies of different cultures and
times lead us to the conclusion that the special problems of adolescence, the ease or difficulty, and the duration of youths' transition to a settled adult status will vary with the economic and
social circumstances and the values of particular cultures. In comparatively simple and undifferentiated societies, the transition to
adulthood may be achieved through various sorts of initiation
ceremonies. At the completion of these ceremonies, which vary
from culture to culture in duration, phase, and the ordeals en-
tailed, the young person may find himself ascribed with adult
status, privileges, and responsibilities with their unmistakable and
serious psychological consequences. [19, 28, 30] The more or less
stable and integrated nature of social organization and cultural
norms displayed in these cultures (more so formerly than now)
are important factors which reduce the perplexities and confusions
that face a youth in his transition to adulthood. In some cultures,
the transition to adulthood may be so clearly and definitely recognized that the boy or girl may be designated by new names at
these initiation ceremonies. For example, the Andamanese girl
acquires a "flower name" at the beginning of menstruation [3,
119]; the Arunta boy who goes through the laborious initiation
ceremonies gets different names at different phases of initiation.
[24, *85 f.*] In one of the Melanesian groups, in which marriage
takes place at a fairly youthful age, both parties relinquish their
former names for a new common name. [25, *347*]

Diverse and not infrequently contradictory economic and social status problems; complicated marriage requirements, considerations, and norms of highly differentiated Western societies usually prolong the transition stage with various kinds of conflict situations and suspensions. In these societies, therefore, it is not hard to find cases of restless old maids or eccentric bachelors who display fantasies and other unsettled modes of behavior more or less peculiar to adolescents.

A glance at the observations of the adolescent period from studies of primitive cultures reveals diverse types of adolescent transitions. Some transitions are rapid, some prolonged. Some are full of painful ordeals; others are comparatively easy. In these and other respects, different gradations, as determined by the economic and cultural characteristics of diverse cultures, can easily be found in the welter of ethnological literature. The social and cultural norms regulating the activities of adolescent boys or girls may considerably reduce puzzling adolescent problems and difficulties. On the basis of Mead's studies, Klineberg [11] generalizes:

> Margaret Mead . . . who has studied Samoan society from this point of view, writes that there the adolescent girl differs from the non-adolescent only in the fact of bodily changes; there is no conflict, no revolt, no mental disturbance or neurosis; only an easy transition to a new status. There are several reasons for this, as Miss Mead points out. The problem of sex, which in one form or another creates difficulties for almost every adolescent in our society, is practically nonexistent. Samoan society permits premarital intimacies, and shortly after puberty almost every young boy and girl enters into a series of "affairs." These can hardly be called "love affairs," because love in the romantic sense in which we know it rarely enters; but they are for that reason no less able to satisfy an urge which in our society is probably the most important single source of torment and disturbance. [11, *308*]

But in view of certain facts that Margaret Mead herself reports [20], adolescent girls even in Samoa seem to face some problems and conflicting situations, unless the psychological principles that operate in them are altogether different from those of other human beings. Thus:

The first attitude which a little girl learns towards boys ıs one of avoidance and antagonism. . . . After a little girl is eight or nine years of age she has learned never to approach a group of older boys. [20, *86*]

Again,

Not until she is an old married woman with several children will the Samoan girl again regard the opposite sex so quietly. [20, *86*]

Following a custom of Samoa, the young man sends "a confidant and ambassador whom he calls a *soa*" to secure intimacy with a girl. [*89 f.*]

But if he chooses a handsome and expert wooer who knows just how "to speak softly and walk gently," then as likely as not the girl will prefer the second to the principal. This difficulty is occasionally anticipated by employing two or three *soas* and setting them to spy on each other. But such a lack of trust is likely to inspire a similar attitude in the agents, and as one overcautious and disappointed lover told me ruefully, "I had five *soas,* one was true and four were false." [20, *90*]

Consequently,

The most violent antagonisms in the young people's groups are not between ex-lovers, arise not from the venom of the deserted nor the smarting pride of the jilted, but occur between the boy and the *soa* who has betrayed him, or a lover and the friend of his beloved who has in any way blocked his suit. [20, *91*]

It would be surprising if, in these intrigues in sexual affairs, even though they may be of short duration, the girl, too, does not face some complications. Also, as Klineberg [12] later indicated:

Certain problems of interpretation in connection with the Samoan material still remain. There is, for instance, the fact that the adolescent girls do not engage in sex activity immediately after puberty; usually there is an interval of two or three years. [12, *493*]

In view of some other observations reported by Mead to the effect that the wives of titled men derive "their status from their husbands" [20, *77*], that "a girl's chances of marriage are badly damaged if it gets about the village that she is lazy and inept in domestic tasks" [33], and that a premium is put on virginity for marriage [98 f.], it seems safe to say that girls who are expected to conform to these norms do have to face at least a few adolescent problems in their transition to adulthood.

In other studies of adolescence in primitive societies, Mead's material indicates that this period, while not universally a period of "storm and stress," does involve problems varying both in intensity and kind in different cultures, depending upon their socioeconomic structure and the superstructure of norms regulating behavior. Another society in which the period might be considered relatively less difficult than in others is that of the Arapesh of New Guinea [22]. Among them certain norms deem "that all human beings, male and female, are naturally unaggressive, self-denying, lightly sexed, comfortably domestic, concerned with growing food to feed growing children." [19, xix] In spite of the fact, as Mead reports it, that children of seven or eight have acquired a happy and confident attitude toward life, a warm affection toward their fellows, and respectful unaggressive treatment of them, the adolescent period involves the formation of new attitudes and entrance into new economic and social relationships. At this time, Arapesh children are for the first time "made culturally self-conscious of the physiology of sex." [22, 62] The parents have been held responsible for the child's growth until then. Now the boy is held to be "the responsible custodian of his own growth." [62] This involves taboos relating to his genitals, including "disciplinary and hygienic use of stinging nettles and actual bleeding with a sharpened bamboo instrument." [62] When the adolescent boy is initiated, he gains important secrets of the tribe, is segregated from women, observes certain food taboos, and is incised.

> They are subjected to a divinatory ceremony to find out whether they have been experimenting with sex or not, something that they know is forbidden because it will stunt natural growth. [22, 75]

The punishment for the guilty boy involves the "deeply felt" humiliation of publicly violating an important taboo. The boy must also stop the oral play in which he has engaged since childhood. On the other hand, certain aspects of these ceremonies are wholly pleasant. The boys are well-fed and usually emerge "almost plump." They now assume many of their fathers' economic and social responsibilities.

When an Arapesh girl is seven or eight, she is engaged to a boy about six years her senior, and lives in his family's home. Here she lives until puberty as she would with her own family. As she "approaches puberty, her parents-in-law increase supervision of her" to prevent premarital sex activities. An elaborate ceremony occurs at the girl's first menstruation, much of the ritual being designed "to cut out the girl's connexion with her past." [93] She fasts for five or six days, takes part in public ceremonies. However, after the ceremonies, "the betrothed girl's life goes on as before." She now comes to think of her betrothed in the role of a future husband rather than in the big-brother role to which she has become accustomed. There is a period of waiting before the actual marriage.

Observations on the Tchambuli [22] are also pertinent for our discussion of ego problems among adolescents of diverse cultures. For among them, according to Mead, there is a variation in the intensity and kind of adolescent problems encountered by the two sexes. In Mead's words:

> The Tchambuli attempt to standardize the personality of the sexes in contrasting ways—they expect men to be responsive, interested in the arts, women to be bold, initiating, economically more responsible. [19, xx]

The situation is made more complicated by the continuation of

> . . . patriarchal forms combined with personalities more appropriate to matriarchy. . . . Such mixed and badly co-ordinated elements cause a good deal of confusion and functional maladjustment, especially in the young men. [19, xxi]

Tchambuli women raise the food, weave the mosquito bags which are valuable both for use and trade, and are in charge of property, although men are the nominal owners. Men, on the other hand, spend their time in art work and preparing for elaborate ceremonials. Until just before adolescence, the boy is cared for lavishly by women. After initiation ceremonies,

He is supposed to spend more time in the men's house, but he still takes refuge among the women whenever possible. He grows gradually into young manhood; his father and elder brothers watching jealously his attitude towards their younger wives and suspecting him if he walks about upon the women's road. [22, 251]

In order to engage in sexual activities, he must be chosen by a woman. But in order to marry, he must get a marriage price from his male relatives. If he is attractive, versed in the dance, soft-spoken, and resourceful, he may be chosen by more than one woman. On the other hand, the older men watch the boys jealously and try their best "to shame and disgrace them before the women." [259]

Although Mead gives less information about the girls, it is evident that adolescent Tchambuli girls have different and decidedly less pressing problems, since from birth they grow up more and more a part of the solid group of women, whose activities are characterized by "comradeship, efficient, happy work" [252] and comparatively little quarreling.

In contrast to the Samoans and Arapesh, the Manus adolescent faces the difficult task of entering an adult world as a strikingly different person from his childhood self. The Manus of the Admiralty Islands are characterized by Mead [21] as

... driven by a harsh competitive system, hard working and with little tolerance for pleasure or art; each man worked for himself and for his own household; the future economic security of one's children was a principal goal. But the children had no part in this adult world of money values and hard work; they were left free to play all day in a pleasant co-operative world where there was no property and no possessiveness. ... And yet, when they passed adolescence, the generous gay co-operative Manus children turned into grasping competitive Manus adults. [19, xii]

From the time the Manus children are three, they are made "ashamed of their bodies, ashamed of excretion, ashamed of their sex organs." [21, 205] When a girl or boy is engaged, she or he can no longer be seen in the presence of relatives of the betrothed. The breach of this taboo involves as much shame as that learned in connection with the body.

Puberty for girls means the beginning of adult life and responsibility, the end of play, careless companionship, happy hours of desultory ranging through the village. [21, *175*]

Because of the taboos, there are few friends available to the adolescent girl and her childhood play groups break up.

> She makes no new friends, but she sees less and less of her old friends. [*175*]
>
> At menstruation the girl's pact with her sex is sealed forever. She learns that not only must she endure first menstruation, but the strange fact, the fact that no man in all Manus knows, that she will menstruate every moon and must hide all trace or knowledge of her condition from everyone. [21, *157 f.*]

This fact "is locked away in the girl's mind as a guilty and shameful secret." [*184*] For several months, the ceremonies attending this event drag on, during which time the girl must stay indoors.

> Past puberty, betrothed, tabu, and respectable, the girl is expected to settle down peacefully to her labours, to submit silently to eternal supervision. The slightest breath of scandal means a public scene and exaggerated ignominy. . . . No girl can manage a long career of rebellion. While she sins, all of her kin, her betrothed's kin, her betrothed, her partner-in-sin, she herself, are in danger of death from the ever observant spirits. [21, *185*]

She is not yet a full-fledged member of society. Ordinarily,

> These years are not years of storm and stress, nor are they years of placid unfolding of the personality. They are years of waiting, years which are an uninteresting and not too exacting bridge between the free play of childhood and the obligations of marriage. [21, *189*]

During these boring years as a "very much inhibited spectator," "she gets the culture by heart." [*189*] Some girls rebel.

When Manus boys reach puberty, their gay play is interrupted for a few weeks to have their ears pierced and to take part in a feast. Then they return to their play. However, by this time, the girls of their age have retired, and the play group is composed only of younger children and male age mates.

> The boys form closer friendships, go about more in pairs, make more of the casual homosexuality current in childhood. There is

much roughhouse, arm linking, whispered conferences, sharing of secret caches of tobacco. [21, *193*]

Because of this absorption in his age-mate group, the boy rebels actively if his parents decide upon his initiation before most of his age mates have theirs.

A year or so later, "all Manus boys go away to work—two years, five years, sometimes seven years—for the white man." [*196*] During this time, the boy may be "lonely and homesick, over-worked, hungry, sulky, shrinking and afraid," or he may have strange and absorbing new experiences and friendships. However, in either case, his experiences in no way prepare him for adult life in his village, "of which he has a fundamental dread." [*200*]

"Now comes the time when the young man must marry." [*206*] Since he is in no way prepared, he must plunge heavily into debt for household and work equipment which no Manus boy pos-sesses. His life undergoes a radical change. He becomes utterly shamefacedly dependent on his backers. Before him lies the op-portunity of regaining self-respect in his society by "hard dealing, close-fisted methods, stinginess, saving, ruthlessness" or continued dependence and shame. [*208 f.*]

> If . . . childhood had never been, if every father had set about making his newborn son into a sober, anxious, calculating, bad tem-pered little businessman, he could hardly have succeeded more per-fectly. [21, *210*]

In another tribe studied by Mead [22], the Mundugumors, ado-lescence is so frequently a period of intensified struggle and pas-sion, that we shall mention only a few of the problems met there.

> They [the Mundugumors] assume that all children, male and female, are naturally aggressive and hostile. [19, *xx*]

As a result of a Spartan-like childhood,

> Pre-adolescent Mundugumor children have an appearance of harsh maturity and, aside from sex-experience, are virtually assimilated to the individualistic patterns of their society by the time they are twelve or thirteen. Initiation comes to girls as somewhat of a privilege granted to them in proportion as they are aggressive and demanding, to boys as a penalty they cannot escape. . . . [22, *212*]

Under such circumstances, the acquisition of adult status could hardly be expected to be a pleasant process for the Mundugumor adolescent.

> There is a premium upon virginity, and a vigorous, positively sexed group of young girls who plan their own affairs in spite of a restrictive chaperonage. There is a social standard which prescribes that the sister is used in payment for her brother's wife, and a continuous flouting of this standard by her father, her brother, and the sisterless lover who attempts to abduct her. [22, 222 f.]

As a result of these practices, the adolescent girl or boy may find himself married to a boy or girl literally years younger than he or she. Even after marriage, the struggle to satisfy basic needs and to gain satisfactory adult status continues.

In his account of the adolescent period of the Kwomas of New Guinea, Whiting writes:

> Next to the weaning period, adolescence is the most turbulent time in the life of a Kwoma individual, a period marked by the learning of many new habits and the facing of many new problems. [31, 65]

Kwoma boys enter adolescence formally with their initiation into the first age-grade group, whereas girls undergo rites at the time of their first menstruation. The period is closed formally at a ceremony in which the boy or girl is cicatrized, at about the age of sixteen or seventeen. The ceremonies for adolescent boys and girls include a period of seclusion for about two months, while the boys undergo painful trials, dancing, and other tests. On this occasion, sexual license is permitted to all except the youngest initiates (pubescent boys). Since the age-grade ceremony for the boys occurs only once every five years, the formal period of adolescence for boys may last from one to three years and may correspond only roughly to his pubescent period. Because these rites give a boy "privileges and immunities which Kwoma culture grants to persons in this category" [67], the disparity between physiological development and status in the group resulting from the infrequency of the ceremonies would presumably be trying for the boy who develops between ceremonies or shortly after a ceremony. The initiation does, in fact, give the adolescent "a defined status superior to those of his *brothers* who have not yet undergone them. Whereas during childhood a command–obey relationship had to be fought out, and was usually established on the basis of size and age, now the relationship is culturally determined." [92]

Economically, the boy or girl now becomes an asset, engaging in tasks prescribed for members of his sex. The adequate performance of these new tasks has a direct bearing on the status of the adolescent, for

> One of the criteria by which a girl chooses a man for a lover or a husband is his ability as a worker. Other things equal, the more industrious a boy is, the more he is sought after by the girls. Lazy lads are shunned. . . . Industriousness on the part of the girl is an even more important criterion of attractiveness than for a boy. [72]

However, full participation in the economic and social life is not yet possible. Restrictions are put on such acts as the performance of certain tasks, on approaches to members of the opposite sex, exposure of certain parts of the body. Philandering before marriage does occur, but it is frequently accompanied by anxiety since the boy faces danger from the girl's relatives, and the girl is under pressure from her *brothers* who fear that if her reputation is poor "her value as a potential wife" will be decreased.

The Kwoma adolescent suffers certain contradictions in status since, at this time, when he thinks of himself and fulfills the activities of a near-adult, he must continue "to behave towards his parents and his paternal uncles and aunts as he did in childhood." Sometimes the adolescent may revolt against this continued authority of elders. An adolescent boy may also retaliate against what he feels as unjust treatment by breaking or threatening to break "his relationship with any adult or adolescent relative." [94]

As another cultural variation of adolescent problems, we summarize briefly a few points from the case of an American Indian. The anthropologist Paul Radin secured and published the autobiography of a Winnebago Indian [23]. This intimate life history, presented in longitudinal sequence, is especially valuable in revealing the reciprocal effects of the impact of culture and the counteracting adolescent impulses. The Winnebago adolescent is required to fast in seclusion for days so that he may be blessed by the spirits. We see in the autobiography how conflicts between cultural norms and the urge for eating take place under the stress of hunger and how the dictates of hunger prevail. Likewise, a psychological situation arising from a Winnebago sexual taboo is interesting. Among the Winnebago,

> Any contact with menstruating women, or even with objects in any way connected with them, will, it is believed, destroy the power of sacred objects or individuals temporarily sacred. [23, 387]

Hence menstruating girls are secluded in lodges. This particular Winnebago Indian gives detailed accounts of how he and other boys took advantage of this seclusion of girls to approach them and of the careful planning and hardships they had to go through to enter the lodges secretly at night.

In a memorable chapter on "The Crises of Life and Transition Rites," Radin [24], who is more concerned with the recurrent human and socioeconomic implications of his material than with exotic presentations, gives a penetrating synthesis of these transition rites.

> Two distinct sets of circumstances, one physiological, the other economic–social, thus conspired to make of puberty one outstanding focus which was to serve as the prototype for all other periods interpreted as transitional. [24, 79]

In short, these rites mark definite shifts in the social and economic status of the individual and the "passing of an individual from the position of an economic liability to that of an economic and social asset." [79] This new status generates new ego-attitudes related to work, to the opposite sex, and to other persons. Taking as his examples the Arunta of Australia, the Selknam of Tierra del Fuego, the New Caledonians, the Ashanti of West Africa, and the Thonga of South Africa, Radin shows variations in transition as determined by the socioeconomic organization and the derivative cultural norms existing in each of these cultures. The relative ease or difficulty and duration of the transition in each case is especially dependent on the particular socioeconomic circumstances of society. To cite another variation from Radin's material, among the Ashanti of West Africa (unlike many other cultures), "only the girls go through a puberty ceremony." [94] The girls are "carried at certain parts of the ritual" because at this period "they are newly born and cannot walk." [94]

Radin maintains that, in spite of all of the variations displayed as steps of transition from adolescence to adulthood, their basic function, the "basic formula," is the same in all of them, that is, rendering the child "an economic and social asset" from a state of dependence and liability. The existence of puberty rites for girls alone among the Ashanti of West Africa is no exception to the basic formula.

> In the case of women the physiological facts—the first menstruation, pregnancy, and childbirth—at first dwarfed the social–economic factors; in the case of men the social–economic factors from the very beginning dwarfed the physiological. This was natural enough at a period in man's existence where woman's position was at best undifferentiated, politically and economically. The social–economic implications of this situation thus being so much more important for the man, it is not surprising that the puberty rites for him have always remained far more complex and differentiated than those for the woman. The latter became progressively more complex as her economic functions became more important, after the introduction of agriculture, for instance. Occasionally, as in some West African tribes, puberty rites exist for her only. [24, 83]

Psychologically, all of these steps, trials—ceremonies and preachings—which achieve the transition of the adolescent to the adult status mean formation of attitudes related to his new relative role in society, his conformity in respecting the property and sex rights of elders and interest groups, his settling down in the place assigned him by the established authority of his society.

But we do not even have to go to Western Africa or the distant Pacific islands to achieve perspective. The social psychologist can also acquire it if he has won a historical sense with respect to his culture. Here is a concrete illustration of this lack of perspective. G. Stanley Hall in 1904 devoted a chapter of 82 pages to the problems of religious conversions connected with adolescence. [8, vol. 2, ch. 14] With respect to religious conversions, Hall states, for instance:

In its most fundamental sense, conversion is a natural, normal, universal, and necessary process at the stage when life pivots over from an autocentric to an heterocentric basis. [8, vol. 2, *301*]

Four decades later, in the same country, Harold Jones [10], one of the outstanding authorities in the field of adolescence, has to correct in more modest terms what Hall had held to be a universal fact.

As a symptom of adolescence, religious "conversion" is probably less common now than in the generation of which G. Stanley Hall wrote. Sometimes, indeed we note the opposite of conversion, in an adolescent revolt which leads to an active repudiation of religious concepts and practices. [10, *108*]

This trend is substantiated by others. For instance, a "Boy Survey" by Middletown's Optimist Club of 3,771 boys in the county indicated that only 39 per cent of boys from 8 to 16 years of age were church members. [14, *304*] A more recent substantiation comes in a survey made by Weaver [29], himself a professor of religion. Weaver asked high school principals, judges, chairmen of church and school boards, and active laymen "in many urban centers" to guess "what percentage of boys and girls in your community 14–18 years of age have an appreciable relationship with the church, church school, or church young people's societies? By 'appreciable' I mean something less than regular attendance but something more than 'just Easter and Christmas.'" The guesses ranged "from 15 per cent to 30 per cent of the youth population." [*159*] On the basis of this and other surveys he reviewed, Weaver concludes:

Youth are less interested and less active in organized religion than in any other major institution of our culture. [29, *156*]

Until recently, it was almost customary, especially in elite circles, to think of young Russian intellectuals as highly introspective and pessimistic, something like the Dostoievsky character, Roskolnikov. But in reality, the behavior of the young Comsomols as observed, for example, by Frankwood Williams [32] even in the early 1930's, and the majority of artistic expressions of Soviet novels and films, such as *The Road to Life,* the *New Gulliver, Zoya,* and Simonov's

Days and Nights, reflect an abounding optimism and good-natured striving. In fact, the Russian generations brought up under the Soviet system reflect characteristics which are almost the exact opposite of morbid introspection, self-pity, or self-justification.

In a highly developed, highly differentiated, and changing social system in which cultural norms of past centuries exist side by side with new norms brought about chiefly by technological developments, adolescents face conflicting values which make their transition to settled adult life more difficult. In their penetrating analysis of *Middletown in Transition,* the Lynds write:

> Today, in the presence of such rigorous tenacity to the "old, tried ways" by part of the population, the range of sanctioned choices confronting Middletown youth is wider, the definition of the one "right way" less clear. That this is the normal situation in the process we call "social change" does not lessen the confusion it entails. . . . If the child up to high-school age associates, by reason of the assignment of each child to a grade school on the basis of residential propinquity, with other children from somewhat similar subcultural backgrounds, this homogeneity of sorts is lost when the children pour from all quarters into Central High School. Here the whole range of cultural tolerances and intolerances grind against each other; the child of parents who think it "cute" and "attractive" for a daughter to enamel her nails, use rouge, have a crisp "permanent," and "learn to handle boys" sits next to the daughter of a family in which the parents are engaged in a quiet but determined campaign to circumvent the influence of the movies and to keep their daughter "simple," "unaffected," and "healthy-minded." This widening of contacts with unevenly sanctioned choices, supported not by outlaw individuals but by groups, means under these circumstances for both parents and children uncertainty and tension. [14, *175*]

To get out of these conflicting situations, in some cases, young people in high school may try to find security in early marriages.

> It is, as noted above, a less uncommon occurrence in these 1930's than it was ten years ago for high school students to marry and thus to seek to hew a path of freedom out of the cultural conflicts, uncertainties, and stubborn parental restraints in which they find themselves. [14, *175 f.*]

In other cases, the difficult economic situations delay marriages. As the Lynds note, during the depression in Middletown, young people just had to "stick around," while "the repetitiveness of this familiar round of life among neighbors may become acutely distasteful if either of man's great peacetime anodynes for routine—marriage and work—are denied him." [486] This was the predicament of "Middletown youngsters." Marriage often had to be delayed because there were no jobs.

As these observations show, a major economic event such as a depression which further sharpens economic differences between the classes may be reflected in a sharpening of the differences among adolescent groups. These conflicts no doubt have psychological consequences. Turning again to Middletown, for example, the Lynds note that the standards for dress in the high school groups were set by the more well-to-do North Side girls. The depression meant that the poorer girls from the South Side were considerably less up to standard than before. These girls were very distressed, "some of them to the point of withdrawing from high-school." [445] The status of these South Side students was further handicapped "by the presence among their number of an increasing number of marginal persons who are going on into high school because they cannot get jobs." [452] One result of this stress on the South Side adolescent was that "some boys and girls now no longer dare brave the front door of the high school 'with the steps crowded with richer students looking you over,' but go around to the side entrance." [452]

The depression seems to have brought about particularly severe social problems for girls. For even if a girl did not have to assume the economic responsibility for the family or engage in serious forms of deviant behavior, she may have had to quit school at an early age "because of runs in her stockings, torn shoes, and worn-out dresses." [13, 95] Or, she might become "afraid to bring any friends of hers to her home" and have to evade their invitations to go out after school hours because she has no money. "Her girl friends don't understand, and she is afraid she is losing their friendship." [96]

A special study of "Youth in the Depression" made by Kingsley Davis [4], gives a realistic picture of the way a major economic event can further aggravate the feelings of insecurity in a great number of young people.

Boys and girls all over the country find nothing but a blank wall in front of them. With their parents suffering, their own futures clouded, the ordinary roads to success closed, they blindly seek a way out. In such conditions youth movements spring up. [4, 12]

If not caught in actual youth movements of various kinds, young boys or girls at least spontaneously develop more or less secret or confidential groups, cliques or gangs, among themselves. From these they derive a certain satisfaction of status and security in a contradictory, apparently hostile, social world.

Extraordinary changes in the behavior of adolescents are also, of course, brought about by war. We already have some significant studies indicating the impact of World War II on adolescents in the United States, a country, we should recall, that was comparatively little affected by the war. Not only did thousands of late adolescents have "maturity thrust upon them" by entrance into the armed services [6, 62], but in the United States alone the adolescent labor force from ages 14 to 18 grew from 872,314 in 1940 to 3,000,000 in 1944, with others working part-time and during vacations. [15] While many quickly became "adult," many others suffered from this aggravated contradiction in status. [1, 7, 33] Adolescent workers in war plants, for example, were sometimes only "tolerated" by adult workers, by adults in the communities, and by parents. [7, 27, 26] In addition to the greater disparity between the values of adolescents and parents created by the acceleration of cultural change brought about by the war, such conflicting situations resulted in increased parent–youth conflict, increased drifting away from home and grown-ups. [2, 39] In particular, the war intensified the problems of the younger adolescents. Although feeling "the restlessness, excitement, and anxiety that war brings," they found little opportunity to share in it all and were often held back by their parents. [38] One result of these conditions for young adolescent girls, who take the "next older group" or "those just older" as their reference group, was the great rise in sex delinquency. [6, 9] This was found even among girls "from families that are of high quality." [7, 30] Additional problems came to those adolescents whose homes were broken by the war, whose families migrated to strange communities, or whose parents worked away from home during wartime. [2, 26]

Davis [5] has given a cogent sociological characterization of the main problems relating to "adolescence and the social structure." He emphasizes the point that, as a result of the conflicting norms relating to such matters as maturity status, profession, marriage, in a society of rapid social change, the problems adolescent boys and girls face "involve strain and inconsistency," making the transition more or less an ordeal, prolonging it to a greater or lesser degree, and in some cases creating inevitable parent–youth conflict.   In a separate study, Davis takes up specifically "The Sociology of Parent-Youth Conflict" (pp. 287 f.).

Davis further indicates the specific social inconsistencies and contradictions of occupational placement, of the institutions and norms regulating sexual behavior, and of the rights and privileges of adolescents.   Calling attention to such contradictions, he writes:

> In our society, even apart from the family, the adolescent finds an absence of definitely recognized, consistent patterns of authority. *Because of the compartmentalization of the culture he is defined at times as an adult, at other times as a child*. [5, 13, italics ours]

In contrast to such casual and contradictory patterns, Davis points out how, in a different society, the Soviet Union, adolescents are an organic part of an integrated social system; how, for example, the youth in school and in the Pioneer and Comsomol organizations play a responsible role in harmony with their maturity level. On the basis of such considerations, he concludes:

> The Soviet system suggests that to make the school an integral part of the political and economic structure, and to give youth a productive role, central planning of the whole economy is necessary. [5, 15]

A study such as this forcefully brings home once more the futility of any study of the social psychology, or of any psychology for that matter, of adolescence without first placing the individual in his socioeconomic setting.   In a later chapter we include a few specific illustrations of individual adolescent behavior in group situations which are in harmony with the general trend of society at large (pp. 338 f.).

The full importance of a knowledge of the setting within which the adolescent develops can be seen if we realize that, under certain conditions, even schooling may be a curse instead of a blessing for youths in the process of becoming grown-ups. A concrete illustration of the point is reported by Majumdar [16] in his study of "A Tribe in Transition," the Ho tribe of the Ghota plateau in India. Among other interesting problems facing this colonial tribe, he reports the effects of schools introduced by the British government. Education in the local schools "does not help the Hos in the least from an economic point of view, unless the students can proceed to the High School at Chaibassa." [*197*]   Even then the student will probably not receive a remunerative job from the British government. However, children of the landowners can return to be "the leaders in the village." The usual reaction of the average Hos who go to high school is to "return to their homes and curse their education for the rest of their lives" after two or three years of moving "heaven and earth to secure a job." [*198*]

As we shall see, adolescents frequently find relief from puzzling inconsistent, confusing situations, by "rebelling" against the dictates of adults in their immediate environment and anchoring themselves in an age-mate world, or, specifically, in age-mate groups (pp. 251 *ff.*). Their behavior is then regulated in an important way by the values or norms prevalent among the age mates to whom they refer themselves. Many of these norms may run counter to those of their parents and other adults. However, this picture, if not completed, leaves an erroneous impression. Undoubtedly, the majority of adolescents in a particular culture eventually become full-fledged adults, abiding by the major norms of their culture, class, and so on, just as the "pleasant co-operative" Manus children become "grasping competitive Manus adults." An adolescent may defy his parents in relation to some more or less important norms of his class; yet later, when he has passed into adulthood and has incorporated norms appropriate to the interests of his class and the status of adults in his particular situation, he may staunchly uphold the very same norms he once so violently repudiated. For example, George Apley of John Marquand's novel [17] outraged his Boston Brahmin family by falling in love with an Irish girl. Only after the onslaught of united family pressure and a trip to Europe did he give up his intentions of marrying her. But years later, George, now in his father's shoes, fought with almost equal intensity his own son's affair with a daughter of a nouveau riche from Worcester.

These few examples of cultural variation could be multiplied by hundreds from the rather disconnected studies of ethnologists. The facts reported here should be enough to give us some perspective and save us from the error of making generalizations based on particular cultures. All in all, a survey of this material indicates that the problems facing the adolescent vary from culture to culture, rendering the transition to adulthood more or less complicated, more or less conflicting, more or less prolonged. Such studies indicate the necessity of using comparative material from different cultures and times, and the necessity of first placing adolescent ego problems in their social settings. For significant variations and factors of social change necessarily reflect themselves in the status problems of the adolescent, who are themselves in a critical and unstable stage of transition. After learning this from the ethnologist, we can return to our own work as psychologists carrying with us the implications of the lesson learned. We should start our work by reiterating a methodological consideration appropriate in this connection. With variations in the social setting, the transitional period of adolescence may be more or less prolonged, fraught with more or less intense problems. However, the basic psychological principles which operate in all of these social settings should be the same. If we abandon the search for these psychological principles, we will be falling into the tragic blunder committed by the Fascist advocates of basic race differences.

REFERENCES

1. BOLL, E. S., Britain's experience with adolescents, *Ann. Am. Acad. Pol. and Soc. Sci.,* 1944, **236**, 74–82.
2. BOSSARD, J. H. S., Family backgrounds of wartime adolescents, *Ann. Am. Acad. Pol. and Soc. Sci.,* 1944, **236**, 33–42.
3. BROWN, A. R., *Andaman Islanders,* Cambridge (England): Univ. Press, 1922.
4. DAVIS, K., *Youth in the Depression,* Chicago: Univ. Press, copyright 1935.
5. —— Adolescence and the social structure, *Ann. Am. Acad. Pol. and Soc. Sci.,* 1944, **236**, 8–16.
6. GARDNER, G. E., Sex behavior of adolescents in wartime, *Ann. Am. Acad. Pol. and Soc. Sci.,* 1944, **236**, 60–6.

7. GROVES, E. R., and G. H. GROVES, The social background of wartime adolescents, *Ann. Am. Acad. Pol. and Soc. Sci.,* 1944, **236,** 26–32.

8. HALL, G. S., *Adolescence, Its Psychology and Its Relations to Physiology, Anthropology, Sociology, Sex, Crime, Religion and Education,* New York: Appleton, copyright 1904.

9. HANKINS, D., Mental hygiene problems of the adolescent period, *Ann. Am. Acad. Pol. and Soc. Sci.,* 1944, **236,** 128–35.

10. JONES, H. E., *Development in Adolescence,* New York: Appleton-Century, copyright 1943.

11. KLINEBERG, O., *Race Differences,* New York: Harper, copyright 1935.

12. —— *Social Psychology,* New York: Holt, copyright 1940.

13. KOMAROVSKY, M., *The Unemployed Man and His Family,* New York: Dryden, 1940.

14. LYND, R. S., and H. M. LYND, *Middletown in Transition,* New York: Harcourt, Brace, copyright 1937.

15. MAGEE, E. S., Impact of the war on child labor, *Ann. Am. Acad. Pol. and Soc. Sci.,* 1944, **236,** 101–09.

16. MAJUMDAR, D. N., *A Tribe in Transition,* New York: Longmans, Green, 1937.

17. MARQUAND, J. P., *The Late George Apley,* Boston: Little, Brown, 1937.

18. McGRANAHAN, D. V., and M. JANOWITZ, Studies of German youth, *J. Abnorm. & Soc. Psychol.,* 1946, **41,** 3–14.

19. MEAD, M., *From the South Seas, Studies of Adolescence and Sex in Primitive Societies,* New York: Morrow, copyright 1939.

20. —— *Coming of Age in Samoa,* in [19].

21. —— *Growing Up in New Guinea,* in [19].

22. —— *Sex and Temperament in Three Primitive Societies,* in [19].

23. RADIN, P., *The Autobiography of a Winnebago Indian,* Univ. Calif. Publications in Am. Archaeology and Ethnology, vol. **16,** April 15, 1920, 381–473.

24. —— *Primitive Religion, Its Nature and Origin,* New York: Viking, copyright 1937.

25. RIVERS, W. H. R., *History of Melanesian Society,* Cambridge (England): Univ. Press, 1924.

26. SKINNER, M., and A. S. NUTT, Adolescents away from home, *Ann. Am. Acad. Pol. and Soc. Sci.,* 1944, **236,** 51–9.

27. SORENSON, R., Wartime recreation for adolescents, *Ann. Am. Acad. Pol. and Soc. Sci.,* 1944, **236,** 145–51.

28. VAN GENNEP, A., *Les Rites de passage,* Paris, 1909.

29. WEAVER, P., Youth and religion, *Ann. Am. Acad. Pol. and Soc. Sci.,* 1944, **236,** 152–60.

30. WEBSTER, H., *Taboo, A Sociological Study,* Stanford: Univ. Press, 1942.

31. WHITING, J. W. M., *Becoming a Kwoma,* New Haven: Yale Univ. Press, copyright 1941.

32. WILLIAMS, F., *Russia, Youth and the Present Day World,* New York: Farrar & Rinehart, 1934.

33. ZACHRY, C. B., Customary stresses and strains of adolescence, *Ann. Am. Acad. Pol. and Soc. Sci.,* 1944, **236,** 136–44.

CHAPTER 9

RE-FORMATION OF THE EGO IN ADOLESCENCE
(Continued)

We have seen that by the time of puberty the child develops to relate himself psychologically to definite groups, such as family, school, age mates, sex groups, church, and other social institutions. We have cited briefly some effects of these diverse identifications. But the child has yet to achieve the status of a full-fledged adult man or woman with all that that status implies in the way of grown-up functions, rights, privileges, and responsibilities. Psychologically, he has yet to be treated as adult by his social surroundings. He has yet to experience himself and behave as adult through the incorporation of the grown-up values of masculinity or femininity, norms of some work or profession (or anticipations thereof), and norms of social status as prescribed by the prevailing values of the economic and social institutions within his reach. Usually, the period of adolescence during which girls and boys reach their major physiological maturity is the period of transition when they face these problems. The relative ease or difficulty, the duration of the transition depends, as was briefly indicated in the last chapter, on the particular economic and social circumstances surrounding the boys or girls. The variations of socioeconomic conditions, the integrated or contradictory character of prevailing norms, the consistency or inconsistency of the treatment and expectations faced, the integration or "marginality" of their own roles as part of the general social scheme, enter in as important factors.

THE DEVELOPING EGO RENDERED UNSTABLE AND, AT TIMES, CRITICAL

Young boys and girls strive to satisfy newly developing desires, to get settled or start getting settled. In the many different ways in which they experience themselves as being involved, they make effective or futile efforts of emancipation or independence. In their strivings to do away with childish things, their "psychological weaning" [1] or drifting away from earlier dependencies is manifested in various ways. In the course of these strivings, there arise instabilities, insecurities, adult–youth conflicts, and crises proportional to the resistances and inconsistencies met in the surroundings. These resulting instabilities and insecurities are, of course, subject to variations due to individual differences.

Our present concern is the impact of these phenomena on the developing ego-attitudes. For the developing ego, which is thus rendered less stable, less secure, wavering, and conflicting in the midst of transition and inconsistent situations and norms, has to be related anew to a constellation of more mature personal and group relationships. It is painful to toss around without some stable anchorage. Even the satisfaction of basic drives, including the newly developed definite sex urges, have to be justified in terms of one's ego-values. Because of the lack of adequate situations provided by the established grown-up world which might make these status anchorings possible, the result, in many cases, is the spontaneous formation of more or less secret cliques, gangs, and similar adolescent groups. We shall designate such groups as *membership groups*. In other cases, crushes or identifications with idolized persons, or identifications with groups of which the adolescent is not directly a member (or even with whom he is not in contact) may serve a similar function psychologically. These latter identifications will be designated as reference idols or *reference groups*.[2] These membership groups, reference idols, and reference groups play an important role in determining the interests, attitudes, and ego links of the adolescent boy or girl. In the remainder of this chapter, we shall give an account of the ego development of adolescents along these lines. Our account will necessarily be sketchy.

[1] This characterization was aptly used and elaborated by L. Hollingworth. [20, *36 ff.;* 21, *882–908*]

[2] The term *reference group* was used by Hyman (pp. 137 *f.*). The exact sense in which we use it will become clear as we go along. Our use of it is not essentially different from Hyman's.

The characterization of adolescence as the period of transition to adult status, and, consequently, to mature or grown-up ego-attitudes certainly needs to be qualified. For under prevailing economic conditions a boy may be drawn to work in a shop, plant, or farm even some years before the advent of puberty; a girl may be imposed with the serious responsibilities of keeping house or taking care of children. In such situations, he or she does develop adult ego-attitudes in these respects. Still, if the age mates of a child in such situations are not undergoing similar experiences, he or she may experience more or less serious conflicts. And, while performing the tasks of an adult, he or she may in other ways be treated as a mere child. Actual observations in several Turkish villages have provided many concrete illustrations of such treatment. Before they were even seven or eight, these Turkish children showed hardly any remnants of childish egocentric speech. In some respects, they behaved and spoke as prematurely grown-up children. The coefficient of egocentricity seemed to be reduced almost to zero under the mature responsibilities they were subjected to. Nevertheless, this premature development in some respects did not save them from adolescent problems after they reached puberty. We observed cases of various kinds of parent–youth conflict, problems related to marriage and sexual activities due to adolescent physiological development. For example, in some cases, forced or mutually agreed-upon elopements, with a great many complications from the family and other sources, ensued as a consequence. These are only illustrations. Many other variations of adolescent problems due to differential inconsistent out-of-phase timings of the various developmental processes may be found.

Changing body and changing self.[3] In observations concerned with the very beginning of ego development, we saw the importance and primacy of the delineation of the baby's body as *his* from surrounding objects, the recognition of his hands, feet, face, as *his*. Up to the advent of puberty, boys and girls are certainly preoccupied with their bodies. As may be seen in examples selected at random from hundreds of cases, boys and girls, during

---

[3] This phrase, used by Zachry [49] as a chapter heading, aptly epitomizes the adolescent bodily changes and their psychological consequences. [31]

adolescence, become acutely aware of their own bodies and even parts of it (besides the sex organs), especially in a society where there is a high premium on physical attractiveness. An adolescent's whole ego concern may at times be focused on the attractiveness or, real or fancied, unattractiveness of even a part of the body. Prevailing norms concerning feminine and masculine attractiveness and the relative importance attached to these norms in the person's reference and membership groups may, of course, determine in significant ways the extent and intensity of ego-involvements focused on the body or its parts.

Studies dealing with physiological developments and their psychological correlates at the period of adolescence are being rapidly accumulated. After mentioning briefly the physiological changes, we shall concern ourselves mainly with their impact on ego development. A few more or less representative accounts of these changes may be found in the references noted.

The bodily changes occurring during adolescence are regulated to an important degree by the endocrine glands. The pituitary, thyroid, adrenal (cortex), and gonads play particularly important roles in the growth phenomena of this period. Adequate functioning of all the endocrine glands, with their proper interrelatedness with each other, with the nervous and the cardiovascular systems, is apparently a necessary condition for normal growth. Under the regulation of the endocrine glands, an increased growth in height and weight generally precedes pubescence. This growth is accompanied by changes in body proportions toward more typically masculine and feminine builds, changes in the size of most of the internal organs, appearance of the secondary sex characteristics (for example, growth of pubic hair; change of voice and growth of beard in boys; breast development in girls). At the same time there is a maturation of the reproductive organs of each sex, ordinarily indicated by the onset of menstruation for girls and the secretion of spermatozoa for boys, together with the growth and development of the genitalia. Such changes do not occur, of course, without some changes in the general functioning of the bodily processes, as indicated, for example, by measurements of basal metabolic rate.

The psychological consequences of these gross changes and the more or less clear-cut differentiation of the sexes at this time are treated later in more detail. However, we should note here for future reference two of the more important facts of physical growth for our problem of the re-formation of the ego at adolescence. First, girls, on the average, mature physiologically a year or so earlier than boys. As we shall see, the psychological consequence of this fact is that girls tend to form attitudes of adult femininity and social maturity earlier than boys of the same age. We sometimes find, for example, that girls tend to drag the boys of their age with them into more mature interests and skills, such as dancing, appropriate to their more mature level of development.

Secondly, not only does variation in time and rate of growth and the onset of pubescence vary from environment to environment, from class to class, but even within a given group, individual variations in development and rate of growth may be marked. And we shall see that marked deviation in either direction from group norms of development has psychological consequences for the adolescent boy or girl who is in such a situation.[4]

With these more striking physiological changes, one's conception of one's ego correspondingly changes. As Zachry [49] aptly puts it, "the body is symbolic of the self." [32] To start with, the very psychological correlates of these changes tend to be felt as extraordinary even independent of their ego relationship. [47] The adolescent's already accentuated awareness and focusing on *his* body becomes even more acute with the more pronounced, somewhat stylized attention of others (for example, parents and other adolescents) on his or her body, with sex desires toward and from age mates now present in a developed way. And with the development of these sex desires and changing attitudes toward one's body there comes an intense awareness of the developing opposite sex. This fact is aptly illustrated by the statements of one boy concerning his changing associations with girls. In junior high school this boy was only "interested" in girls. However, he writes:

[4] These bodily changes during adolescence are described in detail in [2, 3, 4, 7, 18, 20, 22, 25, 37, 39, 47, 49]; the earlier development of girls is discussed in [2, 4, 7, 39, 49]; variations of growth are shown in [1, 2, 4, 20, 49].

It was in high school that I began to date in the true sense of the word. It was now that girls were beginning to attract me in a different light. It was no longer their intelligence or athletic ability or tom-boyishness which attracted me, but it was the way they wore their makeup, the way they moved their hips when they walked, and the way they snuggled up close when we danced that I began to notice. It was all new, strange, scary, but terribly interesting and exciting. [48, *12*]

As a consequence of these changes, the adolescent cannot help but preoccupy himself and, especially, herself with comparisons in relation to the prevailing norms of body proportions and growth, and, more specifically, in relation to the girls or boys of his own group. Zachry mentions the case of a girl who, being slightly "larger and heavier than most of her contemporaries," became so conscious of her body that she covered herself up most of the time "in a voluminous smock." [49, *63*] Frequent letters appear in the interesting magazine *Seventeen* to this effect:

How about showing some clothes for the short, chubby teen-ager? We all want to look like the rest of the crowd—but you know how some of us look in sweaters and skirts.

Or

You put too much emphasis on the petite junior miss and leave her skyscraper cousin out in the cold!

The adolescent boy or girl may try very hard to incorporate in himself or herself and to conform to the particular norms of femininity or masculinity fashionable in the surroundings when sexual maturity has been reached. At first these efforts may be clumsy or affected. And all of these strivings tend to produce feelings of uncertainty about one's own self.

In nearly all the representative works on adolescence, there are many concrete illustrations of the changing body and the changing self, and a more or less acute focusing of the whole conception of one's self on the body in general, or even on some part of the body. This may become psychologically so exaggerated as to become a major ego concern and may have a major influence in regulating the adolescent's social behavior. Even anxieties and insecurities in other respects may be reflected in such a concern. Peter Blos [5] gives the following illustration:

At the age of thirteen or fourteen years, Betty begins to be very concerned with her looks. The *mole on her cheek,* which is somewhat noticeable, becomes *the focus of her self-consciousness.* Worry about her appearance increases and finally motivates her to avoid dances or parties until the mole will have been removed by an operation. She has read about operations which have succeeded in improving the looks of women, and has set her hopes on this surgical work. [5, *93*, italics ours]

To cite just a few other cases of the body or its parts becoming a major focus of the adolescent's ego, the following statements, communicated to the writers recently by a former student of a large Midwestern University, are relevant:

All through my grade school years, I was the tallest girl in the class, and, as a matter of fact, was rather proud of it. However, the summer before I entered Junior High School at the age of thirteen, I grew to just an inch below my present five-feet-eight. I towered above every girl and boy in our class; and it seemed to me that I was the tallest girl in the world. *None of my family's comforting words made it easier for me to walk across the room at school.* In high school, two girls taller than I entered the class. *But they weren't in our crowd,* so I continued to feel like a giraffe when I went out with the girls. I suppose the fact that several of the boys grew to six-footers helped dispel that shrinking feeling. But the crowning touch came in the spring of my junior year. The school paper published a list of characteristics of a composite "Ideal Girl." Lo and behold, my name was listed after "Ideal Height." I haven't felt too tall since. [italics ours]

Averill [1] mentions another case of a comparatively tall girl who walked stooped and with round shoulders in order to appear shorter. [*32*] Hollingworth [20] mentions several examples, including the absorption of some adolescents with pimpled or blemished skin. [*8*] One boy began to walk on tiptoes because his feet seemed so large [*12*]; another was so conscious of his changing voice that he refused, even under pressure from the teacher, to sing in school [*13*]; and still another sat "with his hand over his mouth and chin much of the time" because he thought he needed to shave and his parents disagreed. [13]

As can easily be seen in the foregoing illustrations, the problems raised in regard to one's self are relative matters; that is, problems arise in regard to one's own stage of maturity and development (height, weight, bodily proportions, and the like), in relation to one's own sex and age mates.   In several studies carried out in the Institute of Child Welfare of the University of California, which has contributed some of the most significant investigations in the field, this result is reported time and again.   For example, Nancy Bayley and R. Tuddenham [4] conclude:

> . . . that being different from their peers seemed to be a potential hazard to adequate adjustment. *The poorest adjusted among the four extreme groups were the early-maturing girls and the late-maturing boys.* As these children attended a coeducational school in which grade placement was largely by chronological age, the two groups who would stand out in the schoolroom as physically most different would be the large, early-maturing girls and the small, late-maturing boys. To be a girl and large, and to be a boy and small, are both contrary to the ideals of the culture, and therefore it seems plausible to expect that some of these children, if they do not have adequate compensations in other fields, might well find their physical difference an emotional problem. [4, *53*, italics ours]

Similarly, Zachry states:

> A boy whose physical development begins rather earlier than that of other boys in his class is apt to feel not only that his body is out-sized. *Perhaps he comes to feel himself a misfit.* [49, *51*, italics ours]

A case cited by Averill illustrates this point.   Harold became pubescent before the boys in his "gang" of which he had been the leader.

> . . . Harold's lengthening arms and legs, and his amazingly enlarging hands and feet have made him decidedly awkward and clumsy. The other boys, not yet pubescent, are beginning to be somewhat shaken in their loyalties to their recent leader. [1, *31*]

Peter Blos illustrates the same general fact conversely.

> The late developing boy or the boy showing inappropriate sex development is handicapped in his social development on account of

group discrimination. It has been observed that *changes in physical status are followed by a changed attitude of the group: thus a boy with retarded maturation was long an outsider until a spurt of growth set in which subsequently led to his smooth absorption in the group.* [5, 253, italics ours]

The self-consciousness due to late maturation in relation to one's own age mates may cause the adolescent greater or lesser degrees of shyness or timidity in his behavior. F. W. Burks [9] reports in a study of the Tugwell High School Clubhouse (1936–37) [5] in California that the "late maturing boys were not able to utilize the clubhouse as a laboratory for practicing techniques for use with girls in quite so free an atmosphere as those who had achieved some proficiency in the Jackson School clubhouse." [12]   In White's account of Joseph Kidd [46] we see a concrete example of the difficulties encountered by a boy who developed later than his classmates, in this case because he was nearly two years their junior. White states Joseph's predicament:

> Being in the same grade with his brother, he had come to depend upon him for companionship, initiative, and even defense. When sexual maturity carried the brother into a new circle of activities, Kidd felt deserted and helpless; he was faced by the new task of making his own way, a task for which his being more than a year younger than the group was at this age a serious handicap. His accustomed social attitudes were now revealed as wholly unsuitable. [46, 196]

The relative standing of the development of an adolescent in relation to his age mates may not be a constant matter; it may mean different things in different situations. Zachry reports an illustration of this point "as described by Lawrence S. Kubie, M.D., at a meeting held by the Study of Adolescents."

> At the age of twelve one youngster may, for example, attain a size more usual to a boy of sixteen. Grouped with other twelve-year-olds in the classroom he may feel quite comfortable, since he is not unlike them in the stage of his intellectual and emotional development. But among the same boys on the playground he is facing a curiously complicated psychological challenge. [49, 50]

[5] We are indebted to Drs. H. E. Jones and M. C. Jones for securing this unpublished report.

In detailed investigations of various aspects of the adolescence of John Sanders, one of the cases studied longitudinally by the Institute of Child Welfare of the University of California [25], we find clear-cut substantiation of the importance of the changing body and changing self in relation to one's own group. John, who was not an unusual boy, whose case was not a dramatic one, and who, incidentally, could get along much better with his father than with his mother, was rated by his classmates as approximately average in different personal characteristics (masculine, happy, popular, and so on) at the age of 12.5 years. John matured physically a year or so later than his age mates.

> . . . during his junior-high-school years John became markedly shorter, lighter, and punier in relation to classmates. [25, *155 f.*]

At the age of 15, John suffered a "disheartening change of status in all the traits represented." [*154*]

> Adult observers agreed that around the age of 15 John was at a low point in, for example, popularity, initiative, and good-naturedness, and at a high point in evidences of anxiety, show-off behavior, and affectation. [25, *155*]

His "adolescent spurt" started at 15, a year or so later than other boys. With this spurt, an upward trend came in his sociability and status in relation to his age mates. By the age of 17.6 he approached the average of his age mates. In his freshman year in college, John was reported as having "a pleasing personality."

In analyzing John's case, Harold Jones states:

> . . . delayed maturing may lead not only to loss of status with others, but also to the anxiety expressed in the question, "Am I normal?" When the biological innovations of adolescence are at last clearly avowed, a turning point may be reached not merely in physiological development, but also in social recognition and in feelings of personal security. The interpretation followed above stresses the social significance of adolescent changes, and implies that the psychological effect of these changes rests upon the degree to which an individual is sensitive to the norms and values of his social environment. [25, *156*]

Incorporation in the ego of norms of masculinity and femininity.
We have seen that as the body changes into one of a mature male
or female, the adolescent's conception of himself or herself also
changes. The adolescent begins to conceive of himself or herself
as man or woman. This includes the social expectations and
values attached to the male or female body. As some of the illustrations in the previous section have indicated, certain values have
to do with desirable body proportions of one's own and of the
opposite sex. These values, when incorporated as part of the ego,
regulate in an important way the adolescent's experience and behavior related to his own body and to his choice of "desirable"
companions of the opposite sex. As we shall see later, these choices
are also defined in terms of ego-attitudes related to norms of the
"right" people for associates, in terms of class, status, and the like.
Whereas girls, prior to adolescence, are prone to be fairly free in
the way they handle their bodies, they now become highly conscious of them, handling them in terms of such culturally prescribed norms as modesty and feminine attractiveness. So, too,
boys handle and treat their bodies in terms of norms of masculine
attractiveness which have now become more acutely ego-involved
for them. Thus, a high school boy may appear casual, athletic, or
whatever stance and pose is suitable to the particular culture and
time. Fashions of male and female dress assume great importance
at this time. This development has been aptly summarized for
200 adolescent boys and girls by investigators at the University of
California. [41]

> Psychologically also the girl feels a necessity of proving to herself
> and to the world that she is essentially feminine; the boy needs to
> demonstrate that he has those masculine qualities which require others
> to recognize him as a man. This characteristic accounts for the girls
> spending a large part of their leisure time in shopping and in personal
> adornment. This is the secret of the manicured nails, painted red to
> match vivid lips. This is why they must wave and curl their hair,
> and, having perfected the process, must pin into it ribbon bows, bits
> of lace, or flowers. This is the reason for the boy's urge to learn to
> drive a car and for his willingness to move heaven and earth to bor-
> row or own one. Along with this development, also, we are told by
> our group that a girl to be popular must be modishly pretty, keep

herself clean and neat, be a good mixer. A boy, on the other hand, must be aggressive and must excel at sports. He must have the ability to dance and to talk easily with girls, and in addition he must show that he can compete readily with other boys; that he can achieve and master. [41, 6 f.]

It may be seen from this summary characterization that not all of the social values incorporated as ego-values connected with masculinity-femininity are directly related to the male or female body. There are also norms regarding the social and economic functions, the statuses of men and women. And there are norms regarding the essential nature of men and women which are more or less appropriate to those particular social and economic functions and statuses. No matter what the contribution of infantile sexuality may be in determining the male or female ego, the ego-values of masculinity or femininity are effectively acquired during adolescence. As Goodenough [17] concludes on the basis of standard studies in America:

> Girls, on the average, earn their most highly feminine score on the M–F test when they are in the eighth grade; boys make their most masculine score during the third year of high school. Roughly, these periods correspond to the usual age at the attainment of puberty. *Perhaps the explanation for the wide divergence of the sexes in psychological traits at that time is a reflection of the adolescent's intense interest in all matters that have to do with the establishment of his status as man or woman.* [17, 486 f., italics ours]

In Tryon's study [44] of certain "factors involved in the task of maintaining status with one's peers," we find some substantiation of Goodenough's last point. Tryon studied 350 boys and girls, first at the age of 12 and later at the age of 15, acquiring their opinions of others in the group by means of a verbal-picture ("Guess Who") test. As Tryon summarized her findings:

> During the period between ages twelve to fifteen, values for girls underwent some revolutionary changes; values for boys underwent relatively minor changes, mainly in terms of slightly shifted emphases. [44, 565]

As an example, the 12-year-old girls with high prestige in the group were described as "neat, attractive appearance; friendly but rather demure and docile social manner; quiet good humor; and controlled behavior conforming to adult standards" [563]; whereas the 15-year-old girl gained prestige "either through buoyant, rather aggressive good-fellowship with both boys and girls, or through sophisticated, glamorous qualities which attract the boys." [565]

As we have seen, girls mature physiologically earlier than boys. In the group Tryon studied [43] "most of the girls had passed through the pubescent period at fifteen years, and probably less than one-half of the boys had." [79] The data illustrate the changing characteristics or "traits" necessary for status accompanying the girls' changing bodies, just as, as we have seen, changing interests come at this time. It would seem entirely possible, as Tryon suggests, that if the boys in this study had been at a comparable level of physiological maturity, a similar shift in "desirable" personal qualities would have appeared for them. Whether or not the shift would be as "revolutionary" as that for girls remains to be answered by a study of the question. It is even possible that a further shift might be found in the girls' values. For, as Tryon notes, the girls who were rated high because of "cordial rather dominating good-fellowship with both boys and girls . . . were very successful with the boys who were just venturing into mixed-sex social situations; the behavior of these girls was enough like that of the boys that it did not alarm the boys." [79]

The adolescent experiences himself or herself and behaves like a man or a woman as prescribed by these norms, whatever they may be in a particular culture. As Conklin formulated it:

> Perceptions of the physical self as male or female and *all the possible meanings which may accrue to those perceptions* must cause a very large twist toward difference in the self concepts of the two sexes. [12, 56, italics ours]

Certainly, norms regarding the conceptions of man and woman, their functions, their status do "accrue" and do vary from culture to culture as determined by their socioeconomic organizations. Consequently, we find, in different cultures, different identifications, behavior manifestations, different problems. As Conklin points out:

If the greater introversion is perceived or believed in by a girl, that will have its reflex upon her self concept and all self-regarding functions. If the boy believes that he has better control than the girl, that will affect his attitudes as much as hers. If any or all of the possible emotional differences between the sexes are brought to the attention and perception of boys and girls, then their self concepts will be affected thereby. [12, 56]

This point, which should be seriously accounted for in any analysis of personality, finds expression again in Wile's statement: [47]

Even the growing differentiation of male dominant aggressiveness and female dominant submissiveness acquires meaning and value only in terms of social standards which set them up as laudable patterns for adolescents. Their particular world defines the processes to which adolescents shall submit and undertakes to guide them into the essential qualities which are deemed socially valuable. [47, 9]

The anthropologists, in particular Margaret Mead, have given accounts of diverse and contrasting norms related to masculinity and femininity in different cultures. Such variations are not peculiarities or distant primitive cultures alone. With variations of socioeconomic systems, the conception of man and woman varies. For example, the Lynds [33] give the following characterization of the conception of man and woman in America:

The worlds of the two sexes constitute something akin to separate subcultures. Each involves an elaborate assignment of roles to its members and the development of preferred personality types emphasizing various ones of the more significant role attributes. . . . But this culture says not only that men and women do different things; they *are* different kinds of people. Men are stronger, bolder, less pure, less refined, more logical, more reasonable, more given to seeing things in the large, but at home needing coddling and reassurance, "like little boys." Women are more delicate, stronger in sympathy, understanding, and insight, less mechanically adept, more immersed in petty detail and in personalities, and given to "getting emotional over things." [33, 176 f.]

In the Soviet Union, this dichotomy of personality characteristics of man and woman is not the case. That such is the fact does not have to be demonstrated by citations from the studies of psychologists. Thousands of concrete illustrations have appeared in printed form about the behavior of Soviet women during the fulfillment of the Five Year Plans and during World War II, not only in the auxiliary armed services and factories, but also in combat situations and guerrilla warfare.

We have mentioned these sociological characterizations of norms concerning man and woman because of their organic connection with our problem. First of all, adolescents are in a transitional period in terms of their status. If, as Zachry and others point out, they at the same time receive inconsistent treatments from grown-ups, they will have further difficulty in stabilizing their egos. Gardner [16] writes of such conflict situations:

> It might be well to note here in the interest of tolerance of the adolescent that as far as the expression of maturity goes, he is "condemned if he does and condemned if he doesn't" show evidence of maturity of sexual interest and outlook, and this even by his own parents. That parents wish their adolescents to grow up and be independent and that at the same time they wish them to continue to be children and dependent upon them has never made the task of the adolescent an easy one. [16, 61]

Now, in addition to such conflict situations, adolescents are put in even more puzzling circumstances by virtue of the fact that many of the norms relating to masculinity and femininity, even in highly developed Western societies, are certainly survivals of past centuries and periods.

Modern technological developments and social changes, recent momentous events of the last decades (such as depression and war) have brought about changes in the social behavior of men and, especially, of women. But the norms concerning the "basic nature" of man and woman, their "real" function and station in society, still survive side by side with the necessary alterations in behavior forced by the impact of these changes. The discrepancy between certain practices imposed by social and technological changes and these norms, which in themselves are contradictory, produces conflict situations which surely have their psychological consequences. Pointing to this discrepancy, the Lynds state:

But the modifications have been in the kind of behavior sanctioned by the culture, not in the belief that men and women are different in character and temperament, and not in the ways in which they are believed to be different. The modifications of the behavior patterns themselves consist in tolerated exceptions rather than in the development of any clear alternatives meeting with group approval. For the individual, the result is frequently either that he is caught in a chaos of conflicting patterns, none of them wholly condemned, but no one of them clearly approved and free from confusion; or, where the group sanctions are clear in demanding a certain role of man or woman, the individual encounters cultural requirements with no immediate means of meeting them. [33, *177*]

Since adolescents are themselves in a more or less critical process of transition, these situations certainly breed adolescent insecurities, conflicts, rebellions, and, at times, inevitable crises. In the process of re-formation of the ego, we should expect to find, as the California study mentioned earlier in this section indicates, that

. . . once the girl has arrived at the status in the group to which she has aspired, or has learned to adjust herself to a version of the universal feminine model which suits her own personality . . . once the boy feels that he is accepted as a man . . . [he and she] become more stable and predictable. Teachers, and parents say that they have "settled down." [41, 7]

However, the problems related to the contradictions found in being male or female in America do not always disappear in early adolescence. We find ample evidence to show that such conflicts, although perhaps lessened for a time, may increase as the adolescent seriously faces the prospects of work and marriage. Such evidence is to be found in such studies as those of Kirkpatrick [26, 27] where he reports that attitudes toward femininity are highly inconsistent, both for parents and adolescents of both sexes.

It also seems to be true that the sex differences in inconsistency tend to be greater in the younger generation. [26, *355*]

The fact that male students "were decidedly more inconsistent than female students" would seem to make the lot of both males and females fraught with difficulties. [27, *551*]

However, it is the female in a bourgeois society who is in most danger of remaining "marginal," of experiencing continued conflict due to the contradictory ego-attitudes and situations in which she finds herself. Kitay [28] found, for example, that girls tend to incorporate the "prevailing views" about themselves maintained by men, "even when they are uncomplimentary." [405] In the areas of work opportunities, these problems are particularly accentuated for girls. As Seward [40] puts it:

> Having provided its boys and girls with the same educational opportunities and vocational motivation, our society then reverses itself, suddenly denying the girls the very rewards it has held out to them throughout the whole course of their development. [40, 178]

In studying college girls' attitudes toward their role in the postwar period, Seward found

> . . . for the group as a whole, an emphasis on equality between men and women in educational and vocational opportunities, working conditions, community activities, and social contacts. Inconsistent with this liberal trend was a reactionary reinforcement of the traditional subordinate feminine rôle as far as wife and mother relationships were concerned. [40, 193]

As would be predicted, those subjects who rejected the latter notions, were found to be more insecure than those who conformed, this apparently being "the price . . . [they] pay for their nonconformity." [190] Further evidence that this conflict is of social, not biological origin, was found in interviews in which the "attitudes and experiences with respect to sexual and maternal activities could not be differentiated from those of the conservatives." [193] This finding would seem to go counter to the psychoanalytic theory that "all women . . . who fail to find complete satisfaction in the role assigned them by contemporary society" have a "masculinity complex." [177] For example, we would expect that girls who handled men's jobs during the war would find it particularly difficult to return to the role conventionally prescribed for women.

The major conflicts and anxieties experienced by girls who are themselves in a state of transition can be traced back to the inconsistent conflicting values and norms in society. This fact was discussed by Leta Hollingworth [20] 17 years ago and has been more recently pointed out by Seward [40].

The changing ego and adult–youth conflict. The recasting of some major ego-attitudes and the formation of new ego-attitudes in relation to one's body, to one's own and to the opposite sex, grown-ups, education, work or profession, standing in the world, and so on, all imply a change in the ego. This change does not occur overnight. The ego reaches its relative (adult) stability only after a period of time, if it reaches it at all. Under some difficult circumstances and for some persons, the striving for relative stability is considerably prolonged. For example, for some old maids or bachelors frustrated during adolescence, the process may continue throughout a whole lifetime.

We have already pointed out that because of the heightened affective and emotional state of the adolescent due to significant glandular changes and to the accelerated growth rate, he is also in a state of flux psychologically. The more or less stable ego-links formed up to adolescence become shaky and precarious. New relationships, links, and aspirations are still in a fluid state and subject to "mercurial" ups and downs (to use Zachry's characterization), on account of the physiological flux and external (social) pressures. The adolescent tosses about and suffers from the lack of stable anchorages until some new ones are achieved. This instability is especially aggravated in a changing social milieu and in different family situations where the adolescent faces contradictory norms and inconsistent expectations and treatments.

The psychological consequences are feelings of inadequacy, insecurity, and anxiety. Various degrees of crisis may ensue, in some cases with grave consequences for the individual. The intensity of the crisis is proportional to the degree of friction and contradiction of the external demands and individual internal factors. The adolescent may feel all alone as he finds himself caught in the whirl of sex desires, striving to amount to something in the midst of contradictory and inconsistent relationships and values. Several expressions of this feeling of aloneness, of being left out and even betrayed, were found in the diaries of Turkish adolescent boys and girls. The writing of diaries, which indicates a turning inward, seems to be more prevalent in a social milieu which does not provide many opportunities for the adolescents of both sexes to mix together frequently in overt activities such as age-mate parties, dancing and sports. That this tendency to turn inward is reduced in a social milieu where adolescents do have more of a chance to mix together is indicated, for example, by the fact that at the present time in the upper middle-class milieu in California very little diary writing is observed. We mention the keeping of diaries only as an illustration in passing. Before we give a brief account of other behavioral indications of the adolescent's striving to amount to something in his changed relationships and values, his effort to reanchor himself, we must examine somewhat closely the implications of adult–youth conflict for our problem.

Adult–youth conflict. The facts reported concerning adult–youth conflict may be taken as a significant index of the instability and, in many cases one might almost say, of the disintegration of the childish ego. Up to the developmental stage of puberty, a more or less stable set of ego-attitudes had been achieved in relation to parents, other grown-ups, the values inculcated, school authorities, teachers, and age mates. With the changing body and changing self, with the changed expectations and treatments from the social surroundings including the family, even these existing relationships may be altered.[6]

Zachry [49] has given an interesting account of these changes in her chapter on "Changing Relationships with Adults." For example, the adolescent sees himself now as grown-up or, at least, as different, whereas the family at times still continues to look at him or to treat him as the baby child. The case of John Sanders [25], referred to earlier, is a good illustration of the point. In relation to John's mother, Jones states:

> It does not appear, however, that she could regard with objective tolerance the preliminary signs of John's adolescent rebellion; to her,

[6] This does not, of course, mean a denial of the special cases of significant changes in parent–youth relationships at an earlier age in unfortunate family situations. In such cases, age mates in the streets, school, or in gang formations may exert a dominant role. Also we are not ignoring prematurely produced effects in those cases where economic responsibilities are imposed on boys and girls at an early age.

these changing attitudes were a source of irritation and were apparently not thought of as related to her son's social maturing. [25, 20]

The "gripes" and "peeves" adolescents have against their parents because of the inconsistent way they are treated are reflected in the following list mentioned by a 16-year-old boy:

Being called in the morning more than twice. Having them tell me what to eat. Being yelled at in the bathroom in the morning. Being asked questions about homework. Being "called down" about my school marks. Having to tell them where I've been on dates, where I'm going and who I'm going with. Always being nagged about the length of time I use the phone, the light I read in, and the radio programs I hear.[7]

Goodenough summarizes this source of parent–youth conflict as follows:

The conflict between old habits and new requirements—represented on the part of the adolescent by his feeling that he is grown up, that he wants to be treated like a grown-up, while he still has habits of acting like a child, and on the parents' side by their recognition that the child is growing up, their feeling that he ought to act more like a grown-up, although from force of habit they continue to treat him as if he were still a child—often makes for a good deal of friction. [17, 494]

Parent–youth conflict is the more general formulation of the facts covered under "psychological weaning," or the tendency toward independence (emancipation) on the part of adolescents. As a result of such situations, the adolescent boy or girl makes implicit or explicit, effective or, most of the time, futile moves toward emancipation and independence. These rebellions may, in some cases, assume serious proportions. Running away from home and wanting to study in out-of-town places, are examples. Illustrations of this parent–youth conflict have been reported by many observers. We can choose at random a few of the many concrete cases.

Among other cases, Averill [1] relates this one:

[7] This is one of the representative interviews collected for us by Carolyn Berl.

Ruth, a sophomore in high school, is known to her classmates as a "goody-goody," an appellation which she greatly resents. At home, she indulges in the wildest temper-tantrums to get her own way from parents who have scant understanding of the social needs of a young girl. . . . Her clothes are neat, but practical rather than particularly becoming. To Ruth they seem ugly, just because they are so practical. She begs to be allowed to choose her own clothing, but is never permitted any voice in its selection. . . . No company is allowed on school nights, and no excuse is sufficient to gain for Ruth escape from her homework. She is never permitted to attend the school parties, and is resentful at the strict prohibitions which keep her from participating in all club and dramatic activities. At school she is accused of lacking school spirit, and suffers agonies in consequence. Of late, her tantrums have been getting worse, and her parents, though counseled to ignore them, are becoming greatly worried. Frequently she is quite ill for a day or two following these attacks, and insists that she has no interest in getting well. [1, 69]

Zachry [49] reports a case which is interesting because of the indication it gives of an adolescent's awareness of the nature of the adult–youth conflict:

A high-school senior whose home was pervaded by an atmosphere of artificial politeness, in which it was almost unthinkable to express resentment openly, wrote in a theme entitled "The Everburning Fire of Youth":

"When the boy and girl first begin to take notice of a current problem they see the cause of the problem with a clearer and cleaner sense of view than do most of their elders, who are too burdened with many worldly ideas. . . .

"It is disappointing to the younger set to find that their elders do not want to coöperate. Many times when a young boy or girl tries to give some advice he is laughed out of the picture by his elders, who feel that youth has no place in the world except to listen and learn. . . .

"As the boy and girl grow older they are given more chance to have their say, but by this time the majority have either forgotten their ideals or else the events have become so muddled that there is no chance of clear youthful thinking." [49, 311]

A case of conflict in an adolescent boy of an average New England family is taken from Healy [19] "out of the hundreds of available illustrations of such conflicts in our records." [*141*]   Both the father and mother are average normal New England folks. There are no unusual disturbing frictions in the situation up to the time of adolescence.

The issues came out so clearly because he began to rebel at their formulae of life by the time he was twelve years old. The stirrings of an unusually fine physique and a very early adolescence, together with a violent rejection of an earlier father identification, led him to phantasy hazardous adventure and to seek out young daredevils belonging to the unacceptable fringe of his neighborhood with whom he engaged in reckless escapades and delinquencies. Undetected in the latter he then, to the utter astonishment of his family, began a series of runaway episodes. "I can't stand it, doing everything just the way they want me to. They are good enough to me, but I can't talk to them about the way I feel," this wholesome appearing lad told us when we saw him after he had been so perplexing his family for a couple of years. [19, *142 f.*]

Adult–youth conflict is such a general phenomenon in modern complex societies that the problem does not have to be subjected to a precise psychological scrutiny to tap its existence. It occasionally occupies the columns of daily papers. Sometimes, these cases are serious indeed; but here we will note a comparatively minor manifestation. For example, a pretty 15-year-old girl recently remarked to a newspaperman:

Teachers and parents make all the plans, and we run all the errands. We're always on the defensive. Grownups don't trust us or give us any responsibilities. Take our city. We're working like dogs to get a youth canteen. We're the ones who'll use it, but do we have anything to say about it? Like heck we do. [36]

Adult–youth conflict may be a good deal more than the mere individual conflicts of individual adolescents of certain families. It may develop into a standardized attitude among adolescents. Such a standardized adolescent attitude was observed by Stolz, M. C. Jones, and Chaffey [41] in one of the many adolescent studies of the California Institute of Child Welfare. From their investigation of "The Junior High School Age," "based upon an intensive study of one hundred boys and one hundred girls which has been carried on during the three-year period that they were enrolled in junior high school," the authors conclude:

> Adult approval or disapproval meant almost nothing to these young adolescents except as it might affect the attainment of their goal. In fact there was a noticeable resistance, not so much to authority, as our rules seldom got in their way, but simply to adults as such. Those girls and boys who were in the throes of establishing themselves socially were the most antagonistic toward adults. They manifested this attitude chiefly by shunning adults and acting as if their presence were a hindrance. Six months later these same pupils were likely to be the ones who hung around and talked to adults as if, being quite grown up now, they needed to talk and associate with other grown persons. [41, 3]

In another California study of social development in adolescence, Cameron [10] states:

> But through it all there appears the steadily rising pressure to break away from the earlier accepted domination of parents in the home and of teachers in the school. It is as though an overwhelming urge were released within many of these youngsters to assert their independence, to explore quite new and thrilling kinds of relationships with each other, and to proclaim their rights to self-expression as individuals. In a sense the clubhouse was misnamed, for no club meetings were held in it. Nor has any desire been expressed for the formation of clubs. The social organization which these adolescents prefer is less rigid, more changeable and fluid. Formalities are forgotten in their quest for more personal relationships. [10, 4]

In a country in transition, in which the discrepancy between the generations is that of different social periods, adult–youth conflict may acquire still greater proportions. In Turkey, which has been going through such a stage of transition, we have collected material since 1937 (through diaries, interviews, and questionnaires) on the social psychology of adolescence with special emphasis on the problems of attitudes and ego formation. Among other material collected were the reactions of over 3,000 boys and girls in different parts of the country to a questionnaire especially designed to tap these problems. The reactions were obtained under controlled conditions.[8] We summarize here only the main results relating to adult–youth conflict. Two of the questions were especially relevant to the present discussion: "Do you think grown-ups understand you as you are?" and "If there are persons who understand you as you are, who are they?"

The principal finding was that younger boys and girls (approximately between the ages 11 and 14) report, in general, that parents, relatives, or teachers understand them. But above this age and in late adolescence, in general the report is that grown-ups do not understand them. Many boys and girls said that only a few of their friends, who are their age mates, understand them as they are. Some reported that nobody understands them, including themselves. Among the introspections they volunteered to write down, many reveal the important issues of transition. We reproduce here as illustrations only two of these introspective reports.

> The grown-ups cannot understand me, because they are people of the last century whereas I belong to this century. Things which do not please them are very pleasing to me.

Another girl wrote:

> We do not think grown-ups understand us. As there is a great difference between the periods in which we have grown up they misunderstand us and frictions come out as a consequence. [35]

These findings hold only for town and city adolescents attending school. The problems of adolescents in rural districts present different characteristics since, until recent years, very few rural children in Turkey attended school and the great majority of them had to participate at an early age in economic life. These qualifying remarks are made to call attention once more to the fact that the psychological problems (as well as other problems) assume different features in countries in transition, according to the tempo of change in different strata and regions of the population. Perhaps the various acculturation studies now going on may furnish valuable data for dealing with the psychology of these problems.

[8] The results of these studies will be published later.

It may be said, in general, that parent–youth conflict increases with the rate of social change. [15] The Lynds [33] observed this trend in Middletown.

> To quote a veteran worker with Middletown's children, "Our parents are realizing the increasingly sharp divergence of their world and that of their children today as never before." And the parents' world strikes back! In many cases they attempt to use the schools as a means of holding the two worlds together. A high-school course in sociology has been dropped because of parental protest over the fact that problems of sex were discussed in class. Over the heads of Middletown teachers, trained according to standards wider than some of the mores of Middletown, hangs at all times the sword of parental conservatism and anxiety. This is rendered the more difficult because, in manners and morals as well as economics, politics, and religion, the local community contains taxpaying parents of widely varying personal standards. The teacher knows and the community knows that the children ranged in their seats are wise in matters not in the curriculum, and that many of these children are rebelliously clamoring for the right to raise questions and to be outspoken in the face of the official and parental restraints. As one teacher said, "I am facing a new problem nowadays: My pupils insist on raising questions I dare not let them discuss though my conscience demands that I not clamp down on their honest questions. The things they say continually keep me on pins and needles for fear some of them will go home and tell their parents. I have an uneasy furtive sense about it all." [33, 233]

All of these observations indicate that new generations growing up in rapidly changing social surroundings resent, and at times rebel against, the efforts of grown-ups to shape them after their own images. However, the impact of these facts concerning adult–youth conflict must be qualified when viewed from the perspective secured through the studies of ethnologists and sociologists. Adult–youth conflict reflects in a significant way the conflicts between the established generation and the younger generation. The intensity of the conflict might be said to be, by and large, proportional to the degree of social change. In a society in which the survival norms constitute the major values of the superstructure (as the Lynds pointed out) and lag behind the material–technological developments ("cultural lag"), no matter how serious the youthful rebellion and restlessness may be, adult–youth conflict will, in most cases, be an intrafamily and intracommunity affair. A concrete case, personally communicated, illustrates the point. An adolescent boy was strongly and, at times, openly critical of everything that his parents (both parents) did. Nevertheless, he shared the major class delineations, political views, and social-distance norms of his upper–middle class parents.

The impact of special socioeconomic events such as depression, the introduction of new industrial developments in a society or even in a particular locality, may produce new problems in adult–youth relationships. For example, in her study of *The Unemployed Man and His Family,* carried on in 1935–36, Komarovsky [29] presents data amply illustrating this point. One important result of unemployment was to undermine "the authority of the father over the adolescent child even more frequently" than his authority over younger children or his authority as a husband. [92] This deterioration of authority came chiefly because money "was frequently used by the parents as an instrument of education and control." [92] In the light of our preceding discussion of the strivings of the adolescent to amount to something as a person in his own right, the meaning of such facts becomes apparent. Also important was the finding that intrafamily and parental conflict increased because "father is a changed man" since he lost his work. [94 ff.] Furthermore, conflict between father and adolescent children was found to be particularly intense when one of the children was working. [97–102]

Such changes in the established parent–youth relationships due to the impact of serious socioeconomic events suggest that the situational determinations of parent–offspring relationships may be more significant at times than the toilet habits or postulated "Oedipus complexes" of early infancy. At least, in some cases of serious economic misery or serious status problems, qualitative changes in intrafamily relationships may be brought about which go beyond the limits of such wholesale formulations as those positing immutable childhood complexes, where, we are told, adverse social circumstances act only as agents which release nothing more than deep-rooted jealousies, hatreds, and loves in the relatively fixed storehouse of the unconscious. (ch. 14)

THE ADOLESCENTS' REACTIONS AND EFFORTS TO RE-ESTABLISH THEMSELVES TO SOME DEGREE OF STABILITY

In our sketchy account up to this point we have indicated how the adolescent's ego undergoes significant changes with his changing body, his altered relationships with grown-ups and age mates; and how varying socioeconomic circumstances bring about corresponding variations that produce feelings of insecurity and aloneness and different degrees and durations of instability in the shaky ego-attitudes. We saw how, as a consequence, strivings for independence and emancipation arise. These lead to the adolescent's "psychological weaning" from grown-ups, and this in turn produces varying degrees and kinds of adult–youth conflict.

Thus, having lost a more or less stabilized ground of ego links, caught in the whirl of new sex and other desires which meet various degrees of resistances from social surroundings to which he has to adjust himself anew, the adolescent is torn away from his more or less solid earlier ego links. In the throes of re-establishing himself as a person in his own right, he may, consciously or unconsciously, resort to innumerable reactions in addition to his striving to satisfy his strengthened and specified desires. The ego and ego links which have become more unstable and insecure must be re-established, at least to some degree of stability with the new grown-up values whatever they may be to him. Being "in a vacuum," being marginal in so many diverse relationships of a differentiated society is painful, especially during a transition stage when the adolescent is so keenly aware of these ego issues in relation to his body, his male and female friends, his parents, and so forth.

In studies of adolescence, hundreds of different kinds of reactions are reported which reveal the painful and critical process the adolescent goes through in re-establishing himself. We shall give some samples of these reactions and then return to our problem more specifically. As Hollingworth [20] points out, some adolescents demand and feel thwarted if they are refused privacy, their "own" room. [187 f.] As already mentioned, some adolescents, particularly girls, keep diaries. Hollingworth [21, 895] and

Bühler [8, *390*] both cite studies indicating that diaries are frequently the recipients of the adolescent's most secret desires, hopes, and dreams. In Turkey where, as we noted, diaries are more common than in countries where adolescents have more opportunity for extracurricular activities providing for ever-enlarging group activities, one girl of 17 wrote in her diary:

> Oh, my beloved diary, I return to you! You alone understand me. I feel so lost and alone in this cruel world. [35]

An adolescent boy or girl may become absorbed in daydreams or phantasies in which, usually, he or she is the central character. [12, 20] Many adolescents are absorbed in the unreal world of Hollywood movies, the idolizing of movie stars. If there is one Mecca for bourgeois youth all over the world today, it seems to be Hollywood.

Sometimes, if conflict is too great, if failure to re-establish oneself occurs for too long or too often, abnormal behavior may result. Thus Ellen Hill, who in Davis and Dollard's *Children of Bondage* [14] was described by relatives, teachers, and friends as having been, as a child, "an especially agreeable girl, 'sweet' in her disposition," "a favorite with her instructors," "very tractable," became, during early adolescence, "impudent," "malicious," "sly," "very belligerent," and finally "definitely abnormal." [*158 ff.*] She talked to teachers only in monosyllables. She dreamed day and night of deprivations or alleviations of her situation, both material and social. Ellen's case is not a simple one. However, the authors make it clear that this crisis came as a result of an intense impact of economic and family difficulties which increased suddenly in her early adolescence and *seriously threatened her standing with her clique.* The combination of factors associated with adolescence, her aspirations to rise even higher in status, and the crushing realities of economic deprivation and disgrace in her family brought on these behavioral symptoms which the authors characterize as "status anxiety . . . which, in the lives of persons who have experienced rapid change in status, either upward or downward, may be viewed as a form of 'status shock.'" [*156*]

Another example of more or less abnormal behavior is that of adolescents who are frequently ill, with no discoverable organic disorders. Several authors have mentioned the relative frequency of the onset of schizophrenia, manic-depressive psychoses, and hysteria during adolescence. [12, 20, 39, 47] Suicide, which is somewhat more common in complex and transitional societies, may be resorted to. Hollingworth [20] aptly described adolescent suicide when she wrote:

> The adolescent prefers death to the torture of his uncertainties and thwartings, and takes active steps to destroy himself. . . . *The self is lost irretrievably.* . . . [20, *199 f.,* italics ours]

Among the many illustrations of adolescents' attempts to re-establish themselves, Hollingworth cites that of a girl who read the Bible and prayed in the morning and rode horses bareback all afternoon, much to her family's consternation. The girl, it developed, was trying to decide between the occupations of deaconess and bareback rider. [*171 f.*] This illustration gives us some clue to Conklin's interesting study [12] of 329 college students who were asked if they had ever experienced more than one "self" at the same time. Twenty-six per cent could immediately recall having experienced two fairly different "selves" at the same time. "Twenty-eight per cent of the above group reported that they had observed the same phenomenon in others." [*143*]

Zachry [49] mentions the case of a girl who threw herself into sports activities and determined to attain perfection because she felt that the female body was physically inadequate. Two adolescent sisters who had no friends among their age mates engaged in work and study as a substitute activity to the point of overworking themselves. Another girl became "over-assertive," pushing herself to the fore in social gatherings. Still other cases are reported who became self-deprecatory, cynical, or weighed down with self-blame and guilt.

In the struggle to re-establish themselves anew, adolescents may choose idols, or certain characteristics of several persons, and strive to emulate them. Sometimes the model may be a movie star, public figure, fictional character or teacher. One adolescent tried to imitate her teacher in every way, saw no faults in her, and allowed no one to speak ill of her. [20, *182*] Crushes are also found between age mates of the same sex, particularly among girls.

It is not difficult to find two adolescent girls who spend most of their time together, dress similarly, act very much alike, protect each other, and, in general, identify with each other, at least for a time. Cases of "puppy love" are epidemic in adolescence. As we noted, adolescents may, under intense stress, undertake the serious business of marriage at an early age as a way out of their conflicts. Some adolescent loves may, indeed, be both intense and lasting. However, many are highly temporary and frequent. Since love can be described as a high degree of ego-involvement with another person in addition to sex attraction and desires, this rapid shifting and changing of adolescent loves is an understandable result of the mercurial state of the adolescent's ego.

The Effects of Age-mate Reference Groups and Membership Groups in the Re-formation of the Ego-attitudes

The developing and increasing adolescent attitudes and interests, itemized in detail in so many works on the subject, gain in psychological meaning and coherence if they are studied in terms of the reference groups and membership groups to which the adolescent relates himself. For many of these adolescent attitudes and interests develop in interaction with and conformity to such groups. The adolescents' most intense strivings for status and approval take place within such groups. Here our main concern is, of course, with ego-attitudes.

Adolescents progressively turn to the closer company of age mates in their transition from childhood to adulthood, in their struggle to establish themselves as persons in their own rights in an adverse adult-made world in which they are marginal in varying degrees. They interact in their own adolescent circles, limited and influenced, of course, by their particular social setting at large. This gives rise to certain norms of behavior, to fashions and fads of dress and amusement peculiar to various adolescent groups. During these years of transition, adolescents achieve immediate status through conformity to the norms of their age-mate groups. For the time being these peculiar adolescent norms of experience and behavior become the adolescent's own values, determining his personal relationships and attitudes to an important degree. It is not a mere accident of phraseology, therefore, that Harold Jones and other authorities in the field refer to the ensemble of these adolescent standardizations as "adolescent culture." These adolescent norms may be of various durations, some may even be seasonal affairs. They may and certainly do change from society to society, even in different regions or districts of the same society. But as long as they last, they demand conformity from the adolescents within the particular reference group to which they apply. The adolescent derives his status, with the age mates among whom he moves to some extent at least, from the fulfillment of expectations prescribed by them. In this connection, we can advance the hypothesis that the degree of influence of age-mate reference groups and membership groups varies directly with the degree of psychological weaning from grown-ups and the intensity of adult-youth conflict.

The effect of age-mate reference groups on ego-attitudes. As we noted, probably proportional to the degree of psychological weaning from grown-ups and strivings for independence, adolescents seek in an increasing way the company of their age mates or peers. The influence of companions in determining the adolescents' likes-dislikes, interests and attitudes, increases correspondingly. His status or ego-values are increasingly derived from age-mate associations. These adolescent values change, of course, from society to society and vary even according to the particular socioeconomic standing of the immediate milieu. We designate the age-mate groups to which adolescent relates himself as his reference group.

Authorities in the field of adolescence, such as Hollingworth, Harold Jones, Zachry, Blos, Goodenough, and others all give interesting hints of the increased influence of age mates during adolescence. Zachry [49] remarks:

> In the desire to be liked by his own group, the adolescent usually does his best to conform to its standards, even at considerable cost to himself. [49, 355]

Consequently, while adamant to the criticisms and advice of parents, the adolescent may be more receptive to the advice of age-mate groups. This is well illustrated by Zachry's concrete observation:

A sixteen-year-old girl was saying she thought she could take criticism from friends which she would not accept from her family. She related that last year she wore bangs. Her mother was not sure she liked them, but the student kept the bangs because her girl friends all said they looked very well. The only negative criticism friends have given her is that she is too loud. "The family have been telling me for years the same thing," she explained. " 'That's enough noise from you,' they say. Lately I've been quiet." [49, 355]

On the basis of such observations Zachry concisely formulates the regulation of the adolescent's values by his reference group:

In the struggle to establish himself as a person in his own right, independent of adults, the adolescent measures his success against that of those whose status is similar to his. The greater success of some of them in one aspect or another of development seems to threaten to impair the solidarity of those on whom he depends. Also it may appear to him a direct challenge to his adequacy. Differences in degree of success in achieving standards that are important to peers (and some of those that are prized by parents and teachers as well) are therefore elements in their emotional relationships. Economic status, social conventionality, ethical standards, religious and political beliefs, academic success, athletic prowess, ability to win the indulgence of adults, or popularity with members of the other sex—any one of these or all together—as he and his peers embody them are to the adolescent measures of his own success in establishing himself in growing independence. [49, 369 f.]

Likewise Blos [5] has given a concise summary of the impact of "peer-culture" in shaping the adolescent's personal values of failure or success:

Group opinion serves, then, as a selective influence for desirable and undesirable behavior, and the approval or disapproval of peers becomes progressively the most influential force in motivating adolescent conduct. [5, 249]

And

This belongingness to the group, which becomes progressively important for the adolescent, replaces family ties to some extent and thus prepares him for new conformities and identifications implicit in the group life of adults. [5, 250]

Blos then goes on to indicate that the attitudes and behavior of the individual cannot be understood properly without reference to his age-mate groups:

The intermediary phase of social development which takes place at adolescence can be properly evaluated only with reference to its intrinsic functions and meanings. One of its most unique functions is to establish a group life with its own standards, values, appreciations. This group life, often referred to as peer culture, has a decisive impact upon the adolescent's development and is indeed far more influential at times than adult opinion or judgment. In fact adults are often unable to comprehend the peculiar logic of adolescent behavior that is perfectly reasonable to adolescents themselves. A girl of 14 expressed herself on this matter and said that sometimes she felt that boys and girls of her age understand each other better than their parents understand them. For instance, she continued, "They'll do some silly thing, and the parents won't understand why it is they're so silly. . . ." [5, 251]

Goodenough's account [17] is in harmony with these:

Unquestionably the influence of his associates upon the way the adolescent thinks and acts is very great; greater, probably than at any previous stage of his life. For the adolescent there can be no stronger argument for having or doing a thing than the fact that "all the others are doing it." Nothing is likely to awaken so great an emotional disturbance or cause so much worry as the feeling that he is in some way different from the others. *"Others" in this case, means the other members of his own particular group; he is not especially concerned about resembling those belonging to some other clan.* A fashion started by the leaders of a group, even though it may happen to be uncomfortable or inconvenient, is faithfully copied by all the lesser members. *Opinions, prejudices, beliefs, likes, and dislikes are likewise determined by the group, and the boy or girl who differs is made to feel the force of group ostracism unless he has sufficient force of personality to bring the others around to his point of view.* [17, 492 f., italics ours]

Such accounts of adolescent groups clarify the observations made earlier, such as those of John Sanders (p. 231) concerning discrepancies in physical and, consequently, in social maturity *as com-*

pared with age mates and the resulting group discrimination against the deviant boy or girl.

It is not difficult to compile detailed items of values concerning popularity and friendship, fads and fashions, and other standards that prevail among adolescent groups and that must be conformed to if an age mate uses such a group as his reference group. For example, Averill [1] gives a two and a half page list of fads prevailing among high school pupils in 1935. [*208–211*] Because of space considerations we cannot, unfortunately, reproduce such lists here. The regulation of adolescent behavior *in relation to* age-mate groups was further verified in a survey made by *Life* magazine. [30] The reporter prefaced his pictures of teen-age girls with this revealing observation:

> It [the adolescent world] is also a world of many laws. They are capricious laws, changing or reversing themselves almost overnight. But while they are in effect, the laws are immutable and the punishment for violation is ostracism, swift and terrifying practise of ancient peoples. Months ago colored bobby sox folded at the top were decreed, not by anyone or any group, but, as usual, by a sudden mysterious and universal acceptance of the new idea. Now no teen-ager dares wear anything but pure white sox without a fold. [30, *91*]

Such observations are not confined to adolescent girls. Another *Life* survey [32] of teen-age boys gives a similar picture:

> Wherever they are seen, teen-age boys have a comfortable, sloppy look. Their sloppiness is not haphazard but is governed by definite though changing sets of fashions. The current style for daily wear as evidenced by the boys of Des Moines consists of a loud flannel shirt, heavy white athletic socks, and, if possible, wavy hair. [32, *92*]

The urgent necessity of age-mate contacts for these teen-age boys is shown in the following comment:

> Many of Des Moines's teen-age boys have jobs after school but all of them feel that life would be unbearable without at least four hours of "fooling around" every day. Fooling around consists of many things: of carrying out some club ritual, of playing rummy or a game of catch or teasing girls or holding a bull session under the awning in front of the drugstore. [32, *96*]

In their intensive study of 100 adolescent boys and 100 girls in California, Stolz, M. C. Jones and Chaffey [41] drew definite conclusions regarding the influence of age-mate reference groups:

> As we look back over this three-year period during which we have measured, questioned, watched these youngsters in the early stages of adolescent development, certain changes in interests, attitudes, and activities seem to have accompanied the physical changes and to be more or less typical of the group. One of the outstanding facts that we have noticed about these children as they grow into adolescence is their preoccupation with social activities. There is an overwhelming desire among these typical junior high school children to be with other children, to understand themselves in their relations to others in their age group. . . . There are several characteristics of this phase of social awareness which distinguish it from the play of younger children and from the social contacts of adults. One of the most potent drives behind this urge for social activity is derived from the youngsters' desire for group approval. To achieve this approval they must adapt themselves to the ways of the group, substituting its standards for those of the home and the school. [41, 2]

It is relevant to our hypothesis to call attention to the fact that these boys and girls are the same adolescents for whom adult approval and disapproval meant almost nothing. (p. 244) The effect of age-mate groups to which the adolescent relates himself may be so strong that the adolescent may even feel apologetic about the interference of his parents. One of the girls studied in this group remarked:

> I am afraid my friends will think I have no controi over my parents. [41, 4]

The more mature group influences start earlier for girls than for boys, paralleling the conclusion reported earlier in this chapter concerning the changing body and changing self. The girls almost drag the boys to social attitudes and interests appropriate to the group. Stolz, Jones and Chaffey [41] state:

> A point to be noted here is that girls begin to display this social awareness and interest in the opposite sex earlier than boys. Probably this age difference would be greater still if boys were allowed to pursue their own course undisturbed. But actually what seems to

happen is this: the girls, feeling the urge to be admired by boys, start hunting for prospects where they are most likely to be found—in the classroom among boys of their own age. Then begins a campaign by the girls to train the boys as good dancing partners and desirable party escorts. Under this tutelage, sometimes resented by the boys, sometimes preeningly accepted, boys develop the required social attitudes about a year later than the girls, many of them earlier, in all probability, than if they were left to their own devices. [41, 5]

The dominance of group interests in the extracurricular activities of adolescents has been observed by Cameron [10] who reports that

> In the fall of the second year no reference to any classroom situation or school subject appeared in our records of conversation or in the "scandal sheets." [10, 23]

In their "self-imposed isolation" from adults, to borrow another characterization from Zachry, appropriate norms may arise due to the group interactions. They may be only short-lived. These norms often seem to serve the function of sanctioning certain activities otherwise prohibited by society at large. The following observation reported by Burks [9] gives a hint in this direction:

> There seems to be a hypothetical danger in the clubhouse institution in the children's lives—a danger that was only suggested by some of the observations. This is the tendency for some of the group (especially the less mature youngsters) to promulgate unacceptable patterns of behavior that *started* in the clubhouse, through association of that behavior with the surroundings and atmosphere of the place where the patterns developed. Such association might lead to a sort of "jelling" of anti-social behavior, which would be further fostered by the inertia of reputation among the clubhouse crowd. [9, 27 f.]

Among the adolescents of families in lower income groups, in which the striving for some sort of social status and the attempt to overcome economic and sex deprivations and unfortunate family backgrounds are all combined together, group conformities may end with more grim consequences. In Cressey's study of the closed dance hall in Chicago [13], he shows how, when deprivations, conflict with grown-ups, thwartings, and uncertainties become strong enough, the adolescent girl may run away to the "closed world" of the dance hall and anchor herself in the groups she finds there. Most of these girls came to the dance hall during adolescence. They came from broken homes and, generally, miserable conditions. Usually, there was severe conflict between the girl and her parents, perhaps because the latter's Old World values were widely divergent from those of the Americanized adolescent. One girl remarked:

> I lived with other dance hall girls, met my fellows at the dance hall, got my living from the dance hall. In fact there was nothing I wanted that I couldn't get through it. [13, *125*]

Another said,

> I don't feel like I belong back in Wisconsin any more. But up at the "school" I just feel at home. . . . I know how things go, I have friends who are always glad to see me come back, and who really are interested enough to spend their money on me. [13, *126*]

Cressey concluded that the "desire for recognition, for status, along with the desire for intimacy or response, and for new experience and excitement, all find some satisfactions in the closed dance hall." [*126*] But, in order to gain these satisfactions, the adolescent girl must become one of the group of dance hall girls. For example, one girl found that the talk in the rest room was disgusting and so she avoided it. As a result, she was razzed by the girls.

> But it didn't take long to get used to things. I gradually got to using their talk and now when I get back there I talk dirty just like the rest of them. [13, *137*]

After she becomes a member of the group, it is not difficult for the girl to turn to prostitution, as frequently happens.

The approval or disapproval of the reference group in regulating the attitudes and interests of adolescents is demonstrated also in the case of youngsters of the leisure class. Here the group attitudes are directed towards maintaining social distinction and class lines. Adolescents tend to anchor themselves in groups composed, for the most part, of boys and girls of their own class. Edith Wharton [45] described such a group in the 1880's:

> Like all agreeable societies, ours was small, and the people composing it met almost every day, and always sought each other out in

any larger company. . . . Our society was, in short, a little "set" with its private catch-words, observances and amusements, and *its indifference to anything outside of its charmed circle*. . . . [45, 79, italics ours]

As Ogden [38] has pointed out, the society sets today have more or less institutionalized the atmosphere in which their children are brought to adolescence through the private boarding school.

The homogeneous character of the student body is conducive to the development of a class sense of cohesion. [38, 34]

Naturally, this limits the choice of friends.

She [the society girl] *is cordial without discrimination to everyone who is accepted in her sphere of society; she is snobbish to outsiders.* . . . She is afraid of the censure of her crowd. [38, 54, italics ours]

When a society girl makes her debut, at eighteen, she may become a member of the Junior League, which, although not requiring a debut for membership, is generally composed of girls who have made debuts. The Junior League, purportedly organized for charitable purposes, seems actually to serve as a meeting ground of friends, where the young girl carves a niche for herself and may stay until she is too old to belong.

Similarly, college fraternities and sororities serve as groups of "distinction." As one writer [6] comments:

The word, "sorority," connoting culture, refinement, social polish, has become synonymous with campus prestige. [6, 31]

This same writer tells of personal experiences in a well-known college sorority in which the importance of maintaining the prestige of the sorority was so great that it was worth severe financial strain. An "unorganized" college man [24] tells how the attitudes generated in the fraternity reference group cut across group antagonisms between fraternities:

I soon found out that the student body was separated by a wide and formidable gulf: the fraternity members as a whole and the independent or non-fraternity group. The first group stalked over the campus as though they were God's chosen children, and in most cases refused to have any association with the despised majority, of which I was one. [24, 30]

Student offices were ordinarily held by fraternity men, elected by the amalgamated efforts of the fraternities. And when an "honor system" with no supervision for examinations was proposed, the "frat" boys united to push it through so that "the scholastic standing of the house . . . [would be] considered honorable." [30]

We must not ignore individual cases of strong identification seen in intense crushes, love, or hero worship. In such instances, ego-attitudes are shaped and oriented in many different ways as determined by the identification with the lover, sweetheart, or hero. Usually, the loved persons are individuals in the reference group or the heroes worshipped are persons with high social prestige, in the current opinion of the reference group. Even in such cases of intense individual identification, the norms of the reference group still exert a significant influence on the ego-attitudes of the individual. However, if the idol is a person out of the reference group, then the individual adolescent becomes a social misfit in his or her immediate adolescent surroundings. Stolz, M. C. Jones, and Chaffey [41] report cases of high school girls who fell in love with older men outside of their own adolescent milieu with the intention of marrying them and who became socially blind to their immediate age-mate surroundings. [7] Not only did these adolescent girls satisfy their sex urges but they established themselves psychologically at least by means of these identifications.

The way in which these strong identifications with persons (living or dead) who are outside the current prestige scale of the immediate age-mate group may make an individual a social misfit in his social milieu is nicely illustrated by a case described by Hollingworth. [20] A 14-year-old boy

> . . . began to appear in his classes and at meals, wearing his hat. He steadfastly refused to remove his headgear at the request of parents and teachers. This idiosyncrasy caused his anxious mother several sleepless nights. Eventually a teacher more discerning than others obtained the lad's confidential account of his peculiar action. He would not remove his hat, because William Penn (his model for the moment) had refused to take his hat off in assemblies! [20, 179]

But even such exceptional cases do not vitiate our hypothesis. For besides any sexual or other functions such outside heroes may serve, they do serve the function of establishing the adolescent psychologically and at least for the time being as a person in his or her own right.

The effect of age-mate membership groups on ego-attitudes. In our account of the re-formation of the ego in adolescence, we first put the problem in its broad social setting. This gave us the perspective necessary to realize the impact of special socioeconomic variations in producing variations in ego problems, making the process more difficult in some societies than in others, prolonging it more in certain societies than in others. We saw how the difficulties and complications involved in the transition from childhood to adulthood led to adult–youth conflict. This, in turn, led to intensified efforts on the part of the adolescents to achieve independence from adults and to establish themselves as persons in their own right. We saw how adolescents gravitate towards each other, forming age-mate groups that become of supreme importance in their lives at least during this transition period. Whatever status value the adolescent genuinely experiences during this time of transition is derived from his standing in this reference group of age mates.

The age-mate reference group, however, defines identifications and personal preferences only in broad outlines and only for standards and fads common to all who relate themselves to these groups. In the "self-imposed" psychological isolation of the adolescent, further differentiation spontaneously takes place. Strong friendships or cliques of two, three, or more adolescents emerge on the basis of common secrets (sexual and otherwise), common desires, common problems, common interests such as those based on family background, school activities, and the like. In such group formations, the members share secrets which they cannot and dare not share with others, especially grown-ups. Certain roles arise prescribing the relative standing of members to each other. Certain expectations are produced which prescribe mutual loyalties and responsibilities. Certain badges of belongingness, certain catchwords, and even norms (though perhaps short lived) arise, leading to attitudes appropriate for group members.

Such cliques, as Jones, Zachry, and others have pointed out, are formed first among girls and then among boys. (Another fact that demonstrates the earlier social maturity of girls following their earlier physical maturation.) The formation of cliques or gangs made up of both sexes may follow. In some cases, the clique formations of two or three close friends may serve as nuclei around which large gangs are formed. Such cliques or gangs may survive for a shorter or longer period owing to the more or less "mercurial nature" of adolescents' relationships. These cliques or gangs may be more or less confidential or secret formations, depending on the character of the activities in which they engage and the degree of conflict with adults and various institutions. The clique or gang gains solidarity in proportion to the resistances it meets and withstands. So long as they last, these cliques or gangs demand conformity and loyalty from their members. Individuals who do not conform are ostracized or discriminated against. The status maintained in the clique or gang is the main source of ego-satisfaction. The sense of group belongingness in the clique or gang brings a feeling of personal stability or security in proportion to the degree of psychological weaning from parents or the intensity of parent–youth conflict.

Many authors in the field of adolescence have given accounts of the importance of such clique or gang formations or have called attention to the way in which they determine the character of adolescent attitudes and identifications. Out of a host of such reports we shall choose only a few representative examples. Goodenough [17] points out the significance of the solidarity and group consciousness that prevail among gang members:

> Not only does the adolescent, as a rule, begin to show a new interest in the opposite sex, but a new element appears in his relationships with persons of his own sex. This is the formation of clubs or gangs. It is, of course, true that long before the age of adolescence children play together in groups and form special friendships that give these groups something of a lasting character. But *in most cases the social groups formed by young children lack the solidarity and the feeling of group-consciousness that characterize the adolescent gang or club.* [17, 491, italics ours]

Wile [47] generalizes as follows concerning the importance of adolescent groups:

Much of adolescent adjustment depends upon the relative degree of self-consciousness and group consciousness. It also rests upon the acceptance of oneself as part of the group and the willingness to identify the demands of the group as in harmony with one's own needs. Herein appears the potential significance of group pressures, seeking to bring about adolescent conformity with the mores of the age. *Every group that invites adolescents to unite with it bids them live in accord with group sanctions—and each group is concerned with its own goals and principles which may not be in the interest of society as a whole. Every social group molds adolescents in direct ratio to their participation.* Adolescent groups naturally are most directive and may be coercive. The gang and the club, as sub-sections of society, exert their influence for or against the ruling principles of the world of grown-ups. The shifting morals of each age help to determine the extent of the fight of society for, and of youth against, specific indoctrinations. Concepts of right and wrong, good and bad, moral and immoral, decent and indecent, constitute a risk for all acceptances extending beyond the simple ideas that continually find favor among adolescents upon the basis of reasonable tradition. [47, 4 f., italics ours]

Zachry [49] points to some of the factors which make gang standards become the adolescent's own standards:

It is significant also that in his compliance with gang standards he is taking a step toward self-determination in conduct, since this group is made up not of those who are much larger and stronger than he but of those who are like him in appearance, capacities, and interests. Thus these standards are more nearly his own than were those which he acquired so early that he does not remember how this came about, and some of which he is now relinquishing for the time being at least. [49, 163 f.]

The formation of adolescent gangs and the function they serve are clearly stated by Peter Blos [5]:

In early adolescence the formation of gangs represents the beginning of a group life which has its own distinctive characteristics. [5, 249]

A few pages later, Blos writes:

It offers him in return a security in group belongingness and in collective responsibility at a time when he is abandoning childhood relationships and reorienting himself in terms of mature goals. *In response to the pressures of peer culture, his family patterns of relationship, identification, and feeling life are gradually modified in the direction of group norms.* [5, 254, italics ours]

Commenting on the resistance these norms and their conforming behavior encounter from grown-ups, Blos points out the difficult state of marginality the adolescent experiences in his efforts to establish himself:

> Such adult indifference or hostility towards the adolescent's treasured peer standards raises a further difficulty: if he is loyal to his group, he denies himself adult acceptance and approval; if he complies with adult demands, evading the possibility of asserting his independence, he loses the recognition of his peers. [5, 254]

We shall be concerned again in the next chapter with the unpleasant consequences of marginality or conflicting identifications.

These representative statements are not mere armchair speculations of authorities. As we shall see from the illustrations in this and the next chapter, they are amply substantiated by factual evidence.

The systematic observations of the social activities and groupings in a high school clubhouse during the years 1936–37 unmistakably show clique and gang formations. We should like to call attention to the fact that the situation in the clubhouse was not altogether free from adult supervision. F. W. Burks [9], who summarized the clubhouse observations, expresses the formation of adolescent cliques or gangs in terms of "social stratification." [9]

> One of the most notable manifestations of the adolescent group, which began during this year, and continued during the following years after the clubhouse was closed, was the differentiation into distinct social strata, between which there was little real intercourse and each of which built up its own barriers, defenses, and feelings of solidarity. [9, 16]

When once formed, these groups, which generated "a growing feeling of cliquishness," demanded that their members behave

[9] We should prefer to save the term "social stratification" to designate major class delineations in society at large in terms of the individual's role in the processes of production, distribution, and the like: for example, as employer or employed.

within the bounds of the group standards and keep in step with them. Those who went beyond these bounds were ostracized or discriminated against.

The approaches made by "novices" to be accepted by those who have already established themselves were observed.

> In addition to the rising stratification on the basis of prestige in the social hierarchy of the school, there were also other bases for discrimination and feelings of superiority. One of the most striking was degree of social maturity, the less mature boys feeling at a disadvantage with more experienced ones, hesitating to assert themselves, or even to stand up for their rights. The less mature were subject to disapproval for some of their activities by the "older" group; and frequently compensated for their feelings of inferiority by swaggering attempts to appear grown-up. [9, 19]

On the basis of such observations, Harold Jones [25] points out the difficulties experienced by non-clique members or leftovers:

> The social stratification encountered in high school affected the girls much more than the boys. Yet it was the boys more than the girls from Jackson Junior High who were outspoken about the treatment which they received at the hands of the cliques. Although certain positions (such as student body president) were available to students who were not members of these exclusive groups, other offices dealing with the school social functions were traditionally filled by a "club" member. [25, 22]

Jones gives a concise and concrete picture of such clique formations in the form of Moreno sociograms obtained from actual data. He titles this section "Group Structures." Here we reproduce sociograms showing the interpersonal relationships of boys and girls approximately 15 years old.[10] It can be clearly seen from Figure 1 that among the girls in the high ninth grade, "the social structure, at this age level, consisted of a number of compact and somewhat separated groups or cliques." [43] This compact

---

[10] These sociograms are reproduced from Campbell's study [11] with the permission of the author. They are also reproduced by Jones [25, 44]. The sociograms were constructed from the results of an item on the "Guess Who" test asking for the subject's "best friends." The dark lines represent reciprocal mentions of "best friends," while the broken lines represent mentions not reciprocated.

cliquishness is not evident in the sociogram for boys at this age level (Figure 2). This fact shows once more the earlier social maturity of girls. It would be interesting to trace the interpersonal relationships of boys a year or so older. We should guess that clique formations among the boys would also increase when they reached a corresponding level of social maturity.

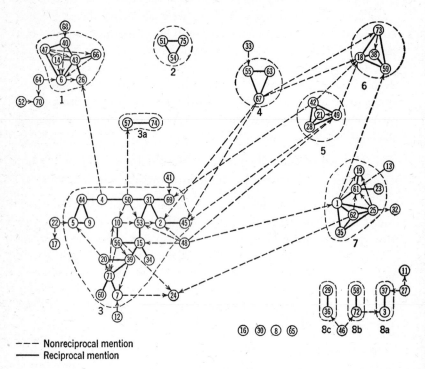

--- Nonreciprocal mention
— Reciprocal mention

FIG. 1. Best friends—girls.

Analysis of the consequences of being "left over," or of having no established standing in the reference group and no membership in a closely knit clique, shows in clear-cut fashion the psychological properties that arise in group membership or from group identification. This is revealed in the case of John Sanders, studied by Jones and his associates. John is the same boy referred to previously in our discussion of the changing body and changing self. In comparison to his age mates, he was retarded a year or so in his physical development. We have already noted the important psychological consequences of such retardment. In Figure 2 John is represented by circle 78 in the upper right corner of the sociogram. As can be readily seen, he was in a peripheral social situation. He felt the unpleasant experience, the insecurity

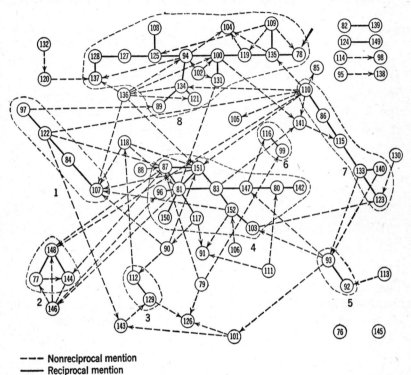

--- Nonreciprocal mention
— Reciprocal mention

FIG. 2. Best friends—boys.

of his peripheral state in relation to his immediate reference group. At this time, he was at the high point of unpopularity among his age mates, in spite of the fact that he made "unsuccessful attempts to gain attention and to identify himself with his classmates." [57]

John is obviously the kind of person with whom no girl would go out, if she thought she had prestige to maintain. Even girls who are fairly independent in their attitudes toward their social position would feel that they *couldn't* descend to go out with John Sanders! Perhaps the chief reason for this is his lack of a functional familiarity with social patterns; he tries hard to conform to these standards of the adolescent culture, but is still an outsider wistfully looking in. [25, 57]

This statement was verified by Tryon's research [44] on the popularity of boys and girls 15 years old in this same social milieu, perhaps these very boys and girls:

> Boys, to be successful with girls, must be admired by boys. . . . [44, 565]

John's "unskillfulness in activities enjoyed by other boys marked him as 'queer'; it made for social isolation, and his response to this lowered status was to develop characteristics which further increased his unpopularity." [159 f.] This social isolation from the group was deeply resented by John himself. As he expressed it to his counselor in his senior year in high school:

> The greatest mistake I ever made was not spending more time on the playgrounds. I should have been made to do it. Boys don't like you unless you can play games. It affects your whole personality. [25, 103]

John was interested in art, perhaps as a compensation for his lack of athletic prowess and other activities popular among the boys of his reference group. And he was pretty good at it. But among his age mates at the early years of adolescence, artistic accomplishment was not a criterion used in judging acceptability. As we saw before, after John's delayed "adolescent spurt" took place, his popularity also jumped up. The consequences for John's popularity of this "adolescent spurt" and the changing interests of the group in later adolescent years are concisely formulated by Jones:

> In later adolescence these deficiencies became of smaller importance, partly because of changing social values and partly also because of a process of maturing that is expressed in social structures as well as in organisms. The naïve likemindedness characteristic of a younger group broadens, at a later age, into a greater variety of special interests. Special sympathies and appreciations in this more differentiated society give the individual a greater range of choice—a greater opportunity to select his own appropriate environment. . . . Thus, the more favorable situation and prognosis for John, as he reached the end of senior high school, were due partly to changes in John as he laboriously caught up with the group, but we must give credit also to

changes in the group as they caught up with John, and as their values and standards of achievement came closer to the sober aspirations which John had always held important. [25, *160 f.*]

In Burks' summary [9] of the Tugwell clubhouse, more evidence of changing values within the adolescent reference group is given. For example, as the group became older, the clubhouse no longer served as the center of activities. As standards of amusement become more sophisticated, such as attendance at night clubs and country clubs, the clubhouse was occupied chiefly by "youngsters who had not been able, because of social immaturity or lack of family 'status' to achieve a place in the various social groups in the high school. . . ." [28] Just as an individual (for example, John Sanders) may be a misfit in his reference group, so too certain cliques may be generally looked down on as "queer." In the clubhouse, the art group "had no prestige with the general crowd," because its activities did not fit into the dominant values current among the larger adolescent group. Whatever the difficulties involved in belonging to a low prestige group, still, as Burks remarks, at least a member would avoid the "thwarted feeling" of having no group at all.

Group formations, such as those found in the California studies, are not artifacts of biased observation. Such groups and cliques can be found in concrete observations of everyday life. *Life* magazine [30] had one of its reporters make a picture survey of an adolescent clique composed of 12 girls from 15 to 17 years old. The survey reveals that all of these girls "go to the same school, take the same courses, know the same people and generally exhibit the passionate uniformity of a teen-age clique." [*92 f.*] These girls spent most of their time together, exchanged confidences, spent long hours on the telephone. Group solidarity and loyalty "keeps the girls firmly united against all protest" from grown-ups concerning their activities or current fads.

Another *Life* survey [31], made in Indianapolis, revealed that the currently prevalent "Sub-Deb Clubs" serve the same psychological function as does any spontaneously formed adolescent clique. Any group of girls may form a Sub-Deb Club which is free from adult supervision. At the time of the survey (1945) there were in Indianapolis 700 such clubs with some 6,000 members.

Sub-Deb Clubs have meetings and initiations and even print news-papers, but their main purpose is to have parties. In Indianapolis they are enormously successful in achieving this purpose. One reason is that single girls might be shy about asking boys to parties but clubs of girls can be downright aggressive. [31, *91*]

This comment of *Life's* reporter is similar to those made by Stolz, M. C. Jones, and Chaffey [41] in California, indicating that the girls, earlier in maturing, tend to "drag" the boys into social activi-ties. These cliques, like many gangs, have names and even pins which serve to strengthen the group and give an identification to in-group members. Some of these names are clues to the changing interests of these adolescent girls. For example, *Swami* stands for "Subtle Women are Most Intriguing"; *Jilts* means "Jump in Line to Smooch"; *Genius, Inc.* refers to the talents of its drama-loving members; while the meaning of *Glama* is the secret of the mem-bers alone.

Although these Sub-Deb Clubs are not exclusively secret socie-ties, the members do share confidences. Goodenough [17] writes:

> The girl's club is less likely to center around any particular activity. Its members, however, share among themselves various "secrets," bits of gossip, and so on to which they often refer mysteriously in the presence of outsiders in the hope of arousing curiosity and envy. [17, *492*]

It has frequently been noted that in the United States there is relatively greater secrecy in the clique activities among girls than among boys, due perhaps to the more conflicting ego-attitudes of femininity.

Campbell's research [11] has already been mentioned in con-nection with Jones's discussion of group structures. Although Campbell specifically studied adolescent opinions of classmates of their own and the opposite sex, her results also have implications concerning the problem of clique formation among boys and girls. Reference to Figures 1 and 2 taken from Campbell's study show that "cliques of two, three or more individuals seem to be fairly descriptive of the girls," while the boys of this age tend to associ-ate in "chains" of friendship, not in cliques. We would be in-clined to agree with Campbell's conclusion that most of these sex differences are related to "the greater physiological and social maturity of the girls," and that consideration of boys of an equal level of maturity would reveal more similar results. However, in line with our hypothesis that the degree of absorption in and the degree of solidarity of age-mate groupings varies with the degree of conflict, some questions posed by Campbell may be considered.

> Do women in our culture feel less security of independent status so that there is greater need of the ego support derived from identification with a group? What is the effect on personality? Are women more conservative in their ideas, more responsive to personal influence and loyalties? . . . Does this type of organization tend toward a stereotyping of personality, interests, attitudes, opinions? [11, *150*]

In view of material on gang formation presented in the next chapter, we can safely say that the greater cliquish tendency found among 15-year-old girls in California in this study is not *always* in *all* strata of society, under *all* conditions, greater than for boys. Additional research on older adolescents comparable to the upper and middle class children in this study would give valuable clues relevant to the preceding hypothesis concerning the degree of absorption in, the solidarity, and the secrecy of adolescent groups.

Like any other group at any age level, an adolescent group, once formed and stabilized, demands conformity and loyalty (identification) from individual members. The status members really experience is derived largely from their standing in the clique or gang and is proportional to the degree of their identification with the clique or gang. Behavior that is *for them* proper and improper, decent and indecent is regulated by the current group norms, as long as they last and as long as the individual enjoys group membership. From an unpublished California study,[11] we cite a concrete case showing the observance of an adolescent girl of rigid norms governing the acceptance of dates:

> With respect to the group codes connected with "going steady" she seems to have accepted all the necessary accompaniments—"I can't go out with Fred on Friday." (Fred was coming to see her for a date she had had for some time.) "So I just told him that I couldn't go

[11] Unpublished material used through the kindness of Harold and Mary Cover Jones.

out with him and if he comes it's just too bad!" When I suggested tentatively the *possibility* of breaking the date with her new "steady" she responded with immediate certainty that that just couldn't be done "because I'm going steady now and I just can't go out with anybody else."

Although activity can proceed at a rapid pace, limits to behavior are prescribed by group norms. If anybody goes beyond these bounds he is put within the bounds again. This is keenly observed by Cameron [10] in his study of 200 junior high school pupils:

> To have news value, the competition of boys and girls for popularity with members of the opposite sex, must be expressed in exaggerated, daring, and exciting terms. But their verbal freedom is in general divorced by a wide margin from their actions; so that, for example, anyone who became really interested in heavy petting was ostracized from this group. [10, 20]

Similarly, the reporter who made the picture survey of a high school clique for *Life* [30] includes pictures showing that a member of the clique runs the danger of ostracism if she is *too* interested in boys, puts herself in their midst ignoring the girls, "necks" at movies, or has *too* many dates. Cameron observes further:

> Let anyone get conceited about his status, or ride too high on a wave of popularity, and without warning a torrent of invectives will be let loose. With merciless directness and intolerance the offending person's prestige is battered into shreds and he is left to fend for himself in getting back into the group. [10, 22]

In the next chapter we shall elaborate our account of the structural properties arising in spontaneously formed groups or gangs. We shall give there concrete illustrations of the impact of these structural properties of groups on the identifications, loyalties, and attitudes of the individual members. Investigators, both in psychology and sociology, who studied the behavior of the individual member in adolescent gangs or groups, have furnished invaluable data which are ripe for a social psychological conceptualization. We include here only a few more examples to show the serious individual consequences that can result from allegiance to group norms.

The concrete cases studied by Thomas [42] highlight the serious effects such group memberships can have on the behavior of some unfortunate youngsters.

> It frequently happens also that a girl is drawn or drifts out of her family and community into a bad gang, as in the case No. 78, becomes identified with them by assimilation, and cannot free herself. She may then be kept by one of the men or sold into a house. Cases No. 79 and No. 80 are typical of the psychology of the girl in this relation. [42, *142*]

Augusta Jameson [23] who actually lived with a group of delinquent girls without identifying herself with the authorities until she secured the girls' confidence, secured 29 autobiographies and questionnaires from 106 delinquent girls. These questionnaires were made through the aid of some of the girls themselves, and were given twice, four months apart. Correlations between the test and retest were "very high." Basing her findings on this material plus "agency, institutional, and court records; and some upon physical, psychiatric, and psychological examinations," Jameson concludes:

> In general there appears to be a vague pattern, an outline of successive incidents, and conditions, in these girls' lives. These various stages do not necessarily occur singly but often in combination with previous or subsequent ones. [23, *30*]

Among these conditions, Jameson lists the following which indicate the effects of age-mate groups:

> Failure of the family and the community to offer normal socially accepted satisfactions for their personal needs. . . . Existence in the community of an apparently congenial group of young people participating in overt sex activity. . . . Initiatory experiences of the girl in the sex group, frequently accompanied by fear and unpleasantness, but necessary as a "price of admission," to this group whose members appear to be having adequate satisfactions. . . . Adoption by the girl of the pattern of sex delinquency defined by the group. [23, *31*]

Jameson then concludes:

> It is the writer's impression that the delinquency of these girls has been a normal, natural process, resulting from the type of social stimuli

to which they have been exposed. From the girls' standpoint, their delinquency has represented an opportunity for securing the human satisfactions which in more conventional social situations are secured in more socially approved forms of conduct. [23, 31]

Such group determinations of more or less consequential types of behavior are amply illustrated in the next chapter.

SOME IMPLICATIONS OF THE FOREGOING MATERIAL FOR OUR PROBLEM

Before closing our sketchy account of the psychology of the re-formation of the ego during adolescence, a concise statement of the main trend that stands out, especially in the last sections, will provide a useful clarification. This trend has serious implications that have to be accounted for in any psychology of what is usually designated in a loose way as "ego drives"—an important domain in the field of motivation. As was hinted before, the appallingly long and disconnected lists of adolescent attitudes and interests will gain a coherent scheme of conceptualization if they are studied *first* in relation to the individual boy's or girl's reference groups in general and membership groups in particular. For the adolescent derives his major attitudes and interests from the reference groups to which he relates himself. As we have seen before, the norms of these reference groups become his attitudes. The major status problems for him arise in relation to his reference groups in general and to his membership groups in particular. His identifications, loyalties, and conformities are, in a major way, determined in relation to them. His main concern, for the time being at least, is to establish himself, to have a standing in his reference and membership groups, even though they may change in different periods. The consequences of this concern define in an important way many aspects of his ego problems.

Of course, any standing in the reference group or membership group will not do. Individual members strive to achieve better standing in their group due to the factors of individual differences in temperament, intelligence, ability, and in many other dimensions. These individual differences may lead to varieties of continuous efforts to better relative standing in the group, may cause frictions among the members, may end in discriminations, ostracisms, and such. However, all of these effects of individual differences take place within the terms of group loyalty and conformity prescribed by the group norms, whatever their character and direction may be in the particular social and class setting in which the individual moves. If he displays behavior altogether incompatible with the bounds of group characteristics, he is simply out; he becomes an outsider. In some cases, any status in the group is of more value to the individual than loss of the sense of belongingness, especially if he is in conflict with unfortunate family circumstances. (p. 298) All of these conclusions indicate that the all important factors of individual differences have meaning in group situations as they relate to the relative standing of the individual member. For the experts in the field of clinical psychology or those who are mainly concerned with the therapeutics of individual cases, behavior difficulties due to individual differences may be the major concern. It surely is our business to keep in touch with the findings of these psychologists. However, for the social psychologist, no matter how unique and colorful these individual factors may be, the main concern *first* should be the situational determinations of group interactions and the psychological properties that arise as a consequence in the individual members. The result of multitudes of experiments have probably made it quite clear by this time that the individual behaves differently in group situations. This fact deserves to be noted, by the social psychologist especially, with the same importance as any fact of individual differences.

If the adolescent's efforts to achieve some stability for an ego which has been rendered more insecure and more unstable during the process of transition, if his strivings to establish himself are studied in terms of the demands of his reference and membership groups, perhaps elaborately formulated lists of drives to account for the ego-strivings of adolescents will become superfluous. For example, in one of the recent accounts of adolescent drives, we find the following items: "Drive for Autonomy, Drive for Social Ties (Social Acceptance), Drive for Achievement, Drive for Recognition, Drive for Abasement, Drive for Aggression, Drive for

'Succorance,' Drive for Control (Dominance), Drive for Escape."
This impressive list certainly looks like a refined elaboration of
McDougall. But by increasing the list of drives or needs and
thus compartmentalizing them, the functional relationships displayed in behavior manifestations aimed at achieving a desired
status are not clarified. We should think rather that they are
obscured.

What an adolescent, with the unstable and more or less transi-
tory state of his ego links and with the more or less confused
character of his ego aspirations, is striving to achieve, is to stabilize
his ego-values—to amount to something or to anchor his ego
securely—*in relation to his reference group, whatever this may be
to him in his particular social milieu.* In order to achieve this, he
has to and he wants to identify himself with the group or groups
in question. He does his level best to incorporate (in his ego
which is, we repeat, a genetic formation) the norms of the group,
whatever they may be in his particular social setting. He has to
and he wants to conform to them in his behavior. If conformity
to these norms is achieved by ruthless competition and individualism, he does his level best to be competitive and individualistic to
the limits of his capacity. If the norms of his group put a great
premium on being co-operative, he does his best to be co-operative.
Within the bounds of these prescribed directions, individual
differences operate, sometimes to extremes of various kinds of
morbidity.

For example, a Samoan, a Zuni, a Bathonga adolescent [34]
will do his best, for the sake of his ego, to display individualistic
behavior as little as possible. Perhaps an adolescent in these groups
would never dream, for the sake of his ego, of exhibiting behavior
displayed by the members of an exclusive fraternity or sorority
oriented towards greater achievements of social distinction and
individuality. In a culture in which cooking is considered a
greater mark of distinction, a woman will be less lured by com-
pliments directed to, say, a Greer Garson.[12] Anybody who is
familiar with behavior manifestations in different societies can

[12] An actual observation communicated to the authors by Irving A. Hallowell
of Northwestern University.

give hundreds of examples of functional variations in ego-striv-ings. In one, self-assertiveness may be effective in achieving the de-sired status; in another, submission and inconspicuousness may be more effective in establishing one's self in his group. In a society in which "male and female human natures" are judged by double standards, strong masculine characteristics may raise one's appeal value as a person. In the same society, coyness and submissiveness may raise a woman's appeal value as a person.

In short the developing ego, which is a genetic formation itself, or the re-forming ego in adolescence, has to be anchored securely and in a relatively high standing in relation to one's group. Whether this will be achieved by being assertive or submissive, by being individualistic or co-operative, by the attainment of this or that sort of personal virtues and accomplishments, will vary ac-cording to the demands and pressures of one's own reference group in general and membership group in particular.

In these chapters, we have given a few functional variations of adolescent strivings to establish one's self in his group. In the next chapter we shall cite some more concrete illustrations. Scientific concepts are certainly the variables with which investigators in various fields deal with their data. However, if the constructs or concepts come in to confuse issues and to compartmentalize arti-ficially the functional relationships of these variables, they render no scientific service, to say the least.

REFERENCES

1. AVERILL, L. A., *Adolescence: A Study in the Teen Years*, Boston: Houghton Mifflin, copyright 1936.
2. BALDWIN, B. T., *The Physical Growth of Children from Birth to Maturity*, Univ. Iowa Stud.: Stud. in Child Welfare, vol. 1, no. 1.
3. BAYLEY, N., The adolescent growth study: III. Skeletal X-rays as indicators of maturity, *J. Consult. Psychol.*, 1940, **4**, 69–73.
4. —— and R. TUDDENHAM, Adolescent changes in body build, *43rd Yearbook, National Society for the Study of Education*, 1944, 33–55.
5. BLOS, P., *The Adolescent Personality, A Study of Individual Behavior*, New York: Appleton-Century, copyright 1941.
6. BRADLEY, P., The touch system among coeds, *Real America*, 1934, **4**, 31 f.
7. BROOKS, F. D., *The Psychology of Adolescence*, Boston: Riverside Press, 1929.
8. BÜHLER, C., The social behavior of children, in *Handbook of Child Psychology* (C. Murchison, ed.), Worcester: Clark Univ., 1933, 2d ed., 374–416.

9. Burks, F. W., *The Tugwell High School Clubhouse* (*1936–37*), unpublished, Univ. California, Inst. Child Welfare.

10. Cameron, W. J., *A Study of Social Development in Adolescence,* unpublished, Univ. California, Inst. of Child Welfare.

11. Campbell, H. M., *Sex differences obtained by the "Guess Who" technique in reputation assessments given and received by adolescent boys and girls,* thesis on file in Library, Univ. California, 1941.

12. Conklin, E. S., *Principles of Adolescent Psychology,* New York: Holt, copyright 1935.

13. Cressey, P. G., *The Closed Dance Halls in Chicago,* thesis on file in Library, Univ. Chicago, 1929.

14. Davis, A., and J. Dollard, *Children of Bondage,* Washington: Am. Council on Education, 1940.

15. Davis, K., The sociology of parent–youth conflict, *Am. Sociol. Rev.,* 1940, **5,** 523–35.

16. Gardner, G. E., Sex behavior of adolescents in wartime, *Ann. Am. Acad. Pol. and Soc. Sci.,* 1944, **236,** 60–6.

17. Goodenough, F. L., *Developmental Psychology,* New York: Appleton-Century, copyright 1945.

18. Greulich, W. W., Promising leads for research in problems of adolescence, *Proc. Second Bienn. Meet. of Soc. Research in Child Development,* Washington, 1936, 13–14.

19. Healy, W., *Personality in Formation and Action,* New York: Norton, copyright 1938.

20. Hollingworth, L., *The Psychology of the Adolescent,* New York: Appleton, copyright 1928.

21. —— The adolescent child, in *Handbook of Child Psychology* (C. Murchison, ed.), Worcester: Clark Univ., 1933, 2d ed, 882–908.

22. Hoskins, R. G., *The Tides of Life,* New York: Norton, 1933.

23. Jameson, A. T., Psychological factors contributing to the delinquency of girls, *J. Juvenile Research,* 1938, **22,** 25–32.

24. Jannis, J., Brothers under the gin, *Real America,* 1934, **4,** 30 f.

25. Jones, H. E., *Development in Adolescence,* New York: Appleton-Century, copyright 1943.

26. Kirkpatrick, C., A comparison of generations in regard to attitudes toward feminism, *J. Genet. Psychol.,* 1936, **49,** 343–61.

27. —— Inconsistency in attitudinal behavior with special reference to attitudes toward feminism, *J. Appl. Psychol.,* 1936, **20,** 535–52.

28. Kitay, P. M., A comparison of the sexes in their attitudes and beliefs about women: a study of prestige groups, *Sociometry,* 1940, **3,** 399–407.

29. Komarovsky, M., *The Unemployed Man and His Family,* New York: Dryden, 1940.

30. *Life,* Teen-age Girls, December 11, 1944, **17,** no. 24, 91–9.

31. —— Sub-Deb Clubs, April 2, 1945, **18,** no. 14, 87–93.

32. —— Teen-age Boys, June 11, 1945, **18,** no. 24, 91–7.

33. Lynd, R. S., and H. M. Lynd, *Middletown in Transition,* New York: Harcourt, Brace, copyright 1937.

34. Mead, M. (ed.), *Cooperation and Competition Among Primitive Peoples,* New York: McGraw-Hill, 1937.

35. Mizanoglu, N., *A Study of Psychological Development During Adolescence,* unpublished, on file in Library, Univ. Ankara, Turkey.

36. *New York World-Telegram,* March 22, 1946.

37. Ogden, E., Regulation of circulation at adolescence, *Proc. of Second Bienn. Meet. of Soc. Research in Child Development,* Washington, 1936, 121–4.

38. Ogden, M. B., *The Social Orientation of the Society Girl,* thesis on file in Library, Univ. Chicago, 1938.

39. Schwab, S. I., and B. S. Veeder, *The Adolescent: His Conflicts and Escapes,* New York: Appleton, 1929.

40. Seward, G. H., Cultural conflict and the feminine role: an experimental study, *J. Soc. Psychol.,* 1945, **22,** 177–94.

41. Stolz, H. R., M. C. Jones, and J. Chaffey, The junior high school age, *Univ. High School J.,* 1937, **15,** 63–72.

42. Thomas, W. I., *The Unadjusted Girl,* Boston: Little, Brown, copyright 1927.

43. Tryon, C. M., Evaluations of adolescent personality by adolescents, *Monogr. Soc. for Research in Child Development,* 1939, **4,** no. 4.

44. —— Evaluations of adolescent personality by adolescents, in *Child Behavior and Development* (R. G. Barker, J. S. Kounin, H. F. Wright, eds.), New York: McGraw-Hill, copyright 1943, 545–66.

45. Wharton, E., *A Backward Glance,* New York: Appleton-Century, copyright 1934.

46. White, R. W., The personality of Joseph Kidd. I. History of an adolescent crisis in the development of ego-structure, *Character and Personality,* 1943, **11,** 183–208.

47. Wile, I. S., *The Challenge of Adolescence,* New York: Greenberg, copyright 1939.

48. Winch, R. F., *Social and Personality Characteristics of Courtship Revealed in College Men,* thesis on file in Library, Univ. Chicago, 1942.

49. Zachry, C. B., *Emotion and Conduct in Adolescence,* New York: Appleton-Century, copyright 1940.

CHAPTER 10

EGO-INVOLVEMENTS AND IDENTIFICATIONS IN GROUP SITUATIONS

It has become almost a truism by now that group interaction produces differential results in the experience and behavior of individuals participating in a group situation. Before we take up the problem of ego-involvements and identifications in group situations, we shall call attention to the psychological properties generated in group situations. Whether organized or not, when two or more (say, five hundred individuals) interact in a situation, psychologically speaking, we have a group. The size of the interacting group will, of course, greatly affect the characteristics of the group, as, for example, its compellingness for the individual members. A group will function differently depending on whether it is spontaneous or organized, homogeneous or heterogeneous. However, without losing sight of special problems these and other variations create, we can still say that essentially the same basic psychological principles are at work in the many variations of group interaction.[1]

At the end of the 19th century and during the first decades of the present century, sociologists were time and again stressing the fact that the individual in group situations no longer experienced and behaved in the same way as he does when in isolation, while psychologists in general preoccupied themselves with a search for the elements of the mind (sensations) before attempting to handle concrete problems of everyday life. Since sociologists received little help from the main body of academic psychology, they tended to formulate their own psychological principles or to advance suprapsychological (supraindividual) doctrines. In the writings of Durkheim [16], Le Bon [24], Blondel [8], Ross [47], Martin [29], La Piere [23], Blumer [9], and others, we find inter-

---

[1] For a discussion of this point, see [56].

esting characterizations of collective behavior. Almost everyone who wrote on collective behavior stressed the general fact that the individual, when in a group, becomes a "different person" than he is in isolation and may indulge in activities not ordinarily expected of him. Some authors emphasize the point that the individual becomes a sadistic beast when in a collective situation (for example, Ross [47]), or releases his brakes altogether to regress completely to the basic instinctive (libidinal) level of psychological functioning (for example, Freud). Others maintained that an individual achieves the highest deeds of altruism while he moves as part and parcel of a collective movement (for example, Durkheim [16]).

Without making a special issue of the positive or negative effects of collective behavior, we shall note in passing that the direction taken by the activities of an interacting group is determined by the factors (motives) that are instrumental in bringing individual members together and the norms arising during the process of interaction. For example, a revolutionary group, emerging as a consequence of disgust felt against reactionary forces and determination to wipe them out, will lead the individuals involved to achieve deeds of genuine selflessness; a lynching party, instigated by reactionary ideology and groups, will commit beastly acts; while an artist or nudist colony in the bohemia of some large city may indulge in acts of orgiastic libidinal satisfactions.

Starting especially with the works of Walter Moede [32] and F. H. Allport [1], psychologists studied differential group effects on many psychological functions (for example, thinking, attention, feeling). In the excellent reviews of Murphy and Murphy [38]; Dashiell [14]; Murphy, Murphy, and Newcomb [39]; we find convenient summaries of the rapidly accumulating investigations concerned with the effect of group situations. In the genetic studies of Piaget and his students, sociometric studies started by Moreno, and the experiments of Lewin and his students, the structural, as contrasted to piecemeal (elementaristic), properties of group situations stand out significantly. We shall review these studies briefly later in this chapter.

Impressed by the fact that in actual social life group norms usually emerge in critical situations, Sherif [55] produced the rise of group norms in an experimentally introduced ambiguous and unstable stimulus situation. (pp. 52 f.) Cantril [11], studying the rise of actual social movements, analyzed the basic psychological principles at work in collective behavior.

If we are ever going to have a social psychology of more or less lasting group situations and group identifications, we must seek the structural properties of group interaction and formation, group products once they are formed, their subsequent effects on the behavior of individual members, and the reciprocal functional relationships between group and individual members. If there are any consistent dynamics involved in group formations and functioning and in the behavior of the individual member, they should be conceptualized on the basis of concrete observations, especially everyday life situations. This should show us the general functional variables of the group–individual relationship in any group situation whatever the particular circumstances may be that give rise to group formations and whatever the particular type of behavior thus determined or altered. Once this is done, it will be comparatively easy to study the specific conditions and factors that enter into the functioning of a particular group and the specific goals to which it is directed.

In this chapter we shall confine ourselves to comparatively small groups and to the rise of norms, ego-involvements, and subsequent identifications in these groups. We shall be concerned chiefly with spontaneously formed small groups (gangs). For in such spontaneously formed small groups, differential group behavior, group products, and identifications are comparatively easily traced. Because of their *relatively* simple nature, adolescent cliques and gangs are in certain respects excellent prototypes of group interaction and formation. We can see in them the emergence of group products, the determination of the behavior of the individual member by group identifications, the generation of group loyalties and pressures. We should, however, make it explicit that gangs are not only adolescent phenomena. Drifting away from the conventional family setting may occur before adolescence, even in early childhood, depending on the degree to which the child identifies himself with his family and other conventional groups or institutions. This identification, in turn, is regulated by complex social and economic factors. However, as we have seen in chapter 7, a certain degree of ego development must take place before a child can relate himself to any group. The rate of this development is undoubtedly affected by many of the same factors influencing the degree to which he later identifies himself with conventional groups.

Already sociologists have amassed many impressive investigations of cliques, gangs, isolated groups, and collective phenomena. These are full of direct implications for the psychological conceptualization of group formation and of those supralocal (supraindividual) properties of group structures which determine the differential behavior of individual members. In their psychological conceptualizations of their own data, sociologists generally have coined their own "psychologies" consistent with the ideas of "human nature" to which their particular ideologies lead them. On the other hand, psychologists, just beginning to face group problems as psychological problems, tend to ignore the vast wealth of sociological data which lend themselves so easily to psychological formulations. It seems that many sociologists, following the erroneous traditional dichotomy between the individual and society, have taken psychology as the apologist of the individual and of "individualism" and have neglected to follow closely the concepts psychologists work with. At the same time, it is surprising that most psychologists investigating group problems have not often bothered to go out of their little worlds and examine the wealth of material already collected by sociologists.

The main theme of this chapter can be briefly summarized here on the basis of the sociological and psychological data, now converging in their implications. The ego of the growing boy or girl develops as a consequence of various contacts with the surrounding physical and socioeconomic milieu. This process defines one's identity as a person, anchors him in a constellation of interpersonal relationships in many capacities. His sense of status and its stability is derived from this constellation of relationships interwoven during the course of genetic development. He carries on his daily activities (for example, his strivings to make a living and still a *better* living) as prescribed by these socially incorporated ego-values. If these ego-values serve the function of regulating his activities in such a way that his basic needs are more or less satisfied and if he feels secure in the constellation of human relationships thus organized, he leads his life as a respectable normal member of the group (subject, of course, to variations due to individual differences). But, if these values or norms do not adequately satisfy his basic needs, or if they produce conflict due to the lack of integration between the values of different groups a person identifies himself with, then he may strive restlessly to anchor himself anew, or he may indulge in daydreams, various sorts of abnormal phantasies, or other "substitutive activities" with their possible neurotic consequences. Individuals who are experiencing basic deprivations, who are tossing around without a secure social anchoring, owing to the contradictory nature of organized social relationships, may gravitate towards each other to form, spontaneously, more or less well-organized groups. And they may then derive their satisfactions from the activities and identifications such informally organized groups make possible.[2]

Most crucial and realistic observations on group psychology are still made, not by psychologists, but by observers who either personally share collective experiences or take a part in the process of group transformation. For, unlike psychologists, these observers cannot afford to make serious mistakes. Concrete illustrations of this point will be seen later in relation to Makarenko's work in the Gorki Colony during the trying days of the early 1920's when civil war was raging in the Soviet Union. In the more or less isolated situations of combat in war where men share misery and dangers in the most elemental and consequential way, there develop spontaneously among them groups peculiar to them alone in which other men of their own army may not be allowed to

----

[2] Although we shall not consider them here, groups which arise because they promise happiness to their members through escapist solutions are good illustrations. For examples see [7, 11, 17, 57]. On the other hand, the experience and observation of misery, class contradictions, social prejudices of all sorts which are derivatives of these contradictions lead many people in all countries to accept more objectively valid explanations concerning the causes of this misery and contradiction. Subsequently, these individuals may take a realistic firm stand in the face of many hardships.

participate. It is just as if the process were regulated by an established norm.

Among his other keen observations of men collectively under stress and reported in words or incisive lines and shadings, Bill Mauldin [31], who shared it all, caught the major properties of such groups:

> While men in combat outfits kid each other around, they have a sort of family complex about it. *No outsiders may join.* Anybody who does a dangerous job in this war has his own particular kind of kidding among his own friends, and sometimes it doesn't even sound like kidding. Bomber crews and paratroopers and infantry squads are about the same in that respect. If a stranger comes up to a group of them when they are bulling, they ignore him. If he takes it upon himself to laugh at something funny they have said, they freeze their expressions, turn slowly around, stare at him until his stature has shrunk to about four inches and he slinks away, and then they go back to their kidding again.
>
> It's like a group of prosperous businessmen telling a risqué joke and then glaring at the waiter who joins in the guffaws. Combat people are *an exclusive set,* and if they want to be that way, it is their privilege. They certainly earn it. New men in outfits have to work their way in slowly, but they are eventually accepted. Sometimes they have to change some of their ways of living. An introvert or a recluse is not going to last long in combat without friends, so he learns *to come out of his shell.* Once he has "arrived" he is pretty proud of his clique, and he in turn is chilly toward outsiders.
>
> That's why, during some of the worst periods in Italy, many guys who had a chance to hang around a town for a few days after being discharged from a hospital where they had recovered from wounds, with nobody the wiser, didn't take advantage of it. They weren't eager to get back up and get in the war, by any means, and many of them did hang around a few days. But those who did hang around *didn't feel exactly right* about it, and those who went right back did it for a very simple reason—not because they felt that their presence was going to make a lot of difference in the big scheme of the war, and not to uphold the traditions of the umpteenth regiment. A lot of guys don't know the name of their regimental commander. They went back because they knew their companies were very shorthanded, and they were sure that if somebody else in their own squad or section

were in their own shoes, and the situation were reversed, those friends would come back to make the load lighter on *them*. [31, *58 ff.*, all but the last italics ours]

Further examples of ego-involved group loyalties arising during critical times are reported in the next chapter.

Judgments, perceptions, and attitudes are referential affairs, consciously or unconsciously related to a framework. If this frame becomes unstable and conflicting, judgments and attitudes related to this frame are consequently apt to lose their stability and integration. The same is true for the genetically formed ego. If we lose our faith in the persons or groups with which we identify ourselves, or if we are estranged from them for various reasons, our feeling of identity becomes unstable and shaky. Under the circumstances, we are apt to strive to anchor ourselves more firmly in a new constellation of human relationships.[3]

The case of the "marginal man," with ambivalent or contradictory group loyalties, or with experiences of successive acceptance and rejection by the groups he is related to, illustrates our point clearly. Such a man usually develops conflicts due to the contradictory components of his loyalties, or to frustrations arising from his alternating acceptance or rejection by the groups he is related to in the social order in which these contradictions prevail. In the works of Park and Miller [43], Park [44], Stonequist [58], Child

---

[3] The cases of more or less isolated groups (for example, in prisons, concentration camps, or involuntary isolation of some sort), their formation, and the products emerging in them may be studied to exemplify our theme. For example, in Clemmer's study [13] of life in a large prison, he notes that, because of uncertainty and confusion about the life they have left and because of the impersonal prison routine, new inmates almost invariably experience a "loss of identity" at first. Some men never recover from this chaotic state. However, the majority come to accept the prison code and even anchor themselves in informal groupings to a greater or lesser degree. They then identify themselves with the prison group, and their behavior is regulated by the code. Other members remain anchored in persons or groups outside of prison and manage to live with a minimum of inner conflict, because their behavior is judged by themselves in terms of a reference group outside. However, some men "have a double or triple allegiance," identifying themselves with the prison group in some respects, the outside world in others. It is these prisoners, the "betwixt and between," who suffer inner conflict, who become "stool pigeons," and whose behavior seems "confused and illogical." These "stool pigeons" are looked down upon scornfully by both inmates and authorities.

[12], and others we find interesting illustrations of such conflict situations. Recently Hughes [20] has given a sociological account of these "dilemmas and contradictions of status," which at times cause frustrating experiences for the individuals caught in them.

Group identifications. Studies of adolescent conflicts, crises, identifications, and cliques give us important psychological clues by means of which we can more adequately examine the intricate problems of ego-involvements and identifications in group situations. We have seen how the adolescent boy or girl tosses in the flux of "unsettledness" and personal confusion with the rise of the sexual urge and the development of other youthful aspirations and longings, with *now* more intensely felt deprivations, emerging interests and values. And we will recall that most of these new adolescent yearnings are not sympathetically shared, in general, by the older generation and are usually not satisfied in what the adolescent regards as a rigid adult world filled with restrictions and prohibitions. The consequences are, in many cases, parent–youth (adult–youth) conflict, leading, for example, to: drifting away ("psychological weaning") from parents and other grown-ups, ending in actual running away from the oppressing family situation in some cases; crises of various kinds in which the adolescent feels that nobody understands him, he is all alone in an unsympathetic sadistic world; or expressed or unexpressed feelings or acts of rebellion against different types of authority.

The kind and the intensity of parent–youth conflict, of psychological weaning, of crisis and rebellion, and of actual behavior that may ensue will vary according to the class structure of the society, the relative stability or instability of the times, the rate of technological changes, and the deprivations the particular adolescent is subject to because of the particular circumstances of his family, class, and so on. A sociological analysis of certain of these important variables determining the amount and degree of parent–youth conflict in a particular culture (as contrasted to universal factors, for example, differences in age between parents and children) has been made by Kingsley Davis [15]. Pointing out that such conflict is minimal or inconsequential in some cultures, Davis emphasizes that, although the physiological changes at adolescence are highly important factors, they are universal and, consequently, cannot in themselves account for variations in the degree of conflict from one culture to another. The four "complex variables" Davis analyzes are: "(1) the rate of social change; (2) the extent of complexity in the social structure; (3) the degree of integration in the culture; and (4) the velocity of movement (e.g., vertical mobility) within the structure and its relation to the cultural values." [535] Viewing contemporary American culture in terms of these variables, Davis comments that owing to the rapidity of sociological change, not only do the norms of adults and youth differ in content, but the complexity of our society with its lack of integration leads to conflicting standards, norms, and goals *"within* the generations" (including, of course, those norms relating to sex).

[The feeling of insecurity, of being tossed around, is painful, as any deprivation is painful. It has its limits of endurance. As a result there is a tendency to anchor one's self some place where an actual or fancied feeling of security is provided. This anchoring may be achieved through various kinds of identifications with persons who have affective value or who stand high in one's eyes; or it may be attained through membership in some clique, gang, club, sect, select neighborhood, or institution.] In "casually patterned" societies of a high degree of development and differentiation, to borrow a concept used by Robert Lynd in his provocative book, *Knowledge for What? The Place of Social Science in American Culture* [28], efforts to get one's self anchored may be directed to contradictory and escapist orientations. These contradictory identifications and affiliations may develop into absurd proportions. Instead of giving a consistent feeling of security, they may only produce further conflicts.[4]

Youngsters who are striving, sometimes desperately, to get out of a psychological crisis situation, to find for themselves an atmosphere of experience and action sympathetic to and in harmony with their yearnings and aspirations, or to satisfy keenly felt deprivations, spontaneously form adolescent groups (cliques, gangs) with kindred souls. The structural properties of such groups—

---

[4] For some accentuated illustrations of this point, see the references on the "marginal man" and ch. 11.

such as degree of solidarity, integration, degree of exclusiveness of loyalty demanded—will vary according to the extent to which each individual member is driven to cast his own personal lot with a group as determined by the locality in which he lives, the degree of mobility possible, economic class, and ethnic affiliations. For economic class and ethnic affiliations are major determinants of significant identifications and anchorages or of the lack of them, especially in bourgeois societies where rigid prejudices prevail (as seen in "social distance" studies).

The goals towards which clique or gang activities will be directed vary according to the character of the major deprivations, the character of the feeling of not belonging, and the aspirations of the individuals in the gang or clique. A certain gang of the type most frequently studied by sociologists may engage particularly in pilfering, "jack-rolling" or stealing. Another gang, whose members are economically above the subsistence level, may specialize in orgiastic or other sexual activities, a third gang or clique may be noted for its acts of "distinction" in assuring for its members an envied *status* in their social world. School gangs or cliques of the latter kind have not attracted so much attention, perhaps because they do not stand out as spectacular. As we saw in the last chapter, college fraternities and sororities almost serve as a prototype of groups engaging in such activities.

THE STRUCTURAL PROPERTIES OF GROUPS

Studies of the spontaneous formations of gangs and the subsequent rise of appropriate *norms* (codes) and *roles* which define the relative. *status* of individual members, give us excellent information concerning the character of group structures, identifications, and loyalties, and their determination of the behavior of the members. The material on gangs is especially helpful in formulating psychological generalizations, since sociologists have published elaborate studies on the formation and functioning of gangs, including case histories of individual members. The group properties, individual identifications, and behavior in gangs found here give us, as we have said, the essential prototype of any group or group behavior.

In these gang studies, a cardinal fact concerning the behavior of individual members *in any collective situation* stands out in high relief: the fact that, once an individual identifies himself with a group and its collective actions, his behavior is, in a major way, determined by the direction of the group action, whatever this direction may be, good or bad, constructive or destructive. Once an individual identifies himself with the group, whether this group is a clique, gang, club, fraternity, sect, or political organization, his ego becomes so involved that he is apt to feel a loss of personal status if he does not keep pace with group activity. His social status as he feels it consists largely of a constellation of these group identifications, whatever the specific character and level in the particular scheme of social stratification may be. Deviations and injuries inflicted on his identifications, either by himself or by others, are usually experienced as a personal loss of prestige. Thus a gang member acquires his real social status in his gang, even though he may have learned by heart all the prevailing norms of society at large.

This fact is nicely pointed out by Zorbaugh: [63]

> The church, the school, and the occupational group, then, as well as the newspaper, play no intimate rôle in the local life of the Near North Side [of Chicago]. . . . The Gold Coast has its clubs; intimate groups gather in "village" studios; the foreign areas have numerous lodges and mutual benefit societies; the slum has its "gangs." Even in the rooming-house area, where group life is at a minimum, occasional cults and sects spring up, and every pool hall and cigar store has about it a nebulous group. And these groups may play an enormously important rôle in the lives of their members. [63, 192]

In Thrasher's work we have an account of hundreds of gangs studied in the early 1920's. Thrasher's book is a mine of rich data for the social psychologist. It is full of material which shows the process of group formation under well-defined economic and social situations, the structural properties of groups, and the rise of appropriate norms (codes) that regulate the behavior of individual members to such an important degree.

Before we analyze the structural properties of "gangs," it is important to note that, no matter what kind of "deviant" activities gang boys engage in, they are generally wholesome and normal human beings, subject only to the usual individual differences found in any school, Sunday school, or club population. Thrasher [60] states that

> Aside from their usual lack of adjustment to the formal demands of conventional social codes, however, gang boys . . . are not morbid or psychopathic as is sometimes the case with boys who are subject to the repressions and punishments of a more artificial situation. [60, *172*]

Other investigators substantiate the fact: we see it in Clifford Shaw's *Brothers in Crime* [52]; [5] in Whyte's *Street Corner Society* [62]; and Zorbaugh's *The Gold Coast and the Slum* [63]. Gangs are formed spontaneously to serve the function of a social institution, to secure a status and a social identity for youngsters not genuinely provided with such an identity by society at large. And perhaps even more important, gangs regulate and encourage activities which satisfy basic human needs, because families and communities have failed to provide many children with the means of relieving major deprivations.

> Gangs represent the spontaneous effort of boys to create a society for themselves where none adequate to their needs exists. [60, *37*]
> It offers a substitute for what society fails to give; and it provides a relief from suppression and distasteful behavior. [60, *38*]

This comes out again and again in representative studies. For example, we see in Zorbaugh's conclusion [63] how restrictions imposed by privileged classes to maintain class lines encourage gang formation.

> The child cannot live and conform in both social worlds at the same time. The family and colony are defined for him in his American contacts by such epithets as "dago," "wop," "foreign," and the like. *He feels the loss of status attached to his connection with the colony.* In his effort to achieve status in the American city he loses his *rapport* with family and community. *Conflicts arise between the child and his family.* Yet by virtue of his race, his manner of speech, the neces-

[5] The clinical summaries contained in this book and made by the psychiatrist, Harold Hanson [ch. 13] are particularly to the point.

sity of living in the colony, and these same definitive epithets, *he is excluded from status and intimate participation in American life.* Out of this situation, as we have already seen, arises the gang, affording the boy a social world in which he finds his only status and recognition. But it is by conforming to delinquent patterns that he achieves status in the gang. And every boy in Little Hell is a member of a gang. [63, *176 f.,* italics ours]

Thrasher [60] begins his study by giving socioeconomic account of the areas particularly conducive to the formation of gangs (gangland). He writes that

The gang is almost invariably characteristic of regions that are interstitial to the more settled, more stable, and better organized portions of the city. The central tripartite empire of the gang occupies what is often called "the poverty belt"—a region characterized by deteriorating neighborhoods, shifting populations, and the mobility and disorganization of the slum. [60, 22]

It is against this situational background that the activities of such gangs become significant. The specific activities of different gangs may vary, as Thrasher points out. The situational determinants in each case must be specifically studied.[6]

Thrasher, like some other sociologists in the field, tends to consider gangs as cases of disorganization. This seems to us a moralistic view of the subject. As Whyte recently noted, activities of slum areas and those of gangs have an internal organization of their own while they last.[7] In Whyte's words:

It is customary for the sociologist to study the slum district in terms of "social disorganization" and to neglect to see that an area such as Cornerville has a complex and well-established organization of its own. I was interested in that organization. I found that *in every group there was a hierarchical structure of social relations binding the*

[6] The almost universal formation of gangs among young boys in certain areas of the population formerly has led certain authors to posit such conceptions as a "gang instinct" (see, for example, J. Puffer [46]). But sociologists like Thrasher and Shaw who are intimately acquainted with gangs have dismissed such untenable psychological positions in favor of situational (environmental) explanations.

[7] We say "while they last" because the impact of the established society, which contributed to the gang's formation, at the same time impinges upon it in the direction of its dissolution. We shall comment on this point later.

individuals to one another and that the groups were also related hierarchically to one another. Where the group was formally organized into a political club, this was immediately apparent, but for informal groups it was no less true. While the relations in such groups were not formally prescribed, they could be clearly observed in the interactions of individuals. [62, *viii,* italics ours]

As we shall see presently, adolescent boys, particularly those who experience economic stress and deprivation, who are actually (if not legally) denied the opportunity to identify themselves organically with society at large, cannot help but gravitate to each other in their common destiny to form *spontaneously* more or less organized groups which provide them with some kind of status, some means of satisfying their youthful deprivations. If these same boys could identify themselves with a group that held opposite values and used other devices to achieve the same ends, they would have formed their loyalties and oriented their activities accordingly.

In chapter 7 we pointed out certain important implications which contact with age-mate groups had on the process of ego development. Thrasher comments:

The majority of gangs develop from the spontaneous play–group. [60, 29]

In the light of our earlier discussion, this fact acquires particular significance. More recently, Whyte [61] further substantiated Thrasher's observation:

The clique structure arises out of the habitual association of members, over a long period of time. The nuclei of most gangs can be traced back to early boyhood years when living close together provided the first opportunities of social contacts. [61]

These observations show in a concrete way the effect of spontaneous age-mate contacts and games on the developing social identity of children. It is immaterial for our argument, of course, whether all gangs develop from early childhood contacts, or whether many of them are products of the adolescent age level. Clifford Shaw reports several concrete cases of gangs which started when youngsters exchanged stories of exciting experiences and began to organize various exploits. These interactions tend to produce a group structure which varies in its stability according to the situation.

In the process of group (gang) formation, the relative standing of one individual to another becomes defined. Each member acquires a relative *status* with appropriate functions of authority and responsibility. The leader himself emerges in the process of interaction in diverse group activities. Thrasher points out:

> There is a process of selection in the gang, as a result of the struggle for status, whereby the ultimate position of each individual is determined. The result of this process depends largely upon the individual differences—both native and acquired—which characterize the members of the group. [60, *334*]

Whyte, who lived in the slums and intimately associated with gangs, formulated in a clear-cut way the crystallization of a relative role or status for each member, as well as shifts of status with changing situations:

> Each member of the corner gang has his own position in the gang structure. Although positions may remain unchanged over long periods of time, they should not be conceived in static terms. To have a position means that the individual has a customary way of interacting with other members of the group. When the pattern of interactions changes, the positions change. [62, *262 f.*]

On the basis of extensive observations of hundreds of gangs, Thrasher states:

> While it may sometimes be true that a gang forms about a leader, the reverse is generally true: the gang forms and the leader emerges as the result of interaction. [60, *351*]

Certainly individual differences in various psychological characteristics of the members, their relatively high or low status in the group, their superiority in diverse abilities may secure a particular member leadership in the gang. Thrasher mentions such characteristics as physical strength, athletic prowess, gameness, quickness and firmness of decision, and imagination as qualities which determine the leadership of a particular member in a particular gang. Which one of these or other qualities will help a person gain leadership in a gang is situationally determined by the particular pattern of activities the gang goes in for. As Thrasher states:

The marks of leadership vary from gang to gang. The type of boy who can lead one gang may be a failure or have a distinctly subordinate rôle in another. . . . Physical and athletic prowess, which stand the leader in such good stead in most gangs, for example, would not be valued in the following type of group. [60, *344*]

Then he cites the case of "The Bandits" who, while carrying on "delinquent" activities, engage as a group in such activities as "social and folk dancing with girls." In another example he notes that

A hunchback was a very successful leader of a gang of healthy boys. [60, *350*]

Studies on personality traits, such as aggressiveness or submissiveness, acquire concrete meaning only when the situational factors in any group situation are given due consideration.

Leadership in a group is by no means an accidental or arbitrary affair. The status of the leader is exercised not simply by virtue of some personality trait, but rather because the leader lives up to certain expectations demanded by the pattern of established relationships. As Thrasher states,

The leader has considerable power over his subordinates *so long as he does not abuse it.* [60, 292, italics ours]

Whyte [61] points out that the higher a member's status is, the *stricter* the expectations are for the fulfillment of his responsibilities and obligations.

Not all corner boys live up to their obligations equally well, and this factor partly accounts for the differentiation in status among the men. The man with a low status may violate his obligations without much change in position. [61, *657*]

But this is not the case for members with high status, including the leader. The leader, as Thrasher says, "goes where others fear to go" in the exploits of the gang.

The number of members in the gang may range from two to several hundred. It is interesting to note that usually the membership does not exceed limits which will make interpersonal contacts difficult or direct face-to-face group pressure on the members impossible. For example, out of 895 gangs Thrasher examined from this point of view, 538 gangs had membership within the range of 10 to 20 members each.

The specific variations in the particular situations that give rise to gangs and the variations in the aspirations produce gangs with different characteristics.

> No two gangs are just alike. The cases investigated present an endless variety of forms, and every one is in some sense unique. [60, 45]

Gangs specialize in certain types of activity:

> Gangs which develop specialized structures and codes for the furtherance of some interest of their own may be regarded as functional types. Thus, groups are organized around such dominant interests as junking, sex, picking pockets, stealing, athletics, gambling, or some special type of crime. In each case they develop their own technique. [60, 291]

These different groups start spontaneously around a more or less diffuse nucleus and become structured and organized in various degrees as time goes on.

All sorts of collective products emerge in the process of interaction in group activities and experiences. The new group products further strengthen the group structure and solidarity, reenforcing group pressure on the individual members. Gang names, such as "Dirty Dozen," "Lilies of the Valley," "Shielders," "Hudson Dusters," "Yakey Yakes," "Five Points," "Vultures," "Forty Thieves," add to the feeling of group belongingness.[8] Gang members are called by special nicknames assigned according to their relative positions in the group. Thrasher says:

> Personalities are recognized by the names applied to the members of the gang. Individual peculiarities, which have an important effect in determining status, are likely to give color to the boy's whole personality. He is named accordingly, and his name often indicates the esteem in which he is held by the group. [60, 339 f.]

[8] These are names of actual gangs taken from [60, 275 f., 281].

In the course of time, the gang develops definite boundaries as its area of activity. Psychologically, this area is appropriated as the gang's own area for operation. Violations of this appropriation by some other gang are on occasion reacted to violently.

> Just as among nations borderline disputes sometimes precipitate disastrous wars, so gangs may be mobilized and led to battle on the same issue. [60, *126*]

Time and again, Thrasher calls attention to the fact that group solidarity, the "we" feeling, is strengthened through outside resistances, collective fights, and alliances with other gangs. In some cases, this outside resistance may come from adults. Thrasher quotes a gang member:

> "This desire to escape family supervision marked the beginning of our feeling of solidarity. Our first loyalties were to protect each other against our parents." [60, *31*]

Similar to the feelings of belongingness in any group, and the development and delineation of attitudes towards the "in-group" and "out-group" members, attitudes develop which define cooperative and sympathetic in-group relationships, various degrees of prejudice and of social distance towards outsiders.

All systematic investigators like Thrasher, Shaw, Zorbaugh, Landesco, and Whyte have observed that appropriate norms arise. These, in turn, regulate the formation of the attitudes and the subsequent behavior of the members. In Thrasher's words:

> Every gang tends to develop its own code of conduct, of which its members are more or less aware and which may be more or less rigidly enforced upon them. The code of the gang is in part reflected from the patterns of behavior in its own social world, in part the result of the development of primary group sentiments, and in part the product of the individual group in its own special environment. [60, *284*]

In a similar way, group slogans arise which formulate gang practices in a short-cut way. Expressive words become standardized for the gang, have special meaning to the members.

The isolated life of gangland leads to the development of a distinct universe of discourse. . . . Like its morality, this argot, too, follows to some extent patterns in its own social world. . . . [60, 266 f.]

As in any social group of any degree of solidarity, these norms are inculcated in the individual members in the very process of interaction, generating feelings of belongingness and loyalty. Also, as in any social group, various sorts of pressures, correctives (such as applause and ridicule), and punishments are applied to keep the attitudes and behavior of the members in line.

Opinion in the gang manifests its *pressure* in the variety of mechanisms through which group control is exerted, such as applause, preferment and heroworshipping as well as ridicule, scorn, and ostracism. . . . In the gang the member who has broken the code may be subjected to a beating or in extreme cases may be marked for death. [60, 291 f., italics ours]

Deviations from group behavior are thus reacted to by the group as a whole with varying degrees of severity. Since "squealing" is the worst deviation, in some cases it is punishable by death. On the positive side, group identification generates at times the highest degree of co-operative and sympathetic tendencies within the delinquent gang. There exists within the gang "a sort of brotherhood and mutual kindliness. This manifests itself in many forms of self-sacrifice. If a member is in serious danger the rest will spare no pains to save his life. One boy will sometimes undergo severe hardships to aid another." [290]

After a boy becomes a good member of the gang, his personal identity is linked to that of the group. His status in the gang is, in a major way, his status as he experiences it. For it is in the gang interaction that he lives his life intimately and intensely. When his ties with the gang are strained, he may feel he is losing his ground. Thrasher aptly puts it:

Any standing in the group is better than none, and there is always the possibility of improving one's status. Participation in gang activities means everything to the boy. It not only defines for him his position in the only society he is greatly concerned with, but it *becomes the basis of his conception of himself.* [60, 332, italics ours]

Consequently, his feeling of personal security is derived from gang membership. This feeling of security "tends *to remove the qualms that might well arise in an individual embarking upon some perilous undertaking on his own account.*" [*296,* italics ours] Here we see the differences, even qualitative differences, between the individual alone, or in one situation, and the same individual in a group with which he strongly identifies himself. Under the pressure of the group situation, the individual's social identity may be transformed.

Thrasher cites many concrete cases of such differential group behavior. In the report on one gang by an ex-member we will see (p. 303) how a member of a gang where toughness was at a premium dropped his ruffian ways and was always quiet and courteous when he went out on the sly with his girl. Here is another example:

> We have one case of an Italian boy, R——, who in the gang can always be counted upon to respond to an appeal for the best for himself and the gang. Outside the gang his record has not been so satisfactory. In the gang he is stimulated by group appreciation; while without he is not. [*60, 295*]

Group loyalty may at times dominate over serious cases of personal injury, as we shall see shortly (p. 301) in the case of a gang member who refused to squeal on another member who had cut his head open by a blow with a lead pipe. Individuals in group situations sometimes become so personally involved in the collective situation that they do not isolate themselves as individuals to figure out what is most advantageous to them personally.

> Whatever we did, we knew would be done as a group. At the end of the season Steve suggested that we enlist as a body (the whole team), and leave at once. Some wanted to join the marines; some the army; but a vote decided on the navy. In order to stay together, we went to the Great Lakes Naval Training Station and enlisted as a group of apprentice seamen, even though some of us could have received ratings had we been willing to quit the others. [*60, 188*]

All of these facts indicate the inadequacy of any approach to personality which posits unchanging personality traits, especially those concerned with social characteristics, without due regard to the determination of behavior by situational factors generated in any collective interaction in a psychologically lawful way. These psychological products emerging in the process of gang formation and conduct are amply illustrated by Thrasher. His account of "The Dirty Dozen" gang, which he characterizes as a fairly typical group, will give us concrete evidence of the structural properties, emergent products, and subsequent attitudes and identifications found in a group. This report was made by a former associate of the gang.

The Dirty Dozen began merely as the result of a dozen or more fellows (from sixteen to twenty-two years of age) meeting casually on a street corner at the entrance of one of Chicago's parks and later on in "Mike's" poolroom a short distance away. Most of the boys were loafers, who spent their time swimming, playing baseball and football, shooting craps, or sitting around and talking. They liked brawls and fights, and the gang helped to satisfy these wants with less personal discomfort than might occur if one fellow alone started hostilities or tried to steal something. Of their various activities, some form of conflict seems to have been the chief.

There was war between the gang and the police, for even though the latter did not always have any particular offense for which the fellows were wanted, they did try to break up the group whenever it congregated on the corner.

The gang as a whole often came into direct conflict with other gangs. One night at the old Imperial Theater, the Dirty Dozen found themselves seated opposite the "Chi" gang, their rival in football and baseball. During the show, which was poor vaudeville, the fellows started to hurl remarks at each other. The verbal conflict grew into a near-riot, which continued until the police came.

The Dirty Dozen, however, was capable of collective action against other enemies than rival gangs. One night while the race riots of 1919 were at their height, the gang, armed with revolvers, blackjacks, and knives, started out to get the "niggers."

At Thirty-fifth and State streets, five miles or more from their own territory, and after some preliminary skirmishes, "Shaggy" Martin threw the trolley of a street car filled with colored people. The rest of the gang, which had increased to about twenty by this time, piled on. "Shaggy," who was left alone at the back to hold the trolley-rope, was standing there with it in one hand and a billy in the other when a colored woman slashed him across the heart with a razor. Then someone hit her, and another fellow "got" her husband.

Shaggy died in the patrol on the way to the hospital. "Swede" Carlson, the only fellow the police caught at that time, said that his last words were, "What will mother say?" The gang took up a collection for flowers, but the direct result of the episode was a desire for revenge. They killed two negroes and "beat up" five more after the death of Shaggy.

The standing of each fellow in the gang was determined by competition and conflict within the group itself. Each member was trying to outdo the others in football and everything else. There was always a struggle for the leadership, which usually went to the best fighters.

"Slicker" Charlie and Ellman were for some reason or other "on the outs," and a fight was arranged to see who was better. The encounter came off in the park. Each fellow had his second, and the time of the rounds was set just as if it were a regular prize fight. Ellman, who won, mauled Charlie severely, and the latter fell into disgrace, at least in his own opinion.

This feeling of his own belittlement caused Charlie much resentment toward the victor and led to another fight in which Charlie struck Ellman with a lead pipe. The blood shot out of a big gash in his head. After they had taken him to the emergency hospital, a cop came in and wanted to know how it had happened, but Ellman would say nothing except that he had fallen and his head hit a rock. The code of the gang was that honor forbade squealing. With this incident the feud came to an end.

An example of conflict of the play type, which had a very tragic outcome, occurred one day in the park. About eight of the fellows went to the lagoon and piled into two tiny rowboats. It was a warm summer evening, and the bunch was feeling pretty good, so they decided to have a battle. Splashing soon led to striking with oars. The battle was raging when one of the boats went over. In it was a fellow called "Steam," who could not swim. The others struck out for the shore, but Steam went down. As soon as they discovered that he was gone, they went out and dived for him until one of them succeeded in getting the body. The fire department came and a pulmotor was used, but to no avail. Before the funeral a collection was taken up, and an expensive floral piece was purchased. The gang turned to the good for one day, and every member went to the church. Steam was never spoken of afterward, for each one of them felt a little bit responsible for his death.

Members of the gang often engaged in shady exploits as individuals or in pairs. Ellman and "Dago" were always managing to make some money in one way or another. At one time Ellman told me of the "booze" ring, for which he and Dago did the delivering. Where they got the booze I never found out, but they made $25 or $30 apiece for a night's work and gambled it away at a place which was a regular Monte Carlo, with tables for crap-shooting, and caller's chips which were purchased from the cashier.

The same pair were involved in the robbery of a golf shelter. Owing to Ellman's carelessness, he was followed and arrested. He was convicted of petty larceny and put on probation, but the police could not make him reveal the name of his pal. By keeping mum he saved Dago a lot of trouble.

Another example of loyalty was an incident which occurred when the gang went to Detroit. Dago gave the money which he was to use for carfare home to a younger fellow. Although it was winter, he himself rode the blind. Since the train took water on the fly, he was frozen to the train when it pulled in.

The gang also enjoyed many quiet evenings. It was the rule for the fellows to meet at Mike's on winter nights to shoot pool and talk. In the summer their hang-out was on the corner at the entrance to the park. There was a tendency to stick together at all times in play, just as in other activities. They often went swimming. Every year they played football, for which they tried to keep in training, and they developed a good team. The older fellows were the leaders in their athletic activities.

One of the exploits of the gang was a migration from Chicago to Detroit when high wages were being paid to automobile-workers. They rented a house there and the whole gang lived together. Even though they were making fabulous wages, they did not save a cent, and finally came back to Chicago—broke. It was this Detroit adventure that made bums out of most of them. They had drinking orgies almost every night at their house, and the crap games took their money.

The gang controlled its individual members, particularly when the group was together. As individuals, and in other group relationships they were not so bad, but in the gang they tried to act as tough as possible. The man who danced, who went out with girls, or who was well-mannered was ostracized. Charlie used to act hard-boiled, and he even wore his cap so that it made him look tough. Ellman, who liked to give the impression that he was a ruffian, was going with a girl on the sly. When he was with the gang he was one of the meanest fellows in it, but when he went out with his girl he was very courteous, quitting his loud talk and dropping his braggadocian air.

In the last few years the gang has disintegrated. There has been a tendency for its members to be incorporated into the more conventional activities of society. The majority of them seem to have become more settled in their mode of life. Some have moved away. Even the fellows who have changed, however, are still pretty low under the polished surface. Gang habits and influences still persist. [60, 46–50]

The reasons for the disintegration of a gang give us further insight into the mechanism of group identification. We have seen that gangs are formed by boys as they strive to relieve deprivations and secure for themselves a stable and genuine social identity. It is not a mere coincidence, then, that "settling down" in conventional society tends to disintegrate gang loyalties or, at least, to cause members to drop out of active gang participation. As the former associate of the Dirty Dozen gang wrote in the last paragraph of his report, there is "a tendency for its members to be incorporated into the more conventional activities of society. The majority of them seem to have become more settled in their mode of life." Desertions from the gang probably vary with the degree of organization and solidarity of the group.

According to Thrasher, a "new activity of settlement, playground, or club" may take away some of the gang members. Thrasher cites marriage, becoming a family man, as one "of the most potent causes for the disintegration of the older groups." [36] Whyte summarizes the process concisely:

To the casual observer the corner gang seems to go on for years without change, but actually changes are always taking place; and, as the men grow out of their twenties, the gang itself tends to disintegrate. Some of the members marry and have children. Even if they continue to hang on the corner, their interests are no longer confined to that social area. With marriage, some move out of Cornerville; and, even when they return to spend time with the boys, they are not the active members they once were. In this period of life the corner boy is expected to "settle down" and find the job that will support him and his family in future years. He becomes a different fellow, and his gang either falls apart or is included in some larger club organization. [62, 35]

Not all gang members "settle down" in the orthodox established life of society after their adolescent years by getting a steady job, marrying, and so on. Some go on to participate in the more grim exploits of the adult gangs.[9] In these adult gangs, group loyalty and conformity are more exacting, perhaps, in proportion to the rewards and punishments gang members face as the consequence of their exploits. As a result, the structural properties and pressures of groups imposed on members of adult gangs become more rigid. Deviations are punished more ruthlessly, in many cases by death. Landesco [21] has given close-range accounts of such adult gangs and of their exacting structural properties in his impressive study of "Organized Crime in Chicago." There he cites concrete instances of death penalties meted out to deviant gang members.

On the basis of his longitudinal and intensive studies of the gang world, Landesco generalizes on the group norms that emerge to determine the attitudes and behavior of the gang. He comments on how gangs at times try to impose their codes on the out-groups with which they are in contact:

> The gang not only has its own code which governs the conduct of its members, but it even goes so far as to impose it upon outside society. In recent years in Chicago, the public has become familiar with the bold practices of criminal gangs in terrorizing witnesses and in exacting the death penalties upon them and upon members of the gang who are suspected of having given information to the police. *An inside view of the attitudes and codes of a notorious criminal gang shows how a closely knit group develops its own standards and is outraged and puzzled by the attempts to deal with them according to the law*. [21, 1055, italics ours]

Landesco goes on to indicate that gang members "form a group dominated by the gangster's code of loyalty," that the "welfare,

---

[9] The study of factors that determine whether a gang member will "settle down" after adolescent years or advance to membership in adult gangs should be of great significance psychologically. We cannot diverge here to make a special issue of the point.

standards, and laws of organized society evoke no response in their hearts and minds." [*1057*] He gives concrete illustrations of "gangsters' mutual loyalty" [*1053*]; of how "a man of character" is defined among the gang members as prescribed by gang norms [*1047*]; and how, once these norms are well standardized and inculcated in the youthful candidates, "a stigma is soon attached to legitimate employment." [*1046*]

Time and again, Landesco emphasizes that it is only by coming into contact with the pressures and punishments of society outside of his underworld that the gang member "gets his first sense of the necessity of justifying his behavior." [*1048*] For within his own group and the underworld which constitutes his real psychological reference group, he derives his relative status through the degree to which he fulfills and surpasses the prescribed expectations of his group. In formulating this point, it seems to us that Landesco has provided one of the best possible characterizations of the psychological properties of more or less closed groups and the subsequent conforming experiences and behavior of individual members.

> The gangster's defense of his mode of life arises only when he comes in contact with the legitimate outside world. Only then does he become conscious of a conflicting way of living. In his own group, on the contrary, *he achieves status by being a gangster, with gangster attitudes, and enhances his reputation through criminal exploits.* His contacts with the police and the courts and his successive confinements in the corrective, reformatory, and penal institutions, beginning with the Juvenile Detention Home, then in turn the Industrial Training School, the reformatory and the penitentiary, *gain him the prestige of a veteran in his group.* His return from the State Reformatory at Pontiac or from the penitentiary at Joliet is the occasion of sympathy and rejoicing from his gang brothers. The bitterness engendered within him by punishment and the feelings of revenge nurtured by his mutual association with other convicts have more deeply impressed upon him the psychology of the criminal world. Then, too, the stigma which society places upon him as an ex-convict *identifies him the more with the underworld.* [21, *1043*, italics ours]

In another interesting study, "The Woman and the Underworld," Landesco [22] reports the case of a high-grade Chicago gangster. This study contains significant hints concerning the psychology of group membership by its inclusion of a concrete case from real life showing the dominance of established group ties over the promise of a settled life with plenty of money and an attractive and refined woman. Among "five women who entered the life of Eddie Jackson," the case of the "Companionate Woman for Whom He Cared" is particularly illuminating from this point of view. The companionate woman "was an American girl, born in the East. She was an attractive looking woman—tall, about five feet eight inches, weighed about 130 or 135 pounds, had studied music and had graduated from a finishing school. She always retained a maid in the house." [894]

> Miss ——'s father was a manufacturer in the east. Occasionally he came to Chicago for a cure, which was known as the "gold cure" and was given for $25 a treatment. He took two or three treatments a week. [22, 895]

Miss —— tried hard to reform Eddie Jackson and to settle down with him in the East. In Jackson's own words:

> She wanted me to quit and go to work. She had plenty of money. We had our trunks packed to go to New York and she wanted to start me in some business. [895]

> She wanted to help me start in any business I might choose. I had some money. I cannot say that I did not have plenty of chances, but I liked the excitement of the racket, the politics, and the fixing—the successes and the failures. [22, 896]

Jackson finally made up his mind to leave for New York:

> Our trunks were packed and I decided to let her go ahead, and follow five days later. I never reached New York. [22, 896]

The successes and failures of his own group had become so well ingrained in Eddie Jackson that they weighed more heavily than the settled life which came so closely within his reach. In Eddie's own words:

> You see, there was a good deal of excitement and interest, and some skill involved in the racket—and it was not so easy to separate from it for the sake of Miss ——. [22, 896]

Landesco's analysis sheds light on the dominance of group identification over other factors in this case:

> Upon his [Eddie Jackson's] release from prison, he went directly to her apartment. She wanted him to leave Chicago, to change his ways and friends. The prison experience had changed her (not him), had sobered her; the lark was over, the feast of freedom embittered. She insisted. He allowed her to leave. *He could not leave his underworld.* [22, *901,* italics ours]

Generality of gang formations. If gangs were a phenomena occurring only in Chicago or a few large cities, there could be no justification for generalizing from gang material about spontaneous group formations, their psychological function for the individual, the rise of group products, and their subsequent role in regulating members' behavior. However, sociological literature gives abundant evidence that spontaneous group formations like gangs, far from being isolated or rare phenomena, occur quite generally—occur, in fact, wherever individuals are under the stress of the various factors already mentioned as important in spontaneous group formation, as, for example, various sorts of deprivation, lack of a stable social identity.

The almost universality of spontaneous group formations under the stress of these factors has been pointed out by Gist and Halbert. [18]

> Ganging is a natural process. *Whether the activities of a gang are perverse or constructive depends upon the character of the habitat of the gang*—upon the culture patterns predominating in the region and upon the sequences of situations that arise in the natural history of the gang. The gang is a form of adjustment that boys, and even girls, make whenever their family or neighborhood do not satisfy their major wishes in a conventional way. [18, *212,* italics ours]

In 1925, Park [42] commented on the generality of spontaneous group formation, tracing much of it back to the play group, which "under the conditions of urban life" is assuming "an increasing importance." [*111*] Such groups frequently evolve into gangs which "have exercised a considerably greater influence in forming the character of the boys who compose them than has the church, the school, or any other communal agency outside of the families and homes in which the members of the gang are reared." [*112*]

In Asbury's book, *The Gangs of New York*, [*5*] we learn that gangs of boys and young men have existed since New York City's early days. He notes, for example, that during and after the Civil War, "as the slums increased in extent, gangsters of all types and ages multiplied in numbers and power." [*238*]   This increase in the number of gangsters was related to the increasing number of gangs often "composed of lads from eight to twelve years of age." [*239*]   He also notes that gangs of similar sorts occur in various ethnic and national groups, including orientals.   From material collected in 20 American cities, Shaw and McKay [*53*] show that the spontaneous formation of gangs which engage in "delinquent" activities occurs wherever the causes already indicated are found to exist.   Basing their generalizations on data from such diverse cities as Chicago, Richmond, Peoria, Denver, Boston, and Spokane, the authors conclude:

"Delinquency—*particularly group delinquency, which constitutes a preponderance of all officially recorded offenses committed by boys and young men*—has its roots in the dynamic life of the community." [*435*, italics ours]   These roots are "products of the operation of general processes more or less common to American cities." [*435*]   Evidence supporting the authors' statement that such statistics may be interpreted in terms of groups is given by a study of boys brought to court in Cook County.   This revealed that

. . . 81.8 per cent of these boys committed the offenses for which they were brought to court as members of groups.   And when the offenses were limited to stealing, it was found that 89 per cent of all offenders were taken to court as group or gang members. [*53, 167 f.*]

In many additional cases, the influence of gang membership was to be seen.

Studies of boy transients and tramps show further how some members of the younger generation drift away from established conventional family life, from institutions such as schools and the church, and gravitate toward patterns of loyalties and identifications that have already been informally created by other individuals who had already found the more established ways of life unsatisfying. A youngster who "takes to the road" may have his eyes opened to the excitement and mobility of this way of life from older and experienced members of transient groups. [2, 256] [3, 300] [4, 786] [41, 64] Many transients take to the road during adolescence. This is significant in view of the factors that contribute to adolescent discontent with the established order of things.

Since there is always a tendency to attribute gang formations to some psychological factors or traits peculiar to the gang members themselves, we stress again the fact that gang formations serve the same psychological function as any membership group does for its members—a school clique, a fraternity or sorority, a club. A gang provides a social identification, a status. Thrasher cites many cases of gangs or embryonic gangs formed in the schools. And we have already seen how adolescents gravitate towards each other to form more or less confidential cliques when conventional settings do not afford them social anchorings or identities in harmony with their developing longings and the values of their new generation. They drift away to form their own intimate social cliques, even though some of these may be short-lived. Under certain conditions these cliques may develop into gangs. Thrasher states that "a clique may serve as the basis for a gang" [60, 320] or "in a certain sense a well-developed clique is an embryonic gang." [320] The objective purposes towards which the group (clique or gang) activities are directed may be quite different, even diametrically opposite. But from the point of view of group formation, essentially the same psychological mechanisms are at work in the various sorts of group formations. So we must draw no sharp and artificial distinctions between cliques and gangs in seeking the psychological principles involved in group formations.

The artificiality of drawing sharp lines in relation to the basic properties of groups, of conceiving them as closed and unchanging entities can be shown in more diverse groups. Taking the examples of a momentary group situation, caused by a serious automobile accident on the one hand, and the organized and lasting group core of a senate body on the other hand, Sapir [48] calls attention to the fallacy of making any arbitrary demarcations:

There is in reality no definite line of division anywhere along the gamut of group forms which connect these extremes. If the automobile accident is serious and one of the members of the crowd is a doctor, the informal group may with comparatively little difficulty resolve itself into something like a medical squad with an implicitly elected leader. On the other hand, if the government is passing through a great political crisis, if there is little confidence in the representative character or honesty of the senators or if an enemy is besieging the capitol and likely at any moment to substitute entirely new forms of corporate authority for those legally recognized by the citizens of the country, the Senate may easily become an unimportant aggregation of individuals who suddenly and with unexpected poignancy feel their helplessness as mere individuals. [48, *179*]

Impact of society at large. In our analysis of the influence of the group and group products in regulating the behavior of individual members, it is important to add that, although once an individual is a member of a group (gang)—once he identifies himself with it—the particular sort of behavior in question (for example, delinquency) is not due *only* to contact with the group (gang). In our discussion of the essentially similar psychological functions served by various spontaneous group formations, and in our demonstration of the effects of group loyalties and identifications on the behavior of individual members, we do not even imply that group formations of this sort have, in the larger sense, any existence independent of the social milieu in which they are formed. For these groups are obviously, in turn, products of economic, ethnic, and other major social situations in the society at large. Thus, Shaw [49] and Zorbaugh [63] have indicated that gangs engaging in delinquent activities are products of the existing social milieu with its social and class structure, as Shaw comments, of "processes more or less common to American cities." Anderson [4], in criticizing his own neglect of larger social conditions in studying transients, recently indicated that the factors giving rise to transiency are inexorably tied together with sociological, technological, and economic conditions and changes. The very factors which give rise to spontaneous groups are inevitably found as features of the larger social system.

By the same token, the particular activities, standards, and the like which provide individuals with social standing, status, or popularity in the larger society or in a particular stratum or locality of that larger society loom as important in the activities of these more or less well-structured subgroups. For example, the preponderance of athletics in the activities of boys' groups in America today reflects the value placed on such activities by society at large. The high premium placed on such things as feminine attractiveness or dancing is reflected in the activities of adolescent girls' cliques. The standard of living in a society has a major influence on the nature of a gang's exploits. Stealing cars assumes wide proportions among delinquent boys in the United States. The luxurious standards of an Al Capone and his gang could be found only in a society which makes possible "conspicuous consumption" of the staggering dimensions found among the leisure class of a Park Avenue or a Gold Coast.

Certain prohibitions in society may provide gangs with a type of activity that seeks definite economic rewards. Zorbaugh [63] mentions, for example, the importance of "bootlegging" and "hijacking" in the gang activities of Chicago at the time of prohibition. [174] In some strata of society, a high economic standing may be so keenly needed and highly valued that the means by which it is acquired may be relatively unimportant to the members of the community. For example, the local boy in the slums who achieves a decent or even luxurious way of life by "hi-jacking" may be regarded as a local hero, whereas outside of his community he is a "crook." In a "higher" level of society, the means by which some financial magnates gain their fortunes may be overlooked by other members of this society.

In the last analysis, the major established standards of success or failure of the gang or the gangster world are derived from the competitive, individualistic, and financially hoarding standards of the society at large. This is clearly expressed by Andrew A. Bruce in his introduction to Landesco's survey of "Organized Crime in Chicago." [21, 815–821] Bruce characterizes the general nature of the behavior of the gang or gangster world as "a rebellion against organized society and the laws under which organized society has chosen to be ruled and governed." [*815*]   He goes on to say that the major patterns of the gang world are derived from the social system in which it functions.

> Not the least of the disclosures that have been made are those of the permanence of the reigns of the lords of the underworld and the introduction of the capitalistic system into their operations. [21, *815*]

When adult gangs develop their enterprises to great proportions, they may become a real force in the economic and political life of the community.   At the same time they still keep the structural properties of the in-group intact.   In such cases, rather close relationships may be established between business men, politicians, and gang leaders.[10]

Similarly, the prevalent intense competition between gang and gang, clique and clique, club and club reflects the intense social and economic competition of the larger culture.   Gang fights between children of various ethnic, racial, or religious groups often seem to reflect antagonisms and prejudices of the adult culture. In other instances, social, ethnic, religious, and racial demarcations may break down when individuals from such groups are brought closely together under the powerful stress of deprivations, similar ego-strivings, identifications, and so on.   These are only some examples that can be cited of the impact of the macrocosm (larger society) upon the microcosm (gangs, cliques, social movements of various sorts).   They cannot be neglected in any discussion of spontaneous group formation.

INDIVIDUAL MEMBERS AS INFLUENCED BY GROUP NORMS AND IDENTIFICATIONS

There is substantial justification for the position of certain psychologists that the social psychology of group interactions and collective behavior in all its phases should be worked out in terms of the experience and reactions of single individuals if it is going to be psychology at all.   In the previous section we gave a brief ac-

---

[10] These relationships are admirably indicated in Landesco's survey [21], especially in chapter 23 on "Racketeering," chapter 24 on "The Gangster and the Politician," and chapter 25 on "Funerals of Gangsters."

count of some of the consequences of interaction in terms of the resulting group properties and their effects on individual members. In this section, we shall analyze in more detail material concerned with single individuals, and the way these individuals identify themselves with and participate in particular groups. As we shall see, when we approach group situations in terms of the single individual, we are led to the same conclusions concerning the social psychology of group interaction that were reached when we started with the properties of the group. Thus we can do away once more with the individual-group dichotomy.

Our illustrations will be derived from "gang" members, not, however, because our main concern is the special type of behavior exhibited in delinquent groups. As we said before, group behavior shown in gangs merely affords psychologists an unusually good opportunity to study group formations and differential group behavior in a rather clear-cut way. Such gang formations (under given conditions) can be traced comparatively easily. And since they are deviations, their major features stand out in bold relief.

With the aid of expert investigators in the various fields concerned, Clifford Shaw intensively studied boys from the point of view of their socioeconomic background, their psychological make-up, and their physical characteristics. For a good many years he followed closely the lives of boys who participated as members of various gangs at different times. These studies are exemplary. They give admirable accounts of the economic–cultural setting in which these boys gravitate towards each other to form their own group and to participate in activities which relieve their deprivations. Shaw secured the "own stories" (informal autobiographies) of some of these boys and checked them against objective information he collected. In this discussion, we are interested chiefly in the group (gang) identifications, their effects in forming appropriate attitudes and in producing differential group behavior. Shaw's studies contain unusually clarifying insights into the problem of spontaneous group formation because of the stress of major deprivations and the lack of or conflict in personal identity.

The "own stories" are especially important for the psychologist. They show the group identifications, the attitudes formed in group situations, and the behavior conforming to these attitudes—all as experienced by the participants themselves. These documents give the "essentially human" or psychological accounts of these gang boys' lives. In the words of Burgess, "In the life-history is revealed, as in no other way, the inner life of the person, his moral struggles, his successes and failures in securing control of his destiny in a world too often at variance with his hopes and ideals." [50, 4] The following "own story" of a gang member furnishes us, for example, with considerable insight into the dynamics of spontaneous group identifications and the inculcation of appropriate norms in the participants of the group:

When I started to play in the alleys around my home I first heard about a bunch of older boys called the "Pirates." My oldest brother was in this gang and so I went around with them. There were about ten boys in this gang and the youngest one was eleven and the oldest one was about fifteen. . . .

Tony, Sollie, and my brother John were the big guys in the gang. Tony was fifteen and was short and heavy. He was a good fighter and the young guys were afraid of him because he hit them and beat them up. Sollie was a little guy about twelve years of age. He couldn't fight, but he was a smart guy and told stories and made plans for the gang. He was the brains of the gang. My brother was fifteen and was bigger than Tony and was a good fighter. He could beat any guy in the gang by fighting, so he was a good leader and *everybody looked up to him as a big guy*. I looked up to him as a big guy and was proud to be his brother. . . .

When I started to hang out with the Pirates I first learned about robbin. The guys would talk about robbin and stealing and went out on "jobs" every night. When I was eight I started to go out robbin with my brother's gang. We first robbed junk from a junk yard and sometimes from the peddlar. Sometimes we robbed stores. We would go to a store, and while one guy asked to buy something the other guys would rob anything like candy and cigarettes and then run. We did this every day. Sollie always made the plans and Tony and John would carry out the plans. . . .

The gang had a hangout in an alley and we would meet there every night and smoke and tell stores and plan for robbin. I was little and so I only listened. The big guys talked about going robbin and told stores about girls and sex things. The guys always thought about robbin and bummin from school and sometimes from home. . . .

Besides robbin, the gang went bummin downtown and to ball parks and swimming. On these trips we always robbed everything we could get. . . .

When I was ten the gang started to robbin stores and homes. We would jimmy the door or window and rob the place. I always stayed outside and gave jiggers. The big guys went in and raided the place. They showed me how to pick locks, jimmy doors, cut glass, and use skeleton keys and everything to get into stores and houses. Every guy had to keep everything a secret and *not tell anybody or he would be beat up and razzed*. The police were enemies and not to be trusted. When we would get caught by the police we had to keep mum and not tell a word even in the third degree.

I looked up to my brother and the other big guys because of their courage and nerve and the way they could rob. They would tell me never to say a word to anybody about our robbin. My mother didn't even know it. Some kids couldn't be in the gang because they would tell everything and some didn't have the nerve to go robbin. *The guys with a record were looked up to and admired by the young guys. A stool-pigeon was looked down on and razzed and could not stay in the gang.* . . .

The guys stuck together and helped each other out of trouble. They were real good pals and would stick up for each other. They were always planning new crimes and new ways to get by without being caught. Everyone hated the police and looked upon them as enemies. Anybody who was friendly to the police was not trusted. The plans for stealing were always secret and anybody who talked about them to fellows outside of the gang or to the police was not trusted and *became an enemy of the Pirates.* . . . [50, *10 f.,* italics ours]

Clifford Shaw published these intensive longitudinal studies and "own stories" in *The Jack Roller* (1930) [50], *The Natural History of a Delinquent Career* (1931) [51], and *Brothers in Crime* (1938) [52]. His work on the "Jack Roller" (Stanley) is an intensive account of a boy who participated in delinquent activities and, at last, settled down to conventional society for good. Checking Stanley's own story against the objective data at his command and his contacts with Stanley for five years, Shaw states that "the sincerity of the story cannot be questioned" and that "the story reveals his fundamental attitudes and typical reactions to the various situations in which he has lived." [50, *47*]   As we shall see, Stanley's account tells us a great deal about spontaneous group formations and identifications when there is deprivation and lack of stable social links.

Stanley was first studied by Dr. William Healy when he was seven years and ten months old. He was found to be a little above the average in intelligence and of about normal physical condition. He seemed

> . . . on the whole to be a very nice boy. During the examination he talked freely. [50, *198*]

He had a "winning smile." [*198*]

> The psychological tests at the age of eighteen showed an intelligence quotient of 1.06. [50, *199*]

Shaw gives a rather detailed account of the social and economic areas of Chicago in which Stanley's family lived at different periods. They were slum areas with a relatively high degree of poverty and with conflicting immigrant and American values. Concerning one of the areas in which Stanley's family lived, Shaw states:

> In the present Polish neighborhood back of the yards, with a population in 1920 of 52.1 per cent foreign-born, there is a definite break between the foreign-born parents and their native-born children. [50, *35*]

Stanley, the American born son of a Polish immigrant worker, was four years old when his mother died. A few months later his father married a woman who brought with her "seven children from two previous marriages."

> The stepmother favored her own children and discriminated against Stanley and his brother and sister. [50, *42*]

Throughout his story, Stanley complains bitterly about the treatment he received from her. With over ten children in the family, they went hungry most of the time.

Under the stress of hunger and other conditions, Stanley started his real life activities in petty stealing, *led by his step-brother and other boys* a few years older. He kept himself away from the restrained and miserable home situation. He entered school at the age of six but played hooky a great deal.

Despite his frequent truancies, he was graduated at the age of thirteen and a half, while in the St. Charles School for Boys. [50, 32]

His genuine psychological identifications and attitudes seem to have been little affected by the school, although it undoubtedly tried to mold him in the usual routine way. His real identification was with a gang he joined at the age of seven. This particular gang "consisted of about twelve members, who ranged in age from six to seventeen years." [44] Membership in this gang and, later, in other gangs gave Stanley a personal status and identity he did not find in his family or school. It was only as a member of the gang that he was not "looked down" upon.

His delinquent activities began while he was in company with this group. As a member of this group and other gangs he advanced progressively from "truancy and petty stealing at the early age of six years, to the more serious delinquency of 'jack-rolling' and burglary, in the adolescent period." [25] Arrests and commitments followed each other, so that Stanley spent almost half his youthful life in correctional institutions.

Our chief concern in Stanley's story is the effect of group membership on his identity and behavior. From this point of view, one of his experiences can serve as a starting point for the further examination of his story:

> One day my partner didn't show up, and right then and there I lost all my nerve. I needed someone with me to steal. I was too cowardly to steal alone. *A companion made me brave and gave me a sense of security. I couldn't to save my soul steal a dime alone.* [50, 86, italics ours]

Without implying in the least that all delinquent behavior is a function of group behavior, this experience of Stanley's is significant. It gives a typical illustration of the psychological qualities of a group situation, irrespective of the direction group activities take. It is not unusual, for example, to hear a war veteran cite the case of some fellow who surprised his buddies by unexpected bravery—for him—during some active combat.

". . . the life in the streets and alleys became fascinating and enticing" to Stanley very soon after he reached school age. In the streets he found two close companions, Tony and William, whom he regarded as heroes. He soon developed so he fit into their pattern, as any growing boy might fit into the pattern of his heroes, whatever their characteristics might be.

To my child-seeing eyes, I visioned Tony as a great leader in the neighborhood, and he directed his gang around with much bravado. He and William were always stealing and talking about stealing and I fell in with them as soon as I began to play around in the neighborhood. [50, *51*]

Stanley identified himself so closely with the gang he happened to belong to at the time, was so anchored in its social setting, that he felt personally secure only in its atmosphere. We see his loss of ego bearings when he was outside this atmosphere.

From the time I used to go to the markets and to West Madison Street with the old gang I had been attracted to throngs of people, not the Loop throngs, but the West Madison and South State Street throngs. *I could not explain this irresistible interest, even if I wanted to.* Perhaps it was the telepathy that is from one derelict to another. I do know full well that this human wreckage was always full of interest and mystery to my dreamy mind. Men of all nationalities and races, from the four corners of the earth, were there and brushed shoulders with the crooks and gunmen of the underworld. They were all attracted there, as I was, by the cheap movies, flophouses, cheap hashhouses, and, most of all, by the human derelicts that make West Madison Street what it is. *When blue and broken-up I would always find an old pal there to tell my troubles to and receive the sympathy that comes through mutual understanding.* All the old bums and human wrecks were my family. We all ate at the same table and enjoyed ourselves at the same theaters. In fact, we consisted of a brotherhood whose object was mutual pity and sympathy. The brotherhood was made up of ordinary "bos," pickpockets, pan-handlers, petty thieves, "jack-rollers," and the other wrecks that compose the underworld. Here was my favorite haunt, because my friends made their rendezvous there. It seemed to me that here the lights gleamed brighter, the lures were stronger, and that there were more bums to hide me from the stares of snobbish people. [50, *79 f.,* italics ours]

But not any kind of a life that appears to be settled is sufficient to make one feel psychologically settled, even though it may afford food, shelter, and luxuries. When Stanley was an adolescent boy, he was taken into the home of the vice-president of a company where he worked for a time. The vice-president who "was married but had no children," even planned to adopt him. But Stanley felt he did not belong there. Something was missing. He longed for his pals, in whose company he felt himself at ease and a person in his own right.

The surroundings in my new home and neighborhood took my breath away. My first day at the foster-home was like a sweet dream. The new luxury seemed to dazzle and blind me. My new father rode with me to work every morning and home in the evening. We had nice lunches together at noon. He talked nice to me, gave me spending money and good clothes, *but I missed my old pals and the gay life we had lived. Here I did not have any boy chums, but had to spend my time playing the victrola.* My foster-parents didn't have much life, but spent their time reading and playing a tame game of cards. They had lots of company of snobbish people, and *they looked down on me.* Even if they were nice, it was because of pity and charity. *There was something missing.* Eating at the table I was ill at ease. I couldn't do the things just right, and my foster-mother looked at my blunders through the corner of her eye. I compared everything with my sister's common fare and poor surroundings, and *finally longed to go back to my friends and pals.* Back home I wasn't dressed up all the time, and could play and romp and gamble and swear. But here I was not free to move and talk as I was in the habit of doing before. Everything was different—strange and stiff. *I felt out of place*—a city waif dependent upon charity. I had been in jail half a lifetime, but now I was suddenly placed in luxury after living in a dirty hovel. *My adventurous spirit rebelled against this dry life and it soon won out.* [50, 87 f., italics ours]

After leaving this home, Stanley was again in the gang atmosphere, in his own element.

The lures and the irresistible call drew me on like a magnet. I was always helpless before them. I was like a canoe on a storm-swept sea, buffeted here and there, helpless and frail. *I had about as much chance of controlling my desires to drift with the current of the under-*

world as the canoe had of braving the storm. But here I mingled with bums and derelicts like myself, and *people did not stare at my rags and misery. Here I felt at home,* for "misery loves company." So I drifted on with the rest of the human driftwood—carried on by the current of West Madison Street's exclusive "Four Hundred" or more. [50, *93,* italics ours]

In this social atmosphere, Stanley enjoyed the prestige acquired from his relative status in his new gang.

There were four of us who hung around together. The other three had been in St. Charles School for Boys while I was there, and that strengthened our faith in each other. *I was looked up to as the hero of the quartet because I had done fifty-six months in St. Charles, more than all the others put together. They naturally thought I was one who had a vast experience and was regarded as one might regard the big social hit of society.* [50, *96,* italics ours]

Once groups or gangs are formed, reciprocal loyalties develop among the members. Norms arise more or less informally but nevertheless become binding within the group and are inculcated as personal values in the ego structure of the members. Stanley speaks of these reciprocal loyalties:

My fellow-workers [in the gang] were fast guys and good pals. We were like brothers and would stick by each other through thick and thin. We cheered each other in our troubles and loaned each other dough. A mutual understanding developed, and nothing could break our confidence in each other. [50, *96*]

In a similar way, an atmosphere of solidarity is established in jail. Cliques or gangs are formed spontaneously on the basis of common interest and in the face of the common opposition to authority.

In the tailor shop [of the penal institution to which he was committed on this particular occasion] were two pals that I had known in Pontiac. So we became friends immediately and helped each other out by exchanging reading materials, tobacco, and by giving each other warnings and inside tips about how to get by. *It was a little mutual aid society,* which is very necessary in prison. The prisoners have to band together for their own protection. [50, *155,* italics ours]

Once incorporated, the norms of this more or less isolated prison group may also be experienced as intensely felt personal values in much the same way that the norms of any social group are experienced. Stanley's account illustrates this point:

> To squawk on a fellow-prisoner is an unpardonable sin and only the lowest characters will squawk. But there were boys who would squawk and they would usually become boy officers, so we did not trust them but harbored hatred toward them. *They were not fit to be associated with decent boys.* [50, 67, italics ours]

We see from Stanley's own account how he made the norms of the isolated prison situation a part of him:

> I fell in the web without any experience, but soon got onto the ropes. My feeling was for the code and against the officials. Don't trust anybody except tried pals who won't squawk. [50, 67]

Group norms may become so well incorporated as personal ego-attitudes that individual group members will observe them at the cost of personal punishment and hardship. This fact is concretely illustrated in Stanley's story:

> One Saturday afternoon all of us were playing on the drill field, and the first lieutenant (a boy) asked me to go to the cottage and bring his harmonica. While I was in the cottage I saw two other boys who had sneaked into the cottage, and they were stealing something. I took the harmonica to the lieutenant and ten minutes later I was accused of stealing some cigars from the basement. I denied the charge, and could have cleared myself by telling on the two boys, but I wouldn't squawk and break the code; consequently, I was given a good beating and forced to do "haunches" another hour. Many times did I suffer because I wouldn't squawk, but I'd die before I'd turn on a fellow prisoner. [50, 69]

And just as good members of any organized group uphold the values or norms of the group, expect the same of other members, and impose various correctives and punishments on those who deviate, so the good members of gangs become conscious of their own norms and react violently against deviants and nonconformists. Stanley believed

. . . that any game should be played according to the rules of the game. Violators of rules should be punished. Crime is a game, and therefore as a rat violates the rules or code by informing the "dicks" and the "screws," he should be punished when caught, just like other criminals are punished. I think everyone will agree with me in my feelings about these low rats. All prisoners who are worthy of the name will agree with me. [50, *112*]

We saw in the last section that when gang members "settled down" in conventional society, they tended to pull away from the gang. This happened to Stanley. Through Clifford Shaw's insightful analysis of the case and his effective help in placing Stanley in situations which contributed to his settling down without making him feel out of place, Stanley eventually conformed to the norms of conventional society. When about 18, Stanley was released from the House of Correction, identifying "himself with the adult criminal group." [*164*] Shaw gave him new clothes and placed him in a congenial home, where, as Stanley reported, "They seemed to accept me and not look down on me." After several trials in jobs, he became a salesman and showed considerable ability in this work, in which there was not much chance to be reminded constantly of his past record. He married a girl who told him that she did not care what he had done, but was interested in what he was going to be. He enjoyed the company of her other young friends. Encouraged by Shaw, he enrolled in evening classes to complete his high school education. But throughout all this period, his old pals in the slum area still exerted influence over him. In Shaw's words:

The influence of these earlier relationships did not begin to diminish until other interests and relationships were established in his new situation. We may assume that the gradual changes which are taking place in Stanley's conduct throughout this chapter reflect changes in his group relationships. [50, *175*]

Since thousands of young men, who may identify themselves with the adult of the criminal group at the end of their release from prison, do not have the expert guidance of an understanding person, it is likely that many of them will follow the lead of their more mature and grim gang identifications with all the consequences until they can be absorbed in work and in interpersonal relationships with society at large through the transformation of ego identifications.[11]

Another case presented in *The Natural History of a Delinquent Career* [51] is particularly interesting, because it traces the effects of gang influence on the identifications, attitudes, and activities of a boy, Sidney, who differed in some important respects from Stanley, the "jack roller." The results of Sidney's intelligence test at the age of 15 indicated "excellent mental development" and placed "him in the group having superior intelligence." His intelligence quotient was reported as 126.

> The physical and neurological examinations were negative. There was no indication of mental pathology. [51, *261*]

The community in which Sidney grew up was one of the worst slum areas in the city. He was the youngest of two children in a poor, often "destitute" Jewish family. Shortly after Sidney was born,

> Because of the father's repeated desertions, the mother was forced to seek employment outside of home. [51, *230*]

His brother, Abe, seven years older, "was in most respects a model person" of "average intelligence."

> The mother exercised much closer supervision of Abe than it was possible for her to exercise in the case of Sidney. [51, *234*]

Abe did not become associated with neighborhood gangs.

Sidney's first social experiences outside of the home were with a neighborhood play group made up of children four or five years older than himself. As we shall see, Sidney rather consistently associated and managed to keep up with groups of boys older than himself. Possibly he was able to do so partly because he was unusually intelligent. His delinquent activities (petty stealing) began at about the age of seven after his entrance into this group. Sidney wrote of these early stealing experiences:

[11] For an account of the development of identifications with the criminal world, as well as for material relevant to gang effects and the impact of the community and larger society on youthful gangs, see [59, *51–81*].

Never a thought occurred to me as to whether it was right or wrong, it was merely an interesting game. *The apple or orange didn't make as much difference as the getting of them.* It was the taking them that I enjoyed. [58]

One night I remember I rounded up a few of my acquaintances and invited them down to one of these fruit stores and showed them how I could get away with things. I stole about a dozen large beets. At another time I stole for the same bunch some tomatoes or something else to eat. *Everyone had a fine time and cheered me on to further efforts. I felt fine at achieving such success in their eyes.* But a few of them tattled to my brother and I never surrounded myself with an audience after that. I don't mean that afterwards I stole by myself. *The fact is that I never stole when I was by myself.* The kick came when there was someone with me and the fun could be mutual. It was a merry, exciting pastime that interested me to the exclusion of all others. [51, 59 f., italics ours]

Shaw verifies the fact that Sidney stole almost exclusively in the company of others and adds that "more than 90 per cent of the stealing offenses in cases brought before the Cook County court are committed by groups of two or more boys." [59]

During this period, Sidney began to play truant from school, not so much because he disliked school as because it seemed dull compared to the thrilling activities of his gang.

Despite his repeated truancy, his school report shows a record of good scholarship. [51, 231]

Because Sidney was much younger and smaller than the other gang members, he seldom got a fair cut of the booty. They would encourage him to pick a fight with an older boy and then enjoy seeing him "take" the bigger boy. But Sidney "didn't like this as *I wanted to be one of them and not the object of their amusement.*" [73, italics ours]

After several experiences in the Parental School for delinquents and truants, Sidney moved with his family to a new neighborhood. His mother bought him his first new suit. For a year, he skated, played baseball, and so on, with the boys in this school and "was a model pupil." But the following winter, he decided to go to work, was picked up by the truant officer who already knew him well, and was sent off to the Parental School again. This was his fourth term in this detention home.

On his release, Sidney started back to school again. The "nice" boys and girls were not intimate with him. As he wrote:

> I was very unhappy and couldn't find anything to do that would interest me continuously. I knew that if I could get in with a gang I would find plenty of excitement and thrills, but I didn't know of any gang. It wasn't my first choice, but it was a good substitute and I knew it was interesting because I had belonged to a gang when I had been younger. Excitement seemed to be my natural impulse and I greatly desired companionship—some one with similar desires as mine. I wanted lots of fun. *I knew how to get it in the legitimate way*, but couldn't. So I wanted to go with some gang who broke the laws because I knew I could soon gain their attitudes because it would be naturally somewhat similar to the attitude of my old gang. [51, *113*, italics ours]

Finally, Sidney "dropped over to the west side to see what became of the old gang." [*117*] Afterward, he met several boys acquainted with older criminals at the Burns Athletic Club, whose membership, according to Shaw, included "some of Chicago's most notorious criminal characters." [*131*] As Shaw notes:

> Prior to Sidney's contact with the Burns Athletic Club his delinquencies had been limited very largely to pilfering, burglary, and shoplifting. . . . It was immediately following his association with this group and while in the company of some of its younger members that Sidney's first experience in the larceny of automobiles and holdup with a gun took place. [51, *232*]

Because he had no "vocational and leisure-time interests" and was not "incorporated" into any more or less permanent group, he easily accepted "the adult criminal pattern of this group."

These criminals were heroes to Sidney.

> The three fellows that I went with lived in the neighborhood all their lives and they told me the history of many of these racketeers. They knew them all personally and of course I got to know them personally. Just knowing them made us feel like big shots and I longed to be able to carry a big forty-five automatic like they carried on their hip. My life had been lawless and I felt that some day to

become a big gangster would be a fine thing for me. I wanted to be one tough guy. [51, *136*]

It is evident that this group of criminals became the reference group with which Sidney and his friends identified themselves.

When he was 16 years old, he was sentenced to 20 years in prison for rape at the point of a gun. From Sidney's "own story" we gather that, until he knew that the police had been informed of this act, he thought of it as an exciting experience, as something to brag about at the Burns Athletic Club. Shaw points out that this offense "was an integral part of his whole criminal-behavior pattern." [*232*]

> It is perhaps important to observe, also, that prior to the first rape episode in which this gang was involved a number of similar cases had occurred in the Chicago district. These cases were known to Sidney and his companions and had been the subject of discussion among them. . . . It may be assumed that his attitudes toward women and sex behavior were defined through his experience with prostitutes and in the course of his conversations with other delinquents. He was never incorporated into a conventional group through which he might *assimilate* the conventional attitudes and moral values of society. For the most part, his contacts with conventional groups were not only casual and infrequent but essentially *formal and external* in character. [51, *233,* italics ours]

This does not mean, of course, that Sidney was ignorant of the norms of larger society concerning sex. But it does indicate that the norms of larger society were not *his.* Identification with the adult criminal group was for him a more potent determinant of behavior than mere knowledge of the norms of society. Without attempting to analyze all the important factors in this case, we can report Shaw's own conclusion after his study of the records of each member of the major gangs Sidney identified himself with:

> The foregoing records suggest that Sidney's delinquencies occurred as part of the activities of the play groups and gangs of which he was a member. It is clear that delinquency was an established tradition in these groups prior to Sidney's contact with them. [51, *41*]

In a more recent publication, Shaw has portrayed the individual cases of the five Martin brothers [52]. Their social and economic background was similar to the Jack Roller's. The psychiatrist who examined the boys concluded that they could be properly classified as both physically and mentally normal. *Brothers in Crime* gives a detailed account of the deviant behavior and of the "settling down" of the five brothers both in verified objective terms and in the boys' "own stories." The general lines of the course of development of their psychological identifications and attitudes and the factors that contributed to their "settling down" in society at large are similar to those summarized briefly in the case of the Jack Roller. In short, they began their early childhood in play groups and embryonic gangs, psychologically identifying themselves with these spontaneously developed groups.

The boys' mother was a devout church member. But as the boys became involved in the activities of their gangs, "they repudiated all institutions which sought to enforce conformity to conventional standards of conduct." [*140*] The compellingness of group values or norms in shaping the brothers' lives was indicated by the "inability of the family, the school, the church, the juvenile court, and family case-work agencies to alter their conduct." [*126*] Through the efforts of their mother, teachers, social workers, and other adults the boys became quite familiar with the norms of conventional society. However, *knowledge* of these norms did not materially affect their identifications, attitudes, and behavior. The boys had clearly incorporated the values and norms of their gangs *as their own*. Consequently, the conflicting norms of society at large had little or no effect in regulating their behavior.

They gravitated towards organic membership in these groups under the stress of basic deprivations and the denial of an integrated personal identity in home, school, church, and other conventional situations. They had to derive their main feelings of personal status from membership in these play groups, embryonic or crystallized gangs. Their basic deprivations were relieved through the activities of these groups. Thus, when John Martin, the oldest brother who set the example for the others,

> . . . was approximately seven years of age, *he became identified with one of the many play groups in his community,* a group composed of at least twelve boys ranging in age from five to twelve years. Their playgrounds were the alleys, streets, and railroad yards; their activities were largely spontaneous, random, and unsupervised; simple

forms of stealing were interspersed with nondelinquent activities with little realization of their moral implications. [52, *109,* italics ours]

The psychiatrist who examined the Martin brothers reports that they "differed in regard to personality traits." But "despite differences in personality, physical stature, and intelligence, all of the brothers engaged in the same forms of delinquent conduct throughout the early periods of their careers." [*325*] It seems clear, therefore, that the similarity of their behavior in early years was due to their membership in similarly formed groups. In later adolescent years their individually deviant behavior differed according to the specific activities of the gang to which each brother belonged.

One of Shaw's generalizations based on keen observation should be of particular interest to any psychologist who wants to see the problems of personality with clear perspective.

It is interesting to observe that the brothers who had the longest careers in delinquency were the ones who possessed personality traits which are usually regarded as being most desirable. John, Edward, James, and Michael are sociable, friendly, and loyal persons who adapt themselves readily to other individuals. Carl, on the other hand, possesses fewer of these traits, yet he continued in delinquency for a shorter period of time than did his brothers. It is suggested that perhaps socially desirable personality traits may be related to satisfactory adjustments in the delinquent group in the same manner in which they are related to adjustments in conventional groups. In short, they may be social assets in both situations. Conversely less desirable traits may complicate the process of adjustment in delinquent and in nondelinquent groups. [52, *313*]

It seems a tragic irony, in the case of the Martin brothers at least, that a less sociable, less friendly, and less loyal "personality" came as a blessing to save one of the brothers from the more prolonged indulgence in delinquent behavior of his more sociable brothers.[12]

---

[12] For another example, see case 1 in *Judge Baker Foundation Studies No. 1* (Boston, 1922). Throughout the complete report of this delinquent boy there are comments by various officials and examiners on his friendly personality. He is described as "thoroughly pleasant, responsive, smiling often" [*26*]; "fond of activity and fun-loving" [*28*]; "friendly, and very cooperative, and frank in his discussion." [*37a*] This boy had nine formal complaints against him in three years' time. As he said, "You do lots of things to make others think you are a great fellow." [*34*]

Shaw's observations of the family origins of gang members should be mentioned for they give further insight into the problem of parent-youth conflict, the subsequent psychological drifting away from the family situation, and the establishment of new ego links. So far the gang members we have mentioned all came from slum areas. However, Shaw states that there are cases of youthful gang members who stem from "the highest income groups in the community." [*101*] Such cases also reflect the consequences of parent–youth friction due to the conflicting identifications of children and their parents. As we have seen before, parents and boys of the new generation may have incorporated values or norms which represent either different or contradictory cultural patterns due in some instances to the rapid transition of the times.

In each of the individual studies, we have seen how the boy very soon embarked once more on delinquent activities after he was let out of a detention home. In their work on delinquency areas in Chicago, Shaw and his collaborators [49] give significant hints concerning the effect of group formations in prolonging the deviant types of behavior of individual group members. In this provocative work, the authors systematically studied the relative contribution of different areas of the city to the total number of individuals brought to court. For our present problem, the results on "recidivism among male delinquents brought before the juvenile court during 1900–1906 and 1917–1923" are important. For among other things, they reflect again the importance of group belongingness or group reference as a cause of the differential rates of recidivism in various parts of the city. On the basis of their analysis, the authors conclude:

> It is clear from the foregoing material that the extent of recidivism is highest in the areas having the highest rate of individual delinquents and that this fact explains the disproportionately high rate of delinquency cases in these areas. This finding suggests that the factors contributing to delinquency in these areas of concentration tend also to give rise to recidivism by increasing both the proportion of delinquents who become recidivists and the number of times the recidivists appear in court. [49, *186*]

In a more recent work, Shaw and McKay [53], using similar statistics collected from 1927 to 1933, reach the same conclusion.

From these findings and other material on gangs already cited, it is clear that continued gang membership is one of the chief factors in the relatively high rate of recidivism in these areas. There is concrete evidence that, if young delinquents after their release from prison could be placed in informal groups where their interests could be directed along other channels and where they could feel they were active participants, the rate of recidivism would decrease. Referring to such attempts undertaken under the supervision of Clifford Shaw in certain Chicago areas, Martin [30] writes:

> Shaw believes it [recidivism] is caused partially by the tendency of an ex-convict's community to shun him when he comes out of prison. Barred this contact with "respectable" people, the ex-con is forced to seek association with criminals. Soon he will go back to prison. The Area Project attempts to reintegrate ex-cons into their communities. The parolees handled by the Russell Square Committee range from youngsters of, say, fourteen years, locked up for the first time, to men of fifty with long criminal records. Of forty-seven parolees dealt with, only one has been returned to prison for parole violation. (The parole agent caught him drunk.) [30]

In this connection, the practical remarks contained in a recent memorandum from Shaw to the board of directors of the Chicago Area Project are pertinent. [54] They imply the psychological fact that the direction of an individual's behavior is not affected in a major way unless and until he becomes ego-involved in social situations. Shaw observed:

> Attempts to produce these changes *for* the community by means of ready-made institutions and programs planned, developed, financed, and managed by persons outside the community are not likely to meet with any more success in the future than they have in the past. This procedure is psychologically unsound because it places the residents of the community in an inferior position and implies serious reservations with regard to their capacities and their interest in their own welfare. What is equally important is the fact that it neglects the greatest of all assets in any community, namely the talents, energies, and other human resources of the people themselves. For these

reasons, these superimposed programs and institutions, while perhaps providing temporary aid to individuals and families, are not likely to exercise any deep and lasting influence in the social character of the community. They are related to the community only in the most superficial manner and thus have not appreciably reduced the volume of truancy, delinquency, and crime. What is necessary, we believe, is the organization and encouragement of social self-help on a cooperative basis. [54, 2]

SOME PSYCHOLOGICAL LEADS

The conclusions reached on the basis of the material so far reviewed are further confirmed by the more psychological analysis of Healy and Bronner [19]. In their study of many delinquent cases who were paired with nondelinquents, the authors investigate from all possible angles the factors contributing to deviant types of behavior. Without denying in the least the contribution of other variables, we shall call attention to the impact of group contact in producing individual delinquency. We repeat that our concern throughout this chapter has been the group determination of this *consequential* type of behavior. For this throws light on group behavior in general. We have not been interested in individual or group delinquency as such.

The chain of causation between basic urges, desires, and wishes on the one hand, and delinquency on the other, runs clear through Healy and Bronner's impressive work. The authors have clearly diagrammed this chain in Figure 3.[18] We see that basic urges, desires, and wishes may be satisfied through "socially acceptable activities" in society whatever the particular norms of the particular society may be. If they are not satisfied, if they are hindered by economic or other situational circumstances, "feelings of inadequacy, deprivations, and thwartings" arise. These in turn are followed by urges for substitute satisfactions. These urges for substitute satisfactions need not necessarily express themselves in delinquent behavior. Between these urges and actual participation in delinquent activity there is the step of "acceptance of ideas of delinquency." In the authors' words:

[18] Reproduced from [19, 4] by permission.

Now what form substitutive activities will take, whether or not they will be antisocial, depends partly on external circumstances, but mainly upon the acceptance of certain ideas. [19, 7]

The process of acceptance is further elaborated in such formulations:

Very few indeed, if any, enter into delinquency as the result of a new born impulse, without previously having had thought about it.

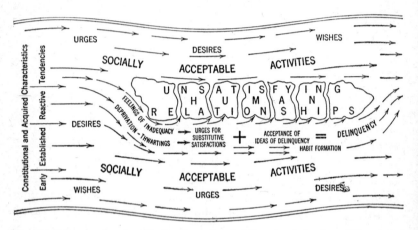

FIG. 3. Diagram showing the development of delinquent behavior. The general life stream of feelings and activities.

There is almost universally some period of incubation of such ideas, generally not thought out to definite conclusions concerning action, but still recurring as part of the mental content. *An educative or assimilative process has been going on, usually under the stimulus of some environmental source or sources, whereby the individual learns about delinquency, its forms and techniques, as he might become informed or educated about, we will say, tree climbing.* [19, 68, italics ours]

The impact of group factors in the "acceptance of ideas of delinquency" is stressed time and again in different connections by Healy and Bronner. For example, they state that *"little delinquency is engaged in without companionship or gang connections."* [63, italics ours] And again, "this particular educative process generally began with information received from youthful comrades—two were taught by older criminals." [66]

In our opinion, the process of acceptance of ideas or norms of delinquency through social contacts will gain clarity and functional usefulness if it is conceptualized in terms of identifications in actual groups or ego-involvements in relation to certain reference groups in general and membership groups in particular. Once identification takes place, whatever the size of the group may be, essentially similar psychological consequences may be expected. Psychologically, it makes a great deal of difference whether praise or ridicule comes from an indifferent group or a group in which we are strongly ego-involved. Once the norms of a delinquent group or any other group are accepted, once identification with a group takes place, the individual is not necessarily content merely to hold the attitudes of the group or to indulge in prescribed activities. He may spontaneously praise the attitudes, spontaneously engage in new forms of behavior consistent with the group line.

The material gathered by Healy and Bronner indicates clearly the way a boy may become identified with a group and the psychological consequences of this identification.

A boy, for example, feeling himself inadequate in other relationships finds himself accepted and gains recognition with a gang if he takes up with the suggestions they give him of stealing with or for them. [19, 8]

They mention in passing the case of a delinquent boy who "previously was effeminate or feminized." The boy gave the rationale of his deviant behavior.

They thought I was no good so I went out to show a cockeyed world that I was a regular guy. [19, 134]

Although the authors do not specify it, the "cockeyed world" the boy referred to is undoubtedly the reference group whose ridicule at last drove him to such action, and in relation to which he wanted to excel as a "regular guy."

In Shaw's account of the Martin brothers, we noted that the brothers who engaged in delinquent activities the longest were the most sociable friendly ones. In this connection, it is interesting to note that Healy and Bronner found that "gregariousness" or "sociability" is clearly more prevalent among the delinquents than among the individuals used as controls. The greater sociability of delinquents may be, at least in part, a product of their striving to anchor themselves in a social setting when social status is denied them by already established groups. The study of Healy and Bronner clearly suggests the psychological function served by the opportunity to anchor one's self in a definite group, even though it may be a delinquent one. For example:

> Under certain circumstances it may be healthier and more normal to join in with the activities and imbibe the ideas of a delinquent crowd than to be a withdrawing, soft, effeminate "mother's boy" or, as in instances already mentioned, to mope at home and develop an abnormal phantasy life. [19, *136*]

SOME VERIFICATIONS OF THE EFFECTS OF GROUP SITUATIONS

Some representative data already presented have demonstrated the effects of group situations on individuals. We have seen how ego-attitudes may be structured or modified in group situations in a lasting or a temporary way. During the past two decades, these findings have been amply verified on the psychological level. We shall limit our discussion here to a brief summary of a few investigations. All of them compel us to call attention once more to the convergence of sociological and psychological formulations. They prove that there cannot be two kinds of psychologies of collective behavior: the psychology of the individual in group situations is valid social psychology, and his social psychology is valid individual psychology.

Since social interaction is possible only when individuals in a situation are able to grasp reciprocal relationships (the point of view of others as well as their own) and when certain rules or norms established as a consequence of human interaction in the past or emerging in the actual situation are observed, the studies of Piaget and his associates, carried out in the 1920's are especially impressive. These investigations conclusively elucidate the genetic development and properties of group interactions and furnish an unique crucible of the psychology of group interaction, the incorporation of social norms in the individual, and their subsequent effects on behavior.

Piaget studied the successive stages of development of (1) the practice of rules and (2) the consciousness of rules. Since his results show that development runs parallel in both respects, we shall not make a special point of presenting his results separately and shall mention only those findings most relevant to our discussion. He specifically examined the development of the individual's morality from the comparatively early years of childhood almost up to puberty. As he puts it, "All morality consists in a system of rules, and the essence of all morality is to be sought for in the respect which the individual acquires for these rules." [45, *1*] After calling attention to this general fact, Piaget starts with a detailed study of "the rules of the game" as played among age mates. These "rules of the game" exemplified by the game of marbles, are among the first rules grasped by the developing child.

During the first years of his life (in the motor stage) the child cannot really participate in a play situation, let alone in more developed levels of group participation. This inability of the very young child to share collective activity of the simplest sort is due to the fact that his ego is not sufficiently differentiated for him to distinguish between what is his own desire and what is external to him. He cannot yet separate fantasy and fact. In short, he cannot recognize his ever-changing mercurial subjectivity as such. Hence, he cannot consistently follow a conversation, a game, or any social activity involving a give-and-take type of relationship. As he grows older, certain rules (norms) are imposed on him by parents, older boys and girls, or other grown-ups. He is made to abide by these rules in the daily routine of life. But even though he abides by them, for the child around 5 or 6 years of age, rules or norms have not yet become an integrated part of his psychology. To him, the rules or norms he is made to follow are absolute, made in an unchangeable way by grown-ups. Even though he abides by them because of the sheer constraint and authority exerted by his elders, he easily lapses to the ever-changing flux of his desires and fantasy when he is not under the grip of external authority. For these externally imposed rules or norms have not yet become *his own* rules or norms.

Only after further development (around the age of 7–8 in the case of Piaget's children) is the child mature enough to grasp consistently the points of view of others, to interact reciprocally and to co-operate in play and other activities with his equals (age mates). As a consequence of age-mate group interactions and co-operations, the group rules or norms become his own norms. In this process he ceases to consider them as the absolute and immutable dictates of grown-ups. In the course of the development of participation in age-mate activities (around the age of 11–12 in Piaget's cases), children reach the stage where they collectively and spontaneously evolve and *codify* appropriate norms for the situation at hand.

These spontaneously emerging norms in collective age-mate activities are among the first norms that boys or girls accept, respect, and abide by as their own. At this point the experience and behavior of co-operation and autonomy as contrasted to authority and heteronomy is first indicated. In Piaget's words:

> From the moment that children really begin to submit to rules and to apply them in a spirit of genuine cooperation, they acquire a new conception of these rules. Rules become something that can be changed if it is agreed that they should be, for the truth of a rule does not rest on tradition but on mutual agreement and reciprocity. [89] Henceforward, he will not only discover the boundaries that separate his self from the other person, but will learn to understand the other person and be understood by him. So that cooperation is really a factor in the creation of personality, if by personality we mean, not the unconscious self of childish egocentrism, but the self that takes up its stand on the norms of reciprocity and objective discussion, and knows how to submit to these in order to make itself respected. . . . Cooperation being the source of personality, rules cease, in accordance with the same principle, to be external. They become both the constitutive factors of personality and its fruit, in accordance with the circular process so frequently exemplified in the course of mental development. In this way autonomy succeeds heteronomy. [45, 90]

Likewise, with the development of co-operative group activities, the unilateral respect and awe felt towards grown-ups and the conforming behavior of early childhood owing to the pressure of external authority alone give way to feelings of mutual respect and "inner responsibility." These conclusions based on rich concrete data and so briefly summarized here, are full of implications concerning the effects of group situations in determining an individual's personal values and loyalties. They substantiate on a more refined level of psychological analysis the evidence that emerged from the gang studies carried out at approximately the same period in a different country. (See pp. 289–304.)

Piaget considers the social and practical implications of his findings in the final section of his study. The upshot of his brilliant discussion is that the individual can only develop a sense of the reciprocal nature of real human relationships through participation in group activities. Only through such co-operative participation does he come to accept group norms as his own and to develop his identification, loyalty, and inner responsibility towards them. If such co-operative participation is lacking, the individual considers the norms imposed on him by sheer authority as nuisances to be evaded whenever possible. Only as an outcome of co-operation in group situations with equals do "the infantile traits that mark the conformist spirit make place for the features that are the outcome of cooperation." [341] "Whence the decline of unilateral respect and the primacy of personal judgment. But in consequence of this, cooperation suppresses both egocentrism and moral realism, and thus achieves an interiorization of rules." [411] At the end, Piaget makes explicit the implications of his results: "It is obvious that our results are as unfavourable to the method of authority as to purely individualistic methods." Piaget specifically criticized the authoritarian sociology of Durkheim and its educational deductions.

> Unfortunately, under the influence of a "pre-notion," hard to account for in a sociologist, and especially in one so methodical, Durkheim thinks of children as knowing no other society than adult society or the society created by adults (schools), so that he entirely ignores the existence of spontaneously formed children's societies, and of the facts relating to mutual respect. Consequently, elastic though Durkheim's pedagogy may be in principle, it simply leads, for lack of being sufficiently informed on the subject of child sociology, to a defence of the methods of authority. [45, 358 f.]

Unlike psychologists who complacently stop after uttering their conclusions on the basis of restricted "closed" situations, Piaget anxiously looks ahead to see if his conclusions hold in concrete situations:

> For, after all, it is one thing to prove that cooperation in the play and spontaneous social life of children brings about certain moral effects, and another to establish the fact that this cooperation can be universally applied as a method of education. This last point is one which only experimental education can settle. Educational experiment, on condition that it be scientifically controlled, is certainly more instructive for psychology than any amount of laboratory experiments, and because of this experimental pedagogy might perhaps be incorporated into the body of the psychosociological disciplines. [45, *413 f.*]

The results of educational processes which give an opportunity for free co-operation among equals in diverse activities and which encourage initiative in positive group undertakings are described in many reports by progressive educators. An outstanding illustration of the emergent effects of democratically organized collective training on individuals is seen in Makarenko's far-reaching work [6]. In 1920, at a time when famine and civil war were still ravaging the Soviet Union, Makarenko started the Gorki Colony, a school devoted to the reforming and training of juvenile delinquents. The first six students who arrived at the colony were, for example, youngsters who had committed quite serious offenses. "Two of them had been found guilty of larcenies, four of armed burglaries. In the institution they acted as a unit. . . . They assumed an attitude of indifference to the rules or to the staff." [38]

After Makarenko had once proved to the youngsters that he could be tough too, he devoted his energies to the creation of a common life in which administration, teachers, and students alike participated. To this end, they all shared in all activities and hardships and in any rewards that came as a consequence of common effort. In Makarenko's words: "In our nervewracking poverty there was one good feature—all of us, teachers and pupils, were hungry and poor alike." The report continues: "Thus in the process of living together, a common formula was being shaped. Events molded both director and pupils, forming the rudiments of a community interest." [6, 39]   In this collective process of working and living together, which effectively transformed the attitudes of the participating individuals, stealing, drinking, and gambling which were common when the institution started, were successfully eliminated.   Once the collective trend of the colony took definite shape, all such objectionable behavior was eliminated, not through the use of punishments, but by putting the matter to the students themselves and securing their active participation.   The positive results emerging in the Gorki Colony were carried to other such institutions.   In these projects the students of the Gorki Colony played no small part.   From the original colony and another carried to its same level by the Gorki teachers and students, three thousand boys and girls graduated. Many of them attained leading positions in industry, the arts, and sciences.   When they assumed responsible work in society at large, they were not treated as exconvicts or "reformed" boys, but as full-fledged citizens.

It may be safe to conclude that the success of this educational experiment in the Soviet Union in transforming the whole life patterns of unfortunate deviant boys and girls into highly useful citizens is due to the fact that the conception and character of the experiment fit in with and, in fact, were encouraged by the whole social system.   During the first decade of the century, exponents of progressive education in many countries spread their enthusiasm for creating an ideal society through the education of new generations.   And, when we consider the Gorki Colony experiment in the light of similar undertakings in capitalist countries, when we relate it to the disillusionment expressed by many progressive educators in Europe and America, its implications become even more striking.   The fate of so many experiments in progressive education tends to show that, in highly differentiated Western societies where individuals must sooner or later face groups with contradictory conflicting functions and values, they are bound to be torn in different directions with inevitable psychological consequences.   Before jumping to any conclusions about the definite effects of a particular group on its individual members, it therefore becomes necessary to investigate at the same time the question of whether or not the groups which an individual sooner or later will face in a major way are integrated in function and values. For groups cannot be taken as closed systems, especially today. The values and directions shaped in one group have serious consequences in the lives of an individual member if they run counter to those of other groups which he is subsequently bound to encounter. It is not difficult to find cases of antagonistic groups in which the degree of in-group solidarity, sympathy and co-operation may be proportional to the prejudices, intolerance, and enmity exhibited towards the members of out-groups. For example, the utmost degree of consideration, democracy, and good will exhibited within the inner bounds of an exclusive club or a Junior League need not be bestowed on out-group persons, especially if the persons in question are members of groups standing at some distance from the club's particular social hierarchy.

Other relevant experimental and research studies of groups have been reported which provide substantial verification of the effects of group situations on the individual member's identifications and ego relationships, on the structural properties of groups, and on the effects of differential group identifications. Here we can mention only a few representative studies, among which should be included the work of Moreno and his associates. Before 1925, Moreno found that individuals assigned in a group to improvise "certain attitudes for typical situations" often committed "the most bewildering acts, although in the realm of fiction, which seem unrelated to their individual selves when we saw them in daily life." [33, 13] In 1934, Moreno [35] summarized a considerable body of research chiefly concerned with interpersonal relationships within various groups. For example, by asking every child from kindergarten through the eighth grade in a public school to choose seat mates, Moreno constructed "sociograms" showing such social relations within each class. He found a progressive development and differentiation in these children's groups. In kindergarten and the first and second grades, children were *seldom sufficiently certain whom to choose.*" [35, 54, italics ours] After about the fourth grade, intragroup relationships were more complex, suggesting that children develop to "exchange emotions readily and freely form partnerships and secret associations." [35, 54] With the development of "cooperative group action," with the "increased differentiation" of children's groups, a "cleavage" from adults occurs, as evidenced by "the declining insight of adults" into the relationships within children's groups. [35, 50] Only after reciprocal relationships developed among children did they accurately practice status distinctions on the basis of grown-up norms. For example, after about the fourth grade "the percentage of heterosexual attractions drops very low." [35, 61] And, at about the same time, choices were made more frequently in terms of the children's own nationality and color groups with simultaneous rejection of outside groups as prescribed by grown-up norms. "This phenomenon could not be observed in the pre-school groups nor in the 1st, 2nd, and 3rd grades although the percentage of members of different nationalities was about the same." [35, 61] The effects of relatively unified groups as contrasted to relatively divided groups are shown in Moreno's study of the New York State Training School for Girls. The standard of conduct and morale of the group and the number of runaways and requests for transfers varied with the degree of interest in the group.

Moreno and his associates have developed ingenious devices, such as the sociogram, and statistical refinements which facilitate the study of groups. [37] Considerable research has been stimulated. To take a recent example, Bronfenbrenner [10] essentially repeated Moreno's studies of school children. One of the significant findings of this study was that the shift in an individual's status "must be interpreted not only in terms of change in individual, social, or psychological adjustment, but also in terms of group developmental trends." [76]

However, the theoretical background presented by Moreno puts the psychologist in the puzzling situation of studying empirical data along with theoretical formulations mixed with mystic notions. For example, in 1943 Moreno [36] wrote: "I have had the good fortune to develop three ideas. The first idea, a study of the godhead, has remained cryptic and misapprehended. The second, a study of man called psychodrama, has aroused some hope that man can train his spontaneity to overcome many of his shortcomings. My third idea, the study of society called sociometry, has given the greatest promise that a measure can be developed for a deeper understanding of society and a key to the treatment of its ills. Many of my friends consider these three ideas one apart from the other. In my own mind, however, all three ideas are of one piece. One has developed out of the other." [*299*] The "study of the godhead" is expressed in *The Words of the Father* [34], a book published in 1941 and listed as one of the "Basic Works of J. L. Moreno" in Sociometry. The preface and commentary of the book are provided by Moreno who points out that "on the title page of this book there is a vacant place: there is no author's name there." [*316*] "The name of the author is given in the title itself—in *The Words of the Father*. [*317*] As Moreno points out in the beginning of his preface "This is an extraordinary book." [*vii*] He continues:

> It is unique because of its premise. Even before a line of it is read—before it is weighted as to its content—its premise is: these are God's own words. [*vii*] . . . God Himself, not only speaks but is shown acting, creating, ruling and judging. God is present. He creates His own universe. He analyzes His own universe. He is in direct communication with every atom of the universe. [*ix*] . . . It would seem that the idea of God has found in this book a final and total expression. [*x*] . . . It is a consolation that the message of the Father comes to the world at this time. There has never been a moment when a word of encouragement was more welcome. [*xxi*]

God's pronouncements cover over 100 pages. The first reads:

> I AM GOD,
> THE FATHER,
> THE CREATOR OF THE UNIVERSE.
>
> THESE ARE MY WORDS,
> THE WORDS OF THE FATHER.

Such prophetic and ecstatic statements are hardly acceptable to the psychologist.

In 1926, the Wawokiye Camp Research Project [40], a study in "experimental sociology," began under the direction of W. I. Newstetter of Western Reserve University. Designed to gain "generalized knowledge of the primary group and the means for its study" [*93*], this long-range study, in the words of its director, "provides devastating evidence that interactions (social behavior) are not the result of measurable 'traits.'" [*104*]   During the early period of the project (1926–28), the approach was slanted chiefly towards the diagnosis and therapeutics of the individual in social situations. "The value of adjustment through group association was demonstrated by practical results." [*vi*]   However, research results were not so satisfactory. "The measures of these supposed traits weighted in some way were intended to yield a score which was taken as an index of social adjustment. This may be a suitable approach for the interpretation of individual reactions, but has been unfruitful as the basis for interpreting social behavior." [*93 f.*]

As a result, the orientation turned toward a study of the group itself as a step forward in achieving a "situational approach." From 1930 to 1933, two five-week camp periods were held each summer. About thirty boys, most of them problem cases, attended each session. Camp life was more or less unplanned, activity and direction generating chiefly from the boys themselves. Among the findings relevant to our discussion were the measurements of status based on weekly reports of preference for companions. By correlating these indices of group status, it was found that each group had a more or less characteristic pattern of stability in status relationships from week to week.

An attempt to discern what sort of behavior is directly related to acceptance by the group was undertaken by Newcomb. [40, *66–92*] As a result of considerable previous experience, cordial and antagonistic responses were chosen as being most inclusive and related to the problem. Observation of free groupings was recorded on a nine-point scale with considerable reliability. The principal finding of this observation was that cordiality *received* was significantly related to group status, while cordiality (or antagonism) *given* bore no significant relation to group status. Attempts to relate ascendance–submission, volubility of expression, and attention to counselors *given* by a member to his status revealed no relationship between the measures, although ascendance–submission *received* was related to group status. "Our principle conclusion, then, is a methodological or technical one. Significant and reliable measures involving interactions of individuals can be obtained from behavior observations, if these interactions are not assumed to flow from traits of individuals." [*92*]

Another valuable series of studies stems from Lewin and his students. In one of their earlier experiments, Lewin and Lippitt [25, 27] undertook to study under relatively controlled conditions the effects of democratic and autocratic leadership and procedure upon "the unity or division of the group structure pattern" of two similarly composed groups of children performing the same activity (mask making). [27, 31] An analysis of extensive records showed that the unity of the club with autocratic leadership was less stable than that with democratic leadership. For the present discussion, comparative results which were taken as indices of "personal ego involvement versus group goal involvement" are highly relevant. [33] For example, of the first-person pronouns used by the autocratic group, only 18 per cent were plural (*we, us, ours*) as compared to 36 per cent used by the democratic group. After the groups had functioned for some time, members were asked to vote as to whether or not the meetings should be continued. All of the autocratic-group members voted to stop, while four of the five democratic-group members wanted to continue. At the same time, the groups voted on how to dispose of the products of their activities. All of the democratic-group members suggested group disposal of one or more of the masks, while the autocratic group members each claimed his own work.

Such examples indicate that members of the group more or less dominated by the leader were less involved with their group than were members of the group in which co-operative relationships among leader and members were fostered. But the distinction made between "ego involvement" and "group goal involvement" seems unnecessary. When one participates as a member of a group, may he not become *personally* involved with the group, its activities, its goals? Or, when one identifies with the group, may not its goals, its rules, its norms become *his*? Lewin and Lippitt comment in connection with these groups of boys: "In spite of the greater spontaneity of expression in the D-situation, the data indicated that the A-members were more frequently observed to be in an overlapping situation where an individual goal conflicted with a group goal and resulted in the member leaving the field of club work." [27, 38] It would seem possible that one reason the autocratic-group member was more often in conflict was that the group goal was not *his* goal, that is, he was less ego-involved than the democratic-group member. Conversely, one factor accounting for "greater spontaneity" of democratic-group members would seem to be greater identification with the group, that is, greater ego-involvement.

Without attempting to summarize the many interesting and relevant findings in this and other studies of Lewin and his students, their substantiation of the sociological material on the differential behavior of members toward in-group and out-group can be mentioned. In the study just cited, "about twice as many social interactions, per units of interaction possibility, occurred between in-group members as between out-group members." [27, 33] In a further study by Lewin, Lippitt, and White [26], fights, reminiscent of "gang wars," developed spontaneously between clubs on two different occasions. One fight occurred between two democratic clubs; the other occurred between a democratic and a *laissez faire* group, where the leader exerted little pressure on the group.

REFERENCES

1. ALLPORT, F. H., *Social Psychology,* Boston: Houghton Mifflin, 1924.
2. ANDERSON, N., *The Hobo,* Chicago: Univ. Press, 1923.
3. —— The juvenile and the tramp, *J. Criminal Law and Criminol.,* 1923–24, **14,** 290–312.
4. —— *Men on the Move,* Chicago: Univ. Press, 1940.
5. ASBURY, H., *The Gangs of New York, An Informal History of the Underworld,* New York: Knopf, 1927.
6. BERMAN, N., The making of Soviet citizens, *Psychiatry, J. Biol. and Pathol. Interpers. Rels.,* 1945, **8,** 35–49.
7. BEYNON, E. D., The Voodoo cult among Negro migrants in Detroit, *Am. J. Sociol.,* 1938, **43,** 894–907.
8. BLONDEL, C., *Introduction à la psychologie collective,* Paris: Colin, 1928.
9. BLUMER, H., Collective behavior, in *An Outline of Principles of Sociology* (R. E. Park, ed.), New York: Barnes & Noble, 1939, 221–80.
10. BRONFENBRENNER, U., *The Measurement of Sociometric Status, Structure and Development,* Sociometry Monogr., no. 6, New York: Beacon House, 1945.
11. CANTRIL, H., *The Psychology of Social Movements,* New York: Wiley, 1941.
12. CHILD, I. L., *Italian or American? The Second Generation in Conflict,* New Haven: Yale Univ. Press, 1943.
13. CLEMMER, D., *The Prison Community,* Boston: Christopher, 1940.
14. DASHIELL, F., Experimental studies of the influence of social situations on the behavior of individual human adults, in *Handbook of Social Psychology* (C. Murchison, ed.), Worcester: Clark Univ. Press, 1935, ch. 23.

15. DAVIS, K., The sociology of parent–youth conflict, *Am. Sociol. Rev.*, 1940, **5**, 523–35.
16. DURKHEIM, E., *Les Formes élémentaires de la vie religieuse*, Paris, 1912.
17. FAUSET, A. H., *Black Gods of the Metropolis*, Philadelphia: Univ. of Pa. Press, 1944.
18. GIST, N. P., and L. A. HALBERT, *Urban Society*, New York: Crowell, copyright 1942.
19. HEALY, W., and A. F. BRONNER, *New Light on Delinquency and Its Treatment*, New Haven: Yale Univ. Press, copyright 1936.
20. HUGHES, E. C., Dilemmas and contradictions of status, *Am. J. Sociol.*, 1945, **50**, 353–9.
21. LANDESCO, J., Organized Crime in Chicago, in *The Illinois Crime Survey*, Illinois Assoc. for Criminal Justice, Chicago: Blakely, 1929, part 3, 815–1090.
22. —— The woman and the underworld, *J. Crim. Law and Criminol.*, 1936, **26**, 891–902.
23. LA PIERE, R. T., *Collective Behavior*, New York: McGraw-Hill, 1938.
24. LE BON, G., *The Crowd, A Study of the Popular Mind*, London: Ernest Been Ltd., 1938.
25. LEWIN, K., Field theory and experiment in social psychology: concepts and methods, *Am. J. Sociol.*, 1939, **44**, 6, 868–96.
26. —— R. LIPPITT, and R. K. WHITE, Patterns of aggressive behavior in experimentally created "social climates," *J. Soc. Psychol.*, 1939, **10**, 271–300.
27. LIPPITT, R., Field theory and experiment in social psychology: autocratic and democratic group atmospheres, *Am. J. Sociol.*, 1939, **45**, 1, 26–49.
28. LYND, R., *Knowledge for What? The Place of Social Science in American Culture*, Princeton: Univ. Press, 1939.
29. MARTIN, E. D., *The Behavior of Crowds*, New York: Harper, 1920.
30. MARTIN, J. B., A new attack on delinquency, *Harper's Magazine*, May 1944.
31. MAULDIN, B., *Up Front*, New York: Henry Holt, copyright 1945.
32. MOEDE, W., *Experimentelle Massenpsychologie*, Leipzig: Hirzel, 1920.
33. MORENO, J. L., *Group Method and Group Psychotherapy*, Sociometry Monogr., no. 5, New York: Beacon House, 1931.
34. —— *The Words of the Father*, New York: Beacon House, 1941.
35. —— *Who Shall Survive?*, Nervous and Mental Disease Monogr., Series No. 58, Nervous and Mental Disease Publishing Co., Washington, D. C., 1934.
36. —— *Sociometry and the Cultural Order*, Sociometry Monogr., no. 2, New York: Beacon House, 1943.
37. —— and HELEN M. JENNINGS, *Sociometric Measurement of Social Configurations Based on Deviation from Chance*, Sociometry Monogr., no. 3, New York: Beacon House, 1945.
38. MURPHY, G., and L. B. MURPHY, *Experimental Social Psychology*, New York: Harper, 1931.
39. MURPHY, G., L. B. MURPHY, and T. M. NEWCOMB, *Experimental Social Psychology*, New York: Harper, 1937.
40. NEWSTETTER, W. I., M. J. FELDSTEIN, and T. M. NEWCOMB, *Group Adjustment: A Study in Experimental Sociology*, School of Applied Social Sciences, Western Reserve Univ., Cleveland, Ohio, 1938.
41. OUTLAND, G. E., *Boy Transiency in America*, Santa Barbara, Calif.: State College Press, 1939.

42. PARK, R. E., *et al., The City,* Chicago: Univ. Press, 1925.
43. —— and H. A. MILLER, *Old World Traits Transplanted,* Chicago: Univ. Press, 1925.
44. —— Race relations and certain frontiers, in *Race and Culture Contacts* (E. G. Reuter, ed.), New York: McGraw-Hill, 1934.
45. PIAGET, J., *The Moral Judgment of the Child,* London: Kegan Paul, Trench, Trubner and Co., Ltd., copyright 1932.
46. PUFFER, J., *The Boy and His Gang,* Boston: Houghton Mifflin, 1912.
47. ROSS, E. A., *Social Psychology,* New York: Macmillan, 1908.
48. SAPIR, E., Group, in *Encyclopedia of the Social Sciences,* New York: Macmillan, copyright 1932, **7,** 178–82.
49. SHAW, C. R., *Delinquency Areas,* Chicago: Univ. Press, copyright 1929.
50. —— *The Jack-Roller,* Chicago: Univ. Press, copyright 1930.
51. —— *The Natural History of a Delinquent Career,* Chicago: Univ. Press, copyright 1931.
52. —— (ed.), *Brothers in Crime,* Chicago: Univ. Press, copyright 1938.
53. —— and H. D. McKAY, *Juvenile Delinquency and Urban Areas,* Chicago: Univ. Press, copyright 1942.
54. —— *Memorandum Submitted to the Board of Directors of the Chicago Area Project January 10, 1944,* mimeographed report.
55. SHERIF, M., A study of some social factors in perception, *Arch. Psychol.,* 1935, no. 187.
56. —— *The Psychology of Social Norms,* New York: Harper, 1936.
57. SHOHLE, R., *The Isolated Religious Sect,* master's thesis on file Univ. Chicago Library, 1923.
58. STONEQUIST, E. V., *The Marginal Man,* New York: Scribner's, 1937.
59. TANNENBAUM, F., *Crime and the Community,* New York: Ginn, 1938.
60. THRASHER, F. M., *The Gang,* Chicago: Univ. Press, copyright 1927.
61. WHYTE, W. F., Corner boys: a study of clique behavior, *Am. J. Sociol.,* 1941, **46,** 647–64.
62. —— *Street Corner Society,* Chicago: Univ. Press, copyright 1943.
63. ZORBAUGH, H. W., *The Gold Coast and the Slum,* Chicago: Univ. Press, copyright 1929.

CHAPTER 11

EGO-INVOLVEMENTS IN CONCRETE SOCIAL SITUATIONS

In our review of experiments and controlled investigations (ch. 6), we saw how various kinds of ego-involvements entered in to shape or modify experience and behavior. We saw how an individual identified himself with certain occupational or status groups, how his role as a member of a class was related to affectively toned attitudes. We found that in some instances experience and behavior were modified by ego-involvements which resulted from the acceptance of *established* norms and values, whereas some ego-involvements resulted from the *momentary* demands of the actual experimental situation in which the individual found himself.

The concept of *ego-involvement* is, of course, not a mere artifact created to account for artificial laboratory situations or for the facts obtained in other controlled investigations. Indeed, the laboratory experiments and other investigations came sometime after observations of concrete social situations had suggested the usefulness and validity of the concept. [4, 5, 41] Equipped with a knowledge of how the ego develops in the child, how it is re-formed in adolescence, how it is constituted and how it affects behavior in controlled laboratory situations, we now have some solid basis from which to view ego-involved activities as they can be seen in concrete social situations.

We can consider only a scattered few of the thousands of examples one might choose for analysis. We shall proceed from relatively simple to more complicated situations. We repeat again that the basic psychological principles are the same, whether they are demonstrated in laboratory experiments, controlled investigations, simple or complicated situations of everyday life.

"The apparel oft proclaims the man." Whatever the origin or

origins of clothes, whatever purposes they serve in different climates, there is little doubt that one of their chief functions is to extend the "self" of the wearer, to enhance his ego, to display his status. Whether it is the simple necklace of the Samoan, the girdle of the Javanese, the earrings of the Siberian Eskimo, the tweed coat of the American college man, or the latest lounging robe exhibited at a fashion show in contemporary Russia, men and women reveal the fact that *they* are concerned about the clothes they wear, the impression clothes make on themselves and others. This is true, of course, only in a relative sense. A destitute person, suffering from the ravages of war, depression, or other circumstances, will be eager enough to get any clothes that satisfy his functional needs. Over a hundred years ago, Carlyle, in his protest against conventions, *Sartor Resartus* [8], wrote:

> Perhaps not once in a lifetime does it occur to your ordinary biped, of any country or generation, be he gold-mantled Prince or russet-jerkined Peasant, that his Vestments and his Self are not one and indivisible; that *he* is naked, without vestments, till he buy or steal such, and by fore thought sew and button them. [8, *40*]

Veblen, in his penetrating *Theory of the Leisure Class* [43], points out that

> No one finds difficulty in assenting to the commonplace that the greater part of the expenditure incurred by all classes for apparel is incurred for the sake of a respectable appearance rather than for the protection of the person. [43, *167 f.*]

When Hurlock asked people the question: "Is your feeling of self-confidence increased by being well and appropriately dressed?" 99 per cent of the women and 94 per cent of the men said "Yes." [19, *46*]

In his well-known book, *The Psychology of Clothes* [14], Flugel states that the great majority of authorities "unhesitatingly regarded decoration as the motive that led, in the first place, to the adoption of clothing." [*17*]

> The essential purpose of decoration is to beautify the bodily appearance, so as to attract the admiring glances of others and fortify one's self-esteem. [14, *20*]

This self-esteem, ego-enhancement, or ego-gratification can, of course, be accomplished in a number of different ways, as Flugel indicates. The most obvious example is the function clothes serve as an indicator of rank in military or religious circles. And in ordinary civilian life clothes provide one of the most concrete expressions of status, especially in those areas of life where status is proportional to the things money can buy. Veblen showed how clothes were used by members of the upper class to demonstrate conspicuous waste and conspicuous leisure. Flugel notes that

> One woman can seriously hurt another, even to the point of making a permanent enemy of her, by being better or more fashionably dressed upon some significant occasion. As long as individuality is permitted, women struggle with one another for wearing the "latest" or most costly frocks. The snobbery of wealth may even take a purely quantitative form, and it may—and often does—become a point of honour to wear a different dress each day (or several different dresses each day, according to the varying occasions of morning, afternoon, and night). [14, *114*]

Another way in which clothes serve to enhance the ego is what Flugel calls the "extension of the bodily self." A person can increase his apparent size, cover up certain physical defects or disproportions, conform more to current norms of beauty by various tricks of dressing. Thus we find today the padded shoulders for both men's and women's garments, padded or supported busts and tight girdles that give women more alluring figures. In extreme cases, we have the long coronation robes of kings and queens, the fancy headdress of the Indian chief, the top hat for the gentleman's evening wear, and the long train of his lady—all of these serve the function of distinguishing the individual from others.

We see ourselves in the movies. It has been pointed out many times that the enormous appeal of motion pictures is due in no small part to the many vicarious satisfactions they provide. By projecting ourselves into the characters and situations, we can escape momentarily from humdrum lives, worries, and cares, the limits imposed upon us by our incomes, our lack of opportunity, our mediocrity in appearance, ability, or talents.

The extent to which this ego-involvement occurs has been recently demonstrated by studies of the tastes and preferences of movie-goers. The upshot of this research is that individuals choose as their favorite movie stars people with whom they can most easily identify themselves—persons of the same sex, of comparable age, and who tend to be cast in roles that represent a person of their income group. Here is a brief summary of the findings, taken from a report (1941) on audience research: [2]

> Most stars do not gain support equally from all groups of theater-goers, but appeal particularly to certain segments of the population. Naturally, the variation is greater in the case of some stars than in others. But the star who is equally popular with both sexes, all age-groups, all income levels, and in all parts of the country, is the rare exception rather than the rule.
>
> Theatergoers have a tendency to project themselves into the situation portrayed on the screen, to imagine themselves in the place of the star, or (perhaps subconsciously) to pretend they *are* the star.
>
> Obviously, it is easier to imagine yourself in Mickey Rooney's shoes if you are a boy of seventeen than if you are a middle-aged housewife. Broadly speaking, that is why Rooney is overwhelmingly more popular with boys of his own age than with any other group of the population.
>
> Many other instances point to the importance of self-identification as a factor in determining marquee values. For example, Judy Garland, Deanna Durbin and Linda Darnell are most popular with girls of their own age. Muni is strongest with men over thirty-one, as are also Lionel Barrymore, William Powell and Edward Arnold. May Robson is particularly popular with elderly females. Joan Crawford, Miriam Hopkins, Irene Dunne, Claudette Colbert and Norma Shearer are most popular with women over thirty.
>
> Seventy-eight per cent of the female stars are more popular with women than with men. . . . By the same token 60 per cent of the male stars are more popular with men than with women. The first thirteen stars, as ranked by men, are all male.
>
> This phenomenon of self-identification can be seen at work in other fields. For example: The old theory that the best way to interest women in an advertisement is to show a picture of a man, or the best way to interest a man is to show a picture of a woman, has no real foundation in fact. The best way to attract women is to have women in the advertisement. The best way to attract men is by having men, or men and women. [2, *14 f.*]

Advertising. The whole "psychology of advertising" can be regarded as an attempt on the part of the advertiser to identify the consumer's self-interest with a particular product. And the interest of the consumers appealed to are in no small part composed of ego-involving values. One of the most brilliant and successful advertisers in the United States has said that "the whole secret of advertising is to get under a person's skin,"—to get a person so interested in and involved with a product that he cannot rest content until he buys it. Anyone familiar with the plethora of appeals made to the public in most countries where competition for business and profits is keen, can, on a moment's reflection, think of dozens of examples of the advertiser's attempt to protect, sustain, and enhance his ego. *Our* involvement with our bodily appearance or its characteristics is demonstrated by the phenomenal success of such advertisements as those which tell us to buy a certain mouthwash to avoid "halitosis" or a certain soap to avoid "body odor." *Our* identification with norms that determine status is fully recognized and exploited by those who imply that, if we use or buy their products, we will be in the same class as the distinguished man or the aristocratic woman shown in the illustration. The manufacturer of a relatively expensive automobile displays a picture of a car with a middle-aged man and woman in it and underneath there is the bold caption, "Here we are being envied"; a hand-lotion concern uses the ad, "Makes working hands look like leisure hands."

Other skillful propagandists as well as advertising experts are well aware of the various attitudes which channel into a person's ego. Analyses of different propaganda campaigns in terms of their effectiveness in arousing ego-involvement would be rewarding.

What's in a name? [1] Although most of us tend to take our names for granted, don't think much about them, still, for nearly all of us, there are occasional instances when we become aware of how much a part of us our names have become. We do not always act with complete neutrality when we see our names misspelled,

---

[1] This discussion of names is largely based on Robert Holt's *Studies in the Psychology of Names* [18]. This unpublished work is the most thorough, well-documented, and systematic treatment of the subject that has come to our attention.

we are flattered when old and casual acquaintances remember our names, *we* are likely to feel hurt if someone we think should know our name has forgotten it, we tend to pass on our names to our children, we sometimes scrawl our names in public places or on historic shrines. The vanity of certain wealthy men is exploited by the trustees of universities, hospitals, and similar institutions who promise that the man's name will be perpetuated in a building or some other memorial if he contributes funds to the institution. The good salesman and the good politician make it one of their first rules to flatter their customers and voters by remembering their names. We saw in chapter 7 how the small child learns that his name is a vehicle around which certain definite things happen and with which he identifies certain values and experiences. In interviews with a great variety of people, Holt found that the overwhelming majority of them felt that their names were a part of them, built in like an arm or a finger, and not a fortuitous possession.

Anthropologists have frequently pointed out that many primitive men make no distinction between the name and the person signified.

> Primitives regard their names as something concrete and real, and frequently sacred. [22, 50]

In some primitive tribes this identification of the name and the person went to such a length that "to be" and "to be named" were synonymous and the child was not regarded as having been completely born until he was named. It is a common practice among primitive peoples to give an individual a new name, or to change his name, at some critical time of life such as puberty or marriage. Among the Dakota Indians, a young man who had distinguished himself in battle was allowed to take on a new and distinctive name; Abram's name was changed to Abraham, the Bible tells us, at the time of the long march to Palestine. Those familiar with anthropological literature could multiply these examples many times.

In the history of surnames the psychologist finds that people who voluntarily chose their names tended to identify themselves with some positive value current at the time. Thus the name

"John," almost unknown in Saxon England, spread widely with the return of the Crusaders; the medieval craftsman, proud of his skill, gratified himself with names such as Shoemaker, Carpenter, Smith, etc.; others took the names of high offices such as Chamberlain, King, Duke. The Reformation, with the King James version of the Bible, had a profound effect on English nomenclature: girls were named Martha, Mary, Phoebe; boys Peter, Paul, Matthew, and so on. The strict Puritans, desirous of standing out from the rest, began the fashion of naming their children after abstract virtues. And so children got such first names as Patience, Prudence, Faith, Hope, etc. This fashion became so extreme that some unfortunate children had whole phrases as their first names. For example, there were three Barebone brothers named: If-Christ-had-not-died-for-thee-thou-hadst-been-damned Barebone; Praise-God Barebone; and Jesus-Christ-came-into-the-world-to-save Barebone. As Holt says, in all of these instances the individual was trying to "identify the self with something with which there was already ego-involvement." [18, 32]

That individuals in everyday life try to get some ego-enhancement from the prestige they hope to associate with their names is revealed by the existence of various organizations which will, for a fee, send to those who write a complete history of their family. In their enticing advertisements, these organizations list such ordinary names as Jones, Baker, Cooper and Smith. A skeptical journalist wrote one of these organizations for a number of these family accounts, each of which they advertised as "separate and distinct works." He discovered striking similarities in them all, similarities which built up the prestige of the recipient, no matter what his name happened to be. He writes:

> In each of 25 manuscripts there occurs a paragraph which flatteringly summarizes the traits and characteristics of ancestors in that particular family. This paragraph, with only the slightest modification of a word or two, reads: "The descendants of these and probably of other branches of the family of America have spread to practically every state of the Union, and have aided as much in the growth of the country as their ancestors aided in the founding of the nation. They have been noted for their *integrity, industry, energy, courage, piety, ambition, initiative, resourcefulness* and *perseverance*." Occa-

sionally, to add a nice touch of distinction to the family history, the order of the words was shifted around. But in 21 of the 25 "separate and distinct works," these italicized virtues were identical. [38]

Further confirmation of the prestige and status significance of names is found in the rather common tendency of persons whose names reflect some unpleasant stereotype or negative value to change their names to something more common and accepted. Jews have had trouble with their names all through their history. In various countries and at various times, they have been forced by law or decree to assume names that would distinguish them from the non-Jews of a society. Such laws were passed in Bohemia in 1787, Napoleon in 1808 forced Jews to adopt certain names, and a Nazi decree required "any Jew having a non-Jewish first name to adopt as an additional given name Israel, if male, Sarah if female." It became a practice for officials to sell names to Jews so that those who were wealthy were able to acquire "good" names such as Stern (Star), Blum (Flower). A young man whose name had formerly been Ginsberg, but who had changed it to Gray, when asked why he had changed his name said:

> It was because of certain associations and meanings connected with the name Ginsberg which did not apply to my family. [18, *115*]

He commented that the former name "suppressed my ego and gave me inferiority feelings."

There are also illustrations of government edicts commanding all people to take certain types of names in the national interest. Thus Edward IV of England in 1465 told the Irish to take English surnames or forfeit their possessions; Philip II of Spain in 1568 forced the remaining Moors in Spain to be baptized with Spanish names. In a decree issued in 1933, all Turkish citizens were ordered to assume a distinct family name of Turkish origin. The names taken by many Turks during this period reveal their ego aspirations. Father Divine urges his "children" to assume new names at the time they join his movement, on the theory that since they have become new persons they should have new names. [6, *128*]

Many people have so identified themselves with their names that they have refused to change them for professional reasons or because of custom. Lucy Stone, one of the early agitators in this country for women's rights, refused to change her name when she was married and believed so strongly that a woman somehow lost her identity by assuming her husband's name that she became the rallying point for the Lucy Stone Leaguers. As one of the Lucy Stoners put it:

> I confess that I believe there is something in names; that one's name is what Lucy Stone called it "the symbol of my identity which must not be lost." The point of view is simply that if you have from your very first conscious thought regarded yourself as Anna Maria Brown, you can't suddenly with any comfort regard yourself as Mrs. Thomas Smith. [18, *110*]

A Southern woman, when asked by Holt how she felt about changing her name at marriage, wrote:

> To be strictly truthful in the matter I shall have to admit that a strong feeling of resentment predominates. I remember it as a distinct shock when I was first called Mrs. Landess. I felt at first a sort of blank bewilderment and then I became almost angry—bristling with resentment. I was always very proud of what Papa made Hilditch stand for—all my ideals (real or fancied) I had cherished seemed tied up in that name and then to have to change it to one vastly inferior, which I came to realize stood for nothing but vulgarity was almost too humiliating. [18, *130 f.*]

Interesting personality comparisons might be made of professional women who change their names when they are married, those who keep their maiden names, and those who adopt the compromise solution of using both maiden and married names together.

The martyr. The pages of history are rife with examples of persons who preferred to die the death of a martyr or a hero than to give up what to *them* were ideals more important than life itself. Giordano Bruno, the Dominican friar of the sixteenth century, was condemned to the flames by the Inquisition because he would not renounce the ideas of God and the universe which the Copernican doctrine had inspired in him. Paul Lafargue and his wife, daughter of Karl Marx, committed suicide when they felt they had outlived their effectiveness as protagonists for Marxism. Joan of Arc, the Maid of Orleans, was tried as a heretic and burned at the stake because of her innocent and unswerving allegiance to the revelations of her "voices" which were not at all in conformity to official Church interpretations. In such instances we have illustrations *par excellence* of the fact that a value can and does become such a central part of the ego, that the individual feels life is intolerable and meaningless if this value cannot be preserved as a part of the self.

World War II brought out in striking fashion—as most wars do—the fact that ordinary soldiers and ordinary common people sometimes prefer to take their own lives, to die for what they believe is a cause (value) rather than be captured by the enemy. The utmost heroism—self-sacrifice—was displayed by men fighting in the various armies. Particularly dramatic illustrations were exhibited by certain Japanese soldiers who chose to blow themselves to bits rather than give *themselves* up; suicide (Kamikaze) pilots volunteered for extinction; there were authentic reports of individual and mass suicides of Japanese civilians. These people died as they did, not because of any innate "Japanese mentality." They had learned thoroughly and felt intensely the particular set of values taught by a chauvinistic religion which held that a life not lived in the service of the Emperor or the State was valueless, while death in the service was noble and would be rewarded in heaven. [37] Heroes in other armies sacrificed their lives for other value constellations.

Ego-involvements determined by situation. We have already pointed out that an individual's behavior may be modified or determined not only because of ego-involvements due to the acceptance of *established* norms, but also because of more or less temporary ego-involvement created by the demands of an actual concrete situation. Thus a person who happens to be at the scene of an accident will often feel that it is *his* responsibility to help an injured person until more competent professional aid arrives. When we take a long ride in the train, get acquainted with the other passengers in our car, a certain camaraderie often develops, we feel that the people in that particular car are members of *our* group as distinct from the passengers in other cars.

In the last chapter we cited an example of group formation from Bill Mauldin's penetrating *Up Front* [29]. At the very beginning of the book, Mauldin describes the identification a soldier makes with his division—a somewhat more permanent identification than one that may be built up with a special outfit assigned to a temporary job but still a group situation brought on by the exigencies of war, not an established group such as the family or the church, characterized by values that remain relatively enduring.

> During the three years I spent in the 45th Division, I was certain that it was not only the best division in the army, but that it *was* the army. Since then I have kicked around in more than fifteen other divisions, and I have found that the men in each of them are convinced that their division is the best and the only division. That's good. [29, 1]

In *Men Under Stress,* a book filled with keen observations, Grinker and Spiegel [16] describe the identifications and loyalties that emerged when men were thrown together in the same air combat team during World War II.

> The most vital relationship is not the purely social. It is the feeling that the men have for each other as members of combat teams and toward the leaders of those teams, that constitutes the essence of their relationship. It is an interesting fact that, *although the members of combat crews are thrown together only by chance, they rapidly become united to each other by the strongest bonds while in combat. . . . The men and their plane become identified with each other* with an intensity that in civil life is found only within the family circle. *Crew members habitually refer to each other as "my pilot," "my bombardier," "my gunner,"* and so on, and their feeling for their plane is equally strong, since its strength and reliability are as important as those of any human members of the crew. . . . *The emotional attitudes the fliers take toward each other have less to do with the accident of their individual personalities than with the circumstances of their association.* . . . The men in the combat teams are brothers by virtue of their constant enforced association, their dependence upon each other, their common ideals and goals, and their relation to their leaders. [16, 22 ff., italics ours]

In another book, *War Neuroses* [17], the same authors show how this identification with a group is one of the strongest forces preventing anxiety in the individual. The group

... becomes the object of considerable love and affection on the part of its members. They are proud of the group, and resent new-comers. They are jealous of other groups, and strive to achieve perfection for their own. ... Not what happens to the individual, but what happens to the group, is the dominant concern. The injury, or even death, of the individual is insignificant, compared to the fate of the group. One pilot with an anxiety neurosis stated this very simply: "I couldn't sweat it out at the field while my crew were over the target. It was worse than going along." Through his identification with the group, the individual shares in the achievement and victory of battle—even if he should be injured or killed. *A part of him continues to live gloriously, as a member of the group, no matter what his personal fate.* This alteration in disposition of the psychological energy by virtue of identification with the group contributes immensely to the capacity of the ego to ward off anxiety. [17, *118*, italics ours]

The loss of morale in the individual soldier and the consequent change in his behavior when his group is broken up and he loses his established loyalties is recognized in the following order issued by General Joseph T. McNarney to all unit commanders of American troops in occupied Germany (April 1946): [36, italics ours]

Due to rapid demobilization and frequent change of station of units and assignments of enlisted men and officers, firm ties of unit-pride have been weakened. The traditional constant concern of officers for the welfare of their men and consequent mutual loyalties have been difficult to maintain during this transition period. Team-work often has been forgotten.

Consequently discipline in certain localities and commands in this theatre has deteriorated to a point of discrediting the fine performance of our troops in general. Indications of this state can be found in:

A. Participation in black market activities and indulgence in drunkenness.

B. A high absent-without-leave rate and excessive incidence of other disciplinary infractions.

C. The high automobile accident rate.

D. The excessive venereal disease rate.

E. The general lack of smartness in appearance and conscientious observance of military courtesy.

F. The complaining attitude toward constituted military authority and those duties essential to maintain high standards of soldierly efficiency. [36]

In chapter 12, dealing with the breakdown of the ego, we shall see further instances of the effect on the individual of the loss of links to other kinds of groups.

Statements obtained from scientists doing strategic work on the atomic bomb during the war revealed that under the stress of circumstances they tended to lose any interest in personal acclaim and identified themselves with the success of the venture as a whole.

> It was the newness and magnitude of the undertaking in time of national crisis which created a spirit of cooperation and teamwork within the group. One only had to note the lights burning in the offices and laboratories far into the night to realize that time was of the essence. These were also times in which there were so many problems of basic scientific detail to be answered that the young physicist or chemist, assigned one question to answer, felt that on the successful resolution of his problem depended the venturing into the next stage of development. . . . Cloistered theoretical scientists, university professors and students, industrial engineers, presidents of companies large and small, army dignitaries and government officials, all these were able to iron out their views and settle differences of policy on which hinged the success of the venture.

Another scientist reported that

> In looking back over my experience with the Manhattan project, I remember a great deal of friction and bitter argument, yet I can hardly remember a case where the basis of friction was personal. I believe the reason why the feeling was so strong in many instances was that the individuals concerned were fighting for the success of the project as a whole and differing only about what course would lead most surely to that success. The very obstinacy with which some maintained their point of view was because they felt that if they gave it up they were giving up something much more important than personal opinions or prejudices. There were many instances in the project of men taking on distasteful jobs merely because they felt they had to be done. Almost universally it was necessary for the directors of the project to keep the professional men from working too hard

rather than to push them. I really believe that there were very few people on the project who were not willing to sacrifice their personal feelings and ambitions for the over-all success. I would estimate that in the professional group over ninety per cent of the men that I know tried and, in large measure, succeeded in merging their egos with the whole work. In many cases this attitude extended down through the clerical and technical groups as well.

By June of 1944, 83 per cent of the people in the United States felt they were personally doing something to help win World War II. Skilled workers, industrialists, housewives—as well as atomic scientists and those in the armed forces—were able to unite their personal values with a larger social value. This identification was determined largely by the circumstances of the war itself, by common threats and the need for all-out effort if all were to survive, and not by any harmony of established values that continued at war's end. Such developments as the wave of strikes that followed the industrial "truce" during the war, controversies over racial discrimination, and the full emergence of party politics indicated that when the war was over there was no longer a unified clearly understood well-directed "cause" for people to identify with. Common allegiances broke down and gave way to separate often conflicting group or class interests which existed in the particular social organization.

An example of the way an astute national leader in a democracy got people to take part in a decision which he had to make but which he knew might be resented is found in President Roosevelt's announcement when he ordered General MacArthur's escape from the Philippines. It was known from a public opinion poll, taken shortly before MacArthur's departure, that half the people in the United States felt General MacArthur should stay with his men in the Philippines to the bitter end. Roosevelt was therefore faced with the possibility that MacArthur would be branded as a deserter by this sizable number of Americans. He could furthermore take it for granted that Axis propagandists would capitalize on the event to show that American generals were yellow and cowardly. The carefully worded statement issued by the President as the first announcement of MacArthur's escape not only soothed what would otherwise have been the ruffled American public but

also made it impossible for the Axis propagandists to make capital
of the event. It can be seen in the statement below how Roosevelt
put the decision up to every American citizen, made them feel it
was *their* decision, and that *they* could choose no other alternative.

> I know that every man and woman in the United States admires
> with me General MacArthur's determination to fight to the finish
> with his men in the Philippines. But I also know that every man
> and woman is in agreement that all important decisions must be made
> with a view toward the successful termination of the war. Knowing
> this, I am sure that every American, if faced individually with the
> question as to where General MacArthur could best serve his country,
> could come to only one answer. [35]

This was the whole announcement.

The effectiveness of "group decision" has been well known
and practiced for years in certain industrial concerns, such as the
DuPont Company in its safety programs, the great TVA development, and the recurrent Five Year Plans of the Soviet Union.
For example, David E. Lilienthal, former Chairman of the TVA,
in his penetrating book, *TVA—Democracy on the March,* reports
that

> From the outset of the TVA undertaking it has been evident to
> me, as to many others, that *a valley development envisioned in its
> entirety could become a reality if and only if the people of the region
> did much of the planning, and participated in most of the decisions.*
> To a considerable degree this is what is happening. Each year,
> almost each month, one can see the participation of the people, as
> a fundamental practice, grow more vigorous, and, although it suffers
> occasional setbacks, it is becoming part of the thinking and the
> mechanics of the development of the Tennessee Valley. [77, italics
> ours]

And Lilienthal's book contains numerous illustrations to show
how group decisions were encouraged as a method of ensuring
maximum co-operation and effectiveness of effort. A demonstration of the same principle is found later in a report by Lewin
of experiments conducted during the war in an attempt to get
people to change their food habits: those who had actively helped
in establishing a group norm felt the decision was *theirs.* As the

report indicates, "the specific effect of asking for a 'group' decision is to heighten the sense of involvement and thus secure greater participation." [23, 9]

Status within groups. We have already reported a number of studies which show the way in which an individual identifies himself with a particular occupation, race, or class, and the effect such identification has on his own conception of status (chs. 4 and 6). And we saw in the last chapter how the individual develops loyalties to particular groups and the important role these loyalties play in defining his ego links. It would, however, be an oversimplification of the real state of affairs if any impression remained that because an individual finds himself placed in some broad category within the social organization, such as "skilled worker," "doctor," "Negro," or "servant," his identification with the group and the status accorded him by other members of the group was identical with the identification and status of all other people who fall within the same general category. For, on closer examination, it will be found that, in addition to the conflicting and ambivalent loyalties already emphasized, there are generally very definite hierarchies and substatus groupings within any broad category. In addition to his general status derived from a broad reference group, an individual acquires a specific status according to his membership character within a given group. Hence, to understand the particular ego constellation of any individual in a precise way, it becomes necessary to know how an individual places himself and is placed by other members of a group *within* any category objectively defined. The point can be illustrated with reference to concrete observations of two commonly used descriptive classifications—"Negroes" and "factory workers."

There is no need here to elaborate the fact that there is a widespread stereotype in the United States concerning the place most white people feel the Negro should have in our contemporary social organization. The existence of the color line was described as follows by the father of an intelligent Negro boy who at the age of 14 was just beginning to be aware of the fact that color made a difference. While sitting on the doorstep of their home in a middle-sized New Jersey city, the father pointed to a tramp who happened to be walking along the street and said to his son, "You see that tramp standing over there, Jim? He's shiftless, common, and no good. However, if he were to bathe, shave, and put on a clean suit, he could gain entrance to any public place in the country. With you it's different. No matter what you do, how well educated you become, you can never be treated on the same social level as that tramp because of your color." [28, *1*]

But within the Negro world itself, one finds approximately the same hierarchy of status according to occupation, education, and so on that exists in the surrounding white macrocosm. This is only one example of a minority group accepting in part the norms of the majority. Negroes who regard themselves as members of the upper class, while denouncing the rigid caste barrier between whites and Negroes will by and large ardently defend a class structure within the Negro group itself. Davis, Gardner, and Gardner, in their study of the *Deep South* [12] indicate that four of the questions asked by upper class Negroes of other Negroes trying to break into the upper class, go somewhat as follows:

> 1) What has been his education? 2) Has he professional or semi-professional status? 3) Are his language, manners, and dress "polished"? 4) Is he black? [12, *246*]

The answer to the last question must be "No." And the same authors further report that "the overwhelming majority of colored persons are considered lower class, *according to the colored group's own standards.*" [222]

A particularly revealing fact about these specific status groupings among Negroes is that the lighter a Negro is in color, the greater chance he has to rise in the social scale. An unusually large percentage of light Negroes is found in the upper class of the Negro world. A young Negress whose very light skin enabled her to pass easily from the Negro to the white world revealed the sensitivity of Negroes about their color when she reported:

> When I am in the presence of dark skinned people, I'm always very careful not to let the word "black" enter into my conversation. I have seen dark people get very angry when anything concerning blackness is brought up. They seem to think that you are belittling or making fun of them. [28, *39*]

This same Negress, a college graduate, observed that many of the "better" Negro sororities definitely tended to exclude girls of very dark skins. It is not unusual for Negroes when filling out documents (such as applications for a marriage license) that require a designation of "color," to be quite specific if they are not themselves black, by inserting "light tan," "brown," and so on. Davis, Gardner, and Gardner describe the way in which light-skinned Negroes tend to form subcliques, and Myrdal reports that

> In such cities as New Orleans, Charleston, Mobile, Natchez, and later Washington, highly exclusive mulatto societies were formed which still exist, to a certain extent, today. Color thus became a badge of status and social distinction among the Negro people. [32, 696]

The same study also reports that

> Darker Negroes who rose from the masses to distinction in the Negro community by getting an education or by conducting successful business enterprises showed an almost universal desire to marry light-skinned women and so to become adopted members of the light-colored aristocracy and to give their children a heritage of lighter color. [32, 697]

An experimental demonstration of this process was reported in Marks's study (pp. 136 f.).

The importance of skin color within the Negro world, together with certain practices such as the attempt of many Negro women to take the curl out of their hair, clearly indicates that Negroes have made many norms of the white world *their* norms, that by and large in contemporary United States these norms taken over from the white world become for them ego-involved in various degrees. Because of his marginal position, various conflicts in values or conflicts of ego identification are bound to be felt by a large proportion of Negroes in our society: their own implicit allegiance to certain bourgeois white standards and white norms tend to run counter to any unequivocal allegiance to aspirations certain Negro leaders may have for racial solidarity and unity and likewise run counter to class allegiances that pay no attention to culture whether white, black, or mulatto.

The hierarchy of status among skilled and semiskilled factory workers has been highlighted in the past decade in the United States by the intense rivalry between the two major labor unions— one organized along craft lines, the other along industrial lines. From the psychological point of view, it is by no means accidental that craft unions got a much earlier start. For workers, identifying themselves with a particular job or skill, could with relative ease join others in the same specific occupation to form an organized pressure group in which all would benefit by the achievement of certain goals. The resistance met by the Congress of Industrial Organizations in breaking down these relatively restricted ego-involvements and transforming them into identifications with persons of other skills in the same industry is well known.

A good description of the specific-status hierarchy felt by workers because of their membership character in the same industry is given in the detailed study of Roethlisberger and Dickson: [39]

In the factory, as in any social milieu, a process of social evaluation is constantly at work. From this process distinctions of "good" and "bad," "inferior" and "superior," arise. This process of evaluation is carried on with simple and ready generalizations by means of which values become attached to individuals and to groups performing certain tasks and operations. It assigns to a group of individuals performing such and such a task a particular rank in the established prestige scale. Each work group becomes a carrier of social values. In industry with its extreme diversity of occupations there are a number of such groupings. Any noticeable similarity or difference, not only in occupation but also in age, sex, and nationality, can serve as a basis of social classification, as, for example, "married women," the "old-timer," the "white-collared" or clerical worker, the "foreign element." Each of these groups, too, has its own value system. . . . Just as each employee has a particular physical location, so he has a particular social place in the total social organization. . . . It is obvious that these scales of value are never completely accepted by all the groups in the social environment. The shop worker does not quite see why the office worker, for example, should have shorter hours of work than he has. Or the newcomer, whose efficiency on a particular job is about the same, but whose hourly rate is less than that of some old-timer, wonders why service should count so much. The management group, in turn, from the security of its social elevation, does not often understand what "all the fuss is about." As was indicated by many of the studies, any person who has achieved a certain rank in the prestige scale, regards anything real or imaginary which tends to alter his status adversely as something unfair or unjust. It is apparent that any move on the part of the management may alter the existing social equilibrium to which the employee has grown accustomed and by means of which his status is defined. Immediately this disruption will be expressed in sentiments of resistance to the real or imagined alterations in the social equilibrium. [39, 555 f.]

And the same authors report that dissatisfaction with wages is due not only to the absolute amount of wages but to what the worker may feel is an unfair wage differential between himself and someone doing a slightly different job.

Complaints arise when wage differentials do not express appropriately the differences in social significance which the different jobs have to the employees themselves. Many workers who expressed a grievance about wages went on to say that the reason for their complaint was not that they were dissatisfied with their own wages but that "it isn't fair." [39, 576]

This is one more example of the fact that judgment is based on a referential scale.

In addition to the mixed loyalties caused by differences in the nature of the jobs themselves, unionization, especially in the earlier days when floods of immigrants were coming into the United States, was made difficult because of the mixed national loyalties of people who became factory workers. MacDonald, in her *Labor Problems and the American Scene* [27], writes that

The foreign composition of the labor force has had a profound effect on the trade unions. The difference in experience, language, and especially skill has made a breach in the ranks of organized labor by creating an aristocratic group with little consideration for the unskilled. The division line between skilled and unskilled has often coincided with that of native and alien. . . . By mixing nationalities to prevent communication, pitting one group against another, playing up the racial and religious antipathies of the Old World, introducing immigrant strikebreakers, employers for a number of years were able to control their labor forces for their own ends. Constant introduction of new recruits tended to keep the labor market in a fluid condition.

No sooner had a labor group settled down and the union movement made an attempt to enlist the workers than another immigrant group was brought in. [27, 237 f.]

Job satisfaction. With increasing technological advancement, the dependence of more and more people on large-scale industrial production and distribution both for a livelihood and for consumer goods, one of the most crucial problems of contemporary society is the attitude toward the job held by those who occupy dependent, wage-earning, or marginal positions. The fact that in the past few decades the rapid industrial development in the United States has enormously changed the occupational distribution of gainful workers can be illustrated by the following census figures: there is a marked decrease of agricultural workers, an increase of workers in jobs concerned with the production or distribution of manufactured goods. Along with this shift in occupation has gone, of course, the familiar shift of the population from farm to urban areas.

PER CENT DISTRIBUTION OF GAINFUL WORKERS IN CERTAIN OCCUPATIONS:
1870 AND 1930 [9]

	1870	1930
Agriculture	53.0	21.4
Manufacturing and mechanical industries	20.5	28.9
Trade	6.8	12.5
Transportation and communication	4.2	7.9

It is unnecessary to point out here that this increasing industrialization has by no means been accomplished entirely by harmonious relationships between management and workers in the United States or most other countries. By and large, workers have "had to fight" for higher wages, lower hours, and better working conditions. A recent survey (1945) has shown that less than one third of skilled and semiskilled workers are satisfied with their incomes, whereas nearly 60 per cent of those in the business and management class say they are satisfied. [10] When Centers asked the question on a national survey, "Do you think working people are usually fairly and squarely treated by their employers, or that employers sometimes take advantage of them?" less than a third of manual workers felt that the working people were being fairly treated whereas approximately half of all business, white collar, and professional people believed workers were getting what was due them. [10]

We are calling attention to the fact that wages and hours are fundamental conditions of work satisfaction to make it quite clear that these must be taken as part and parcel of any more general consideration of what constitutes work satisfaction. However, in addition to the more important structural properties of economic organization, it is apparent that "work satisfaction" involves psychological factors that form a context within which satisfaction with wages and hours is judged.

We cannot survey here in any detail the vast literature that has accumulated on the problem of incentives in industry. Summarizing a number of studies on work satisfaction (1939), Watson concludes:

> We have provided psychologically satisfactory employment for a large proportion of the people in professional and managerial occupations, and for a majority of the middle–class workers in small towns. We have been much less successful in the mines, factories, and unskilled trades. [45, *123*]

And he points to the problem that concerns us here when he observes that certain investigations on the subject of job satisfaction have shown that there is "most distress over ego injuries." H. J. Ruttenberg, research director of the Steel Workers Organizing Committee, expressed the workers' point of view in answer to a question put to him at an industrial conference:

> I live in a district where the workers live, and spend almost all of my time with them, and they are emotionally dissatisfied, intellectually dissatisfied, and economically dissatisfied . . . because of having to respond to technical changes which they did not originate, and in contrast to [workers] who increased production when they were consulted on technical changes. . . . One of the most fundamental impulses in a man in a shop is self-expression. If he is denied that in determining his wages, he feels much dissatisfied. If he is permitted expression in the production set-up, then he feels that he has made a contribution to the whole. [34, *133 f.*]

From his review of industrial leadership, McGregor concludes that "opportunities to participate in the solution of problems and in the discussion of actions which may affect him, the opportunity to assume responsibility as he becomes ready for it" are two of the conditions necessary if an industrial worker is to feel satisfied and secure. [30, 63]   When the British Institute of Public Opinion asked the question (January 1946) "Apart from wages and security, what do you need most in a job for making you feel contented whilst at work?" 40 per cent of all respondents gave answers that revealed their desire for more active participation in the total job— answers such as "cooperation between management and employee," "appreciative employer."   Most of the other answers given were very general ones such as "good working conditions," or concern with specific desires for shorter hours.

Roethlisberger and Dickson conclude from their careful investigation that [2]

It is not possible to treat, as in the more abstract social sciences, material goods, physical events, wages, and hours of work as things in themselves, subject to their own laws.   Instead, they must be interpreted as carriers of social value.   For the employee in industry, the whole working environment must be looked upon as being permeated with social significance.   Apart from the social values inherent in his environment the meaning to the employee of certain objects or events cannot be understood.   To understand the meaning of any employee's complaints or grievances, it is necessary to take account of his position or status in the company.   This position is determined by the social organization of the company: that system of practices and beliefs by means of which the human values of the organization are expressed, and the symbols around which they are organized—efficiency, service, etc. [39, 374]

It is clear beyond any shadow of doubt that the satisfaction an individual has in his job can never be complete unless he feels that the work he is doing is *his* job, unless there is some way in which *he* can participate through his job in some activity that will bring him satisfaction.   This satisfaction may be relatively restricted as in the case of a man who feels the importance of his work in rela-

[2] The failure of most American industrialists to take adequate account of some of the conclusions that can be derived from these and other empirical studies is pointed out by Elton Mayo of the Harvard Business School in his book, *The Social Problems of an Industrial Civilization.*

tion to others in his factory unit; it may involve the larger satisfaction he feels as an important cog in the whole industrial plant; or a worker may identify himself and his job with the fate and progress of a whole social organization or with workers in all countries.

It is not our task here to discuss the relative effectiveness with which this job identification can be accomplished under different systems of economic organization. But we can learn something of the psychological components of job satisfaction among industrial workers in the United States if we examine a concrete case where job satisfaction seems to be extremely high. We take as our example the Lincoln Electric Company which has received a great deal of publicity. Just what conditions prevail in the Lincoln Electric Company to make for job satisfaction? Why does it stand out as a plant where there appears to be complete harmony, cooperation, and mutual confidence between "labor" and "management"?

A report issued by the United States Department of Labor on incentive wage plans (1942) states that the grievances workers have against scientific management

> . . . are attributable to the tendency of management engineers to consider labor as impersonal and as a part of the machine process. Workers feel that they are being treated as abstract "labor" rather than human beings at work. [21, 7]

The undeniable success of the Lincoln Electric Company seems to be due basically to the feeling of its President that "labor is an individual not a commodity." [24, 203] And for Mr. Lincoln the statement was more than words handed out by a public relations department or aired at a management–labor conference. He proceeded to try to create the conditions within which the individual could participate as an individual in the total job of the plant. One of the first things he did was to encourage the formation of an advisory board chosen from the entire personnel of the plant, one man being elected from each department by all members of that department. The men on the board, together with the plant superintendent and Mr. Lincoln, who acts as chairman, serve as the board of directors of the plant. Here are a few of the decisions this advisory board has put into operation: installed a piece-work incentive plan with rates guaranteed by the company and with the worker having the right to challenge the rates set; insured all workers for the equivalent of a year's wages without cost to the individual worker; provided two weeks vacation with pay, closing the entire factory for the purpose; issued stock to the employees who want it (over half are stockholders); established a suggestion system and provided that anyone whose suggestion for more efficient production is accepted will receive half of the net estimated savings for the first year of use (approximately 50 new suggestions are turned in every month and about one tenth of them prove useful); inaugurated a bonus system whereby each worker receives what is regarded as his share of the bonus according to his value to the company; installed an annuity plan and a trust fund; set up an employee association to provide for social and athletic activity and which has, for example, a sick committee whose members have among their duties the obligation to visit within 48 hours anyone who has not reported to work because of illness.

Some of the claims which the Lincoln Electric Company can make (in the early 1940's) are the following: Lincoln workers produce more per hour than any organization making a comparable product in the world; Lincoln Electric factory workers are the highest paid employees in industry anywhere in the world. In 1943 the average annual earnings for all employees was $5,539. Approximately 90 per cent of Lincoln employees own their own homes. There is practically no labor turnover: of 260 employees on the payroll ten years ago, 203 are still with the company. Lincoln selling prices are less than those of any company making a comparable product.

Lincoln himself describes his plan as one based on "intelligent selfishness." [25] What he means by this is that each individual in the plant sees his relationship to the plant as a whole and realizes that "he is a vital part of one going whole." The worker knows that the company's success is *his* success and Lincoln employees do not seem to share the fear so common in many industries with incentive wage plans that they will either work themselves out of a job or that rates will be cut. According to Mr. Lincoln, the plan under which his company operates

> . . . has changed our workers from people who are working at a job at so much an hour into people who feel their success is tied definitely, completely and proportionately into the success of the company itself. They are not working at a job so many hours a day at so much per hour. They are working to get a job done. This change of attitude from working so many hours a day for so much money into the desire of working to produce a certain result produces unbelievable results in efficiency of production. [33, *21*]

An employee of the company puts it as follows:

> I know that the more I make, the more my company is able to make. Every time any of us increases our efficiency, the amount saved is proportioned between me and the rest of my business partners. [47, *4*]

This particular employee regards himself as a business man with definite status:

> For some reason or other, a lot of people seem to be impressed with the idea that because you work where the labor of production gets your hands dirty, you have no right to be paid more than so much a year. . . . Most of these fellows work with their hands and get them pretty dirty sometimes, too. Yet no one ever questions whether they are worth the incomes they make. I look at welding as a kind of professional business, an art I have to be good at in order to keep up with the rest of the businessmen who work around me here at Lincoln. [47, *4*]

The Lincoln Electric Company, as we pointed out, is unusual. The particular combination of factors that makes it what it is also makes it something of a little world of its own. The company's practices deviated so much from the usual ones in American industry that during World War II it was kept busy justifying its methods to government committees and departments. There is no union in the Lincoln Electric Company and the employees, therefore, regard themselves more as "businessmen," identify themselves with the company and its welfare, not with other working people in the larger world outside. In other words, employee identifications with their jobs can be regarded as occurring within a relatively restricted and isolated industrial microcosm: a microcosm with its own norms and values. Hence the Lincoln employee, in identifying himself with his particular organization, does not simultaneously and automatically identify himself with more widespread values common to the whole social organization within which his company is but a small part. Just what would happen to the Lincoln plan and just what identifications Lincoln Electric workers would make if there were a major depression are moot questions.

Lilienthal's report of the development of the TVA clearly reveals the sense of identification and participation an individual worker can obtain if conditions are such that it is apparent to him that in working for a whole regional project he is benefiting himself. He writes:

> In pouring concrete so that the Douglas Dam could be built on a world-record schedule, in tending the glow of the giant electric furnaces at Muscle Shoals, or in stringing aluminum and copper cable along the line of march of transmission towers, TVA workers know, and show they know, that in thus working for their valley they are working for themselves; they build for themselves. [91]

And as Lilienthal points out, incentives based on identifications with group norms can be stronger than incentives based on the "profit motive" alone:

> Whether in private business or public service a man's conviction that he is performing an important service for others, that he is part of something far more important than himself, is a measure to him of the importance of that job. It is this, I think, that accounts in considerable part for the continued enthusiasm of the TVA technical staff long after the newness of the undertaking has passed, a spirit that has been observed and remarked upon by a long succession of visitors from other parts of the country and the world. The notion is naïve that only by the incentive of pay or profit do men "keep on their toes" and do their best work. Many of the TVA's key staff members are earning less than in the posts they left to join this job. [122]

At the present time, the identification of a worker with his job in a factory, mine, or farm, and his *simultaneous* identification with the larger values and purposes of the whole social organization *through his job* can be best illustrated with reference to the role of the worker in the Soviet Union. In a socialist organization where all means of production and exchange are owned and operated by the state, the possibility exists for each worker, no matter what his job, to identify himself with the purposes and aspirations of the whole society. Socialism and Communism are constantly held up to the people of modern Russia by their leaders as the goals toward which each member of the society should strive. The principles of socialism and Communism, as defined by Stalin, are as follows:

> The principle of Socialism is that in a socialist society each works according to his ability and receives articles of consumption, not according to his needs, but according to the work he performs for society. This means that the cultural and technical level of the working class is still not a high one, that the distinction between mental and manual labor persists, that the productivity of labor is still not high enough to ensure an abundance of articles of consumption, and, as a result, society is obliged to distribute articles of consumption, not in accordance with the needs of the members of society, but in accordance with the work they perform for society. Communism represents a higher stage of development. The principle of Communism is that in a Communist society each works according to his abilities and receives articles of consumption, not according to the work he performs, but according to his needs as a culturally developed individual. [42, 6]

In other words, the aspiration is that the standard of living and the cultural level of all workers should eventually be raised to the level enjoyed by the most advanced technicians or professionals. This is the ultimate goal which, as Stalin says, is now far from realization.

The point that concerns us here is the fact that such a general goal exists, is explicitly stated, and that a great effort is made by the Government and party members to keep the goal constantly before the eyes of the people. Status and social approval are measured in terms of the usefulness of an individual's labor in achieving the common goal. Particularly efficient workers are praised in the press and honored with medals. Their photographs appear on special bulletin boards of their factories. They become "Heroes of the Soviet Union." For example, during World War II, hundreds of official decorations were awarded to workers in the rear as well as to members of the fighting forces. Special distinctions are bestowed on factory or agricultural units that show particular initiative or efficiency. Similarly every effort is made to turn public opinion against those who do not seem to be doing their share.

It is in this general context that the Stakhanov movement, developed in the middle 1930's, assumed its particular significance. Although from a technical point of view, it introduced no methods not known and practiced in more advanced industrial countries [26], and although the zest with which Stakhanovism was taken up developed certain weaknesses and exaggerations because of hasty application [13], there can be little doubt that the solid achievements it represented in the long run were largely possible because the individual Stakhanovite in trying to raise his own production standards was not only increasing his income but helping to achieve a national goal that he understood and identified himself with. In becoming a Stakhanovite, an individual was becoming a national hero. For example, Molotov told the All-Union Conference of Stakhanovites:

> Do we not know that the most popular representatives of the Stakhanov movement are rank-and-file working men and women? Yesterday they were still unknown to many even in their own factories, yesterday they were on a level with the other rank-and-file working men and women. But today the whole working class of the Soviet Union knows the names of its new heroes, the names of those working men and women who have become the standard-bearers of the new movement in the fight for socialism. [31, 4]

Stakhanovism was regarded in the Soviet Union as a new form of "socialist competition." There was not only competition between individual workers but competition between factories, factory departments, mines, and collective farms. This socialist competition, the general principles of which were laid down by Lenin in 1918, holds the possibility of leading to cohesion rather than to a division of interest. For the competitor, whether he acts as an individual or as a member of a larger unit, competes *within* the larger framework of a *common* goal which is constantly made clear through the press, over the radio, and in organizational meetings. "The resultant change in the psychological atmosphere," as Ward observed it, "is one of the things that causes the visitor to realize that he is in a new world." [44, *133*].

In a speech to the members of the First Conference of Stakhanovites held in the Kremlin in 1935, Stalin told them:

> People in our country do not work for exploiters, for the enrichment of parasites, but for themselves, for their own class, for their own, Soviet society, where government is wielded by the best members of the working class. That is why labor in our country has social significance and is a matter of honor and glory. . . . Here the man who labors is held in esteem. Here he works not for the exploiters, but for himself, for his class, for society. Here the man who labors cannot feel neglected and solitary. . . . And if he works well and gives society all he can—he is a hero of labor and is covered with glory. [42, *13*]

This identification of the Soviet worker with the Communist goal is seen in reports revealing the conviction of the Soviet citizens that what the state accomplishes, *he* accomplishes; that what the state owns, *he* owns; that *his* standard of living will be raised by collective effort. An American observer writes that "The Soviet people have learned from experience that 'what's ours is mine.'" [44, *40*] A system of ownership has been developed "which makes it true that when a man works for others he is also working for himself." [*43 f.*] A British engineer working in Russia has said that

> For an engineer, a maker of machines, work in a Soviet factory offers tremendous satisfaction. The commercial principle that holds sway in capitalist industry very often forces engineers to spend their energy, strength, and knowledge for nothing, several factories turning out one and the same article, each striving when an order comes to secure the contract. All making new designs but only one obtaining the order. The other designs are wasted. In the Soviet Union, on the other hand, all tasks are linked up with the development of the industry and the engineer knows that the plan he has drawn up will be used. [20, *24*]

The conversations Pearl Buck reported with a Russian-born and educated girl are revealing. This young woman, who had come to the United States with her husband, was not a Communist. Buck reports:

> I discovered after our first conversation that she was even rather vague about the political theories of communism. She judged her country solely by pragmatic tests. What was good she knew because it had been good for her and her family. What was bad was bad because it had not lived up to her expectations. [3, *10*]

Here are a few excerpts from the conversations.

> "What did the village do with the kulak's brick factory?" I asked.
> "It belonged to the collective farm," Masha said. "Those who wanted to work there instead of in the fields could do so. *The people now felt the brick factory was theirs,* and they worked harder than ever and the production was higher than before. I worked in this brick factory in the summer for several seasons, and of course, if you are interested in profits, you compete, and we actually did two days' work in one. Whoever produced the most was respected by others. It was interesting and good work, and our collective farm took the profits and in this way we built new cow barns, and we bought new machines for the fields and to work on the flax." [*49*, italics ours]
> "But I want to tell you about the evening school. Those people worked all day and they came directly from the factory to the school, which was in a barracks. During the little free time before school began, they read and studied. Sometimes they discussed the day's work, and I remember they spoke especially about quotas of work, whether this shop or that factory had lived up to its program. *They felt the responsibility for the work. . . ."* [3, *94*, italics ours]

A Stakhanovite girl who had broken many production records in the textile mill said to an American observer:

> We work in *our own* mill, we work for ourselves, without any bosses, for our country . . . and that is why we are able to tend such a large number of looms. [15, *13 f.*]

This possible identification of the Soviet worker with the values of the whole social organization has been very neatly stated by the Soviet psychologist Rubinstein:

The very fact of social life and social division of labor naturally, by an internal necessity, brings it about that the activity of man is directly aimed at the satisfaction not merely of his own personal needs but of those of society as well. To satisfy his own needs, a man must make the satisfaction of social needs the direct goal of his actions. . . . *The socially important, becoming the personally important while still remaining the socially important,* arouses in the individual tendencies and forces of great strength . . . *the socially important, becoming personally important for the individual, arouses in him forces much more powerful than those evoked by personal desires alone, and different from them in their content, origin and significance.* [40, *195,* italics ours]

Special attention should be drawn to the last part of Rubinstein's statement. For he brings out here a fact we have repeatedly emphasized, namely, that in new social situations new norms and values often arise, that the individual identifies himself with these emerging values and exhibits a behavior which qualitatively as well as quantitatively can and often does differ from the behavior "characteristic" of him—"characteristic" only because of the particular constellation of social determinants in his more usual environment, and which can change radically when those determinants are altered.[3]

In this particular publication, Rubinstein gives no psychological underpinning for his observation that what is socially important can be personally important and vice versa. And he himself poses as "one of the greatest tasks of psychology" the study of "how these moral motives arise and operate, how the individual rises above the merely personal to the socially important, and how the socially important becomes personally important for him." [*195*] It seems to us that the answer to this question is found in the genetic formation of the ego, the incorporation of social values into the ego structure of the individual, the identification of the self with established values of a group or with new norms that may arise in new social situations. There will be "harmony," "integra-

[3] We repeat again that we are not ignoring here individual differences in temperament and ability and certain characteristic tendencies of behavior which they determine. But the relationship of these personality characteristics and traits to the social environment and to particular constellations of situational determinants cannot be analyzed in detail here.

tion," "adjustment" between the individual ego and the values of various groups or the common values of a whole social organization insofar as the established values of groups or social organizations are objectively compatible with one another.

In a society where the values of different class, status, occupation, religious, racial, or nationality groups conflict, in which dilemmas are produced by conflicting statuses, an individual almost invariably finds himself placed within two or more of these conflicting groups. He will almost inevitably be torn in his loyalty, ego-involved to a greater or lesser extent with values that he cannot make jibe with each other. Hence he will feel subjectively torn, frustrated, maladjusted. This conflict of loyalties was clearly indicated, for example, in a study of the attitudes of U. S. coal miners made by the Office of Public Opinion Research in early May 1943. [7] At that time the miners' leader, John L. Lewis, was threatening to call a strike. A temporary truce had been arranged while negotiations continued. The war was raging, and, if a strike were called, government seizure of the mines seemed inevitable. The workers were asked if they would favor or oppose calling a strike. The representative sample voted two to one against a strike. They gave as their chief reason their desire not to let down the war effort, their confidence in President Roosevelt as a man who would give them a square deal. They preferred, almost two to one, to follow Roosevelt's orders as Commander-in-Chief to orders of their union leaders. At the same time, however, over three fourths of them said that, if a strike were called, whether they wanted it or not, they would go out—they couldn't let their union and their union leaders down. As Roethlisberger and Dickson point out in their impressive studies of workers in an American industry, there is in the United States often considerable conflict between an individual's personal values and the values accepted by him and his immediate coworkers, the values held by management, or the values the worker encounters outside the factory when he assumes the role of a citizen. They conclude:

> Where the social conditions of work are such as to make it difficult for a person to identify himself or his task with any social function, the worker is also liable to obsessive responses and hence to a diminished capacity for work. [39, 328]

And they state further that the ultimate significance of an individual's work

> ... is not defined so much by his relation to the company as by his relation to the wider social reality. Only in terms of this latter relation can the different attitudes of satisfaction or dissatisfaction of individuals who are presumably enjoying the same working environment and occupational status be understood. [39, 376]

In a revealing study on some of the factors that make for work satisfaction, W. T. Watson concluded from his analysis of the case histories of a variety of workers that "some form of restlessness or mental dissatisfaction seems always to be present" if workers are separated "in spirit and objective," if they cannot see some general meaning or value in their job. [46, 255] All these results confirm Cooley's earlier observations concerning the importance of the various roles a worker plays in society in addition to his role as a producer. [11]

On the other hand, the worker in the Soviet system has the possibility of finding an extension of the values held by his local factory unit to the whole factory or the collective operation and, in turn, to the larger goal of the whole social organization. Thus the values which are for him personal values and which give him status in his own eyes and the eyes of his fellow workers are part and parcel of or reflections of values of larger social organizations of which he and his immediate group regard themselves a part.

The upshot of all this is, then, that the individual will feel *consistently* and *harmoniously* ego-involved in proportion to the objective consistency and harmony of the many social situations and values which form his particular ego constellation. Without understanding the relationship of the values which constitute the ego, the extent of conflict between or overlapping of those values, we cannot understand either the dynamics of industrial morale or the reasons for the differential participation of a given individual in his job and the gratification that job provides him. The "active" and "reactive" egos of industrial workers described by G. W. Allport [1] become meaningful when there is an understanding of the relationship between values that have become personal and value judgments encountered in actual working conditions.

This conflict between the values of small social units or between the values of small social units and those of larger organizations could be schematically represented somewhat as follows. Figure 4 could represent the loyalties of a typical American factory worker in 1946. He will have definite loyalties to his family; these may conflict with his loyalties to his union (as, for example, when his family suffers if he goes out on strike); the loyalties to his union may oppose some loyalty and identification he may have to the industry in which he works; the precepts he has subscribed to as a Christian he will find at times contradicted by racial discrimina-

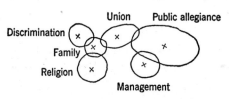

FIG. 4. Conflict of values and identifications.

tion which he may practice or condone; if he thinks of the consumers' welfare or of the progress of the "nation as a whole" he may feel that some of the organized pressures which he has to exert along with other workers in order to maintain or improve his position as a worker are in conflict with the over-all welfare of the public of which he is a member, and so on. Just what conflicts become emphasized, what degrees of overlapping in values occur, what identifications are strongest at the moment will be likely to vary enormously with the changing demands of situations. In brief, there is no clear-cut overlapping of the values that have become part of him.

By contrast, in a situation where there is no contradiction either between the values of different groups or between the values of single groups and a larger social organization, the possibility exists of complete overlapping so that what is socially important can and will become personally important and what is personally important can and will be socially important. The schematic picture would then be somewhat as in Figure 5.

It is clear from all this that the common cliché "human nature can't be changed" has no basis in fact. "Human nature" is inconceivable unless it develops in some social environment. Any social environment includes values or norms which vary in their uniformity and their duration. What the individual is and what he feels himself to be are largely conditioned by the particular con-

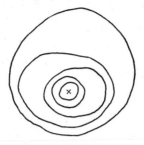

Fig. 5. Overlapping of values and identifications.

stellation of values he learns and that become a part of him. To begin with, "human nature" as represented by any single individual or any group of individuals is not something that follows any fixed pattern laid down by inexorable laws of nature; it is, rather, a complex of potentialities subject to enormous differentiations, emerging in new forms and evolving to new adjustments in a constantly changing world.

REFERENCES

1. ALLPORT, G. W., The psychology of participation, *Psychol. Rev.,* 1945, 53, 117–32.
2. AUDIENCE RESEARCH INSTITUTE, INC., *Increasing Profits with Continuous Audience Research,* New York: Am. Book, 1941; reprinted by permission of G. H. Gallup.
3. BUCK, P. S., *Talk About Russia* with Masha Scott, New York: John Day, copyright 1945.
4. CANTRIL, H., The prediction of social events, *J. Abnorm. & Soc. Psychol.,* 1938, 33, 364–89.
5. —— *The Invasion from Mars,* Princeton: Univ. Press, 1940.
6. —— *The Psychology of Social Movements,* New York: Wiley, 1941.
7. —— How the Miners Feel, unpublished report, Princeton, 1943.
8. CARLYLE, T., *Sartor Resartus,* Oxford: Clarendon, copyright 1913; first published in *Fraser's Magazine,* 1833–34.
9. CENSUS, BUREAU OF, *Industrial Distribution of the Nation's Labor Force: 1870 to 1930,* October 23, 1938.
10. CENTERS, R., *Psychological aspects of socio-economic stratification: an enquiry into the nature of class,* Princeton Univ.: thesis to be published.
11. COOLEY, C. H., *Social Process,* New York: Scribner's, 1918.

12. Davis, A., B. B. Gardner, and M. R. Gardner, *Deep South,* Chicago: Univ. Press, copyright 1941.

13. Dobb, M., *Soviet Planning and Labor in Peace and War,* New York: International, 1943.

14. Flugel, J. C., *The Psychology of Clothes,* London: Hogarth, copyright 1930.

15. Friedrich, G., *Miss U.S.S.R.,* New York: International.

16. Grinker, R. R., and J. P. Spiegel, *Men Under Stress,* Philadelphia: Blakiston, 1945.

17. ———— ———— *War Neuroses,* Philadelphia: Blakiston, 1945.

18. Holt, R. R., *Studies in the Psychology of Names,* thesis on file Princeton Univ. Library, 1939.

19. Hurlock, E. B., Motivation in fashion, *Arch. Psychol.,* 1929, **17,** no. 111.

20. Johnson, H., *The Secret of Soviet Strength,* New York: Workers Library, copyright 1943.

21. Labor, Department of, *Incentive-Wage Plans and Collective Bargaining,* Washington: 1942, Bull. 717.

22. Lévy-Bruhl, L., *How Natives Think,* London: Allen and Unwin, copyright 1926.

23. Lewin, K., *The Relative Effectiveness of a Lecture Method and a Method of Group Decision for Changing Food Habits,* State Univ. Iowa, Child Welfare Research Station, 1942.

24. Mr. Lincoln's formula, *Fortune,* February 1944, 143–206.

25. Lincoln, J. F., *Intelligent Selfishness and Manufacturing,* Cleveland: Lincoln Electric Co., 1942.

26. Littlepage, J. D., and D. Bess, *In Search of Soviet Gold,* New York: Harcourt, Brace, 1937.

27. MacDonald, L., *Labor Problems and the American Scene,* New York: Harper, copyright 1938.

28. Mangum, W. R., *Class and Status Determinants within the Negro Caste,* thesis on file Princeton Univ. Library, 1946.

29. Mauldin, B., *Up Front,* New York: Henry Holt, copyright 1945.

30. McGregor, D., Conditions of effective leadership in the industrial organization, *J. Consult. Psychol.,* 1944, **8,** 55–63.

31. Molotov, V. M., *What is Stakhanovism?,* New York: International, copyright 1936.

32. Myrdal, G., *An American Dilemma,* New York: Harper, copyright 1944.

33. National Industrial Conference Board, Inc., *Wage Incentive Practices,* Studies in Personnel Policy, No. 68, published by The Conference Board, 247 Park Avenue, New York 17, N. Y., 1945.

34. National Research Council, *Fatigue of Workers—Its Relation to Industrial Problems,* New York: Reinhold, copyright 1941.

35. *New York Times,* March 18, 1942, statement by President on ordering Mac-Arthur to leave the Philippines.

36. ———— April 26, 1946, order issued by McNarney to all unit commanders of American troops in occupied Germany.

37. Newell, T. E., Neuropsychiatry in the Japanese Army, *J. Am. Med. Assoc.,* 1944, **126,** 373 f.

38. *Reader's Digest,* June 1937, **108,** anonymous.

39. ROETHLISBERGER, F. J., and W. J. DICKSON, *Management and the Worker,* Cambridge: Harvard Univ. Press, copyright 1943.

40. RUBINSTEIN, S., Soviet psychology in wartime, *Phil. and Phenom. Res.,* 1944, **5,** 181–98.

41. SHERIF, M., *The Psychology of Social Norms,* New York: Harper, 1936.

42. STALIN, J., *The Stakhanov Movement in the Soviet Union,* New York: Workers Library, copyright 1935.

43. VEBLEN, T., *The Theory of the Leisure Class,* New York: Modern Library, copyright 1934; quotations by permission of Viking Press.

44. WARD, H. F., *The Soviet Spirit,* New York: International, copyright 1944.

45. WATSON, G., Work satisfaction, in *Industrial Conflict: A Psychological Interpretation* (G. W. Hartmann and T. Newcomb, eds.), New York: Cordon, 1939, ch. 6.

46. WATSON, W. T., *Division of Labor: A Study in the Sociology and the Social Psychology of Work Satisfaction,* Ph.D. dissertation, Univ. Chicago, 1930.

47. WILSON, N. F., Charlie Wilson, businessman, *Adventures in Business,* 1944, **II.**

Chapter 12

BREAKDOWNS OF THE EGO

The ego cannot be regarded as a fixed, rigid, or permanent entity. For no matter how well formed or "integrated" the ego may seem to be, it can be and sometimes is considerably altered by stresses and strains and upheavals of one sort or another. These pressures may be due either to the impact of concrete situations which have various degrees of compellingness, or they may be rooted in the physical organism and due to motivational (instinctual) tensions or to organic disturbances. Even though an individual builds up a relatively well-formed ego in the course of life, even though he may have a number of firmly established ego-attitudes which determine or affect his judgment and behavior, even though his particular constellation of ego-involved values has a fairly stable continuity of personal identity, and even though the individual experiences the continuous flow of his own identity from day to day and from year to year, and others around him have consistent expectations as to what he will or will not do under various conditions—in spite of all this—sufficient pressure of one kind or another can break down the ego in varying degrees.

There will, of course, be wide individual differences in the particular way any given person is affected by the same pressure or pattern of forces. We have repeatedly pointed out that ego-constellations vary according to social and personal values and that they vary not only in their range of inclusiveness but also in their intensity. Undeniable individual differences in temperament, ability, and organic functions all affect ego stability. Nevertheless, the variety of individual differences, whatever their cause, in no way alters the fact that the ego can be radically changed; can break down; can expand, shrink, dissociate, or regress if a situation is so compelling as to be crushing, if the deprivation of an instinctual need is so severe as to be "unbearable," or if an organic disturbance is so great as to make "normal" behavior impossible.

The whole problem of the breakdown of the ego, and we repeat again, an ego that is genetically formed, deserves much more detailed and elaborate consideration than space allows here. But in this chapter we can at least indicate with examples, some of the circumstances under which the ego is altered in one way or another, beginning with relatively normal instances and ending with pathological cases.

Dissociation of the Ego from the Body

The child has to learn and does learn that his body is part of himself. And he learns the norms that constitute modesty, physical attractiveness, and morality. A constellation of values, both social and personal, associated with his body—its appearance, well-being, sanctity—become an integral part of the genetically formed ego (ch. 7). *We* feel inferior if our physical attractiveness, strength, or poise is not more or less up to standard; *we* feel embarrassed if we overhear someone say that we smell badly or don't keep our fingernails clean.

In her revealing autobiography [10], Sheila Cousins, a London prostitute, pointed clearly to the distinction between her body as an integral part of her person and her body as something men used.

> I have moments when I realize that I am a person to no one, that to the male I am just a body, to the policeman a chance of promotion, to the rest simply a problem. [2]
> However lofty their protestations, men were, in the end, only after my body. [10, *145*]

"I wasn't a good prostitute," she writes. "I hadn't sufficient detachment from what I was doing to be able to pretend feeling for my clients . . . the act of sex I could go through because *I hardly seemed to be taking part in it.* It was merely something happening to me, while my mind drifted inconsequentially away. Indeed, *it was scarcely happening even to me: it was happening to something lying on a bed that had a vague connection with me, while I was calculating whether I could afford a new coat or impatiently counting sheep jumping over a gate."* [10, *150 f.,* italics ours]

Personal interviews with ten prostitutes in New York City confirmed Cousins' observations that, when participating in the sex act *as a prostitute,* a woman, *as a person,* does not usually seem to be involved.[1] Of the ten young women interviewed, only two said that they put "themselves" into the sex act when being paid for it. Both of them described themselves as "over-sexed." For the other eight, any "enjoyment" was only a pretense put on for business reasons. Here are some typical statements from the conversations with prostitutes:

> *The less personal you become the easier it is on you.*
> I think I can honestly say that any emotions I might display to a man are just pretense. *I never become aroused.* Afterwards I am tired and a great deal disgusted with the horrible habits men acquire. But I guess I am no better than they are or I wouldn't be with them.
> I *almost always pretend* that I am having some sort of response. After all these men are paying money to be kidded. The least I can do is see to it that they are not cheated. How good an act do I put on? I suppose all the things we do in this are acting to some extent. I kid and laugh with them before I get down to real business, this makes them think I'm a pretty good sport, but believe me sometimes I could choke them. I don't care what anyone says, it's not as easy as some people think.
> *Do I put myself into it? No, I don't.* Any man who has to go out and pay for it, is not worth the effort it would take to try and respond.
> *It doesn't mean anything at all to me.* How could it mean anything when you make your living at it? This is a business just like any other. You can't be sentimental in this racket. The men want you to go down and that is all. So you get as much as you can out of them and put as little as you can into it.

But when these prostitutes were with their husbands (and quite a number of them were married) or went out with their sweethearts or boy friends, the sex act took on a very different character; the women reported that *they* took part in it as individuals, that it was happening to *them,* not just to their bodies.

[1] These interviews were all made privately and confidentially by a young woman personally acquainted with the prostitutes. Her assistance was obtained through the kind interest of a New York physician.

Sheila Cousins reports her feelings after she first met Richard whom she later married.

> I liked Richard. I felt at once he wasn't out to buy me. That first day he got me a pair of gunmetal stockings and a pair of gloves after lunch, but I knew that there would be no account to settle in a fumbling taxi going home. There was a friendly shyness about everything he said or did. . . . I discovered that he was not only in love with me, he respected me. I think he was the first man who ever had. [10, *136 f.*]

> In a life where sex is merely a commodity, casually traded over the counterpane daily, the faintest spark of personal affection grows to be worth a fortune. [10, *182*]

The same thing appears in the conversations with New York prostitutes. When they go out with their lovers or boy friends, they indulge in characteristic feminine resistances. Their egos are involved, and they want to defend them with the feminine wiles appropriate to the norms of their society. And if they do have intercourse, their reaction is more complete, *they* feel involved.

> When I meet a man whom I would really like as a lover, I flirt with him. If you choose a man, that does not mean he is necessarily attracted to you. So it is only natural that you have to assert yourself in order to interest him in you. When I have finished with a man who pays me, I feel tired. I feel like leaving him as soon as possible. But when I am with my boy-friend it's so different. He comes to my house. I always meet the other men outside. When my boy-friend comes we make a real time of it. We eat and drink and fool around. We talk and have fun. I flirt with him for I want him to keep interested in me.

> I have many affairs with men who do not pay me. *If a man is nice and I am attracted to him I see no reason why I should not indulge myself.* I don't believe I flirt with them openly but I do try to attract them. Doesn't every woman try to attract men to her with what she considers her feminine guiles? As for any such affair being automatic, that is for animals, not people.

The same lack of ego-involvement—the separation of the physical needs of the body from the self—can be seen from the accounts of men describing sex relations they have had with women who were not their sweethearts or wives. Here is an account of the sex life of officers and men overseas with the U. S. Army during World War II written for us by an American officer who spent nearly four years abroad.

> During my time overseas I talked intimately with many officers and men of the American Army. Most of them were in their twenties. Quite a number were married, many not long before they had been ordered abroad. Although some of these marriages were either on the rocks or obviously about to break up, the majority of the boys seemed very much in love with their wives. They would talk to me for hours about their wives, their children if they had any, and their plans for the future of their family.
>
> Frequently, however, the morning after one of these talks, they would tell me in jocose fashion about some gal they had slept with the night before. There was no embarrassment whatever about such confessions and probably a few hours later they would be telling me again how much they loved their wives.
>
> The explanation, I am sure, lies in *the complete dissociation in the minds of these particular soldiers between their wives and families, on the one hand, and the necessity of relieving their glandular pressures on the other. In their eyes, there is no connection between these two things.* While the man might sleep temporarily—and perforce by necessity—with sluts and prostitutes, there is never any doubt in his mind where his love and major values lie: with his wife and his home. In following the necessitous path of extramarital relationships, he does not feel that he is doing his wife any harm (short of contracting a disease), and feels quite clear that his behavior has nothing to do with what will be his life when he returns home again. This is not true, of course, for all soldiers, but did seem to be the state of affairs for most of those who indulged in extramarital relations.

All of this points again to the ancient and well-recognized conclusion that the physical sex act can be regarded as an act of "love" in proportion to the extent the partners merge their egos, identify themselves with each other. Van de Velde has expressed it in his famous book *Ideal Marriage:*

> What husband and wife who love one another seek to achieve in their most intimate bodily communion, and, whether consciously or unconsciously, recognize as the purpose of such communion is: a means of expression that makes them One. [42, *321*]

THE EGO MAY TEMPORARILY DISSOLVE

Under certain conditions an individual may merge his own ego with another person's, feel that he—as a single identifiable person —has ceased to exist and that he belongs to and is a part of some-one else. In the next chapter we cite illustrations from literature of this mergence of one ego with another, of lovers who, together, feel as one but who, alone or separated, feel personally torn apart. This same melting away of the ego is also experienced by certain creative artists who "lose themselves" in their work. The dancer, Martha Graham, has said, for example, that an artist must first "destroy himself" if he is to be creative. [5, *142*] In elaborating this statement of Martha Graham's, a commentator writes:

> It was not merely a matter of sloughing off this manner and that technique. A whole self had to be danced out and away. [5, *142*]

The ego may also temporarily "break down" under the influence of alcohol or various drugs. There is an apt definition of the "superego" as "that portion of the personality which is soluble in alcohol." Since we will indicate later (pp. 492 *f.*) that there seems to us no reason to use the term superego as something distinct from the ego, we can just as well apply this definition to the ego itself. Everyone knows that when a man gets drunk he is likely to say or do things which surprise those who know him well. After consuming sufficient alcohol, a "gentleman" or "lady" may clearly lose some of his normal behavioral characteristics because some of the restraining influences of his ego—personal or social values which are part of himself—have collapsed. In the inter-views with prostitutes, we have seen how these young women often dissociated their bodies from their persons in their work. The prostitutes were also asked if alcohol had any effect on the ease with which they could give their bodies to a customer. Among those who drank, the consensus of opinion was that a few drinks before intercourse for business did facilitate separation of the "self" from the body. Here are some of their statements.

> Drinking to me is a boon. I naturally am a reticent person, and alcohol brings me out of myself. I become quite bold.

Another reports:

> Alcohol makes me feel like being more entertaining. Some of the girls get all ginned up, so that they can take anything that comes along.

Another girl said:

> This job of mine is not as easy as some people think, so a little nip now and then does the trick.

Those who have studied inveterate drinkers known as alcoholics seem generally agreed that the underlying reasons for the addiction is its acceptance by the individual as a method of escaping or overcoming some unpleasant situation or emotional conflict, or its use to make it possible for an individual to play some role denied him in normal life. [33, ch. 12] A penetrating analysis of alcoholics has been written by Bales who states that

> The alcoholic is a man divided against himself. No matter how genuinely he may agree with those who condemn him, there is another part of him which fights back . . . the drinker becomes more and more isolated, "desperately alone," "misunderstood," more and more bound up with his own circular reasoning and self-destructive tendency. . . . The alcoholic "loses his perspective," as some of them put it, and finds himself "bucking the whole world." [4, 16]

It might be mentioned in passing and in connection with the function of groups as described in chapter 10 and the overlapping of identifications discussed in chapter 11 that the most successful cures for alcoholics seem to be those which enable the individual to reintegrate his broken ego "with a social group of which he feels truly and basically a part, a group which understands him thoroughly and sympathetically." [4, 17] The current success of the organization known as Alcoholics Anonymous seems due, for example, almost entirely to the fact that the members of the organization are all ex-alcoholics, that "the new candidate in such a group intuitively recognizes that he is among friends" [18] and that in such a group "the alcoholic obtains recognition and response through the admission of thoughts and activities which, before, he had been desperately trying to hide, even from himself." [18]   In summarizing the success of Alcoholics Anonymous, Bales writes:

> As a member of a solidary group in which the desired ideas are held as group convictions, they come home to the individual with a personalized, tailored-to-fit quality, and with an emotional intensity and repetition impossible to duplicate in any other way. In the matrix of a concrete group with which the individual is closely identified, and in which he has a particular role, the ideas and desired behavior patterns can be thoroughly integrated with his social goals, tied up immediately and directly with those emotions and needs which can only be activated and satisfied in a social context. [4, 21]

In describing the use of the drug pentothal as an aid in relieving neuroses created by war experiences, Grinker and Spiegel speak of "the sedative effect of the drug on the ego" [22, 436] and state that it "serves to desensitize the ego." [383]   Without necessarily accepting the psychoanalytic implications of these authors, we find their description of the effect of the drug highly pertinent to our discussion here. For they point out how pentothal, combined with intelligent psychotherapy, can bring together different portions of the self into a more normally integrated ego. Under the influence of pentothal "the relationship between regressive dependent needs and self-respecting ego forces and even overcompensations often becomes quite clear as the different portions of the personality are expressed in associations." [391]

> Under the influence of the drug and during the process of abreaction, although not fully conscious, the ego, devoid of the stress of anxiety, synthesizes some and often much of the important isolated and pathogenic material into its main body. It is as if the emotions or the memories had been separated from the active ego forces as in a hysterical dissociation, because they had been too threatening to the ego's stability or productive of terrifying and unendurable anxiety. [22, 392 f.]

BREAKDOWNS OF THE EGO UNDER EXTREME DEPRIVATION

If an individual is long denied the satisfaction of an instinctual need, then there is a considerably greater chance that he will transgress the established norms which under more usual conditions are part of *his* ideas of good conduct and with which he would normally identify himself. Enforced sexual continence may lead to such results as obscene acts and homosexuality; prolonged hunger may lead to theft or to some other form of anti-social or at least undignified behavior.

Bill Mauldin, in describing the "abject poverty and hunger of the Italian refugees" encountered by the United States Armies in Italy, has pointed out the very unladylike behavior of old Italian women under such conditions.

> It would take a pretty tough guy not to feel his heart go out to the shivering, little six-year-old squeaker who stands barefoot in the mud, holding a big tin bucket so the dogface can empty his mess kit into it. Many soldiers, veterans of the Italy campaign and thousands of similar buckets, still go back and sweat out the mess line for an extra chop and hunk of bread for those little kids. But there is a big difference between the ragged, miserable infantryman who waits with his mess kit, and the ragged, miserable civilian who waits with his bucket. The doggie knows where his next meal is coming from. That makes him a very rich man in this land where *hunger is so fierce it makes animals out of respectable old ladies who should be wearing cameos and having tea parties instead of fighting one another savagely for a soldier's scraps.* [31, 66 ff., italics ours]

Another American soldier told how norms of decency broke down in Italy and Sicily to such an extent that formerly respectable women sent children out on the streets to solicit Allied soldiers for them, to circumvent the stringent penalties imposed on public prostitution. These observations are particularly significant since the soldier who reported them had lived in Italy for some time before the war, spoke fluent Italian, had seen the country under normal conditions and knew that the behavior he observed was nothing "typical" of Italy but due to the extraordinary conditions created by war.

> While in Palermo, I saw little children soliciting trade for their sisters, cousins, aunts, or mothers. They would stop soldiers on the street with such remarks as "Hey, Joe, wanna gal, verra clean, only one dollar," or they would use some American slang to mention perversions that made the trade sound more interesting. In one instance, I observed a mother with her daughter carrying on "trade" in a single

dark room on a squalid street on the outskirts of the city with another G.I. outside, waiting. From all accounts I could gather, these women had originally come from the servant class who now found a more profitable way to spend their time. On other occasions, I encountered women of higher class means inviting officers to their homes, hoping to acquire some political favor or food. Their "trade" was more formal and practiced with little publicity. War widows or those who had their husbands in Allied prison camps were especially among the latter type. On still other occasions, one found young girls who were out to have a "good time" and the disruption of family life spread a sense of "devil may care" attitude. Most of these women had been bombed out of their homes and had lost their cherished possessions. Many had had relatives killed. They had been forced out of their normal home environments and the fear of ostracism from the social pattern indigenous to that environment no longer existed. It was no wonder they had become cynical, hard-bitten and had chosen this profession out of economic necessity. I had spent considerable time in Italy before the war. What I saw during the war was a real shock to me because it was so very different from what I had previously known.[2]

A German physician, once an inmate of the Belsen concentration camp, has reported how the ordinary self-respecting and law-abiding citizens of normal life "resorted to cannibalism to avoid starvation." The account of his testimony states:

> He told how human beings fought like animals for food, how they carried human flesh around in their pockets, and how the SS (Nazi Elite Guard) ordered those who practiced cannibalism hanged or beaten to death. [35]

Further evidence that the ego is not a mystical entity, that it is related to the organism and affected by physical deprivation is seen in changes of personality such as feelings of unusual exhilaration and well-being, loss of judgment, emotional outbursts, the impairment of critical ability and self-criticism, if an individual breathes air which lacks the amount of oxygen normally required (Anoxia). [40, 585 f.] Recent studies have also shown that even a slight deficiency of vitamin B has marked influences on a per-

---

[2] These observations were given us by R. V. Botsford, Princeton '48, who was with the American Army in Italy.

son's behavior and the conduct he would normally feel befitting to him. Summarizing a number of studies, Shock reports:

> One of the symptoms of even slight vitamin B deficiency in human subjects is their increased irritability, moodiness, lack of cooperation and "meanness." With more severe B-vitamin deficiency such mental states as apathy, depression, and emotional instability have often been observed. A most striking study is that of Williams, *et al.* (1942) who restricted the B-vitamin (thiamin) intake of eleven women to .45 mg. daily, which is an amount little, if any, below that obtained in many American diets. Within six or eight weeks the subjects began to show such symptoms of emotional instability as irritability, moodiness, quarrelsomeness, lack of cooperation, and vague fears progressing to agitation and mental depression. When thiamin was restored to their diets, or even when riboflavin was reduced in the presence of adequate thiamin, no such symptoms were observed.[3] [40, 598 f.]

THE EGO MAY BREAK DOWN IF ESTABLISHED NORMS COLLAPSE OR ARE NO LONGER IN FORCE

If an individual has identified himself, made part of himself, certain social values which are suddenly and completely upset or destroyed by some major cataclysm, then that portion of the ego composed of those values may itself be destroyed, and the individual may exhibit behavior quite out of keeping with what he or his friends would regard as normal or right for him. Two illustrations, both dealing with the collapse of norms in Germany as a result of Allied advances, will suffice here to show how behavior can be radically altered when normal ego-involving standards are suddenly withdrawn.

A vivid description of the looting of a German castle was written for us by Lewis F. Gittler. The important part of the story for our present interests is put in italics. It shows how respectable middle-class Germans in one moment condemned the looting of the castle by others, even by other Germans who happened to be peasants, but in the next moment themselves indulged in looting when they

[3] The study referred to by Shock is [45].

learned that there was something they wanted badly and could now steal without fear of legal action or particular social disapproval.[4]

Near the Weser River east of Paderborn was a large modernized castle dominating a town of about 350 inhabitants. A cavalry reconnaissance squadron on its way to the river passed by the castle about 8 P.M. one evening. There had been no American troops in the town as yet and there was no resistance on the part of the Germans. It was an out of the way town, reachable only by a dirt road thru a forest. As the column of jeeps, half-tracks and armored cars passed the castle, they decided to spend the night there. The major sent in an officer to negotiate with the Baroness. He asked for two floors for his troops. She could remain in her own quarters and the upper two floors. She began protesting, complaining it would not be feasible and generally became such a nuisance about the thing that the Major ordered the castle evacuated by its occupants in two hours. The old Baroness left and the toughened reconnaissance troops moved in. The castle was jampacked with goods and clothes and furniture and foods of all kinds. The troops disturbed nothing outside of the wine cellar. There they found 1,000 bottles of French champagne and cognac. Until 4 A.M. they drank and finally left at dawn with every bottle of liquor, camera, souvenirs, etc. At dawn, the townspeople woke up to find the Americans gone. Many came back from the fields where they had hidden in terror. There was no authority left in the town. The old Baroness (known locally as the Alte Hexe, "old witch,") was in another chateau about 15 miles away where Army trucks had taken her and her servants. The Baroness had been the power and the mainstay in that village. Her grounds and acreage had about 200 Poles and Russian slave laborers.

I had come in with the reconnaissance squadron and after they left I stayed behind. At about 6 A.M., the Russians came into the courtyard and seeing no one around went into the castle and came out loaded down with clothing. The Poles were next. They went in and came out with hundreds of jars of conserved foods. The German peasants went in next and carted out lamps and bedding. In the house where I was staying were several refugees from Krefeld and Duesseldorf. They were of the substantial middle class and had used this as their summer house. One was an art dealer, another a soap manufacturer,

---

[4] This incident was first reported to us by Donald V. McGranahan, former major, AUS, who suggested we get in touch with Mr. Gittler.

another a publisher. We watched the looting going on and as it became more and more intense, *these Germans were outraged by the filthy Poles and the thieving Russians and the stupid peasants. They talked about dignity and honor and how Americans should prevent this sort of thing* and if the Alte Hexe comes back there would be hell to pay. *Just then, the sister of one of the men in the house came in breathlessly saying, "Someone just opened the big room with the silverware."* It had been known in the town that the hexe had thousands of Solingen flat ware in a special room, and all kinds of kitchen utensils, boxes and boxes of them. *The soap manufacturer and the art dealer nodded and a moment later muttered something about going downstairs. I saw them go into the castle with a dozen other respectable-looking Germans. A minute later they came out with their arms full of canopeners, knives, forks, scissors and pots.* The cycle of looting was completed and the castle was quiet again with only a few Poles scavenging around.

Members of the German army during World War II were generally regarded as highly disciplined troops, with great love and respect for the Fatherland. However, documents found on German troops, captured during the last months of 1944 after the Germans had been pushed back on their own territory and when it was becoming clear that defeat was inevitable, revealed warnings from German commanders against looting by German soldiers on German territory. The documents indicate in no uncertain terms that the considerable looting going on during that period was entirely inconsistent with the duty and honor of a German soldier.[5]

In the last chapter we noted that some individuals identify themselves so completely with certain established values that they prefer to die the death of a martyr or a hero rather than live in a world in which these values are taken away. Such people refuse to compromise, and by destroying themselves they preserve what they regard as *their* integrity. For them there is no breakdown, no dissociation, no alteration of the ego. The implication is that those who do not follow the logical course of the martyr must make readjustments if they are to live in peace with themselves. As Dublin and Bunzel remark in their study of suicide [11, *281*] "self-

[5] The writers wish to thank Donald V. McGranahan for sending these captured documents.

destruction seems the only solution of intolerable difficulties," and they cite notes left behind by suicides which show how impossible it has been for them either to alter themselves or escape from themselves.

Bettelheim has described the case of a prominent German politician who had been kept in a concentration camp by the Nazis and who saw that adaptation to the camp was only possible if a basic change occurred in his personality and value relationships. The man killed himself rather than live on as essentially another person.

> He declared that according to his experience nobody could live in the camp longer than five years without changing his attitudes so radically that he no longer could be considered the same person he used to be. He asserted that he did not see any point in continuing to live once his real life consisted in being a prisoner in a concentration camp, that he could not endure developing those attitudes and behaviors he saw developing in all old prisoners. He therefore had decided to commit suicide on the sixth anniversary of his being brought into the camp. His fellow prisoners tried to watch him carefully on this day, but nevertheless he succeeded. [7, 438]

THE EGO MAY REGRESS, DISSOCIATE, OR BECOME RE-FORMED UNDER EXTREME SITUATIONS OF STRESS

Comparatively few individuals, however, choose self-destruction to self-modification. The more likely effect of extreme stress caused by pressures from the environment is some change of the ego formed during the course of life. This may be clear and drastic or it may be relatively hidden and subtle. Numerous examples of such alterations have been observed during the past few years under the many varieties of social upheaval concomitant with the rapid social change in most Western societies.

From studies made on the psychological effects of unemployment, for example, it can be readily discerned that if an individual is not provided the opportunity or right to work, the constellation of values constituting his ego may deteriorate radically, causing a shift in his aspiration levels and a breakdown of former group loyalties. We should emphasize that in this discussion we are not generalizing that these *are* the inevitable effects of unemployment and depression alone, but that unemployment and depression sometimes can and do cause these effects as well as others that do not concern us here. And obviously, how any single individual will react to unemployment will depend in part upon personality factors such as temperament and on the length and circumstances of unemployment.

Autobiographies written by unemployed people in Poland in the early 1930's and reported by Zawadski and Lazarsfeld [46] vividly reveal the "feelings of degradation and superfluousness" experienced. A youth writes, for example,

> I become something absolutely superfluous in my own family. I am nineteen years old, and I define my part quite clearly as that of a sponger. [46, *240*]

An unemployed man tells how he no longer feels that he is an integral part of society:

> Of the many unemployed who have committed suicide lately, many did it, as I believe, under the influence of the fixed idea that they had become superfluous in the world. Really, every unemployed person is excluded from the creative life. For instance I had, as long as I worked, although I did it for the wages, the definite feeling that I participated in the antlike, productive activity of mankind. [46, *240 f.*]

The effect of this ostracism on the normal feeling of self-respect is clear. One of the unemployed writes, for example,

> I look for a job. *I bow with servility, I ask, I beg, I humble myself and lose my ego.* I become a beast, a humiliated beast, excluded from the realm of society. [46, *238*, italics ours]

Another says:

> Life has made a coward of me. Sometimes I would like to bend myself in an humble way before the world and beg, "Buy me! Buy me!" [46, *238*]

The effect of unemployment on one's own conception of his social status and his loss of status in the eyes of others is exemplified by the statement of a 43-year-old mason who wrote:

How hard and humiliating it is to bear the name of an unemployed man. When I go out, I cast down my eyes because I feel myself wholly inferior. When I go along the street, it seems to me that I can't be compared with an average citizen, that everybody is pointing at me with his finger. I instinctively avoid meeting anyone. Former acquaintances and friends of better times are no longer so cordial. They greet me indifferently, when we meet. They no longer offer me a cigarette and their eyes seem to say, "You are not worth it, you don't work." [46, 239]

After reviewing numerous studies made on the psychological effects of unemployment (1938) Eisenberg and Lazarsfeld point out

. . . that the last stage of unemployment consists of a general narrowing of activities as well as of outlook on life. There is also a narrowing of wants and needs. Yet there is a limit beyond which this narrowing cannot go; otherwise a collapse occurs. [12, 378]

The effect of unemployment on the status relationship held by different family members provide particularly neat illustrations of the way an individual's role and position can change if he loses one of his main and traditional functions, in this case if the father in an American family is unable to carry out his role as the breadwinner. Summarizing the analysis of 65 case studies collected in Newark during the depression of the early 1930's, Stouffer and Lazarsfeld, in their monograph on *The Family in the Depression* [41] state the following "hypotheses" concerning the shifts in family loyalties and authorities:

1. If an unemployed father loses authority with his wife he is very likely to lose authority with his children.
2. Conversely, if an unemployed father loses authority with his children he may or may not lose authority with his wife.
3. If the father is unemployed, an adolescent daughter is more likely to rebel against deprivations than an adolescent son, who gets unusual ego satisfaction if he can be treated like a grownup as the result of even slight contributions to the family budget.
4. The presence of an unemployed father in the home, unless there is great irritability and conflict, tends to increase his companionship and authority with very young children.

5. If the mother takes a job, after the father loses his, authority over the children tends to be transferred to the mother.

6. The conflict between father and son tends to be greater if the son returns home unemployed after a period of employment than if the son had never been employed.

7. If the father is employed and especially if he has some influence with his friends outside of the family, a depression tends to increase the dependence of a son on the father, since such a father is likely to be the best means of getting the boy a job.

8. Authority based on categorical orders and punishment is more likely to deteriorate, in the family of an unemployed father, than authority based on intimacy and an attempt at mutual understanding. [41, *116 f.*]

In Angell's *The Family Encounters the Depression,* dozens of examples can be found of the restriction of the ego due to unemployment. The following case, taken almost at random, describes what happened to one of the older sons of a family who, together with his father and sister who were once wage earners, had lost his job: [2]

He has completely lost his *role.* He is unable to face what he considers an exposure. He considers himself a failure. His inadequacy stands revealed to himself. He has previously sensed it, but never actually experienced it. Without his shield of a good job he cannot face the rest of the world. Occasionally he "talks big" but has lost all his braggadocio. Very often he talks deprecatingly of himself. Sometimes he will sit for hours and do nothing but stare. He lacks initiative of any sort. He hates activity of any kind, hates to look for work.

Sometimes he will tirade against every one—the government, church, home, friends. One feels a tension, a conflict, a strain when he is about. Sometimes when this strain is too great he "goes to pieces" in a most pitiable, horrible way. All his inhibitions, his restraints, are lifted and he reveals all his hurts, his disappointments, frustrations— till it is more than others can bear. He once became involved in such a scene in the presence of several young nieces. All the children were weeping and utterly torn with sympathy. He is now incapable of making the least decision for himself—for instance, to wear or not to wear a coat is a source of conflict. [2, *201 f.*]

Many other effects of unemployment on ego standards and values can be listed from a review of the literature on the subject.

A common finding is that levels of aspiration are definitely lowered [26]; some unemployed who never before touched liquor may take to drink [46, 237 f.]; some may lose all former respect for those whom they once regarded as their superiors and their bosses [242 f.]; some lose all national loyalties [249]; and, if unemployed workers are not highly organized, class-conscious, or in some way cared for by their union or other group, their solidarity with other workers is apt to deteriorate and to be replaced by feelings of hostility toward each other and by individualistic competition and the like. [244 f.]

In their article, *Personality Under Social Catastrophe,* Allport, Bruner, and Jandorf summarize an analysis of 90 life histories of persons who experienced various degrees of persecution and suffering in Germany after the Nazi rise to power on January 30, 1933. [1] The authors state as one of their summary conclusions:

> Even catastrophic social change does not succeed in effecting radical transformations in personality. Before and after disaster, individuals are to a large extent the same. In spite of intensification of political attitudes (toward extreme opposition) and in spite of growing awareness and criticism of standards of judgment and evaluation, the basic structure of personality persists—and, with it, established goal striving, fundamental philosophy of life, skills, and expressive behavior. When there was change in our subjects, it did not seem to violate the basic integrations of the personality but rather to select and reinforce traits already present. [1, 19 f.]

But they also point out in their conclusion that, in addition to the stability of these traits:

> *Besides* aggressive responses, direct or displaced, *we find defeat and resignation, regression, conformity, adoption of temporary frames of security, changes in standards of evaluation, lowering of levels of aspiration, heightened in-group feeling, increased fantasy and insulation, and, above all, increased planning and problem-solving.* [1, 20, italics ours]

Now just what "personality" is and just what changes in thought and behavior have to take place before personality can be considered to have "changed" is a problem we cannot go into here. However, we have already cited in previous chapters numerous instances of profound alterations in behavior and attitude due to new situations in which an individual finds himself. Without in the least denying the fact that manifestations of temperament, abilities, or organic characteristics often show an amazing consistency under different conditions, any conception of personality which leaves out ego-involvements seems quite inadequate for social psychology and, what is more important, quite unsupported by the facts of the laboratory and everyday life which show so clearly the effect of these ego-involvements in determining behavior. This point of view seems supported by the Allport–Bruner–Jandorf study itself. In commenting upon the changed attitudes toward National Socialism as the movement became more and more powerful and ubiquitous in Germany, the authors note "the inevitable desertion of neutral attitudes as the social crisis verged into personal catastrophe" [9], and they quote from one case study the remark:

> "Everything was appraised according to pro- or anti-Nazi; there was simply no possibility of being objective. *You had to belong to one group.* We individualists instinctively felt the loneliness of our position outside any group." [1, 9, italics ours]

They also point out that "great anxiety and feelings of insecurity were practically universal," [11] and that the most frequent cause of this anxiety was "uncertainty of future status." [12] Another of their findings is that

> As the months of persecution went on, 42 per cent of the cases for whom data are available betrayed an increased fatalism in outlook. . . . *Others made attempts to come to terms with the situation through alterations in their scale of values.* . . . In some cases, for example, moral standards were disturbed. [1, 16, italics ours]

Such terms as "resignation," "regression," "adoption of temporary frames of security," "changes in standards of evaluation," "lowering of levels of aspiration" obviously have no meaning if the implication that these psychological conditions are related to the ego is taken away.

Just what did happen to the egos of German citizens when they were put in very extreme situations has been brilliantly described by Bettelheim in his report of his own experiences at the German concentration camps of Dachau and Buchenwald and his observations and conversations with other inmates. [7]   Bettelheim is careful to point out that "there were great individual variations" and that his statements must be regarded as generalizations. However, it is quite apparent from his account that there were limits to individual variations and that generalizations were, therefore, quite possible.

Summarizing the effect of the initial shock of being taken prisoner and deprived of civil rights, Bettelheim states:

> It seems that most, if not all, prisoners tried to react against the initial shock by mustering forces which might prove helpful in supporting their badly shaken self-esteem. Those groups which found in their past life some basis for the erection of such a buttress to their endangered egos seemed to succeed. Members of the lower class derived a certain satisfaction from the absence of class differences among the prisoners. Political prisoners found their importance as politicians once more demonstrated by being imprisoned. Members of the upper class could exert at least a certain amount of leadership among the middle-class prisoners. Members of "anointed" families felt in prison as superior to all other human beings as they had felt outside of it. [7, 428 f.]

The initial effort was, then, an attempt to preserve the established constellation of ego-attitudes.

When the prisoners were removed from the prison to the concentration camp, every effort was made by the Gestapo "to break the prisoners as individuals." [418]   The Gestapo principle was "to force the prisoners to feel and act as a group, and not as individuals." [434]   In pursuance of this policy the Gestapo "insisted that none of them [the prisoners] was any better than the others." [447]   Among other methods of achieving the purpose was

> . . . the hostage system and the punishment of the whole group for whatever a member of it does; not permitting anybody to deviate in his behavior from the group norm, whatever this norm may be. [452]
>
> If a prisoner tried to protect a group, he might have been killed by a guard, but if his action came to the knowledge of the camp administration then the whole group was always more severely punished than it would have been in the first place. In this way the group came to

resent the actions of its protector because it suffered under them. The protector was thus prevented from becoming a leader, or a martyr, around whom group resistance might have been formed. [7, *436*]

In addition to various tortures administered, other methods of destroying individuality were systematic and crude attempts to get the individual to dissociate himself from established norms and values. Prisoners were forced

> . . . to hit one another, and to defile what the guards considered the prisoners' most cherished values. For instance, the prisoners were forced to curse their God, to accuse themselves of vile actions, accuse their wives of adultery and of prostitution. This continued for hours and was repeated at various times. [7, *429*]

Bettelheim noticed that new prisoners who had not yet been broken or had not resigned in any way were unusually sensitive to any news from the "outside" world which reflected any change in their social position.

> Even the smallest change in their former private world attained tremendous importance. . . . Their desire to return exactly the person who had left was so great that they feared any change, however trifling, in the situation they had left. Their worldly possessions should be secure and untouched, although they were of no use to them at this moment. [7, *439 f.*]

The general feeling seemed to be

> *If nothing changes in the world in which I used to live, then I shall not change, either.* . . . The violent reaction against changes in their families was then the counterpart of the realization that they were changing. What enraged them was probably not only the fact of the change, but the change in standing within the family which it implied. [7, *440*, italics ours]

Bettelheim notes how particularly disturbing and "unforgettable" experiences were that could not be related to some existing frame of reference.

> It seems that *camp experiences which remained within the normal frame of reference of a prisoner's life experience were dealt with by means of the normal psychological mechanisms. Once the experience transcended this frame of reference, the normal mechanisms seemed*

*no longer able to deal adequately with it and new psychological
mechanisms were needed.* [*433*, italics ours]

The psychological reactions to events which were somewhat more
within the sphere of the normally comprehensible were decidedly
different from those to extreme events. It seems that prisoners deal
with less extreme events in the same way as if they had happened
outside of the camp. For example, if a prisoner's punishment was not
of an unusual kind, he seemed ashamed of it, he tried not to speak
about it. A slap in one's face was embarrassing, and not to be discussed. One hated individual guards who had kicked one, or slapped
one, or verbally abused one much more than the guard who really
had wounded one seriously. In the latter case one eventually hated
the Gestapo as such, but not so much the individual inflicting the punishment. Obviously this differentiation was unreasonable, but it
seemed to be inescapable. One felt deeper and more violent aggressions against particular Gestapo members who had committed minor
vile acts than one felt against those who had acted in a much more
terrible fashion. [*7, 435*]

As time went on and as one torture followed another, the author
consciously felt the pressure on his ego and realized the inadequacy
of established frames for the interpretation of camp experiences,
and the danger that his body and its daily life might somehow
become split off or detached from what he really regarded as
himself. He states:

If the author should be asked to sum up in one sentence what, all
during the time he spent in the camp, was his main problem, he
would say: *to safeguard his ego in such a way, that, if by any good
luck he should regain liberty, he would be approximately the same
person he was when deprived of liberty.* He has no doubt that he
was able to endure the transportation, and all that followed, because
right from the beginning he became convinced that these horrible
and degrading experiences somehow did not happen to "him" as a
subject, but only to "him" as an object. [*7, 431*]

This observation was confirmed by others and not limited to
Bettelheim's own introspection as a psychologist. He writes:

The importance of this attitude was corroborated by many statements of other prisoners, although none would go so far as to state
definitely that an attitude of this type was clearly developed already

during the time of the transportation. They couched their feelings usually in more general terms such as, "The main problem is to remain alive and unchanged," without specifying what they meant as unchanged. From additional remarks it became apparent that what should remain unchanged was individually different and roughly covered the person's general attitude and values. [7, 431]

Bettelheim goes on to describe this detachment he felt:

It was as if he watched things happening in which he only vaguely participated. Later he learned that many prisoners had developed this same feeling of detachment, as if what happened really did not matter to oneself. [431]

During the transportation the prisoners developed a state of detachment, feeling as if what happened did not really happen to them *as persons*. [7, 433, italics ours]

If an individual was unable to keep his ego intact, was unable to view what was happening as something not happening *to him,* then the only alternatives were to commit suicide or suffer a breakdown or dissociation of the ego and a subsequent re-formation that made conditions bearable. We have already cited the case of a man who was conscious of these alternatives and who chose suicide as the lesser of the two evils. Bettelheim reports that the suicides that did occur were confined mainly to middle-class prisoners who were particularly anxious

. . . that their status as such should be respected in some way. What they resented most was to be treated "like ordinary criminals." After some time they could not help realizing their actual situation. Then they seemed to disintegrate. [7, 427]

For the majority of prisoners it seemed that this ability to remain detached was lost. The Gestapo was successful in breaking down individuality. Old norms disappeared, and new ones took their place. Bettelheim reports, for example, that

Prisoners who died under tortures *qua* prisoners, although martyrs to their political conviction, were not considered martyrs. Those who suffered due to efforts to protect others were accepted as martyrs. [7, 436]

And he notes that

. . . as time went on the difference in the reaction to minor and major sufferings slowly seemed to disappear. [*437*]

There was a general "regression to infantile behavior" on the part of nearly all the prisoners who "asserted their power as a group over those prisoners who objected to deviations from normal adult behavior." [*444*]   The prisoners began to live

. . . only in the immediate present. . . . Friendships developed as quickly as they broke up. Prisoners would, like early adolescents, fight one another tooth and nail, declare that they would never even look at one another or speak to one another, only to become close friends within a few minutes. They were boastful, telling tales about what they had accomplished in their former lives, or how they succeeded in cheating foremen or guards, and how they sabotaged the work. Like children they felt not at all set back or ashamed when it became known that they had lied about their prowess. [7, *445 f.*]

The relapse of more adult attitudes under the strain of some deprivation, the stress of conditions that seem irreconcilable with established attitudes, or the internal conflicts and contradictions between various attitudes is a relatively common form of ego-breakdown. We will note it again in the cases of war neuroses cited later in this chapter. This regression to a more infantile level of adjustment frees a person from what has become his intense and trying effort to maintain his more usual consistent status. Often quite "normal" people resort to it temporarily for relief. Bettelheim notes that, once this regression had taken place:

No longer was there a split between one to whom things happened and the one who observed them . . . everything that happened to them, even the worst atrocity, was "real" to them. [7, *437*]

The extent to which the original ego had broken down is indicated by Bettelheim's statement that

Once this stage was reached of taking everything that happened in the camp as "real," there was every indication that the prisoners who had reached it were afraid of returning to the outer world. [*437*]

Old prisoners did not like to mention their former social status or their former activities, whereas new prisoners were rather boastful about them. [7, *443*]

Bettelheim reports that

> Some of the indications from which one could learn about the changed attitudes were: scheming to find oneself a better place in the camp rather than trying to contact the outer world, avoiding speculation about one's family, or world affairs, concentrating all interest on events taking place inside of the camp. [*439*]

> Old prisoners did not like to be reminded of their families and former friends. When they spoke about them, it was in a very detached way. [7, *442*]

It is particularly significant that these "broken" prisoners did not become completely disorganized chaotic individuals. They became, on the contrary, re-formed individuals. Their repeated experience and constant exposure to the values in the microcosm of the concentration camp gave them new frames of reference, new anchorages which determined in large part their thought and behavior and with which they identified themselves. Bettelheim states that *"a prisoner had reached the final stage of adjustment to the camp situation when he had changed his personality so as to accept as his own the values of the Gestapo."* [*447*, italics ours] Examples of this identification with the Gestapo's values are cited. For instance,

> Practically all prisoners who had spent a long time in the camp took over the Gestapo's attitude toward the so-called unfit prisoners. . . . So old prisoners were sometimes instrumental in getting rid of the unfit, in this way making a feature of Gestapo ideology a feature of their own behavior. [7, *448*]

If a "traitor" was found in the midst of the old prisoners, he was slowly tortured to death just as the prisoners themselves were tortured by the Gestapo, instead of being summarily eliminated. The old prisoners tried to get hold of and wear pieces of Gestapo uniforms, tried to make themselves look like the guards. Accepting the Gestapo criticism of American and English newspaper accounts of cruelties committed in the camps, the old prisoners "would insist that it is not the business of foreign correspondents or newspapers to bother with German institutions." [*449*]

When erecting buildings for the Gestapo, controversies started whether one should build well. New prisoners were for sabotaging, a majority of the old prisoners for building well. [7, *449*]

The old prisoners took particular delight in standing smartly at attention during the daily roll-call, prided themselves on being tough, and even imitated in their own games one of the games played by the guards which consisted of discovering "who could stand to be hit longest without uttering a complaint." [*450*] The old prisoners accepted the Nazi race theory; they believed in the need for German Lebensraum. They accepted "as expression of their verbal aggressions, terms which definitely did not originate in their previous vocabularies, but were taken over from the very different vocabulary of the Gestapo." [*447*]

This study of behavior in extreme situations gives us, then, an unusually vivid cameo sketch of an individual's initial attempt to defend and protect his ego, his attempt to preserve some detachment, his eventual regression to a more primitive childlike level of adjustment, and the reconstruction of his ego along lines determined by his experiences and the prevailing values of those in complete authority in the little world in which he found himself.

There is no need to spell out the fact that the methods of modern warfare create conditions for the man in active combat which place on him enormous, sometimes overwhelming, strain. Fortunately for psychology, the effects of these harrowing conditions on individuals were carefully observed by trained psychiatrists during World War II. In their two outstanding books, *War Neuroses* and *Men Under Stress,* Drs. Grinker and Spiegel who served with the Army Air Forces have reported their work in considerable detail and have documented it with numerous case studies. It is especially significant that these two volumes, the second of which prompted General Eisenhower to award the authors the Legion of Merit, were both written while the war was still going on, while the authors were still on active duty, not, therefore, constructing their impressions after a lapse of time and formulating their interpretations in any library or remote office. [21, 22] Under these conditions and with the men they were

treating close at hand, the authors use as their own central theme
the effect of war-created situations on the ego. In the preface of
War Neuroses, they write:

> Opportunity is furnished by the violent, severe stress of war to
> observe the ego's capacities to handle the rapidly and intensely mo-
> bilized biological and physiological drives signaled by anxiety. [21, *vii*]

Elsewhere they state:

> The appearance of the symptoms of a neurosis of war is the signal
> that the weakened ego, no longer able to cope with the accumulated
> anxiety, has begun to sacrifice a part of its normal functions. [21, *123*]

They are careful to point out that the syndromes they encountered
showed enormous variety with no two being exactly alike. Because of this fact the authors show a healthy disregard of any rigid
classification or pigeonholing.

In reviewing the accounts of Grinker and Spiegel, we should
remind ourselves that all of the men they treated were already
preselected. They had already undergone psychological and psychiatric tests. And although such tests, as the authors point out,
still leave much to be desired, (since, for one thing, the psychiatrist has "no laboratory means of duplicating the stress to which an
individual will be exposed in combat" [22, *16*]), still there is little
doubt that the young men selected for the Army Air Force could
be regarded as above the average in the total population in general
emotional stability.

It should also be noted that although the publisher's jacket for
War Neuroses states that the book is "based on no preconceived
theories," the authors' treatment of the ego follows a psychoanalytic interpretation which, however, they do not particularly elaborate or defend. As they employ the term, they do, however, fall
into the psychoanalytic error of reifying the ego, endowing it with
an autonomy all its own. They use such phrases, for example, as
"the ego interprets," [22, *126*] "the weakened ego can no longer
appraise reality," [*136*] "the ego twists and turns under the pressure." [21, *137*] As we point out in chapter 14, any such conception of the ego seems to us quite invalid and unnecessary. But in
spite of this loose use of the term and disagreements we would

have with many of the authors' more detailed interpretations of specific cases, their rich and penetrating observations and their placement of these in an ego context make their studies particularly pertinent for our purposes here.

The authors state that "one of the most frequently heard remarks in our wards was, 'I took it as long as I could; I can't take it any more.'" [21, 69] In a very real sense, this simple everyday statement of the G.I. sums up the problem of ego-breakdown. The job of the psychologist is, of course, to determine precisely what the "I" and the "it" mean. Both of these volumes contain eloquent, if horrible, testimony of the fact that the "it" produced by combat conditions can and often does break down the "I." Grinker and Spiegel use the apt phrase "situational psychotic breakdown" in describing the relationship between the individual and his immediate environment. Just what the authors mean by "situational psychotic breakdown" is shown in the following statement where they point out that under conditions of great stress an individual loses his intellectual capacity to make discriminations, indulges in behavior not at all characteristic of himself, and may gradually regress to a less mature level of adjustment:

> As the pressure on the ego increases, its inhibitory and intellectual functions begin to disappear. Inhibition of the vegetative and motor signs of anxiety becomes impossible. Try as he may, the soldier cannot prevent the appearance of tremor, tachycardia, tachypnea, and restlessness. This is the situation in the moderate anxiety states. A little more pressure of anxiety, and the intellectual, appraising functions of the ego begin to yield. Thought becomes confused and concentration impossible. Discrimination—so important in the danger situation—becomes lost, and when this happens there occurs a further increment to anxiety, because now an accurate evaluation of traumatic stimuli cannot be made, and all stimuli seem equally dangerous. Caught in this deadly vortex, the ego twists and turns in a desperate effort to prevent its complete disintegration. Often patients—or soldiers on the field—express this need in the verbalization: "I've got to get a grip on myself"; and this impulse sometimes finds a motor outlet when the patient clutches the nearest object tightly and squeezes it as if his life depended on it. As the ego functions give way further, various released motor expressions appear: uncontrollable laughing and crying, aimless running about. Sudden failures of muscular

innervation occur, comparable to the intellectual failure; and the patient may fall down and be unable to arise, because of weakness. The loss of ego function appears to be a biological retreat or regression to steadily more immature and primitive levels of ego development. This is not a strategic retreat, but a disorderly rout, under the overwhelming pressure. [21, *124 f.*]

We can include here only portions from a few of the case studies selected by Grinker and Spiegel which provide the evidence for this statement. The following case of severe anxiety shows how a man "lost control of himself" due to dissociation:

A 32 year old infantryman had taken part in the severe fighting in Northern Tunisia. Nothing was known of his past history beyond the fact that his company had been subjected to heavy mortar fire and dive bombing, while attempting to take a height strongly defended by the enemy. When brought into the hospital, he was unable to speak, and presented the typical picture of severe terror. He had coarse, persistent tremors of the hands and lips and started violently when any part of his body was touched. At times he seemed about to speak, but nothing came of it except inaudible whispers. He made no effort to get out of bed or to help himself in any way but lay in a flexed posture with his body curled up like an intra-uterine fetus. The diagnosis on his field tag was schizophrenia, as was the tentative diagnosis made by the admitting officer. It was determined to give the patient a few days' rest, sedation, and adequate nourishment before specific therapy was initiated.

At the end of two weeks the clinical picture had undergone considerable change. The patient was now out of bed, but walked with a peculiar simian gait. His knees were bent and his shoulders stooped, his arms hung lifelessly at his side to below the knees, and his head and neck jutted forward at a peculiar angle. His facial expression was one of anxious, puzzled apprehension. He squinted and frowned at his attendants as if trying to make out who they were and what he had to fear from them. If an attendant made a sudden or unexpected motion, the patient would start back with fear. With much stammering, he asked simple questions in a childlike fashion about who he was, where he was, what had happened to him. He asked these questions over and over again, never receiving satisfaction. From time to time a fatuous smile would cross his face, he would laugh and, leaping upon his cot, he would jump up and down on the springs and shout "Dive bombers! Dive bombers!", as if it were a huge joke. Apparently an accomplished accordion player in the past, he had his instrument with him and enjoyed playing it. He repeatedly played the song, "Maybe," singing the words to his accompaniment without a trace of his usual stammer. When he sang, his whole face lit up in a kind of ecstasy, tears ran out of his eyes, and the apprehension disappeared, only to return as soon as he put away his instrument. There was considerable stereotypy, and various bizarre mannerisms reappeared in a regular routine.

After treatment, this patient made a good recovery. He was able to reconstruct his battle experience, and to orient himself in relation to his past life. Before his breakdown he had been worried concerning his wife's pregnancy, and it appeared that the song, "Maybe," was her favorite melody. The bizarre behavior disappeared, and, although much anxiety and depression in relation to his battle experience remained, there was no longer any question of a diagnosis of schizophrenia. It was obvious that the patient was in a severe anxiety state with much regression and disintegration of the ego. As is typical in the severe anxiety states, recovery of the ego's functions proceeded rapidly after treatment. For a few weeks the gait continued to be somewhat shuffling and stooped, without the normal swinging of the arms. The facial expression was masked, the skin of the face oily, and the eyelids blinked rarely. A moderate tremor of the extremities persisted, which was associated with rigidity of the cogwheel type. Without a knowledge of the past history of this patient, one would have been tempted to diagnose an organic lesion of the extrapyramidal system. After four weeks of psychotherapy this patient recovered from his depression, and the facial expression became spontaneous and lively and the gait normal. Anxiety disappeared except during air raids. The patient was able to assume duties in the ward and about the hospital, and was eventually discharged. [21, 5 ff.]

We have already noted (pp. 285 f.) how individual men in combat tend to identify themselves with *their* combat unit or division. Grinker and Spiegel particularly emphasize the important role played by ego-involving group loyalties in forestalling dissociation and regression. If the support of this identification with a group is undermined either by the loss in battle of many group members or by the inability of a group to act as a team under overwhelming odds, then the individual feels deserted and more alone, and regression is much more likely.

Thus, the problem of anxiety in this context centers about the position of the ego in regard to mastery, independence and freedom of activity. In the anxiety problems of early childhood which form the core of the usual neurotic process, the ego is peculiarly helpless because of its inexperience and its complete dependence on the family figures which constitute the threat. In combat, the ego is often helpless because of its position in the group and the nature of the danger situation. The combat personality surrenders a great deal of its freedom of activity to the group, which is then relied upon for protection. The efficient functioning of the team is the guarantee of safety, and this applies equally to the efficient functioning of equipment, such as the aircraft, which must be maintained by teams. *As long as the group demonstrates its ability to master the dangers fairly effectively, the individual feels sufficiently protected and competent in the environment. But when combat losses are high and close friends have been lost, or when the individual has experienced repeated narrow escapes or a traumatic event, the group is no longer a good security, and the ego learns how helpless it is in the situation.* There is no one to rely upon. At the same time, it cannot overcome the dangers by its own efforts because of the actual dependence on the group.

The ego is thus in a regressed and relatively impotent position, reminiscent of childhood. Its difficulties accumulate as it withdraws more affection from the group and develops greater concern for its own fate, only to find that this fate is less and less under control. Confidence in the activity of the ego is further shaken by the loss of friends with whom there is much identification, when the thought arises: "He and I were exactly alike; if it could happen to him, it can happen to me." Confidence is diminished in addition by physical fatigue and illness and loss of sleep. A vicious circle is established, leading to the progressive destruction of confidence in the ego's ability to master the dangers. Out of the ensuing helplessness is born the intense anxiety. Thus severe anxiety is always secondary to regression and dependence of the ego, and its meaning is that in its regressed position the ego has been deserted by all the forces which could help and protect it; nothing can be done, and the only possible method of avoiding complete dissolution is by flight. [22, *129 f.,* italics ours]

These reports of the effect of an individual's participation in a group under conditions imposed by war is consistent with and further confirms our discussion of ego-involvements in group situations in chapter 10.

Ego-breakdowns in Abnormal and Pathological Cases

The vast literature of abnormal psychology is filled with examples of individuals who, for one reason or another, change from their usual socially acceptable and predictable selves to individuals whose behavior, perception, judgment, thought, or imagination has become disorganized, so incompatible with reality, so dissociated or so idiosyncratic that they are no longer classifiable as "normal." Case studies reported by Janet, Prince, Sidis and others have by now become classics in the field. No matter what classification the psychologist or the psychiatrist may use to describe a particular patient (and these classifications do not concern us here), the general underlying symptom is that these "abnormal" individuals exhibit in one way or another a distorted ego reference, can no longer adjust themselves to the objective conditions around them. In a short paper on *The Psychopathology of the Ego System,* Kisker and Knox [27] show how certain mental disorders can be considered as ego disturbances. Basing their discussions on Koffka's conception of the ego, they note that "the ego has of necessity been postulated in psychology for the same reason that astronomers were forced to postulate a previously unknown planet" [*66 f.*] and they believe that "a large number of functional mental disorders are matters of the ego and its relationships." [67] Such mental disorders mentioned are regression, "a detached ego, split ego, excessive development of the 'myness' system, and ego-isolation." [68]

This breakdown of ego reference is vividly seen in what has come to be called "depersonalization." In William A. White's *Outlines of Psychiatry* [44], widely used as a basic text in the field of abnormal psychology, the author sets the stage for his discussion of "Disorders of Personality" as follows:

The individual, besides receiving certain information from the environment and forming certain ideas, has beyond this a consciousness of self, a feeling that all his perceptions and ideas are experiences of a single self, a self that maintains its own individual identity throughout, and which the individual calls "I." This problem of self-consciousness, although the riddle of psychology, presents certain features useful in elucidating the problem in hand. [44, 69]

And in this discussion, after indicating what is meant by "transformation of the personality," White describes "depersonalization":

A lesser degree of the same sort of process results in a disorganization, a breaking up of the personality. This is seen in many conditions and is associated with a *feeling of unreality,* and occurs as a part of the *delirium of negation.* The patients proclaim that they are changed, they are not themselves. One of my patients would look in the glass and stare in wonder at her reflection, saying her eyes were not hers, they were cat's eyes. Another patient affirmed she had no head, no arms, no body, no mind, nothing. The feeling of personal identity in these cases has become disrupted, the personality disorganized. [44, 70]

Another description of this significant concept (depersonalization) may be cited from Schilder: [39]

It is known that cases of this type [depersonalization] do not experience other people as personalities, but as inanimate automatons and dolls. Furthermore, the outward world looks dreamlike and unreal. Their own selves seem to have disappeared. The patients feel that they themselves act mechanically. They do not acknowledge their perceptions, feelings, and emotions. "There is no real me. I seem to myself like a puppet." [39, 188 f.]

Persons who are described by the very general label of "schizophrenic" are characterized by the radical breakdown of the more usual frames of reference they had developed to give meaning to their environment. Somehow these frames have become inadequate and inconsistent. When these standards for judgment and action collapse, the ego collapses, because these frames with all the emotional overtones of value judgments they contained were so integral a part of the self. A case study by Faris [13] gives a good example of how and probably why a young man was committed to a state hospital with the diagnosis of schizophrenia. Faris points out that

> In the course of Albert's life there arose a number of conflicts and problems which were a great source of torment. These tore at his mind in a variety of ways. *The confused mores in his culture, the contrasting groups to which he held partial loyalty, and the inconsistencies of promise and achievement in his career—such elements form the contribution of social disorganization to the personal disorganization he was suffering.* His behavior during the period of his psychosis represents an adaptation to these problems. It was a poor adaptation, since it did not fit him to survive in the competition of the contemporary civilization; but it was organized and for a time seemed to promise better things. [13, *135 f.,* italics ours]

Among other conflicts Albert suffered were these:

> He had acquired in his youth a violent anti-Semitic prejudice, only to discover in his adulthood that his family was of Jewish descent. . . . He had acquired a strong moral objection to commercial art, which he considered "prostitution" of his talent; but he could earn his living only by means of that kind of art. . . . During the first part of his career his economic success was satisfactory and rapid, and within five or six years after his start he was earning as much as $400 a month and had plans for projects which he hoped would carry him further. His failures after the collapse of the Florida boom and in the later major depression gave him considerable torment. [13, *136*]

As Faris notes, the patient's

> . . . conception of his status was derived not from a harmonious social group of which he was a primary member but rather from distant and mixed sources and partly derived from his reading and daydreaming. . . . *He could not find a group in which he could achieve an integrated and harmonious personality.* . . . *Albert was, in a sense, lost, since he was culturally marginal in several respects.* . . . The conflicts produced in Albert internal strains and an intolerable sense of being internally divided. . . . The solution he found, while undesirable from the point of view of survival in society, did have a logical relation to the nature of Albert's particular problems. It did not demand a change that he could not make. It resolved the conflicts so that he could have unity in his character without pulling himself

out of trouble by his bootstraps. An internal war thus came to a sudden end, and the conflicting elements temporarily came to rest. [13, *136 f., italics ours*]

The particular solution this patient adopted to relieve his marginal status was to identify himself with a certain mystical semireligious philosophy which the reading of a certain book stimulated his imagination to create. Thereafter he acted as quite a different person, claiming superhuman strength, the ability to stop any speeding car or bullet, the ability to "be" any person he desired, and so on.

Angyal describes another "schizophrenic" who had lost all the ego reference of his experiences, especially those based on muscle sensation: [3]

In my patient, as in many schizophrenic patients, the basic differentiation between the ego and the external world is grossly impaired. Parts of the patient's body and of his mental and physical activities are excluded from self-awareness, *are not experienced as belonging to his ego.* The patient complains that the jaw he has is not his jaw, "it is only set in." He complains that his arm feels "lifeless," does not belong to him; that he has "no real skull but only a wooden frame"; that his teeth are "false," etc. Some of the thoughts he has are not his thoughts; "somebody gives them [to him] silently; they put them into [his] head." Sometimes some words come to him; he does not think them, "the words just show up in [his] system." It seems to him also as if some one else thinks in him, "as if I had two or three people with me." He has also the experience of having an alter ego (*Doppelgänger*). Sometimes even his emotions are experienced as disconnected from his ego: "In my stomach there is something, it feels like anger." "In the teeth it feels like anger, as if they would want to bite, to grab everything." Another time he said: "They put some glorious feeling inside of you, as if you had done something great." [*1035 f., italics ours*]

In analyzing this particular case, Angyal writes in part as follows:

The outstanding feature in the psychopathologic picture of the patient is profound disturbances of self-awareness. *The psychologic experiences of the patient have partly lost their usual relation to the ego:* He feels that parts of his body, his thoughts and his feelings do not belong to his ego but are things foreign to him.

Analogous disturbances are to be observed in regard to the psycho-motor activity. The patient's actions have partly lost their usual relation to the ego. They are excluded from the self and appear to the patient not as his own actions but as something "done" to him. The muscular activities or tendencies to such activities generate changes in the muscle tonus, which, because they have lost their ego-reference, are psychologically accounted for as foreign forces acting on the body. . . . Analysis of these symptoms clearly indicates their origin in muscular activities which have become disconnected from the ego. . . . The loss of ego-reference of muscular activity is a manifestation of a more general disturbance of self-awareness. The latter is not further analyzed in this paper but is taken as a descriptive fact. *From the psychologic point of view, the loss of ego-reference seems to represent a special kind of defense mechanism.* [3, 1052 f., italics ours]

Some individuals are classified as "abnormal" when they become so elated and euphoric that their behavior transgresses the boundaries of social tolerance. In such instances the usual ego-involved standards of conduct and behavior dissolve. An illustration can be taken from McDougall: [32]

A professional man in middle life, of good heredity, had shown no previous trace of instability. His history would justify classing him with the cyclo-thymic type. He had, when young, suffered some periods of very mild depression and apathy, such as might be called merely prolonged moods of discouragement. And at other times he had displayed an almost excessive activity and energy, working extremely hard in preparation for examinations and achieving athletic feats that required tremendous endurance and energy. He became actively engaged in a Presidential campaign. He had long been keenly interested in politics and in certain planks of his party's platform; but he had never before taken an active part in electioneering, whether State or Federal, and had never spoken in public. He approached his new task with considerable diffidence; but he very soon found that he was an effective campaign orator. He was immensely pleased, stimulated, and elated by his success. He worked with extreme enthusiasm and energy. He sought and seized every opportunity for addressing public gatherings. At first his colleagues in the particular local campaign were full of admiration; but after some days they were obliged to communicate with his relatives and ask them to remove him from the scene. For his conduct had begun to pass the bounds of the normal and the decorous, and he was beginning to make himself a nuisance to them. He angrily resented all their suggestions to the effect that he needed a rest and had done his share; he was utterly impervious to their arguments and persuasion. Instead of taking a long night's rest after his hard day's work, he would get up very early in the morning and, appearing at the window of his hotel bedroom, would gather a crowd in the street by his animated and somewhat strange behaviour, and deliver to them a fiery address, freely exchanging jokes and pleasantries with his auditors. As he afterwards put it, he felt like a god; for he could sway his audience as he wished, evoking enthusiastic agreement and applause. Such admiring response from public gatherings is, as we know, strong drink for any man. Even men long and gradually accustomed to such successes suffer a kind of intoxication on such occasions; and, as with drugs, they acquire a morbid need and craving for ever new and larger doses; they cannot live without the "lime-light." And in this hitherto quiet and retiring professional man the intoxication went to the point of throwing him off his balance. He was brought home by the exercise of much tact and patience. He refused to submit to medical examination, declaring that he had never before been so fit and strong. [32, *358 f.*]

Cases of split and multiple personalities are, perhaps, the most dramatic and well known in the abnormal literature. The same individual can be two or more quite different "persons," each may have complete amnesia for the experiences of the other and not even recognize the other self. Franz's *Persons One and Three* [14] can be taken as fairly typical. The individual involved had apparently suffered various harrowing experiences during World War I and was brought to Dr. Franz's office by the police who had picked him up in a completely confused state of mind. "He did not recognize his surroundings, he asked to have his name supplied to him, and he did not know the approximate date." [1] The fascinating story of Franz's successful effort to bring together "persons One and Three" need not concern us here. (Person Two was represented by a period of time separating persons One and Three and remained a complete blank in the patient's consciousness.) What does concern us is that the individual as person One was quite a different individual from what he was as person Three.

> When asked about his nationality and birthplace he replied that he did not know where he was born, nor how old he really was, although he could approximate his age within a few years. He had no idea what his father's occupation was, nor did he know what he himself had been doing prior to April, 1915, at which time he became conscious of himself. [14, 26]

Even self-recognition was lacking:

> Later I led him into another room in which there was a mirror, and I suggested that he look at himself in the glass. He appeared to be greatly upset at his appearance, and after having taken one look, he said: "My God, is that me?" [14, 62]

Habit systems were altered, as the following indicates:

> Twice also Jack was found to have purchased cigars, and to have smoked them. In his so-called "normal" state he did not smoke cigars. He had not smoked them since 1914. When, therefore, Jack reverted to his first personality the old habit came to the fore. [14, 131]

Franz's description of the first meeting of persons One and Three is revealing. While the doctor was going over a map with the patient in an attempt to help him reconstruct the course of his wanderings as a soldier in World War I:

> Suddenly he stopped, and with his finger directed to a point and a name, said, "Voi! I was there. I had a monkey." His emotion was obvious. He was greatly excited. Memory was trickling through. The walled-off memories could not be kept impounded. The face of the dam gave way, and there was an onrush carrying all before it. It was irresistible. The memories were eddying, and tossing one over another. His remarks came too rapidly to be recorded. He traveled from Africa to France, to the United States, to England, and to Ireland, back and forth. Ideas were tumbling about in their mad rush to come to the surface. In a few minutes he had lived fifteen years. *He had met, and he had recognized, himself.* [14, 79, italics ours]

Although Franz was unable to learn much of the early history of his strange patient, he writes at the end of his account that

... it is worthy of note that every change which had been observed, or of which we have had reasonable information, was known to be preceded by a period in which he was under what is commonly called "emotional strain." He was worried financially, or he was irritated, or he was fearful, or he may have been too happy. [14, *188*]

An example of several selves living together simultaneously in the same person is seen from the following account which a schizophrenic wrote of himself: [6]

> I am a peculiar person. In fact I do not know rather [whether] you would call me a person or not. I did possess four (4) bodies that were me. Unlike the twin Severins I do lack the middle brain they possess. I do not know the origin of my specie or of any other specie. I do know people call our specie Gouls. I have lined [linked?] eyes; that is, when the four of me took hands we could see in four directions at once. I have heard the Twin Severins lack duplicate eyes and bodies. I did possess thought transmission. As far as my early life is concerned I do not recall very much; but about three years I can remember all of my other segiments. When I was about 6 years old I lost three of my segiments and received a braining at the same instant. I do not imagine any of you people can understand the mixure of being in different bodies and places at the same time. I have forgotten all about not being like other people.

After a very careful review of the "psychological deficits" of psychotics, Hunt and Cofer [25] conclude that "we should like to conceive this deficit in capacity in terms of a rigidity of set and a reduction in the number of tasks or lines of activity that can be sustained simultaneously or synthesized into a single complex operation." [*1014*]

> *The deficit in the "functional" psychoses, and particularly in schizophrenia, we conceive as an extinction of standards for performance and of thought skills that have been socially rewarded.* [25, *1022*, italics ours]

This conclusion is entirely in line with our formulation: "set," "standards for performance," and "thought skills," are familiar to

---

[6] This is taken from one of a number of essays Professor Wendell Johnson of the University of Iowa has collected from institutionalized people and which he has kindly let us examine.

us as anchorages, standards of judgment, frames of reference, or attitudes which have become ego-involved and whose "extinction" is therefore bound to bring about the extinction of the normally functioning ego.

Organic disturbances. So far in our discussion of abnormal cases, we have considered instances commonly labeled as functional rather than as organic. With the rapid development of neurology toward the end of the 19th century, psychologists began to look for the psychological effects of organic disturbances in the brain. In this effort, Ribot was one of the pioneers. Stimulated by Charcot's work in psychopathology, Ribot [36, 37] brought to his work the physiological knowledge of his day. Although the neurology of Ribot's time seems to us now somewhat crude, and although Ribot tended to regard all psychoses as organic, he was among the first to point out that disorders of brain functions could cause a "dissolution of the personality" and a disintegration of the unity of the ego (Le Moi). The ego was central in Ribot's formulations. He regarded it as a "sum of conscious states" subjectively known from coenaesthesis and from memory.

"An organic lesion," he wrote in 1881, "may transform the coenaesthesis, substituting for the normal sensation of existence a condition of melancholy, mental distress, and anxiety, of which the patient is unable to discern the cause; or, on the other hand, producing undue joyousness, exuberant emotions, and extreme content." [36, *109*] Anything that affects the vital processes upon which "the sum of actual states of consciousness" depends will necessarily affect the ego.

> Feelings form the self; amnesia of the feelings is the destruction of the self. It is logical, then, that a period should arrive when disorganization becomes so great as to disintegrate personality. [36, *121*]

Ribot pointed out that gross injuries to the brain could and did cause disturbances and deteriorations of the higher more abstract mental processes (ideas and memories), and in this process of deterioration he observed that it was the more recently acquired most highly developed intellectual abilities that tended to disintegrate first with the adjustments and memories of childhood "the last to disappear."

With the increased precision of our knowledge of physiology and with the development of more refined psychological tests, the effects of more or less localizable lesions have become amenable to more rigorous investigation. There is no need to review this work here in detail.[7] The outstanding work of Gelb and Goldstein is especially relevant to our problem of ego-breakdowns. [17]

From their tests of color discrimination among patients who had suffered lesions in the frontal region as the result of war injuries, Gelb and Goldstein concluded that there was a very definite impairment of the ability to generalize or to make abstractions. The patients tended to be limited to what the authors described as a "concrete attitude." This effect of organic brain injuries on abstract thinking has been confirmed by Weigl [43], Rylander [38], Halstead [23] and others. Goldstein and Scheerer have more recently reported the results of further tests devised to study this loss of the "abstract attitude." [20] Without taking sides one way or another in the controversy concerning Goldstein's terminology, it is significant for us to notice that in the description of the "abstract attitude," Goldstein and Scheerer place as the first characteristic in their list the loss of ego reference. All of the other characteristics they describe refer in one way or another to the deterioration of normal frames. They state:

> The abstract attitude is the basis for the following *conscious* and *volitional* modes of behavior:
>
> 1. To detach our ego from the outerworld or from inner experiences.
>
> 2. To assume a mental set.
>
> 3. To account for acts to oneself; to verbalize the account.
>
> 4. To shift reflectively from one aspect of the situation to another.
>
> 5. To hold in mind simultaneously various aspects.
>
> 6. To grasp the essential of a given whole; to break up a given whole into parts, to isolate and to synthesize them.
>
> 7. To abstract common properties reflectively; to form hierarchic concepts.
>
> 8. To plan ahead ideationally; to assume an attitude towards the "mere possible" and to think or perform symbolically. [20, 4]

[7] Thorough reviews of the literature on the psychological effects of brain lesions will be found in [9] and [28].

The illustrations used by Goldstein and Scheerer to exemplify these various characteristics of the abstract attitude which is lost by those with a cerebral pathology are so illuminating that we shall quote here in full the examples given of the deterioration of the first three modes of behavior previously mentioned.

1. *To detach our ego from the outerworld or from inner experiences.*

Patient F. is asked to take a comb from a table and bring it to the examiner. She cannot do this without combing her hair ("forced responsiveness"). A patient of Head says, "With me it's all in bits, I have to jump like a man who jumps from one thing to the next; I can see them, but I can't express them." Patient Sch. is asked to repeat the sentence: "The snow is black." He states he could not say it, that it was not so. The examiner explained to him that such senseless phrases can be repeated even though they are not true, and then urged the patient to repeat the sentence. Now the patient repeated the requested sentence, but mumbled immediately afterwards: "No, the snow is white." The same patient could not be induced to repeat the sentence "the sun is shining" on a rainy day. Patient Schor. with a paralysis of the right arm was unable to repeat the sentence "I can write well with my right hand." He replaced the word "right" by the word "left." Another patient was well able to use eating utensils while eating, whereas given these objects outside of the eating situation, he produced only a jumble of senseless movements with them. Another patient was unable to drink water out of a glass on command, unless he was really thirsty.

2. *To assume a mental set willfully and consciously.*

A patient is unable to set the hands of a clock to the demanded hour, but can recognize what time it is immediately if presented with the clock. Another patient, whom the examiner started off on a continuous task, *e.g.,* counting or writing letters, is unable to proceed spontaneously if once interrupted; he is unable to initiate an action on his own, to assume a mental set willfully. A patient of Woerkom could give the *series* of the week days and months of the year correctly, but if the examiner named a *particular* day or month, the patient could not give the name of the one preceding or following.

3. *To account for acts to oneself or to others.*

A patient is well able to throw balls into three boxes which are located at different distances from him. He never misses. Asked which box is further and which is nearer, he is unable to give any account or to make a statement concerning his procedure in aiming. Another patient points correctly to the source of a noise, but cannot state the direction from which the noise originated. To do this requires an abstract grasp of spatial relation and the concomitant capacity to account for this understanding by verbalization. [20, *4 f.*]

Their characterization of the "concrete" attitude indicates the central position of this loss of ego reference.

We surrender to experiences of an unreflected character: *we* are confined to the immediate apprehension of the given thing or situation in its particular uniqueness. . . . *We* surrender to the immediate claims and particular uniqueness of thought and feelings in the same way as to the outer world claims. [*2 f.*, italics ours]

Goldstein and Scheerer are careful to point out that the abstract attitude must be regarded as a relatively recent evolutionary development, as a "new emergent quality." [22]   And that Goldstein is not using the concept of the ego in any loose psychoanalytic sense as a mysterious autonomous entity is indicated in another of his publications [18] in which he writes, in a discussion of repression:

The factor, which actuates the so-called repressing, is formed neither through prohibitions from without, nor by a censor, nor by an ego, nor by a super-ego. Rather, through maturation, new patterns of the organism are formed, conforming to the human species in general and to the cultural pattern of that particular milieu in which the child grows up. *Of course, one can call this development "ego-formation," and of course, the prohibitions, just like other processes in the environment, are co-determining factors in this formation.* [18, *320,* italics ours]

A revealing illustration of the effect of a temporary concussion on the ego is given by Koffka when he cites the report of a mountain climber who had lost consciousness after falling into a chasm. [29]   The climber reported his "awakening" as follows (Koffka's literal translation):

". . . fog . . . darkness . . . fog . . . whirring . . . grey veil with a small lighter spot . . . fog . . . faint dawn . . . a soft humming . . . dull discomfort . . . fog . . . something has happened to somebody . . . gloomy fog, and always that lighter point . . . a shivering shudder: something clammy . . . fog . . . how was it? . . . an effort at thinking . . . ah, still fog; but besides that light point there outside, there emerges a second point inside: right, that is *I!* . . . fog, dull ringing sound, frost . . . a dream? . . . Yes, indeed, a wild, wild, wild dream!—It has dreamed—no, rather *I* have dreamed. . . ." [29, *323 f.*]

As Koffka remarks:

Phenomenally quite a long period of time passed without an Ego. . . . The Ego did not even emerge with the first articulation of the field, the light point, not even with the first feeling of discomfort, and apparently not even with the first conscious thought, though it was this which led very soon to the momentary establishment of the Self, which was, however, as yet quite unstable. [29, *324*]

In his summary of the effects of brain lesions on personality, Stanley Cobb [9] indicates that severe concussions or contusions of the brain, while they have comparatively little effect on the "intellectual" functions such as memory, are very likely to extinguish those personal and social standards of judgment which determine an individual's moral codes.

Persons who have had several concussions or contusions of the brain often develop a clinical picture that is quite characteristic: after each injury, but usually more conspicuously after the third or fourth, the patient has persistent headache, increased by using the eyes or exposure to the sun; transient diplopia is common. He avoids lifting or leaning over because of increased headache and dizzy feelings. After a few months this state becomes one of general invalidism with many aches, easy fatigability, lack of initiative, and varying degrees of apathy. Close psychiatric supervision may keep him socially acceptable, but he usually drifts off, becomes a "rolling stone" and "irresponsible." Alcohol affects him strongly and may precipitate epileptic attacks of various kinds. Psychological examination shows little intellectual deficit in such fields as memory, retention, and alertness, but as the process goes on, such symptoms of deterioration may appear. *During the first year of his disorder the patient seems to be simply unreliable; later he becomes incorrigible, a pathological liar, always taking the easy way out and avoiding sustained effort. Some*

of these patients are difficult to distinguish from the "ne'er do well"
and chronic delinquent diagnosed "psychopathic personality" and
"moral imbecile." [9, 557, italics ours]

In this same discussion, Cobb also reports the changed personality brought about by encephalitis (an "inflammatory reaction within the brain due to invasion by micro-organisms"). [559]

The patient may come first to the physician complaining of fatigue and nervousness. . . . The family will complain that the patient is becoming coarse and ill-mannered, irritable and forgetful. The jovial megalomania so often described may be present, but it is not the rule; a mood of depression is not uncommon instead of the textbook euphoria. But when the elated, expansive mood is present, it is a most remarkable phenomenon: one sees a man in the prime of life, who has previously been modest and reliable, rather suddenly break forth with ideas of omnipotence and actions dishonest and spectacular. The usual picture, however, is less striking, with emphasis on the gradual loss of culture and memory.

I remember well, when acting as clinical clerk at Queen Square for Kinnier Wilson, I saw him present a new case to a group of students in the out-patient clinic. I was seated at the table taking notes, Wilson was standing, having just dismissed a patient, and there was an empty chair beside my table. Wilson rang for the next patient, the door opened and a man entered, followed by his wife. He walked across the fifteen feet of classroom, smiled at the students and at me, and sat down. Wilson turned to me instantly and said, "Write down G.P.I. as the diagnosis." Probably my jaw dropped, for he went on, "Well, Cobb, what else could it be? Here is a middle-aged man coming to a nerve clinic. He enters the room smiling, pushes ahead of his wife, does not take off his hat, takes the only chair without asking and likes an audience!" Subsequent neurological and serological studies proved the correctness of the diagnosis. [9, 559 f.]

Cobb remarks that the striking thing about those suffering from general paresis is their loss of "good manners and culture" at the outset of the disease. [560]

We saw in earlier chapters how the ego develops in childhood and adolescence. We can see in cases of senility how the ego breaks down and deteriorates in old age. Muncie describes senility in his chapter dealing with "the acquired organic deficit reactions" [34, ch. 10], and Kraines indicates that

The essential pathology of senile dementia is an abiotrophy of the ganglion cells of the cerebral cortex. [30, *382*]

The senile reaction

... is a gross caricature of the normal aging process with its *circumscription of interests, the backward glance at things long past,* and the garrulous reminiscences. [34, *409*, italics ours]

Muncie describes how the "frontier of memory" is "pushed steadily backward with the progress of the disease." [*409*]

Closely related to this disturbance of intellectual functions are changes in personality which "are extremely common" according to Kraines. Among these changes are increasing irritability, outbursts of anger and resentment, increasing egotism, acute excitement or depression. Commenting on a senile patient whose case he describes, Muncie summarizes as follows:

A simple decline in the assets, especially those of memory and judgment, living in the remote past, and disoriented for the present. The speech showed loss in the reverse order of its acquisition and finally was reduced to unintelligible jargon. Emotional lability, with fairly good social preservation; evasion and confabulation were marked features. [34, *413*]

This "second childhood" characteristic of so many senile patients clearly shows the regression to a relatively simple narrow level of ego functioning, the disintegration of the ego-attitudes of the more normal adult.

How the ego is affected by surgical insult to the frontal lobes. Brickner's well-known study of the effect of the removal of part of both the frontal lobes of a New York stockbroker (referred to as *A* in the following quotations) shows beyond the shadow of a doubt that the loss of these higher areas of the brain also brings about a loss of ego-involved standards for behavior and thought. A mere listing of some of the title headings of chapters that contain detailed recorded conversations with the patient indicates the generalizations derived from hours of close observation: [8]

Impairment of Restraint in Controlling or Concealing Emotion.
Impairment of Restraint as Indicated by Boasting or Self-Aggrandizement.

Impairment of Restraint as Indicated by Reminiscing Which Is Utilized for Self-Aggrandizement.

Impairment of Restraint as Indicated by *A*'s Free Expression of Mild Hostility.

Impairment of Restraint as Indicated by the Free Expression of Angry, Aggressive, Negativistic, Puerile Impulses Employed for Superarrogation, Sometimes Combined with Hostility. [8, *xiii f.*]

Brickner concludes from his detailed analysis that

The most prominent symptomatic mark of *A*'s conduct is the relatively free exhibition of emotional and instinctive phenomena. The three constantly recurring themes of *A*'s action are self-aggrandizement, hatred and sexuality.

A's exaggerated need for ego aggrandizement is easy to perceive. [*275*]

There is nothing about *A*'s impairment of restraint which is not to be found in any young child who has not yet learned enough about the requisite appreciations to make choices and to plan his behavior. [8, *280*]

And he notes that "such highly derived attainments as 'moral sense,' 'social sense,' 'character' and 'personality'" are dependent on "judgment, critique, abstractive ability, generalizing capacity, appreciation of situations, sense of humor and others." And it is apparently these psychological capacities that were "removed" along with the sections of *A*'s frontal lobes. The author notes that many earlier writers on the subject have used the term "inhibition" to describe the psychological consequences of frontal lobe symptoms. Among these earlier writers were Elder and Miles (1902) who stated that frontal lobe symptoms

. . . are exceedingly difficult to analyze and are even more difficult to describe. The absence of such symptoms renders a man what he is . . . [their] presence . . . alters the *ego* of a man, takes away his special mental characteristics and reduces him to a lower level. [8, *276*]

Freeman and Watts have used frontal lobotomy as an admittedly last resort cure for what they describe as "overwhelming consciousness of the self." [15] Summarizing the results of 66 such operations, they write:

Prefrontal lobotomy bleaches the affective component connected with the consciousness of the self. Patients who are afflicted with a distressing consciousness of the self (either as a unit of society or as a collection of organs) and whose preoccupation is fixed and unyielding, will secure from prefrontal lobotomy definite relief even though certain of their ideas and actions may persist for a long time. Reduction of the affective component allows the personality to appear in purer form, divested of certain restraining features, but essentially unchanged in regard to energy and intelligence, the principal change being an alteration in the direction of interests from within, outward. Prefrontal lobotomy is radical treatment, not only figuratively but literally in that it reaches down to the roots of the personality. If the neurosis or psychosis has its roots in an overwhelming consciousness of the self, and if this consciousness is intractable and disabling, then prefrontal lobotomy may bring peace to the warring mind and a new lease on life. [15, *118 f.*]

Here are some of their illustrations of the alteration in personality after prefrontal lobotomy: [8]

A timid, restrained hypochondriacal woman now joins in the party with her daughter, is able to dance until after midnight with her daughter's friends, cook supper for them, and send them home in the midst of jests and wise cracks. She is no longer conscious of the fatigue nor is she very much aware that there is such a thing as dignity in the presence of young people. She boasts that the boys come to the house on account of her. A former school teacher, having suffered from involutional depression for six years, sits unconcernedly among a group of physicians while we are describing to them her suicidal attempts, chronic alcoholism, her erratic behavior, and hare-brained plans for an artists' colony, her alcoholic father, and her psychotic mother and sister, and then smilingly states to the doctors: "I have to drink alone because I get perfectly nasty in public."
[15, *116*]

Bennett, Keegan, and Wilbur have reported successful use of the operation in four cases of "aggressive paranoid schizophrenia." [6] And Hebb and Penfield have written of a patient who developed epileptic seizures after being struck on the forehead, who

[8] Other detailed accounts of the effect of the operation on social behavior will be found in [16, ch. 13].

was "irresponsible, childishly stubborn, restless and forgetful" [24, 422], and who showed considerable restoration of his normal personality and intellectual capacity after a partial lobectomy which removed approximately one third of each frontal lobe. The different effects of surgical insult reported by Brickner as contrasted to those reported by Freeman and Watts, Hebb and Penfield, and other variations found in the literature are generally agreed to be due to the particular nature of the operation performed. In spite of the physiological mysteries that still baffle the expert concerned with the mechanisms of the brain, there is no disagreement on the fact that even partial removal of the frontal lobes can and does significantly alter an individual's personality, significantly change the behavior and thought that makes him his normal "self."

In this chapter we have seen that the genetically formed ego, which is re-formed during adolescence and which is for the adult so largely composed of a constellation of personal and social values, can and does disintegrate, dissolve or break down, under certain conditions. Definite signs of ego-deterioration or breakdown are observable. These vary according to the particular situation to which a person is exposed and, within limits, are subject to individual differences of temperament, ability, and the like. The few examples of ego-breakdown reviewed here give further evidence that the ego is not an innate entity, that it is not fixed and static, and that its change and dissolution, like its formation and re-formation, result from the relationship between the individual and his social environment. And the cases of ego-breakdown resulting from definite organic disturbances or physiological imbalance are further evidence of the fact that ego-striving is rooted in the human organism, is made possible because of its potentiality for functioning on a conceptual level, and is therefore neither a primary instinct in the sense of hunger or sex nor the manifestation of some mystic force.

REFERENCES

1. ALLPORT, G. W., J. S. BRUNER, and E. M. JANDORF, Personality under social catastrophe: ninety life-histories of the Nazi revolution, *Character and Personality*, 1941, **10**, 1–22.

2. ANGELL, R. C., *The Family Encounters the Depression,* New York: Scribner's, copyright 1936.

3. ANGYAL, A., The experience of the body-self in schizophrenia, *Arch. Neurology and Psychiatry,* 1936, **35,** 1029–53.

4. BALES, R. F., Social therapy for a social disorder—compulsive drinking, *J. Social Issues,* 1945, **1,** 14–22.

5. BEISWANGER, G., Martha Graham: a perspective, in *Martha Graham,* by Barbara Morgan, Duell, Sloan and Pearce, copyright 1941.

6. BENNETT, A. E., J. J. KEEGAN, and C. B. WILBUR, Prefrontal lobotomy in chronic schizophrenia, *J. Am. Med. Assoc.,* 1943, **123,** 809–13.

7. BETTELHEIM, B., Individual and mass behavior in extreme situations, *J. Abnorm. and Soc. Psychol.,* 1943, **38,** 417–52.

8. BRICKNER, R. M., *The Intellectual Functions of the Frontal Lobes,* New York: Macmillan, 1936, quotations by permission of the author.

9. COBB, S., Personality as affected by lesions of the brain, in *Personality and the Behavior Disorders* (J. McV. Hunt, ed.), vol. **1,** New York: Ronald, copyright 1944, ch. 18.

10. COUSINS, S., *To Beg I Am Ashamed,* New York: Vanguard, copyright 1938.

11. DUBLIN, L. I., and B. BUNZEL, *To Be or Not To Be,* New York: Smith & Haas, 1933.

12. EISENBERG, P., and P. F. LAZARSFELD, The psychological effects of unemployment, *Psychol. Bull.,* 1938, **35,** 358–90.

13. FARIS, R. E. L., Reflections of social disorganization in the behavior of a schizophrenic patient, *Am. J. Sociol.,* 1944, **50,** 134–41.

14. FRANZ, S. I., *Persons One and Three,* New York: McGraw-Hill, copyright 1933.

15. FREEMAN, W., and J. W. WATTS, The frontal lobes and consciousness of the self, *Psychosomatic Med.,* 1941, **3,** 111–19.

16. —— —— *Psychosurgery,* Baltimore: Thomas, 1942.

17. GELB, A., and K. GOLDSTEIN, Psychologische Analysen hirnpathologischer Fälle: X. Über Farbennamenamnesie, *Psychol. Forsch.,* 1925, **6,** 127–86. (*Zbl. ges. Neurol. Psychiat.,* 1925, **60,** 577.)

18. GOLDSTEIN, K., *The Organism,* New York: Am. Book Co., copyright 1939.

19. GOLDSTEIN, K., and A. GELB, Psychologische Analysen hirnpathologischer Fälle: I. Zur psychologie des optischen Wahrnehmungs- und Erkennungsvorganges, *Z. ges. Neurol. Psychiat.,* 1918, **41,** 1–142. (*Zbl. ges. Neurol. Psychiat.,* 1919, **18,** 105–08.)

20. GOLDSTEIN, K., and M. SCHEERER, Abstract and concrete behavior: an experimental study with special tests, *Psychol. Monogr.,* 1941, **53,** no. 2.

21. GRINKER, R. R., and J. P. SPIEGEL, *War Neuroses,* Philadelphia: Blakiston, copyright 1945.

22. —— —— *Men Under Stress,* Philadelphia: Blakiston, copyright 1945.

23. HALSTEAD, W. C., Experimental analysis of the effects of pre-frontal lobectomy in man, *Psychol. Bull.,* 1938, **35,** 687.

24. HEBB, D. O., and W. PENFIELD, Human behavior after extensive bilateral removal from the frontal lobes, *Arch. Neurol. Psychiat.,* 1940, **44,** 421–38.

25. HUNT, J. McV., and C. N. COFER, Psychological deficit, in *Personality and the Behavior Disorders* (J. McV. Hunt, ed.), vol. **2,** New York: Ronald, copyright 1944, ch. 32.

26. ISRAELI, N., Distress in the outlook of Lancashire and Scottish unemployed, *J. Appl. Psychol.*, 1935, **19**, 67–9.

27. KISKER, G. W., and G. W. KNOX, The psychopathology of the ego system, *J. Nerv. and Ment. Diseases*, 1943, **96**, 66–71.

28. KLEBANOFF, S. G., Psychological changes in organic brain lesions and ablations, *Psychol. Bull.*, 1945, **42**, 585–623.

29. KOFFKA, K., *Principles of Gestalt Psychology*, New York: Harcourt, Brace, copyright 1935.

30. KRAINES, S. H., *The Therapy of the Neuroses and Psychoses*, Philadelphia: Lea and Febiger, copyright 1943, 2d ed.

31. MAULDIN, B., *Up Front*, New York: Henry Holt, copyright 1945.

32. McDOUGALL, W., *Outline of Abnormal Psychology*, New York: Scribner's, copyright 1926.

33. MOWRER, E. R., *Disorganization: Personal and Social*, New York: Lippincott, 1942.

34. MUNCIE, W., *Psychobiology and Psychiatry*, St. Louis: Mosby, copyright 1939.

35. *New York Times*, September 29, 1945.

36. RIBOT, T., *Diseases of Memory*, New York: Appleton, copyright 1881.

37. —— *Les Maladies de la personnalité*, Paris: Alcan, 1895.

38. RYLANDER, G., *Personality Changes after Operations on the Frontal Lobes: A Clinical Study of Thirty-two Cases*, Copenhagen: Ejnar Munksgard, 1939.

39. SCHILDER, P., *Goals and Desires of Man*, New York: Columbia Univ. Press, copyright 1942.

40. SHOCK, N. W., Physiological factors in behavior, in *Personality and the Behavior Disorders* (J. McV. Hunt, ed.), vol. **1**, New York: Ronald, copyright 1944, ch. 19.

41. STOUFFER, S. A., and P. F. LAZARSFELD, *Research Memorandum on the Family in the Depression*, New York: Social Science Research Council, Bull. 29, 1937.

42. VAN DE VELDE, TH. H., *Ideal Marriage*, New York: Covici Friede, copyright 1931, quotations by permission of Random House.

43. WEIGL, E., Zur psychologie sogenannter Abstraktionsprozesse: Untersuchungen über das "Ordnen," *Z. Psychol.*, 1927, **103**, 2–45; trans. by M. J. Rioch, *J. Abnorm. & Soc. Psychol.*, 1941, **36**, 3–33.

44. WHITE, W. A., *Outlines of Psychiatry*, New York: J. Nervous and Mental Disease Publishing Co., 1913.

45. WILLIAMS, R. D., H. L. MASON, R. M. WILDER, and B. F. SMITH, Induced thiamine (B_1) deficiency and the thiamine requirement of man: Further observations, *Arch. intern. Med.*, 1942, **69**, 721.

46. ZAWADSKI, B., and P. LAZARSFELD, The psychological consequences of unemployment, *J. Soc. Psychol.*, 1935, **6**, 224–51.

Chapter 13

SOME ILLUSTRATIONS FROM LITERATURE

It has often been pointed out that novelists and playwrights seem to be better observers of "human nature" than professional psychologists. And there is little doubt that in the vast storehouse of literature the psychologist would find nearly all of his observations anticipated. But the very nature of the psychologist's job, unlike that of the novelist, dramatist, or poet, imposes on him the obligation of going beyond his observations, accounting for them with consistent scientific concepts. His intellectual burden is lightened only insofar as he can verify his observations, see what general psychological principles can be drawn from them.

In literary works produced in different countries at different periods of time, there is abundant illustration that novelists and playwrights were fully aware of the fact that many a person's interests and desires are ego-involved. Through the characters or situations they build up, they reveal in dramatic proportions properties of the ego that are similar in their characteristics to those we have already found in controlled investigations. And so, on the basis of these controlled studies and the knowledge we have gained of the development and components of the ego, we are in a position to handle systematically the psychology of ego-involvements as these appear in various literary works. We must, of course, always recognize the subtle shadings and nuances given by any author to the feelings, passions, and situations he portrays; we must bear in mind that the literary artist is by and large dealing with particular and unique qualities of personal experience. But through the variety of intricate and distinct episodes and characterizations, we can find underlying psychological principles reflected.

In this chapter we must limit ourselves to a few of thousands of examples that might be given in a more exhaustive analysis.

A thick book could be written on the use which Shakespeare's genius alone made of the psychology of ego-involvements. We shall proceed here, as we have before, from relatively simple to relatively complex situations.

We saw in an earlier chapter how the boundaries of the child's ego gradually expanded to include his body, his room, his clothes, his toys, his house, and so on. Most of us, whether children or adults, feel that there is some little space we can call ours, that is part of our own psychological world, included in our own ego-boundaries. The space may be some corner of a room where we have a favorite chair, it may be some glade in the woods to which we make recurrent visits, it may be a barrel in the woodshed we like to sit on in the evening after dinner. Whatever it is, we come to feel that that space is not only ours but is a part of us. If it is pre-empted by someone else, destroyed, or intruded upon, *we* are annoyed, we feel that *our* privacy, *our* selves have been violated, injured, or insulted.

This ego-involvement a person has with a space which through usage and association has become *his,* is illustrated in John Steinbeck's *Of Mice and Men.* [14] Crooks is a Negro stablehand who had his own little bunk in the harness room; Lennie, a big, kindly, almost moronic individual who has a temporary job on the place, looked after by a faithful friend, but generally isolated from the rest of the men.

> Crooks sat on his bunk. His shirt was out of his jeans in back. In one hand he held a bottle of liniment, and with the other he rubbed his spine. Now and then he poured a few drops of the liniment into his pink-palmed hand and reached up under his shirt to rub again. He flexed his muscles against his back and shivered.
>
> Noiselessly Lennie appeared in the open doorway and stood there looking in, his big shoulders nearly filling the opening. For a moment Crooks did not see him, but on raising his eyes he stiffened and a scowl came on his face. His hand came out from under his shirt.
>
> Lennie smiled helplessly in an attempt to make friends.
>
> Crooks said sharply, *"You got no right to come in my room. This here's my room. Nobody got any right in here but me."*
>
> Lennie gulped and his smile grew more fawning. "I ain't doing nothing," he said. "Just come to look at my puppy. And I seen your light," he explained.

"Well, I got a right to have a light. *You go on get outta my room.*
I ain't wanted in the bunk house, and *you ain't wanted in my room.*"
[14, *118 ff.*] [1]

The favorite theme in the literature of all ages and all peoples
is, of course, the love of a man and a woman. Many authors have
shown that all-embracing passionate complete love means essentially that a lover has merged his or her ego with the person loved,
that the self of one person includes the self of the other, that what
is one's is also the other's, that the separation of the lovers means
a separation of the self of each. Shakespeare, at the very end of
his *Measure for Measure,* has the duke say to his Isabel:

> *What's mine is yours, and what is yours is mine.* [Act V, Scene 1]

And in *Romeo and Juliet,* Juliet tells Romeo that the more she
gives to him the more she has:

> **Juliet.** What satisfaction canst thou have to-night?
> **Romeo.** The exchange of thy love's faithful vow for mine.
> **Juliet.** I gave thee mine before thou didst request it; And yet I
> would it were to give again.
> **Romeo.** Wouldst thou withdraw it? for what purpose, love?
> **Juliet.** But to be frank, and give it thee again. And yet I wish but
> for the thing I have: My bounty is as boundless as the sea,
> My love as deep; *the more I give to thee, the more I have, for both
> are infinite.* [Act II, Scene 2]

In Emily Brontë's *Wuthering Heights* [1], Catherine reveals her
complete identity with Heathcliff, the man she loves:

> . . . *he's more myself than I am.* Whatever our souls are made of,
> his and mine are the same . . . *My great miseries in this world have
> been Heathcliff's miseries,* and I watched and felt each from the be-
> ginning: *my great thought in living is himself. If all else perished,
> and* **he** *remained,* **I** *should still continue to be; and if all else re-
> mained, and he were annihilated, the universe would turn to a mighty
> stranger: I should not seem a part of it.* My love for Linton is like
> the foliage in the woods: time will change it, I'm well aware, as win-
> ter changes the trees. My love for Heathcliff resembles the eternal
> rocks beneath: a source of little visible delight, but necessary. *Nelly,*

---

[1] All italics in literary passages quoted are ours. Words in bold type italicized
in originals.

I *am Heathcliff!* He's always, always in my mind: not as a pleasure, any more than I am always a pleasure to myself, but *as my own being.* [1, *68 f.*]

Eugene O'Neill in *The Great God Brown* [10] at the end of the play shows the undying love of a wife for her dead husband. In this scene, Margaret, the wife, on a moonlight night nostalgically revisits the scene where her husband, Dion, proposed to her. She asks her boys to leave her, and in the last scene of the play she says:

So long ago! And yet I'm still the same Margaret. It's only our lives that grow old. We **are** where centuries only count as seconds and after a thousand lives our eyes begin to open—(**she looks around her with a rapt smile**)—and the moon rests in the sea! I want to feel the moon at peace in the sea! I want Dion to leave the sky for me! I want him to sleep in the tides of my heart! (**She slowly takes from under her cloak, from her bosom, as if from her heart, the mask of Dion as it was at the last and holds it before her face**) My lover! My husband! My boy! *You can never die till my heart dies!* You will live forever! *You are sleeping under my heart! I feel you stirring in your sleep, forever under my heart.* (**She kisses him on the lips with a timeless kiss.**) [10, *98*]

The feeling of passionate lovers has been caught by Ernest Hemingway in his moving story of the Spanish Civil War, *For Whom the Bell Tolls* [4]. Robert Jordan, an American fighting with the Spanish Republican forces, and the Spanish girl, Maria, whom he affectionately calls "Guapa" and "Rabbit," are lying together at night in the open woods.

Then they were together so that as the hand on the watch moved, unseen now, *they knew that nothing could ever happen to the one that did not happen to the other,* that no other thing could happen more than this; that this was all and always; this was what had been and now and whatever was to come. This, that they were not to have, they were having. They were having now and before and always and now and now and now. Oh, now, now, now, the only now, and above all now, and there is no other now but thou now and now is thy prophet. Now and forever now. Come now, now, for there is no now but now. Yes, now. Now, please now, only now, not anything else only this now, and where are you and where am I and where is the other one, and not why, not ever why, only this now; and on and always please then always now, always now, *for now always one now; one only one, there is no other one but one now, one, going now, rising now, sailing now, leaving now, wheeling now, soaring now, away now, all the way now, all of all the way now; one and one is one, is one, is one, is one, is still one, is still one, is one descendingly, is one softly, is one longingly, is one kindly, is one happily, is one in goodness, is one to cherish, is one now on earth* with elbows against the cut and slept-on branches of the pine tree with the smell of the pine boughs and the night; to earth conclusively now, and with the morning of the day to come. Then he said, for the other was only in his head and he had said nothing, "Oh, Maria, I love thee and I thank thee for this." [4, *379*]

And at the end of the book when Jordan takes his final leave of Maria, this identity of the two lovers as one is again brought out.

"Guapa," he said to Maria and took hold of her two hands. . . .

"Listen. We will not go to Madrid now but *I go always with thee wherever thou goest.* Understand?"

She said nothing and pushed her head against his cheek with her arms around him.

"Listen to this well, rabbit," he said. He knew there was a great hurry and he was sweating very much, but this had to be said and understood. *"Thou wilt go now, rabbit. But I go with thee. As long as there is one of us there is both of us.* Do you understand?"

"Nay, I stay with thee."

"Nay, rabbit. What I do now I do alone. I could not do it well with thee. *If thou goest then I go, too.* Do you not see how it is? *Whichever one there is, is both."*

"I will stay with thee."

"Nay, rabbit. Listen. That people cannot do together. Each one must do it alone. *But if thou goest then I go with thee. It is in that way that I go too.* Thou wilt go now, I know. For thou art good and kind. *Thou wilt go now for us both."*

"But it is easier if I stay with thee," she said. "It is better for me."

"Yes. Therefore go for a favor. Do it for *me* since it is what thou canst do."

"But you don't understand, Roberto. What about *me?* It is worse for me to go."

"Surely," he said. "It is harder for thee. *But I am thee also now."*

She said nothing.

He looked at her and he was sweating heavily and he spoke now, trying harder to do something than he had ever tried in all his life.

"Now you will go for us both," he said. "You must not be selfish, rabbit. You must do your duty now."

She shook her head.

"You are me now," he said. "Surely thou must feel it, rabbit."

"Rabbit, listen," he said. *"Truly thus I go too.* I swear it to thee." [4, *463*]

In the libretto written for Richard Strauss's opera *Der Rosenkavalier* by Hugo von Hofmannsthal [15], Octavian in talking to the Marschallin at the beginning of the first act, describes the fusion which occurs between the "I" and the "You" of lovers.[2]

> . . . You, you—what means this "you"? or "you and I"?
> What sense has this?
> These are words, mere words, are they not? It is for you to say!
> But still, there is something in them;
> A dizziness, a pulling, a longing and urging,
> A languishing and burning;
> The way my hand approaches yours,
> The will toward you, the embracing of you,
> I am what "wills" toward you;
> But the "I" is lost in the "you" . . .
> I am your boy, but when I lose sight and hearing—
> Where is your boy? [15, 2]

In a familiar passage from the balcony scene of *Romeo and Juliet,* Shakespeare shows how ego-involved a person's name can become, how his name stands for his identification and status, how difficult it is to separate the person from what his name stands for, and how the fate of two people who loved each other was affected by the established value judgments of families that were bitter enemies. Romeo's ego is one constellation as a member of his family, a different constellation as a lover. [Act II, Scene 2]

> **Juliet.** O Romeo, Romeo! wherefore art thou Romeo?
> *Deny thy father, and refuse thy name;*
> *Or, if thou wilt not, be but sworn my love,*
> *And I'll no longer be a Capulet.*

[2] This passage was called to our attention by Oliver Strunk who also made the English translation for us.

Romeo (aside). Shall I hear more, or shall I speak at this?
Juliet. *'Tis but thy name that is my enemy;*
Thou art thyself though, not a Montague.
What's Montague? it is nor hand, nor foot,
Nor arm, nor face, nor any other part
Belonging to a man. O! be some other name:
What's in a name? that which we call a rose
By any other name would smell as sweet;
So Romeo would, were he not Romeo call'd,
Retain that dear perfection which he owes
Without that title. *Romeo, doff thy name;*
And for that name, which is no part of thee,
Take all myself.

In a story of Frankie, a 12-year-old girl just entering adolescence, Carson McCullers gives a penetrating account of the acute feeling of isolation Frankie experienced as a result of the situation she lived through during a summer. Frankie was too young to be in girls' clubs; too old for John Henry, the six-year-old cousin she had to be with; confused and angered by Berenice, the Negro maid who talked about her four husbands and made fun of Frankie. When her older brother returned from Alaska, married a girl from Winter Hill, a city 100 miles from the home town, Frankie identified herself romantically and completely with the brother and his bride. McCullers shows us how Frankie's formerly lonely world suddenly expanded to include the bride and groom, how for the first time in her life she felt she could now regard herself as part of a "we," and how the newly extended self seemed to dissociate when this "we" she had become went to stay in Winter Hill. [7]

For a long time now her brother and the bride had been at Winter Hill. They had left the town a hundred miles behind them, and now were in a city far away. They were them and in Winter Hill, together, while she was her and in the same old town all by herself. The long hundred miles did not make her sadder and make her feel more far away than the knowing that they were them and both together and she was only her and parted from them, by herself. And as she sickened with this feeling a thought and explanation suddenly came to her, so that she knew and almost said aloud: **They are the we of me.** Yesterday, and all the twelve years of her life, she had only been

Frankie. She was an **I** person who had to walk around and do things by herself. All other people had a **we** to claim, all other except her. When Berenice said **we**, she meant Honey and Big Mama, her lodge, or her church. The **we** of her father was the store. All members of clubs have a **we** to belong to and talk about. The soldiers in the army can say **we,** and even the criminals on chain-gangs. But the old Frankie had had no **we** to claim, unless it would be the terrible summer **we** of her and John Henry and Berenice—and that was the last **we** in the world she wanted. Now all this was suddenly over with and changed. There was her brother and the bride, and it was as though when first she saw them something she had known inside of her: **They are the we of me.** And that was why it made her feel so queer, for them to be away in Winter Hill while she was left all by herself; the hull of the old Frankie left there in the town alone. [7, 50]

The importance of ego-involvement with the same values if a friendship or love relationship are to be lasting can be illustrated in Sinclair Lewis' *Cass Timberlane.* [5] The following passage is part of a conversation between Cass Timberlane and his wife, Jinny, just after Jinny has admitted to Cass that she had become Bradd Criley's mistress. She has told Cass she is going to leave him and go back to Bradd whom she intends to marry. Here Lewis points out how the allegiance of one person to a set of norms another person does not respect makes for incompatibility; how behavior (in this case Bradd's truthfulness) can be judged only within a referential frame.

[Jinny] "Does charm seem to you such a bad quality for a girl to have in a husband?"

—I'm not coming off so well in the argument. And this is a life-death struggle to hold her, not just a squabble. [Thinks Cass to himself]

"Yes, I think it **is** bad, when it's deliberately turned on and off, as it is with a blackguard like Criley."

"You mean 'heel,' don't you? You know, when you say he's a heel, you're talking like a man and it doesn't mean a thing to a woman, unless she's half-man herself. Very few women care a hang about the laws or the social rules. What they love in a man is the feeling that he isn't merely **with** them, but that he **is** them, and feels and thinks as they do before they've finished thinking it. What people like you detest about the heels, the outlaws, is that they don't give a hoot for the idiotic rules that you've set up to protect your own awkwardness, which comes from your never really being completely one with a woman, but always remaining a little aside from her, noticing how good you are or how bad. And expecting her to do what—Bradd just **laughs** when I'm unpunctual, and maybe **you** can't trust what he says, but with me he's **always** truthful!" [5, *335*]

In the same book is exemplified the substitute ego-gratification one person can have through another person's success. In this instance, one woman puts herself in the place of another woman who has won the affections of the man she herself loves. The following conversation takes place at a dinner party given for Cass Timberlane and Jinny. Cass asks his hostess to seat him beside Chris Grau, a woman who loves him and whom everyone in town had expected him to marry.

> "Cass! Are you a competent husband for any girl as fine and winning as Jinny?"
> "I don't know. I hope so."
> "You've got to be! For my sake, too. Cass, she's my understudy. No, she's me; she represents me, she **is** me, in the only love-affair I'll ever have. Are you gentle enough for her and tolerant enough and imaginative enough and flexible enough?" . . .
> "Cass, you do love her, don't you! I'm glad. *Do love her. If you ever for one minute wanted to love me or anything in me, then love me now in her.*" [5, *179 f.*]

A more complicated variation of this same theme is found in *The Great God Brown* where Dion, shortly before his death, taunts Brown for his love of Margaret, Dion's wife, and her children, and for buying off Dion's mistress because they all love him, Dion. Brown has just admitted his love for Margaret. Dion antagonizes Brown by suggesting that Brown can have the love of Margaret and the children only if Brown can make Margaret and the children feel that Dion still lives through him.

> **Dion** (**with a terrible composure**). No! That is merely the appearance, not the truth! Brown loves me! He loves me because I have always possessed the power he needed for love, because I am love! . . .
> **Dion** (**sinking in his chair, more and more weakly**). I'm done. My heart, not Brown— (**Mockingly**) My last will and testament! *I leave*

Dion Anthony to William Brown—for him to love and obey—for him to become me—then my Margaret will love me—my children will love me—Mr. and Mrs. Brown and sons, happily ever after! (**Staggering to his full height and looking upward defiantly**) Nothing more—but Man's last gesture—by which he conquers—to laugh! Ha— (**He begins, stops as if paralyzed, and drops on his knees by** Brown's **chair, his mask falling off, his Christian Martyr's face at the point of death**) Forgive me, Billy. Bury me, hide me, forget me for your own happiness! May Margaret love you! May you design the Temple of Man's soul! Blessed are the meek and the poor in spirit! (**He kisses** Brown's **feet—then more and more weakly and childishly**) What was the prayer, Billy? I'm getting so sleepy . . . [10, *64 f.*]

In our formulations, the devotion one person has for another is due to the fact that this other person is included within one's own ego boundaries, has become a personal value constituting part of one's own ego. Thus if our friend suffers, *we* suffer with him; if he is successful and achieves a fame he desires, *we* are happy and proud. Great friendships recorded in history or literature or seen in everyday life, involve a mutual devotion, reveal an overlapping or inclusion of one person's ego with the other's. In his tragedy *Hippolytus* [3], Euripides portrays the devotion of a nurse for her mistress. The mistress, Phaedra, has fallen passionately in love with Hippolytus, a proud individual, symbol of chastity and asceticism. Phaedra, a married woman, has vowed to die rather than let her passion for Hippolytus overcome her and disgrace her. The nurse is ignorant of the cause of Phaedra's determination to die. Phaedra sees that her own death will bring death to her devoted nurse.

[Nurse] There then I cover thee; but when will death hide my body in the grave? Many a lesson length of days is teaching me. Yea, mortal men should pledge themselves to moderate friendships only, not to such as reach the very heart's core; affection's ties should be light upon them to let them slip or draw them tight. *For one poor heart to grieve for twain, as I do for my mistress, is a burden sore to bear.* Men say that too engrossing pursuits in life more oft cause disappointment than pleasure, and too oft are foes to health. Wherefore I do not praise excess so much as moderation, and with me wise men will agree. . . .

(At the mention of his [Hippolytus'] name Phaedra's attention is suddenly caught.)

Phaedra. Oh! Oh!

Nurse. Ha! doth that touch the quick?

Phaedra. Thou hast undone me, nurse; I do adjure by the gods, mention that man no more.

Nurse. There now! thou art thyself again, but e'en yet refusest to aid thy children and preserve thy life.

Phaedra. My babes I love, but there is another storm that buffets me.

Nurse. Daughter, are thy hands from bloodshed pure?

Phaedra. My hands are pure, but on my soul there rests a stain.

Nurse. The issue of some enemy's secret witchery?

Phaedra. A friend is my destroyer, one unwilling as myself.

Nurse. Hath Theseus wronged thee in any wise?

Phaedra. Never may I prove untrue to him!

Nurse. Then what strange mystery is there that drives thee on to die?

Phaedra. O, let my sin and me alone! 'tis not 'gainst thee I sin.

Nurse. Never willingly! and, if I fail, 'twill rest at thy door.

Phaedra. How now? thou usest force in clinging to my hand.

Nurse. Yea, and I will never loose my hold upon thy knees.

Phaedra. *Alas for thee! my sorrows, shouldst thou learn them, would recoil on thee.*

Nurse. *What keener grief for me than failing to win thee?*

Phaedra. *'Twill be death to thee; though to me that brings renown.* [3, 769 ff.]

In one of Phaedra's speeches, Euripides reveals the tense and tragic conflict that arises when sexual passions run counter to highly cherished values that have become a part of one's self. In the following speech we find Phaedra, convinced that she will not be able to master and subdue her love for Hippolytus, deciding on death rather than a life in which she could no longer identify herself with values that to her were paramount. These values include her status and position as the member of a noble family, her adherence to the norms of marital fidelity, her love for her children, and the unstained reputation she wants to leave behind when she dies.

When love wounded me, I bethought me how I best might bear the smart. So from that day forth I began to hide in silence what I suffered. For I put no faith in counsellors, who know well to lecture others for presumption, yet themselves have countless troubles of their own. Next I did devise noble endurance of these wanton thoughts, striving by continence for victory. *And last when I could not succeed in mastering love hereby, methought it best to die;* and none can gainsay my purpose. *For fain I would my virtue should to all appear, my shame have few to witness it.* I knew my sickly passion now; to yield to it I saw how infamous; and more, I learnt to know so well that I was but a woman, a thing the world detests. Curses, hideous curses on that wife who first did shame her marriage-vow for lovers other than her lord! 'Twas from noble families this curse began to spread among our sex. For when the noble countenance disgrace, poor folk of course will think that it is right. Those too I hate who make profession of purity, though in secret reckless sinners. How can these, queen Cypris, ocean's child, e'er look their husbands in the face? do they never feel one guilty thrill that their accomplice, night, or the chambers of their house will find a voice and speak? *This it is that calls on me to die, kind friends, that so I may ne'er be found to have disgraced my lord, or the children I have borne;* no! may they grow up and dwell in glorious Athens, free to speak and act, heirs to such fair fame as a mother can bequeath. For to know that father or mother has sinned doth turn the stoutest heart to slavishness. This alone, men say, can stand the buffets of life's battle, a just and virtuous soul in whomsoever found. For time unmasks the villain soon or late, holding up to them a mirror as to some blooming maid. 'Mongst such may I be never seen! [3, 774]

Both laboratory experiments and other controlled investigations have shown us how the particular constellation of social values that forms so large a part of our egos gives us our particular status, our anchoring and our identity in the network of social relationships around us. Our standing in a group or community, our reputation, generally stems from judgments made by others of our status. If we are relatively satisfied or proud of the status or anchoring we have achieved, then any reflection or disparagement of our status disturbs our ego, upsets *us,* makes *us* feel insecure, angry, deflated. Shakespeare shows this in the well-known passage, spoken by Iago in *Othello:*

Iago. Good name in man and woman, dear my lord,
Is the immediate jewel of their souls:
Who steals my purse steals trash; 'tis something, nothing;
'Twas mine, 'tis his, and has been slave to thousands;
But he that filches from me my good name
Robs me of that which not enriches him,
And makes me poor indeed. [Act III, Scene 3]

In those primitive and more advanced societies where class or caste lines exist, we find that in nearly all established communities one of the determinants of a person's status is the family he belongs to. The particular place one's own family has in the hierarchy of community values can and very frequently does provide an ego-anchorage. Hence one of the quickest and surest ways for an individual in these societies to rise in the social scale is to marry into a family already solidly established in a superior position. To guard against a breakdown of class and status lines, it was the accepted practice in many societies in earlier years for parents to choose the husbands or wives for their children. Although this custom has generally broken down in advanced countries, there are still subtle and indirect methods parents can and do use to minimize the danger that a child will fall in love with someone "beneath" him and to maximize the opportunities for social intercourse between children of the same class: A family will live in the "right" neighborhood, children will be sent to the "right" school or summer camp, and so on. But when, in spite of these precautions, a child from a "superior" class breaks out of bounds and decides to marry someone beneath him, considerable consternation is likely to arise. Parents feel that *their* status will be lowered by any such action, *they* suffer an ego-disturbance, an ego-failure.

The difficulties and conflicts arising either from the attempt of a person to marry into a class he regards as "higher," or the threat to the ego of a person in a "superior" class because a child is going to marry "beneath" him, has been a recurrent theme in literature, especially in American novels in the past few decades. We will cite here only two of these more recent examples.

The first is from Marquand's *The Late George Apley.* [6] The Apleys could count themselves among the uppercrust of Boston society—they lived on Beacon Hill, sent their sons to Harvard, and so on. For generations this had been the case, and George Apley had sufficient independent means to maintain his position well. His son John had secretly married the recently divorced Louise McCullogh. The father was shocked when he heard the news for, as he said, he had always believed that "John was basically sound." He thought Louise came from a "reasonably good" New York family. On learning of John's marriage, George Apley wrote to a close friend:

> "I had hoped better things of John but now that he has in quite a real sense left us, I feel more than ever a sense of responsibility toward the family." [6, *307*]

Later on George Apley learned more about Louise's family, and his whole estimate of her changed. The following paragraph is taken from a letter he wrote to John after acquiring the added information:

> *"I cannot for the life of me see why you did not tell me in the first place that Louise, whom I am growing more and more anxious daily to set eyes upon, was one of the Hogarths of Connecticut. This, of course, makes a very great difference,* foolish, perhaps, in your eyes, but not in mine. *It has always been a most important thing with me to place a person.* Many of us are accused unjustly of being snobbish. This is not the case. The so-called snobbishness is generally due to one's inability to place the subject of it in the accepted social scale. *Louise's being a Hogarth places her perfectly.* I am sure that the man McCullogh must have been a very bad hat." [6, *308*]

Christopher Morley, in his *Kitty Foyle* [9], outlines in bold relief the thoughts and feelings of an independent self-sufficient girl, Kitty Foyle, the daughter of a former cricket club coach and night foreman at a machine shop, who falls in love with Wynnewood Strafford VI, son of an old Main Line Philadelphia family. Although Wyn also loves Kitty, she refused to marry him because of her class consciousness and class pride, and he married a Philadelphia socialite in the approved fashion. The following excerpts are from a few of the scenes Kitty recalls some years after Wyn's marriage.

Wyn wanted to take me out to Darby Mill. He had planned it all beforehand, they were throwing a house-party out there and I'd had a note from his mother. Naturally I had some sense, I could even see in the way her handwriting went up and down it was a fever chart, but Wyn wouldn't take No.

It was a mistake. Of course Wyn had done what any man would, told everybody to be lovely to me and they were so god damn lovely I could have torn their eyes out. *I was the only one that wasn't in the union.* That crowd, if they stopped to think about it, would reckon that Ben Franklin was still a boy from the wrong side of the tracks, so what would they think about me. Somebody wanted to know if I was one of the Iglehart Foyles from Baltimore or the Saltonstall Foyles from Pride's Crossing. I said no pride ever crossed our family, except when the old man carried his bat against Merion C. C. . . . . *I knew either I or the rest of them didn't belong,* and the embarrassment went around the dinner table all wrapped up in a napkin like that wine bottle the butlers carried. [9, *187 f.*]

Later in the book, Kitty recalls another episode.

"Well then I've got to tell you," Wyn said. "Uncle Kennett has a big idea, he wanted to explain it to you himself. He says you're just exactly the girl for me, Kitty, and the girl the family needs, and he wants to send you back to college for a year and then maybe go abroad a year and meanwhile I'll try to get some education myself and be ready for you."

Oh Jesusgod I don't know exactly how you said it, Wyn. It was something like that. My poor baby, how could you know what that would do to me the way I was just then. Maybe that nice old man with his **thee** talk could have sold it to me; I don't know. I had a kind of picture of some damned family conference and the Straffords and their advisers trying to figure out how the curse was going to be taken off Kitty Foyle. So that was it, they were going to buy the girl with an education, and polish off her rough Frankford edges, were they, and make her good enough to live with stuffed animals' heads and get advertised in the **Ledger.** I can still see your face, my poor baby, when I turned on you. I felt hot inside my throat and on the rims of my ears.

"You can tell Uncle Ken he's a white slaver. Listen, Wyn Strafford, I'll be your girl whenever I feel like it because I love you from hell to breakfast. *But I wouldn't join the little tin family if every old Quaker with an adding machine begged me to.* No, not if they all went back to college and got themselves an education. *So they tried to sell you the idea they'd trim up Kitty so she could go to the Assembly and make Old Philadelphia Family out of her, hey? Cut her out of a copy of Vogue and give her a charge account and make a Main Line doll out of her.* They can't do that to Kitty Foyle. Jesusgod, that's what they are themselves, a bunch of paper dolls."

. . . By God, I'll improve **you** all I want but you can't improve **me**. *[9, 241 ff.]*

The way in which a person's status or role in society, rather than any intrinsic characteristics or qualities of his personality, determines how others react to him, and, in turn, how he is deeply influenced by them in his ego-inflations has often provided the basis for comedy, tragedy, and for literature that aims to convey a "moral." G. H. Mead has pointed out that we frequently judge people by projecting ourselves into the status role we attribute to the person being judged [8]. George Bernard Shaw seems to take particular pleasure in showing up hypocrisy by bringing into his plays pointed references to this effect of status on our evaluation of an individual. In *The Devil's Disciple* [11], Richard Dudgeon, who has been regarded by his mother and the rest of the Puritan community as a renegade and dubbed "The Devil's Disciple," is found unexpectedly to have inherited his father's property. When Richard obeys the summons of the Presbyterian divine, Anderson, and visits the latter's house, he finds to his surprise that he is treated quite civilly for only recently Anderson had roundly condemned him for his sins. Just before the following incident, Richard is apologizing to the minister and his wife for the wetness of his coat, due to his walk in the rain:

Anderson. Take it off, sir; and let it hang before the fire a while: my wife will excuse your shirtsleeves. Judith: put in another spoonful of tea for Mr. Dudgeon.

Richard (eyeing him cynically). *The magic of property, Pastor! Are even you civil to me now that I have succeeded to my father's estate?*

Judith throws down the spoon indignantly. [11, Act II]

And not only is our judgment of a person affected by the status he holds, but his own judgment of himself, what he regards himself to be, can be and often is determined by the reactions of others to him. If a person is treated *as though* he were a person with high status, then *he* is likely to regard himself as such (at least for the time being); if he is treated *as though* he had a low status in the particular hierarchy of values used as the referential framework, then *he* is disappointed, insulted, and so on. Shaw calls attention to this form of ego-involvement in his *Pygmalion* [12]. A poor London flower girl, Liza, is made into a lady by the speech expert, Higgins, who teaches her in his Wimpole Street studio to speak and act like a lady. Higgins treats Liza as an experimental subject and he is, as Shaw describes him, "careless about himself and other people, including their feelings." Participating in the experiment is a visiting speech expert, Pickering, a sensitive man with the qualities of a gentleman. Just before the following dialogue takes place, Liza is telling Pickering, in front of Higgins, that although Higgins did teach her to speak as a lady would "it was just like learning to dance in the fashionable way: there was nothing more than that in it." Liza continues with the question:

But do you know what began my real education?

Pickering. What?

Liza. Your calling me Miss Doolittle that day when I first came to Wimpole Street. That was the beginning of self-respect for me. And there were a hundred little things you never noticed, because they came naturally to you. Things about standing up and taking off your hat and opening doors—

Pickering. Oh, that was nothing.

Liza. Yes: things that showed you thought and felt about me as if I were something better than a scullery-maid; though of course I know you would have been just the same to a scullery-maid if she had been let into the drawing room. You never took off your boots in the dining room when I was there.

Pickering. You mustn't mind that. Higgins takes off his boots all over the place.

Liza. I know. I am not blaming him. It is his way, isn't it? But it made such a difference to me that you didn't do it. You see, really and truly, apart from the things anyone can pick-up (the dressing and the proper way of speaking, and so on), *the difference between a lady and a flower girl is not how she behaves, but how she's treated.* I shall always be a flower girl to Professor Higgins, because he always treats me as a flower girl, and always will; but I know I can be a lady to you, because you always treat me as a lady, and always will. [12, Act V]

A frequent theme of tragedies is the portrayal of the fate of individuals who, obeying the edicts of their conscience or what they regard as a higher law, run up against man-made laws or established norms of their community. The individual in these situations is shown to have so identified himself with a particular value that compromise is impossible and death is preferable to a life in which a radical realteration of the ego structure would be forced. This is the situation in Sophocles' play *Antigone* [13]. Creon had assumed the throne of Thebes and had issued a proclamation that the corpse of one of Antigone's brothers who had led an armed force against the city and who had been killed in combat should remain unburied on the battlefield. Because of the emphasis placed by the Greeks upon the necessity of proper funeral rites, this action of Creon's was regarded with particular terror; it ran completely counter to the divine laws accepted by the people at that time. Antigone, deliberately disobeyed Creon's proclamation by performing the necessary burial rites for her brother's body, out of respect for her brother and for a higher law emanating from the gods she believed in. For this action, Creon condemned her to be buried alive in a vaulted grave. The following excerpt is from a speech of Antigone after she learned Creon's judgment:

Tomb, bridal-chamber, eternal prison in the caverned rock, whither I go to find mine own, those many who have perished, and whom Persephone hath received among the dead! Last of all shall I pass thither, and far most miserably of all, before the term of my life is spent. But I cherish good hope that my coming will be welcome to my father, and pleasant to thee, my mother, and welcome, brother, to thee; for, when ye died, with mine own hands I washed and dressed you, and poured drink-offerings at your graves; and now, Polyneices, 'tis for tending thy corpse that I win such recompense as this.

And yet I honoured thee, as the wise will deem, rightly. . . .

And what law of heaven have I transgressed? Why, hapless one, should I look to the gods any more,—what ally should I invoke,— when by piety I have earned the name of impious? Nay, then, if these things are pleasing to the gods, when I have suffered my doom, I shall come to know my sin; but if the sin is with my judges, I could wish them no fuller measure of evil than they, on their part, mete wrongfully to me. [13, *447 f.*]

To give up life for what is regarded as a "higher" life, is, of course, found in the precepts of various religious leaders. The individual who completely accepts the principles of these religious prophets, is promised a "new" life. In the Gospel of St. Matthew, Christ's teaching is reported:

Then said Jesus unto his disciples, If any **man** will come after me, let him deny himself, and take up his cross, and follow me.

For *whosoever will save his life shall lose it: and whosoever will lose his life for my sake shall find it.*

For what is a man profited, if he shall gain the whole world, and lose his own soul? or what shall a man give in exchange for his soul? [*Matt.* 16: 24–26]

And the disciple, Paul, in his epistle to the Galatians, tells of the new life he has after his conversion.

For I through the law am dead to the law, that I might live unto God.

I am crucified with Christ: nevertheless I live; yet not I, but Christ liveth in me: and the life which I now live in the flesh I live by the faith of the Son of God, who loved me, and gave himself for me. [*Gal.* 2: 19–20]

The transformation of personality under condition of extreme stress, the deprivation of instinctual needs, or organic changes furnish the story of many famous literary characters. Samuel Butler in *The Way of All Flesh* [2] observed in simple language one of the psychological conditions for the breakdown of the ego.

All our lives long, every day and every hour, we are engaged in the process of accommodating our changed and unchanged selves to changed and unchanged surroundings; living, in fact, in nothing else than this process of accommodation; when we fail in it a little we are stupid, when we fail flagrantly we are mad, when we suspend it temporarily we sleep, when we give up the attempt altogether we die. In quiet, uneventful lives the changes internal and external are so small that there is little or no strain in the process of fusion and accommodation; in other lives there is great strain, but there is also great fusing and accommodating power; in others great strain with little accommodating power. [2, *343*]

In Hamlet, Shakespeare portrays Ophelia's madness in part by having her appear before the King and Queen and behaving in quite unseemly fashion. Clearly her standards of respect for these high personages had broken down as had her standards of decent conduct. After Ophelia is ushered into the presence of the King and Queen, the following scene occurs:

Ophelia. Where is the beauteous majesty of Denmark?
Queen. How now, Ophelia!
Ophelia. How should I your true love know
From another one?
By his cockle hat and staff,
And his sandal shoon.
Queen. Alas! sweet lady, what imports this song?
Ophelia. Say you? nay, pray you, mark.
He is dead and gone, lady,
He is dead and gone;
At his head a grass-green turf;
At his heels a stone.

O, ho!
Queen. Nay, but, Ophelia,—
Ophelia. Pray you, mark.
White his shroud as the mountain snow,—

(Enter King)

Queen. Alas! look here, my lord.
Ophelia. Larded with sweet flowers;
Which bewept to the grave did go
With true-love showers.
King. How do you, pretty lady?
Ophelia. Well, God 'ild you! They say the owl was a baker's daughter. Lord! we know what we are, but know not what we may be. God be at your table!
King. Conceit upon her father.
Ophelia. Pray you, let's have no words of this; but when they ask you what it means, say you this:

> Tomorrow is Saint Valentine's day,
>   All in the morning betime,
> And I a maid at your window,
>   To be your Valentine:
> Then up he rose, and donn'd his clothes,
>   And dupp'd the chamber-door;
> Let in the maid, that out a maid
>   Never departed more.

King. Pretty Ophelia!

Ophelia. Indeed, la! without an oath, I'll make an end on 't:

> By Gis and by Saint Charity,
>   Alack, and fie for shame!
> Young men will do 't, if they come to 't;
>   By Cock they are to blame.
> Quoth she, before you tumbled me,
>   You promis'd me to wed:
> So would I ha' done, by yonder son,
>   An thou hadst not come to my bed.

King. How long hath she been thus?

Ophelia. I hope all will be well. We must be patient: but I cannot choose but weep, to think they should lay him i' the cold ground. My brother shall know of it: and so I thank you for your good counsel. Come, my coach! Good-night, ladies; good-night, sweet ladies; good-night, good-night. [Act IV, Scene 5]

Shakespeare's Hamlet, one of the most complicated and complex characters in all literature, is many-sided. And Shakespeare has Hamlet himself aware of the different constellations and patterns of values which constitute the changing pattern of his ego, a fact which further adds to the complication. Depending upon his mood and the situation in which he finds himself, Hamlet is a different person at different times. Right after his famous soliloquy, "To be or not to be," the following dialogue takes place between Hamlet and Ophelia:

Ophelia. My lord, I have remembrances of yours,
>   That I have long longed to re-deliver;
>   I pray you, now receive them.

Hamlet. *No, not I;*
>   *I never gave you aught.*

Ophelia. My honour'd lord, you know right well you did;
　　And, with them, words of so sweet breath compos'd
　　As made the things more rich: their perfume lost,
　　Take these again; for to the noble mind
　　Rich gifts wax poor when givers prove unkind.
　　There, my lord.
Hamlet. Ha, ha! are you honest?
Ophelia. My lord!
Hamlet. Are you fair?
Ophelia. What means your lordship?
Hamlet. That if you be honest and fair, your honesty should admit
no discourse to your beauty.
　Ophelia. Could beauty, my lord, have better commerce than with
honesty?
　Hamlet. Ay, truly; for the power of beauty will sooner transform
honesty from what it is to a bawd than the force of honesty can trans-
late beauty into his likeness: this was sometime a paradox, but now the
time gives it proof. *I did love thee once.*
　Ophelia. Indeed, my lord, you made me believe so.
　Hamlet. You should not have believed me; for virtue cannot so
inoculate our old stock but we shall relish of it: *I loved you not.* [Act
III, Scene 1]

And again at the end of the play, just before he duels with
Laertes, the one Hamlet asks Laertes forgiveness for any wrong
another Hamlet has done:

Hamlet. Give me your pardon, sir; I've done you wrong;
　　But pardon 't, as you are a gentleman.
　　This presence knows,
　　And you must needs have heard, how I am punish'd
　　With sore distraction. What I have done,
　　That might your nature, honour and exception
　　Roughly awake, I here proclaim was madness.
　　Was 't Hamlet wrong'd Laertes? Never Hamlet:
　　If Hamlet from himself be ta'en away,
　　And when he's not himself does wrong Laertes,
　　Then Hamlet does it not; Hamlet denies it.
　　Who does it then? His madness. If 't be so,
　　Hamlet is of the faction that is wrong'd;
　　His madness is poor Hamlet's enemy.

Sir, in this audience,
Let my disclaiming from a purpos'd evil
Free me so far in your most generous thoughts,
That I have shot mine arrow o'er the house,
And hurt my brother. [Act V, Scene 2]

These are only a few scattered examples from literature of the ways in which the novelist and playwright have pointed to the problem of ego-involvement. We have seen how people have become attached to certain values, how these values have become a part of them in the various situations described. The allegiance to conflicting values within an individual is the basis of ego-disturbance, ego-conflicts, just as the mergence and overlapping of values within the single individual or between individuals is the basis for ego-satisfaction, ego-expansion. Detailed and systematic analyses of the literature of all peoples, both ancient and modern, would surely pose for the psychologist wide varieties of ego-involving situations, intricate patterns of ego constellations, stark and subtle modifications of behavior due to ego-involved attitudes. The self-appointed job of the novelist, the playwright, and the poet is to portray life, analyze it impressionistically as a sensitive observer. The self-appointed job of the psychologist is to explain systematically and scientifically the thoughts, feelings, and actions of men. Since so much of life is filled with ego-involved experiences, the literary artist and the psychologist are bound to have this common meeting ground.

REFERENCES

1. BRONTË, E., *Wuthering Heights,* New York: Dutton, copyright 1907.
2. BUTLER, S., *The Way of All Flesh,* New York: Dutton, copyright 1916.
3. EURIPIDES, *Hippolytus,* in *The Complete Greek Drama* (Whitney J. Oates and Eugene O'Neill, Jr., eds.), trans. of E. P. Coleridge, New York: Random House, copyright 1938.
4. HEMINGWAY, E., *For Whom the Bell Tolls,* New York: Scribner's, copyright 1940; quotations by permission of the publisher.
5. LEWIS, S., *Cass Timberlane,* New York: Random House, copyright 1945; quotations by permission of the publisher.
6. MARQUAND, J. P., *The Late George Apley,* Boston: Little, Brown, copyright 1937; quotations by permission of the publishers.
7. McCULLERS, C., *The Member of the Wedding,* Boston: Houghton Mifflin, copyright 1946; quotations by permission of the publisher.

8. MEAD, G. H., *Mind, Self and Society*, Chicago: Univ. Press, 1934.
9. MORLEY, C., *Kitty Foyle*, Philadelphia: Lippincott, copyright 1939; quotations by permission of the publisher.
10. O'NEILL, E., *The Great God Brown*, New York: Boni & Liveright, copyright 1926; quotations by permission of Random House.
11. SHAW, G. B., *The Devil's Disciple*, in *Three Plays for Puritans*, New York: Brentano, copyright 1906; quotations by permission of the author.
12. —— *Pygmalion*, New York: Dodd, Mead, copyright 1916; quotations by permission of the author.
13. SOPHOCLES, *Antigone*, in *The Complete Greek Drama* (Whitney J. Oates and Eugene O'Neill, Jr., eds.), trans. of R. C. Jebb, New York: Random House, copyright 1938.
14. STEINBECK, J., *Of Mice and Men*, New York: Modern Library, copyright 1937; quotations by permission of Viking Press.
15. VON HOFMANNSTHAL, H., Libretto for Richard Strauss' opera *Der Rosenkavalier*, Berlin: Adolph Fürstner, copyright 1910.

CHAPTER 14

THE EGO IN PSYCHOANALYSIS

In casually patterned societies a social lag is created by the impact of technological developments on established institutional controls; on religious, political, and economic ideology; and on norms of behavior. This is reflected in the turmoil that goes on within the individual when he tries to make a satisfactory life adjustment. Personal dilemmas, uncertainties, and crises are invariable by-products of periods of social change. In recent years, laymen who have wanted some "scientific" help in meeting their personal problems have turned to psychology. The psychology they appeal to is very often some form of psychoanalysis. It is perhaps the only kind of psychology they have ever heard of or, at least, the only variety of psychology that seems to hold out any promise of explanation or eventual resolution of their difficulties. And many social scientists, too, quite properly thinking psychology should be able to help in accounting for anthropological, economic, or political phenomena, have turned especially to psychoanalysis and, like the layman, have tended to equate it with psychology.

Psychoanalysis has, therefore, a tremendous vogue. Its appeal seems to increase with the general acceleration of social change. This appeal comes partly from the fact that psychoanalysts have had the courage to deal with problems of general interest and concern to laymen and to social scientists, and that they attempt to explain phenomena of everyday life experienced by the individual or observed by the social scientist. The appeal is also due no doubt partly to the fact that they use a dramatic and alluring method, one that deals with "hidden" and unconscious motives, with sex and with love, with hate and with fear. Once an individual has been initiated into the psychoanalytical approach and terminology, the search for the causes and cures of personal and social problems takes on all the thrill and excitement of detective story fiction.

If psychoanalysis were concerned only with individual therapy, we would not need to discuss it in social psychology. But psychoanalysis does become relevant and important for us because it deals with the problems of social psychology, offers explanations of the various social phenomena that are the concern of the social psychologist—with groups and institutions, with religion and other ideologies, with war and revolution.

Here is the scope of psychoanalysis as seen by some of its exponents.

The relationship of psychoanalysis to social psychology was made explicit by Erich Fromm. In 1930 he noted that psychoanalysis made no false distinctions between individual and social psychology. The basic method of social psychology is, he held, the same as the method of psychoanalysis, an extension of Freud's early emphasis on the importance of the environment to the child. [22] Fromm felt that psychoanalysis, by making a comprehensive analysis of the nature of man as it works itself out in a social process, could be particularly useful in enriching and giving a psychological basis to the historical materialism of Marx and Engels. [23, 45 f.] Others have made less cautious statements. Jones writes that "the prevailing muddle" we see in man's social relations is due more than anything else to ignorance of "those unconscious forces on the nature of which psychoanalysis is throwing so much light." [35, 194] Alexander relies on psychoanalysis as the cure for our present social problems:

> The methods and principles of dynamic psychology created an entirely new field—the science of human relationships. . . . In the face of the present wholesale manifestation of irrational forces, all eyes turn for an explanation to psychiatry, the science of irrational human behavior. [4, 22 f.]

Kardiner tells us that if the conclusions he has reached in applying psychoanalysis to the study of various cultures prove to be correct "then it can be safely said that it has opened up a new chapter in the understanding of human society." [37, 252]

It is clear, then, that psychoanalysts have staked a claim to the territory of social psychology. Because of this, psychoanalysis must be watched carefully and checked for its scientific validity.

FREUD'S FORMULATIONS [1]

Freud begins his group psychology with the statement:

The contrast between Individual Psychology and Social or Group Psychology, which at a first glance may seem to be full of significance, loses a great deal of its sharpness when it is examined more closely. [18, *1*]

From the very first Individual Psychology is at the same time Social Psychology as well. [2]

Whatever else the social psychologist may think of Freud's formulations, he must acknowledge at once that the distinction made by Freud between social demands on the one hand and the instinctual urges of the individual on the other is to his everlasting credit. This distinction between the superstructure of society and the needs of the individual was not one of a rigid sharp dichotomy. Although Freud did not carry the dialectics of his own methods to its logical conclusion, did not follow through all its implications,

---

[1] *Note on Adler.* We are deliberately centering our attention here on Freud and psychoanalysts who stem from Freudian tradition. Our final evaluation of the validity and adequacy of the psychoanalytic interpretation of social phenomena will, in its fundamental respects, also apply to Adlerian psychology. For, although Adler rejects Freud's emphasis on sexual instincts and on the Oedipus complex, there is for Adler, as for Freud, a universal explanation of behavior: As the result of the child's feeling of inferiority to his parents and to the world at large, he develops a longing for superiority, *"this fiction of a goal of superiority so ridiculous from the viewpoint of reality, has become the principal conditioning factor of our life as hitherto known.* It is this that teaches us to differentiate, gives us poise and security, molds and guides our deeds and activities and forces our spirit to look ahead and to perfect itself." [1, *8*] This goal of superiority *"introduces into our life a hostile and fighting tendency."* [8] In addition to this goal of superiority Adler believes that the individual has an "eternal, real and physiologically rooted *community-feeling."* It is from this community feeling that we develop "tenderness, love of neighbor, friendship and love, the desire for power unfolding itself in a veiled manner and seeking secretly to push its way along the path of group consciousness." [9 *f.*] The ego develops as a result of this early feeling of inferiority, of the compensating longing for superiority and the impact of community feeling in the child.

he recognized the close interrelationship between social pressure and the dynamic forces at work in the single individual. He pointed out that the interaction of social demands on the individual was a process profoundly affecting his thought and action: "an individual in a group is subjected through its influence to what is often a profound alteration in his mental activity." [18, *33*] He saw that opposing forces were at work within the unity of a single individual.

> If a Psychology, concerned with exploring the predispositions, the instincts, the motives and the aims of an individual man down to his actions and his relations with those who are nearest to him, had completely achieved its task, and had cleared up the whole of these matters with their inter-connections, it would then suddenly find itself confronted by a new task which would lie before it unachieved. It would be obliged to explain the surprising fact that under a certain condition this individual whom it had come to understand thought, felt, and acted in quite a different way from what would have been expected. And this condition is his insertion into a collection of people which has acquired the characteristic of a "psychological group." [18, *5 f.*]

The social psychologist is impressed, too, with Freud's honesty, his willingness to follow his observations into whatever theoretical formulation he thought they led him. He hesitated neither to break away from the scientific and philosophical traditions of his day, nor to disagree with his own earlier concepts when he thought new evidence called for revisions.

Since the publication of Freud's *The Ego and The Id* (1923) the ego has become especially important for psychoanalysis. Anna Freud's *The Ego and Mechanisms of Defence* published in 1937 further highlighted the concept so that modern psychoanalytic literature seems to be concerned with the ego to a significant degree. After a sketch of Freud's own basic formulations we shall see where this led him and his followers in their attempts to explain social phenomena.

According to Freud, we begin with the unorganized, unrefined *id*—the source of all instinctual, primal impulses, the original initiators of thought and activity. It is not necessary for us here to review the changes in Freud's own thinking concerning the nature and number of instincts or to subscribe one way or another to the often heated discussions of psychoanalysts concerning the relative importance of the sexual instinct, the death instinct, and the like. Freud himself has said that "there is obviously a great opportunity here for arbitrary choice." [17, 66] Our concern here is with the general formulation that the infant begins life with an undisciplined id, the core of his personality, the instinctual source of energy. These instincts seek immediate gratification so that the infant, before he has been affected by social processes, by social pressures, is completely dominated by the pleasure principle. "In the psychoanalytical theory of the mind we take it for granted that the course of mental processes is automatically regulated by 'the pleasure principle': that is to say, we believe that any given process originates in an unpleasant state of tension and thereupon determines for itself such a path that its ultimate issue coincides with the relaxation of this tension, i.e. with avoidance of 'pain' or with production of pleasure." [19, 1] The child, then, is constantly motivated to reduce the tension created by instinctual energy.

The ego develops when the child bucks up against the outside world, when the instinctual impulses of the id cannot be immediately gratified.

> The ego is that part of the id which has been modified by the direct influence of the external world. [21, 29]

The ego is able to modify the id because the ego is affected by perception—both by the "external perceptions" from the outer world and by the "internal perceptions" yielded by sensations from the id. The job of the ego, then, is that

> . . . of bringing the influence of the external world to bear upon the id and its tendencies, and endeavors to substitute the reality-principle for the pleasure-principle which reigns supreme in the id. In the ego perception plays the part which in the id devolves upon instinct. [21, 29 f.]

The ego sizes up for the individual his relation to the environment, it has the capacity to suppress immediate pleasure (the reality principle), to differentiate between the impulses coming from the id and those coming from the outer world, and to distinguish between those impulses of the id whose immediate gratification will cause pain and those that can be gratified without fear of punishment.

Perception for Freud "is not a merely passive process; we believe rather that the ego periodically sends out small amounts of cathec-tic energy into the perceptual system and by their means samples the external stimuli, and after every such groping advance draws back again." [20, *370*] Thought and judgment are, for Freud, extensions of this perceptual process of "groping forward." The perceptual function of the ego has been clearly summarized by Alexander:

> What can be said with certainty about the ego is that it is a forma-tion of two perceptive surfaces, one directed toward the instinctual life (inner perception), the second directed toward external reality (sense perception). One main function of the ego is to confront the facts of inner perception with the results of sense perception, i.e., to bring subjective demands in harmony with the external circumstances. Its tendency is to find satisfaction for as many of the subjective needs and wishes as possible under existing external circumstances. [3, *147 f.*]

The end result is, according to Freud, that what we know as mind can be looked upon "as an unknown and unconscious id, upon whose surface rests the ego, developed from its nucleus the perceptual-systems." [21, *28*] This ego is constantly defending itself from the pain it fears from the instincts to which it is antag-onistic. [15] Freud's ego includes consciousness and by controlling "the approaches to motility, i.e. to the discharge of excitations into the external world" it "regulates all its own constituent processes." [21, *15 f.*] It is the source of repressions. Alexander has summed up the operation of the ego:

> The functioning of the whole mental apparatus can be described approximately as follows: Instinctual needs and tendencies arising in the id tend to become conscious because the conscious ego controls the motor innervations on which the satisfaction of the needs is de-pendent. A great part of the instinctual demands becomes immedi-ately conscious and finds its acceptance or rejection after a process of conscious deliberation. This deliberation involves an estimate of the external situation and a comparison of the inner demand in question with other conflicting tendencies present in consciousness. [3, *148*]

The ego, then, gradually gets more and more control over the id. And the particular pattern of the ego's adjustment of instinctual forces to the external world becomes the fundamental trait of any personality. [43]

The id, however, does not easily relinquish the objects which will give it immediate gratification. The repression of instincts, especially of erotic trends, is painful. In order to make "it easier for an object to be given up" [21, 36] the ego substitutes one object for another so the id can achieve cathexis. Thus the ego becomes "a precipitate of abandoned object-cathexis" and "contains a record of past object-choices." [21, 36]

"The ego is formed to a great extent out of identifications taking the place of cathexes on the part of the id which have been abandoned." [21, 68] If the ego's object-identifications become too numerous and too incompatible with one another, intense pathological conditions result, but even for the relatively normal individual these "conflicts between the different identifications into which the ego is split up" [21, 39] are accompanied by definite affective properties.

The ego can gradually get control over the id through this process of transforming erotic object-choices. Libido is gradually withdrawn from the id as the object-cathexes of the id are turned into "ego constructions." [21, 82] The ego thus becomes "the true and original reservoir of the libido." [19, 66] This flow of the libido into the ego gives rise to the Freudian mechanism of secondary narcissism. For Freud, not only self-love but love for others is derived from this libido within the ego; being in love means "that the object draws a part of the narcissistic ego–libido to itself." [18, 125]

The earliest and the most important identification a child makes is with the parents who are "the first object-cathexes of the id." [21, 69] When the child discerns that one parent is an obstacle to the gratification of the sexual desire it has with respect to the other parent, then the Oedipus complex appears. The ego's transformation of this "first and most important identification of all" [21, 39] precipitates within the ego itself a "special office" [68] —the superego. The superego is the "heir to the Oedipus complex." [21, 69] The cornerstone of the superego is, as Bychowski has expressed it, "the Images of persons who have guided the child and were its source of norms." [9, *313*]   Since the child was dominated by its parents and compelled to obey them, the super-ego becomes the arbiter of what shall and shall not be allowed, the source of authority and prohibitions. When the superego functions in consciousness it is known as conscience or guilt.

This precipitate, the superego, has for Freud a special position within the ego:

> The broad general outcome of the sexual phase governed by the Oedipus complex may, therefore, be taken to be the forming of a precipitate in the ego, consisting of these two identifications [father identification and mother identification] in some way combined together. This modification of the ego retains its special position; it stands in contrast to the other constituents of the ego in the form of an ego ideal or superego. [21, *44,* italicized in original]

Freud maintained that the Oedipus complex is universal. He believed that the id could be inherited, that in it "are stored up vestiges of the existences led by countless former egos" [21, *52*], that the identification with the father (parent) "takes place in the prehistory of every person." [21, *39*]   Although many analysts do not subscribe to Freud's phylogenetic theory, the universality of the Oedipus complex derived from early parent–child relationships is still a basic tenet for most psychoanalysts today.[2]   In a review of the history of the Oedipus complex, for example, Boehm discusses the fields of literature, biography, and the primitive myths reported by modern ethnologists and concludes that all these various types of data support the Oedipus complex as a phenomenon that pervades everyone's unconscious. [7]

The commanding position of the superego in mental life is, for Freud, due to the fact that it represents "not merely a deposit left by the earliest object-choices of the id; it also represents an energetic reaction-formation against those choices." [21, *44*]   To repress the Oedipus complex is "no easy task" for the individual. The child sees the father "as the obstacle to realization of the

---

[2] Some notable and important exceptions of the pervading psychoanalytic view concerning the origin and function of the Oedipus complex are considered later in this chapter.

Oedipus wishes." [21, 45]   In order to carry out this extraordi-
narily difficult repression, "the child's ego brought in a reinforce-
ment" [21, 45]: it created within itself the character of the father
to repress the Oedipus complex.   And the more tense the Oedipus
complex was in the beginning and "the more rapidly it succumbed
to repression (under the influence of discipline, religious teaching,
schooling and reading) the more exacting later on is the domination of the super-ego over the ego—in the form of conscience or
perhaps of an unconscious sense of guilt." [21, 45]   The ego attempts to free itself from the dominance of the superego by substituting new persons or new relationships as representative of the
parents or parental relations that lie behind the superego.   The
result is that "conflicts and struggles which had evolved during
childhood repeat themselves albeit between other players and in a
new shape." [9, 313]

In spite of Freud's characterization of the superego as something
with a "special position" within the ego, as something that "stands
in contrast to the other constituents of the ego," psychoanalysts and
even Freud himself sometimes seem to have difficulty in making a
clear distinction between ego and superego, in telling where one
leaves off and the other begins.   For example, in correcting his
earlier view that the superego has the function of testing the reality
of things, Freud said:

> The view that the testing of reality is rather one of the functions
> of the ego itself *would fit in perfectly* with what we know of the
> relations of the ego to the world of perception. [21, 34, italics ours]

And what Freud refers to as the "double aspects" of the ego ideal
(superego) inevitably introduces certain confusion in terms: for
the superego not only results from the repression of the Oedipus
complex but is itself the mechanism which effected the repression.
It is not infrequent to find the ego or the superego referred to in
psychoanalytic literature in the form of (super) ego. [33, 307]
Anna Freud says that the superego can be distinguished from the
ego only when it is obvious that the former is critical of the latter. [15]   Alexander, referring to his earlier distinction between
the unconscious superego and the conscious ego ideal, says:

It seems to me questionable whether one should consider the ego-ideal more closely connected with the super-ego, as its continuation in the consciousness, or more allied to the actual ego . . . the ego-ideal is not a completely separate unit, since it is hard to differentiate between conscious values, ideals, guiding principles and the rest of the ego. On the other hand, it is also difficult to make a sharp distinction between the entirely unconscious, almost automatic influences of the super-ego and those more or less conscious ones which direct our decisions and general conduct. [3, *145 f.*]

Fromm believes that the difference between the ego and the super-ego is that the latter has an emotional character derived from the incompatibility of instinctual impulses and social necessities. [25, 95] Horney, rejecting Freud's conception of the origin of the Oedipus complex, feels that the superego should be regarded as a special need for neurotic individuals rather than as an agency within the ego itself. The individual's standards of behavior which Freud derives from the superego are, for Horney, "not ego-alien but are an integral part of the self. To them the 'super-ego' has but a superficial resemblance." [30, *230*]

WHERE FREUDIAN THEORY LEADS IN SOCIAL PSYCHOLOGY

Our brief sketch of Freud's theory of ego development has been necessary to give us a background for understanding the application of his formulations to social phenomena. As we said previously, from the point of view of the layman and also of some social scientists, one of the great attractions of psychoanalysis is its apparent ability to explain almost any behavior—whether on the individual or social level. We will cite here a few examples of Freudian interpretations of problems that concern the social psychologist.

Consider, first of all, Freud's own interpretations of the formation and function of groups. Individual participation in a group is one way in which a person can release his instinctual impulses. All groups have, therefore, a "libidinal constitution." [18, *79 f.*] It is instinctual energy that makes group formation possible.

A group is clearly held together by a power of some kind: and to what power could this feat be better ascribed than to Eros who holds together everything in the world? [18, *40*]

In group activity individuals substitute for their own ego ideals a common object with which they identify themselves—hence individual members of a group identify themselves with one another.

Social feeling rests on the foundation of identifications with others, on the basis of an ego-ideal in common with them. [21, *49*]

Freud thus accounts for institutional groupings such as the army and the church. Since each individual "has built up his ego ideal upon the most various models" [18, *101*], an individual can become part of a number of different groups. For Freud, identification with more or less lasting groups (that is, racial or nationality) is explained by his belief that the id can be inherited and that "when the ego forms its superego out of the id, it may perhaps only be reviving images of egos that have passed away." [21, *52*]

For Alexander the whole process of an individual's adjustment to his social environment is to be thought of in terms of the incorporation of parental images into the personality:

This process of identification with the parents and the incorporation of their image into the mental apparatus is the process which we usually call adjustment to the social environment. [3, *143*]

For Reik all social tendencies are transformations of the selfish and aggressive drives of the ego, so that the ego seeks further gratification in attempting to overcome group, nationality, and class differences. [46, *155*] The highest fulfillment of this particular function of ego-striving is, for Reik, what we call love. Love is the projection of our ego-ideal, it is "an escape from oneself" [46, *89*], so that we really fall in love with people whom we would like to be.

Another example of a psychoanalytic interpretation concerned with one feature of social life is Fenichel's carefully worked-out account of the function of money in our society and our desire to accumulate it. [12] Disagreeing with Ferenczi and Róheim that money was originally invented for the specific purpose of satisfying an erotogenic (anal) instinct, Fenichel regards money as a social institution first external to the individual. The reason the individual in our society reacts to money as he does is as follows. The infant considers its mother's breast and later its own faeces as parts of its ego. Denial of the breast and loss of faeces therefore become identified with injury to one's own bodily ego.

The desire to possess a great deal appears thus to be a direct expression of the narcissistic need to enlarge as much as possible the compass of one's own ego. [12, *79 f.*]

Our possessions therefore "are an expanded portion of the ego." [*80*] The accumulation of possessions is seen connected primarily to anal eroticism because "in the anal sphere holding back and accumulating can afford an experience of erogenous pleasure." [*82*] The same author accounts for social class, the division into "haves" and "have-nots," by the efforts of the "have-nots" to regain their lost feeling of infantile omnipotence. This they can do by identifying themselves with persons who represent characterizations of their own superego. [13]

A psychoanalytic explanation of war has been offered by Waelder [54]. All mass formation, he believes, is a process of regression where external principles or authorities take the place of more mature internalized demands which the individual's conscience imposes upon him as a substitution, in their turn, of the earlier commands and prohibitions of parents. In mass formations, then, men can act like children again, giving vent to the impulses of hate and destruction inherent in them. Social conflicts, including wars, are therefore due to the "frailty of human reason" [*46*] caused by this infantile regression.

The psychology of revolution has been given special attention by Ernest Jones. [35] The characteristic of revolutionary change is, he says, destructiveness. And the reason for this destructiveness is the impulse "to displace the old, or, more specifically, the Oedipus wish to kill the father." [*198*] Jones recognizes the important role of revolutionary leaders whom he feels are people with no qualms about murdering the "father figure." This is true of revolutionary leaders, because they possess in high degree the paranoid's mechanism of projection which is for them a "defence against sex inversion, or—more strictly—against the incorporated 'bad objects' resulting from this inversion." [*201*] Led on by leaders with these homosexual tendencies, participants in a revolutionary movement substitute the "concept of society" for their own parents whom they alternately loved and injured. Revolutionary leaders have the appeal they do in critical times, because it is during these critical times that individuals become most sensitive to their own "deep seated sense of guilt."

The rise of Fascism has been accounted for on the basis of the prolonged infantile sexuality said to be especially characteristic of the working people and the *Kleinbuergertum*. The general frustrations of this group led them to accept the authority of a leader as a compensating identification. [44] Their normal "id-drives" were increasingly denied expression and the authority of the superego was diminished. Hence people indulged themselves in ways formerly forbidden. But such indulgences only created new guilt feelings which demanded in their turn self-punishment or sadistic punishment. The personal satisfaction accompanying this punishment became itself a further reason for unconscious indulgence. By creating enemies that could be chastised and attacked, therefore, Naziism was able to restore the feeling of self-righteousness. All the hate and destructiveness of the infant was transferred to new objects. In Hitler, the *Kleinbuerger* found an adequate parental symbol and by identification with Hitler was able to forget the weakness of his own infantilism. [51, *106–109*] Those most susceptible to Nazi propaganda were "those who have neither securely established their own manhood and independence of the Father nor have been able to combine the instincts of sexuality and love in their attitude towards the Mother or other women." [34, 6]

Another modern application of psychoanalysis is Jones's account of the psychology of Quislingism. [34] The Quisling identifies himself with the formidable father image which is so irresistible that the individual by "devious and desperate devices" [4] transforms the image of the evil father into the image of a good father. In this process of self-deception the attempt is made to appease the real enemy by "making suitable concessions." [5] Quislingism thus becomes an "exquisitely homosexual" solution. [5] The treachery and betrayal associated with Quislingism is due to the fact that alliance with the enemy is a sadistic attempt "to overcome the incest taboo by raping the Mother instead of loving her." [6]

The psychology of anti-Semitism has been variously treated along psychoanalytic lines. One explanation is that anti-Semitism is an "unconscious hostility" directed to Jews who are recognized as the proponent of the "monotheistic God (superego God)"

whose acceptance has forced the renunciation of the instincts. [39]
A recent study of the personalities of anti-Semitic women concludes that their prejudice is due to a very strict and conventional
superego in harmony with parental images so that instinctual
impulses must find their outlet in very devious expressions such as
anti-Semitism.

> Our puritanical anti-Semites project their id impulses onto the Jew.
> [14, *286*]

The solution of anti-Semitism, according to these authors, therefore lies in the direction of a more intelligent and more lenient
child training on the part of the parents which would result in
greater emotional security and more psychological insight.

An apologist for a rigid Freudian interpretation of the development and continuation of culture is found in Róheim. [47]
Although Róheim rejects Freud's contention that the collective
unconscious can be inherited, he feels that all of man's culture has
been developed "as a sublimation or reaction–formation to infantile
conflicts." [*149*] He substitutes an ontogenetic theory of culture
for Freud's phylogenetic theory. He notes that the distinctive
feature of man as contrasted to other animals is his prolonged
infancy. This plus the retarded development of dentition with
the consequence that there is in the infant considerable activity
unrelated to the acquisition of food, together with the "relatively
precocious sexual development" of the human infant, all adds up
to the fact that the long process of human maturation and the
characteristics accompanying it produce a set of conditions from
which culture develops. Institutions and ways of life not directly
connected with the acquisition of food are regarded as sublima-
tions of the infantile situation. His view is "that the bulk of
human culture, even in its adaptational or ego–aspects, arises out
of play or ritual activities. The reason for these activities lies in
the infantile situation, and they acquire survival values secondarily
by assimilating a part of the environment to man's needs." [*163*]

> Therefore in the development of human adaptations the tendency
> is for adaptations that are based on the infantile situation to replace
> in an ever decreasing degree those based on the stimulus–reaction
> pattern. [47, *163*]

For example, according to Róheim, the art of making fire is "a displaced play repetition of the genital act or of masturbation." [163] Differences between different cultures are accounted for on the basis of variations in the infantile situations which are themselves "probably based on constitutional variations of human groups." Changes that occur within a culture are due to the fact that a culture provides for the sublimation of only some of the id trends and defense mechanisms of the individual and that what tendencies the culture fails to sublimate provide the "psychic background" which makes for reform and change. But over the course of generations, the culture adapts itself to the characteristics of the infantile situation so that, even when the individual is affected by the institutions of a culture, these institutions must be regarded only as representing "the petrified strivings of past generations of human beings." [166]

Fenichel is highly critical of Róheim's ontogenetic theory of cultural development. He believes that social institutions, first created by human beings who were satisfying their needs, then become external realities themselves, part of the outer stimuli "that modify the instinctual structure of mankind." [12, 70] The process of socialization for Fenichel is a reciprocal action where social influences modify the instinctual structure and the modified instinctual structure itself "reacts again upon social reality." [71] As we have seen in Fenichel's account of the drive for wealth, he accepts the orthodox view concerning man's instinctual structure and regards culture and its institutions essentially as furnishing objects for the displacement of instinctual impulses and their infantile derivatives. For him the ego is a direct development of the instincts as they are influenced by the outside world. He objects to the psychoanalyst, such as Horney, who "takes from psycho-analysis its biological basis—that of instinctual needs." [11, 418]

MODIFICATIONS WITH CULTURAL EMPHASIS

In the early 1930's there was increasing recognition on the part of some analysts of the cultural variations of Freudian formulations, a sensitivity to the data and concepts so rapidly accumulating in anthropology and ethnology. Analysts such as Fromm, Sperber, and Horney took vigorous exception to some of Freud's formulations which, they argued, showed a neglect on Freud's part to follow through the implications of the fact that the individual develops in and is modified by a social environment already fairly well structured when the individual is born into it, an environment that itself has certain characteristics and peculiarities the psychoanalyst must be aware of if his explanations are to have any degree of universality.

In 1927 Malinowski published his *Sex and Repression in Savage Society*, the first part of which appeared as two articles in 1924. Here he specifically directed his evidence against the fundamental Freudian tenet of the Oedipus complex as a universal human phenomenon existing independently in any social environment. Malinowski based his argument on his study of the Trobriand Islanders who lived in a matrilineal society and who developed a matrilineal complex "entirely different in its genesis and its character from the Oedipus complex." [40, *83*] Malinowski could find no evidence among the Trobrianders of rivalry or friction between the father and the son. If there was any ambivalent attitude of love and hate it was "felt between a man and his mother's brother, while the repressed sexual attitude of incestuous temptation can be formed only towards his sister." [*80*]

Malinowski's interpretation of the cultural relativity of the Oedipus complex was vigorously attacked by Jones [32] who maintained that Malinowski's findings could be interpreted "as a mode of defence against the primordial Oedipus tendencies." Malinowski felt that orthodox analysts such as Jones who place "a certain causal or metaphysical stress" [40, *139*] on the Oedipus complex as the cause, rather than as the effect, of a social structure were unnecessarily divorcing psychoanalytic theory from empirical anthropology which, to Malinowski, clearly shows that "the nuclear family complex is a functional formation dependent upon the structure and upon the culture of a society." [*143*]

Other anthropologists, looking toward a fruitful and productive relationship between psychoanalysis and anthropology, urged psychoanalysts to adapt themselves to the implications which the fact of cultural variation had for their discipline. Sapir was an early and outstanding protagonist of this point of view. In a series of brilliant articles, he pointed out that the mechanisms with which the psychoanalyst was concerned should not be regarded as "closed systems imprisoned within the biological walls of isolated individuals" [49, *233*] and could be studied realistically only when related to deeply ingrained cultural patterns and the various subcultures and personal interactions with other people that constitute the external social world for the single individual. [48, 49, 50]

An early and particularly vigorous attack on psychoanalysis and psychotherapy in general for its neglect of man's social relationships was made by Sperber in 1932. [53] Sperber's criticism is from a Marxist point of view, and it is not without significance that the editor of the journal in which his article appeared felt obliged to point out to the readers that, although Sperber's comments took on the nature of a political tract and therefore were unusual for a scientific journal, it was only proper that a "bourgeois" journal should show it could tolerate this attack.

Sperber maintained that the intellectual efforts of any given period always function in the interests of the ruling class. He saw modern psychotherapy as a strictly bourgeois outgrowth with its emphasis on the individualism produced by capitalist society and its complete neglect of the fact that personality and individual consciousness are socially determined, are not a product of irrational forces working themselves out in isolated individuals. Since life in the bourgeois capitalist class is traditionally regarded as a battle against competitors, neuroses become inevitable: for the goal of individualism is itself an anachronism, incapable of fulfillment. The individual can only be understood, then, as a part of the whole social process. In neglecting this, modern psychotherapy has become a mystical quest for drives, not a real social psychology. Therapy has become related to a sentimental code of ethics, not to any real understanding of the need to socialize the individual, to show him how he is a product of society, to help him understand the particular role he is playing in this transitional period. It is no wonder then, says Sperber, that the formulations of current psychotherapy, which approach the problems of mass psychology from an individualistic point of view, have failed to create any valid explanation of social behavior, have substituted in their stead shadowy theories of a collective unconscious which separate the individual from social reality.

One of the most systematic and closely reasoned revisions of Freud's formulations to accommodate the psychoanalytic neglect of social and cultural influence is that of Erich Fromm. Beginning in 1930 with his account of the function of religion, Fromm has carefully spelled out what he regards as the weaknesses and blindspots of Freudian theory and what must be done by psychoanalysis to remedy them. [22–26]

Fromm points out that for Freud man was regarded as a closed system endowed with certain drives which "were looked upon as eternal forces rooted in the biological constitution of man." [26, 11] Although Freud understood the biological–physiological conditions of drive, Fromm feels that Freud did not comprehend the extent to which drives could be modified by social factors. [23, 34] Because of the naïveté of Freud and most of his disciples concerning the actual development and functioning of social processes, Fromm believes that most of Freud's "applications of psychology to social problems were misleading constructions." [26, 9] Freudian mechanisms such as the super-ego and the ego, sadomasochistic impulses, Fromm regards not as givens of human nature but as end products resulting from particular social structures. [25, 92] He denies the universality and inevitable development of the Oedipus complex, arguing that this psychoanalytic construction is based on false sociological assumptions. The Oedipus complex can only be seen as a development in a particular type of culture. [23, 38 f.; 25, 88] He notes that there are many societies where the father is not a sexual rival of the child or an all-powerful authority. But even though the psychoanalytic supposition concerning the Oedipus complex is false, Fromm believes that this error should not be laid against psychoanalytic method as such—the essential failure of psychoanalysis was that it did not carry its methods far enough and study the interdependence of the individual in groups, classes, and cultures. [23, 38] In their emphasis on the family, their tendency to equate the family to society, psychoanalysts have failed to see that the family is only a carrier of a particular culture. Hence they have tended to identify society as a whole with the bourgeois capitalist family, and they have failed to see the enormous implications of their error.

The psychological make-up of members of any group or any social situation can, according to Fromm, only be understood if the common experiences of group members are studied, if we know how the social, political, or economic structure of a society affects the individual.

> The key problem of psychology is that of the specific kind of relatedness of the individual towards the world and not that of the satisfaction or frustration of this or that instinctual need *per se.* (26, *12*]

Particularly important for Fromm is the necessity of recognizing the objective economic conditions that dominate the particular society in which an individual lives.

> Thus the mode of life, as it is determined for the individual by the peculiarity of an economic system, becomes the primary factor in determining his whole character structure, because the imperative need for self-preservation forces him to accept the conditions under which he has to live. [26, *18*]

In one of his earlier papers [23], Fromm pays tribute to Marx and Engels for pointing out how objective conditions determine mentality. He holds that the interrelatedness of man to his social environment is a dialectical process, that society has not only a suppressing function but also a creative function.

Fromm points out that, since psychoanalysis must itself study the conditions of a society and the way they affect an individual, it cannot jump suddenly from individual to social psychology and transfer bodily to social phenomena explanations that may be satisfactory in dealing with certain individual neuroses. He severely criticizes those analysts who, reasoning by tenuous analogy, reconstruct the psychology of men by studying their ideologies in a vacuum: we cannot reconstruct men from their ideology, we must learn how and why specific ideologies arise as products of men. [22] A particularly prevalent error of psychoanalysts, Fromm notes, arises from their assumption that their own bourgeois society is "normal." They have dealt primarily with neurotics within that class and have assumed that the particular background common to these bourgeois neurotics is identical to social background in general. [23, *35 ff.*]

> Different societies or classes within a society have a specific social character, and on its basis different ideas develop and become powerful. [26, *279*]

Karen Horney's criticism of Freud and his orthodox followers closely parallels Fromm's. In her several widely read books she has clearly and ably stated her qualifications of Freudian theory. [29-31] Freud, she writes, "has assumed that the instinctual drives or object relationships that are frequent in our culture are biologically determined 'human nature' or arise out of unalterable situations (biologically given 'pregenital' states, Oedipus complex). Freud's disregard of cultural factors not only leads to false generalizations, but to a large extent blocks an understanding of the real forces which motivate our attitudes and actions. I believe that this disregard is the main reason why psychoanalysis, inasmuch as it faithfully follows the theoretical paths beaten by Freud, seems in spite of its seemingly boundless potentialities to have come into a blind alley, manifesting itself in a rank growth of abstruse theories and the use of a shadowy terminology." [29, *20 f.*] She sees Freud's blindness to cultural factors "in his inclination to regard certain environmental influences as the incidental fate of the individual instead of recognizing the whole strength of cultural influences behind them." [30, *170*] And she notes with Fromm that psychoanalysis has stemmed from the study of middle-class neurotics of our western civilization and has assumed that the trends pervading in this particular class in this society are biological factors inherent in human nature. [30, *168 f.*]

More recently Abram Kardiner, Coordinator of Psychiatry with the Social Sciences at Columbia University, has also rejected Freud's contention of a specific and variable instinctual basis behind all human nature but defends psychoanalysis as the only technique that can fruitfully study problems of personality and culture. Kardiner believes that his concept of basic personality structure—"the precipitate of the reactions of the individual to specific institutions in the order in which they affect him"—is the key to our understanding of social problems.

Freud did not regard this concept of basic personality as necessary because it was assumed to be the same in all human beings irrespective of culture. [36, *484*]

The task of the psychologist who wants to understand social problems and the relation of the individual to his society is for Kardiner that of discovering the basic personality structure formed in a given society and then tracking down the influences of this basic personality structure on the culture itself. [36, 37]

WHY PSYCHOANALYTIC FORMULATIONS MUST BE REJECTED

In evaluating psychoanalytic formulations, it should be pointed out that if we are to have a real science of psychology we must always avoid any theory or concept which either does not have or does not sometime seem capable of having a naturalistic explanation. The ultimate source of explanations for the scientist must come from his knowledge of the real world. It cannot be the product of unbridled imagination.

From his *Survey of Objective Studies of Psychoanalytic Concepts,* Sears concludes that

By the criteria of the physical sciences it [psychoanalysis] is not a *good* science. . . . The experiments and observations examined in this report stand testimony that few investigators feel free to accept Freud's statements at face value. The reason lies in the same factor that makes psychoanalysis a bad science—its method. Psychoanalysis relies upon techniques that do not admit of the repetition of observation, that have no self-evident or denotative validity, and that are tinctured to an unknown degree with the observer's own suggestions. These difficulties may not seriously interfere with therapy, but when the method is used for uncovering psychological facts that are required to have objective validity it simply fails. [52, *133*]

Sears ends his report with the statement "that other social and psychological sciences must gain as many hypotheses and intuitions as possible from psychoanalysis but that the further analysis of psychoanalytic concepts by nonpsychoanalytic techniques may be relatively fruitless so long as those concepts rest in the theoretical framework of psychoanalysis." [*143*]

Freud's original formulations have undergone and are still undergoing considerable modification and extension with the growing realization on the part of certain analysts of the impact of social realities on the individual and the close interrelationship between the individual and the immediate society around him. So psychoanalysis at the present time is in a state of flux and development. It is apparent from the tone of many of the articles and reviews appearing in its journals that the divergency of some members of the psychoanalytic family from Freud's original precepts is not calmly accepted. Debate is often acrimonious, innuendoes are frequent, and criticism of one analyst by another is not always restrained. We mention this situation here only because it seems to reflect a fundamental inability to agree on formulations which can be scientifically verified, which will stand up on their own merits as demonstrable and unequivocal, and which cannot be shaken or reinterpreted by this or that observation of a given analyst.

Simple and sovereign principles. One of the noteworthy and startling impressions left from a reading of psychoanalytic literature is the ease and glibness with which the more orthodox analysts juggle their various concepts around to explain quite diversified phenomena. By appealing to the same mechanisms, they explain such opposites as love and hate, aggression and submission, the development and function of contrasting ideologies such as Fascism and Communism, Catholicism and atheism. They never seem to be stumped in finding a cause for any variety of thought or behavior, whether on the individual or the social level. Furthermore, a great many of them (persons of Fromm's and Horney's stature excluded) seem able to explain the cause of social phenomena without having to make detailed and painstaking investigations of the phenomena they are accounting for. We saw previously, for example, how comparatively easy it was for the psychoanalyst to explain war and revolution, Quislingism and Fascism.

Sometimes, to be sure, their reasoning seems particularly tortuous but they wind up in the end with the phenomenon to be accounted for neatly placed on top of the pedestal which they have built by putting together their simple and sovereign principles. Sapir noted that the cultural anthropologist's quarrel with psychoanalysis was due to the fact that

> The psychoanalyst has confused the archaic in the conceptual or theoretical psychologic sense with the archaic in the literal chronological sense. . . . The service of cultural anthropology to psychiatry is not as mysterious or remote or clandestine as psychoanalytic mysticism would have us believe. [49, 235]

Murphy, Murphy, and Newcomb point out that

> The psychoanalyst digs into the details of infinitely complex symptom complexes (syndromes) and invariably comes up with a "cause," which, just as invariably, is only another symptom (another part of the same syndrome). Because these symptoms are parts of a syndrome they are always found to be correlated and present at the same time or in a certain sequence; they are then thought to be cause and effect. [41, 306]

Freud posited certain instincts and mechanisms he regards as universal. Without reviewing here the old controversy concerning instincts, we should point out, however, that Freud's various conceptions of instinct (that is, death and destruction and other dramatic instincts) seem particularly abstract, particularly difficult ever to find a definite locus for in the organism. And no solid contribution to our understanding of motivation seems to be served by indulging in the verbal magic of creating a whole host of needs, each endowed with motivational properties, as has been done by Murray and his followers. [42]

We have already noted that evidence from anthropology indicates that Freud's Oedipus complex, so crucial in his derivation of the "superego," can be regarded only as a product of a particular set of cultural conditions. Furthermore, various empirical studies reviewed by Sears concerned with parent preferences and other heterosexual cathexes in our own culture "cast doubt on the alleged universality of the Oedipus situation" [52, 44] and lead Sears to the summary conclusion that

> These data again argue against any universal pattern and re-emphasize the point that has proved itself time and time again in the exam-

ination of such studies as these—that the structure of the little societies in which people grow up are too detailed ever to permit of the kinds of generalizations that Freud has made concerning the role of specific members of the family. [*43*]

Freud has assumed the Oedipus relationship to exist universally, and while other investigators have found instances of it, no indications of a universal cross-sex parental preference have been discovered in either children or adults. [52, *134 f.*]

While Sears finds that infantile sexuality as such is supported by various investigations, he writes that

> There is no evidence, however, to confirm Freud's assumptions about the inter-relationship between the various erotogenic zones. Whether one zone can serve as a substitute for another is still undetermined. [52, *135*]

Sears also reports from his survey:

> There is no indication that the castration complex is common. Quite the contrary. Children whose sex information is adequate show little tendency toward fears or curious beliefs about the sexual process. It seems probable that Freud's notion about children's attitudes toward sex were based on a small sample that was far from characteristic of contemporary American children. [52, *136*]

Furthermore, in chapter 9 we saw that the ideas of masculinity and femininity are largely culturally derived and that variations in adult–youth conflicts significantly affect attitudes toward sex.

In spite of the divergence of some analysts such as Fromm and Horney, who seem to have worked out the most careful and cautious reformulations of Freud, and the great advance they have made in their formulations by taking cultural influences into account, they have still by no means sufficiently emancipated themselves from Freudian influence to arrive at motivational concepts much less abstract, or much less sovereign than Freud's.

Fromm's great contribution is his recognition of the fact that character structure within a society develops from a set of economic conditions. But he accepts a general Freudian interpretation of the dynamics of character as the only useful one. [25, *80*] And he subscribes in general to the psychoanalytic thesis that the foundation of character is determined by the sublimation of drive as a result of childhood experiences. [24, *254*]   In brief, Fromm does not seriously question Freud's basic formulations or Freudian mechanisms such as the libido, masochistic and sadistic strivings, but he does feel that these mechanisms develop as end products of particular social structures; that they cannot be regarded merely as human endowments.   Basic in Fromm's own formulation is the concept of libidinal structure, derived from instinctual energies, especially sexuality.   The particular libidinal structure of any individual can only be understood with reference to his early conditioning and the particular pattern of economic and social pressures in the society in which he lives.   The libidinal structure, then, shifts with objective conditions. [23]   Because of the push of these libidinal forces, there is in everyone a "need to avoid aloneness"—a need "not rooted in bodily processes but in the very essence of the human mode and practice of life." [26, *19*]   Fromm feels that the development of industrial capitalism and the emergence of the religious freedom of Protestantism have greatly increased the individual man's sense of aloneness and isolation. Various neurotic strivings as well as social phenomena are, then, for Fromm to be explained as attempts to escape from this feeling of loneliness which increased freedom brings.   Love and work are seen as types of spontaneous activity which make it possible for the individual to satisfy his need to avoid aloneness by uniting himself with others. [26, *260*]

In accounting for man's "tendency to grow, to develop and realize potentialities" [26, *287*] Fromm posits two abstract and universal motivational mechanisms—the striving for justice and the striving for truth.

> The striving for justice and truth is an inherent trend of human nature, although it can be repressed and perverted like the striving for freedom. [26, *288*]

Fromm recognizes that in making these assumptions he is on theoretically dangerous ground.   But he feels these drives can be accounted for.

> Every individual in childhood goes through a period which is characterized by powerlessness.   It seems to us that in this state of powerlessness traits like the sense of justice and truth develop and

become potentialities common to man as such. We arrive therefore at the fact that, although character development is shaped by the basic conditions of life and although there is no biologically fixed human nature, human nature has a dynamism of its own that constitutes an active factor in the evolution of the social process. [26, 289]

We can thoroughly agree and applaud Fromm's point that the feeling of aloneness characteristic of modern man is a by-product of the mode and practice of life. But the analysis needs to be brought up to date in terms of the complications, differentiations, and conflicts found in contemporary social life. For example, we saw in chapter 10 that sociologists have accumulated a wealth of material dealing with the marginal position, the conflicting statuses experienced by many people today. Furthermore, if such mechanisms as the "need to avoid aloneness" and the Oedipus complex can be shown to be by-products of social relationships, why should Fromm not also apply this same derivation to the strivings for "justice" and "truth"? For these, too, when found, result only from the reciprocal relationships of social life. As previously noted (pp. 334 ff.), Piaget has shown that such concepts of "morality" can and do develop spontaneously as a child begins to see its own place in a constellation of social relations.

Horney, too, in spite of her reformulations, is weighted down with her allegiance to Freud who has, she believes, "shown us the direction in which to move." [29, 61] Although highly sensitive to Freud's lack of a cultural orientation, she is so anchored to Freud's basic approach that, like Fromm, she is forced into the creation of new abstractions in order to free herself from Freud's libidinal approach. Her fundamental concept is that of "basic anxiety" which results from the conflicts, insecurities, and hostilities the individual meets in society, an anxiety generated by the individual's feeling of lonesomeness in a competitive world. On the basis of this hypothesis, she undertakes to reformulate familiar Freudian mechanisms such as masochism, narcissism, and the Oedipus complex. Anxiety she sees as the driving force behind or accompanying two "guiding principles"—safety and satisfaction— that also "rule" man. [30, 73] She only questions Freud's derivation of these concepts, not their validity.

Kardiner accepts uncritically Freud's statement of problems and attempts to find cultural derivations for the traditional Freudian mechanisms. Kardiner's own abstraction—basic personality structure—seems, however, much less precise, less consistent than Fromm's need to avoid isolation or Horney's basic anxiety. Unlike Fromm and Horney, Kardiner does little more than pay lip service to social determinants. He resorts to rather orthodox Freudian mechanisms in accounting for the basic personality structure of any society—the Alorese are what they are largely because "maternal care is sporadic, inconsistent, and undependable," whereas Plainvillers are what they are largely because maternal care is good. And once Kardiner uncovers some psychoanalytic key by perusal of ethnological data, it seems a relatively simple matter for him to account for almost any and all behavior: the quest for prestige and wealth, the genesis and function of rivalry and authority, the appeal of ideologies.

From our point of view, as we emphasized in chapter 5, a particularly dangerous abstraction is that of ego drive. Freud's own writings are rife with such phrases as "the ego strives," the "ego tries," or "the ego introjects into itself." Bychowsky writes that

> The Ego tries in vain to liberate itself from contributions which it had received from its environment a long time ago. [9, 324]

Alexander says that

> One main function of the ego is to confront the facts of inner perception with the results of sense perception. [3, 147]

Reik constantly speaks of "ego-drives." [46] We have seen in previous chapters that the ego is a genetic formation, made up in large part of social values. To reify the ego, endow it with its own drive, is to indulge in a psychological redundancy which completely obscures the real genesis, characteristics, composition of the ego, and its functional role.

Neglect of emergent qualities in personal and group interactions. A fundamental reason why psychoanalysis seems to us not to account in any realistic way for the variety and contrast of social phenomena, for the relative strength and permanency of some social developments, the weakness and transiency of others, for the rise of new norms, for social change, and the like, is due to its complete failure to recognize the real relationship between the individual and his environment, especially the fact that new social products, new social values, as well as new individual orientations, can and do emerge in the continuous process of social evolution. Social change can best be seen as a series of successive stages with each new stage derived from or heaved up by what have proved to be the limitations or contradictions of an earlier stage. Because of this failure to recognize that emergence can and does take place on the psychological and social level as well as on the physical and biological level, analysts have been forced to create their various abstractions and to account for individual and social behavior with circuitous derivations. Indeed, as we pointed out at the very beginning of this chapter, the problems of the neurotic with whom psychoanalysts are primarily concerned, as well as psychoanalytic formulations themselves, can be seen as emergents of a particular set of conditions that obtain in a particular form of society at a particular point in man's history.

Freud himself minimized this fact of the emergence of new qualities with new characteristics and explained what he termed "apparently new characteristics" as only fresh manifestations of unconscious mechanisms.

> From our point of view we need not attribute so much importance to the appearance of new characteristics. For us it would be enough to say that in a group the individual is brought under conditions which allow him to throw off the repressions of his unconscious instincts. The apparently new characteristics which he then displays are in fact the manifestations of this unconscious, in which all that is evil in the human mind is contained as a predisposition. [18, 9 f., italics ours]

In this statement Freud not only neglects the mutual dependence and the reciprocal relationship between the individual and other individuals that constitute the group; he neglects too the facts of cognition and perception which, as we saw in previous chapters, unequivocally demonstrate the relatedness of one stimulus to another, of one experience to another.

For Freud, the whole psychology of judgment is regarded essentially as a

> . . . derivation of an intellectual function from the interplay of the primary instinctual impulses. Judging has been systematically developed out of what was in the first instance introduction into the ego and expulsion from the ego carried out according to the pleasure-principle. Its polarity appears to correspond to the opposition between the two groups of instincts which we have assumed to exist. Affirmation, as being a substitute for union, belongs to Eros; while negation, the derivative of expulsion, belongs to the instincts of destruction. [20, *370*]

Although the relationship between the individual and his social environment has been explicitly recognized by analysts such as Fromm and Fenichel, their failure to take into sufficient account the characteristics of stimulus situations (relatedness, degree of structuration), their failure to recognize the full implications of the fact that well-structured situations can and do develop cognitive frames for the individual, together with their failure to take full account of the consequences that arise when old frames prove inadequate to account meaningfully for new objective conditions with the consequent high suggestibility of the individual faced with an ambiguous stimulus, all boil down to the generalization that even those reformulators of Freud who are anxious to give due place to social influences are either neglectful of or ignorant of established facts in the psychology of perception. Fenichel writes, for example,

> The statement that the production and dissemination of the ideology of a society must be understood from the actual economic conditions of this society, the "super-structure" of which is the ideology; that further they are to be understood from the fact that this "super-structure," by means of the actions of human beings, reacts back again upon the "foundation," the economic conditions modifying them— these statements are correct but general. They become more specific when we succeed in comprehending scientifically the details of the mechanisms of these transformations, and only psychoanalysis is able to help us in that. [12, *94*]

Without denying in any way the tremendous insight Freud has provided us for the understanding of unconscious motivation, it is our contention that these "more specific" and more scientific details Fenichel quite properly feels are necessary, can only be provided when the psychology of cognition, together with a realistic psychology of motivation, are brought together.

It is instructive, in this regard, to see how the psychology of perception and cognition is handled by Kardiner. It is clear from the preface of his first volume [36] that Kardiner equates psychology with psychiatry or psychoanalysis and that in his cursory review of psychological approaches and his defense of psychoanalysis later on in the book he specifically states "we are omitting the experimental psychologies." [356] On page 1 of his first book devoted to his basic orientation, he writes:

> A psychology which elects to study the cognitive and apperceptive functions of man does not make contact at any point with sociology. [36]

This statement is, at best, plausible only if we accept as "psychology" a narrow 19th century variety. Any modern elementary textbook of psychology will show that cognition and apperception cannot be thought of as distinct and isolated processes somehow insulated from affectivity and emotion or that somehow occur independent of temperament or of motivational factors, many of which are socially determined. We can refer back here to our discussion of F. C. Bartlett's impressive experiments (pp. 32 ff.) and repeat again his conclusion that

> It [the perceptual reaction] is directed by interest and by feeling, and may be dominated by certain crucial features of the objects and scenes dealt with. [6, 31]

On the first page of his book Kardiner also says:

> On the other hand, a sociology whose chief concern is to correlate the phenomena resulting from the behavior of human beings in groups does not need psychology. [36]

This would seem to mean, then, that for Kardiner the whole problem of frame formation and the effects of frame formation on perception and judgment are irrelevant. Yet Kardiner himself, in the final chapter of this book dealing with principles and techniques, is forced to include as one of the major elements of personality "perception: of the outer world, of oneself, and of oneself in relation to the outer world." [461] And he further states that

The complicated forms of attitudinized perceptions both of other individuals and of oneself are the most important for our consideration. [36, 463]

In his second volume Kardiner writes that

Direct experience involves all the coördinative functions, such as discrimination and judgment. [37, 8]

And he uses as the only source of data other than his "psycho-dynamic" approach the Rorschach technique, a technique wholly designed to study apperceptive functions. Thus Kardiner bows to perception and cognition as important psychological processes to be taken into account, employs enthusiastically a technique to study perception, but deliberately omits any examination of the rich literature on perception found in experimental psychology. It is no wonder that he fails completely to see the relevance the psychology of perception has for any valid and systematic account of the relationships that he himself has posed as the objects of investigation.

We have already shown how the first stage in the actual formation of an attitude is a perceptual stage, how an individual can and does evolve some frame of reference when repeatedly faced with a stimulus situation, how the structuredness of a stimulus situation must be regarded as a gradation where the less ambiguous the stimulus situation itself is, the more likely is it to compel the formation of a frame. On the other hand, the more ambiguous the stimulus situation itself is, the more likely is the frame to be generated by internal and internalized factors. And in addition to the gradation of structuredness in the stimulus field, the selectivity of perception is often determined by the organism's instinctual tensions and by other motivational and affective factors as was stressed in earlier chapters.

The fact that the individual's perception of new relationships between himself and the environment does cause the emergence of new, perhaps "uncharacteristic," reactions has been observed by Murphy, Murphy, and Newcomb in their review of experimental social psychology. They write:

> It is all too often forgotten that the condition of general arousal or excitement brought about by any object may not only permit new forms of experience but tap new drives, leading to intense activity in reference to the object utterly different from that prevailing the moment before. [41, *105*]

We have already discussed in some detail the outstanding studies of Piaget on the development of a constellation of reciprocal relations in which an individual locates himself psychologically. (pp. 334 *ff.*) Piaget's conclusions must be mentioned again here since they bear so pointedly on the psychoanalytic conception of the development of the "superego." As the result of painstaking investigation on hundreds of cases, Piaget showed that the first stage in the development of the child's morality was, indeed, a result of his identification with grown-ups and his acceptance of their standards as the criteria of what is right and wrong—the stage of moral realism. However—and this is the important part of the story for psychoanalysis—the child's morality does not remain on this level alone. It merges, rather, into what Piaget regards as a different stage where rules and regulations lose their reified reality and where right and wrong are judged in terms of a feeling of reciprocity that develops under the influence of group situations. From this stage there emerges still another stage where increasing maturity and further social relationships developed in Piaget's children a sense of equity. What is happening here is that the original frames derived from the parents sooner or later prove themselves inadequate for any satisfactory adjustment to the group situation. These frames are, then, at least in part, discarded in favor of new standards imposed on the individual by his relationship to others in the group.

Piaget's studies are exceedingly well documented and, within the framework of the culture in which they were made, exceedingly convincing. Norms that arise in the group situation become interiorized in the individual as *his* standards: they become part of *his* ego. These results of Piaget, together with the data from cultural anthropology which show the extreme variation of the Oedipus complex even within a single culture, indicate that the psychoanalytic concept of the universal development of a "super-ego" in human beings has no basis in fact as a special part of the ego with a special function.

It is significant that, although Piaget's studies are extremely well known and generally highly regarded by psychologists, they are very seldom referred to by psychoanalysts. Analysts are either ignorant of Piaget's work or else refuse to come to grips with its implications. Either state of affairs is inexcusable in a discipline that has scientific pretensions.

We have seen that one of the inevitable psychological emergents of an individual's participation in a group is his group consciousness, his awareness of his relationship to the group, and the modification of his own frames or attitudes by group norms (ch. 10). We have seen how the individual becomes extremely suggestible to new formulations, new orientations, new anchorages if and when he becomes aware of a wide disparity between his old frames and new situations or if he is confronted with new and unstructured situations which none of his established frames give meaning to or adequately serve as a readiness for response. Change is one of the outstanding characteristics of the world in which men live; sometimes change follows long periods of comparative stability; sometimes it is violent, sometimes relatively gradual. New inventions, new technological developments, new discoveries of nature's resources and secrets continually affect and bring into new relationships the external stimuli that constitute man's environment. Under the impact of such events and occurrences, old frames frequently prove inadequate for interpretation or adjustment: new frames take their place or modify them, new frames formed either as the result of the perception of well-structured stimulus situations or as the result of the acceptance of new norms, new orientations provided by a leader or emerging as a product of social intercourse. As we have said earlier, these new formulations either may or may not account objectively for the new situations. What happens when new formulations do not adequately account for new situations cannot be gone into here. Nor can we consider in detail now the psychological conditions that give rise to new norms. Here we are only pointing out the fact that new norms do emerge, that in critical times the role of leadership as a source of new orientations is accentuated, that the individual is by no means always unaware of changes taking place in his external world.

A typical explanation of this process of social change by an outstanding orthodox Freudian psychoanalyst, Ernest Jones, is as follows:

> The outstanding discovery of psycho-analysis in this context [evolution and creative change] has been that many—and some analysts would be inclined to say all—of the original discoveries and betterments and improvements of all kinds that previously were attributed to the action of purely creative impulses *are rather to be regarded as by-products resulting from the action of certain defensive mental mechanisms. The endeavor to escape from unconscious guilt and anxiety* leads to infinitely varied mental activities, some of which produce what may socially be called "improvements." To the idealism and self-esteem of mankind it is a chastening reflection that so much of what he is most proud of is merely *an accidental result of the flight from fear and pain,* that a bad conscience should prove to be one of the prime motors in even our loftiest strivings. [35, *203,* italics ours]

There is here a complete neglect of the fact of emergence on the social level and of demonstrable psychological principles that at least in part explain this emergence. It is no wonder then that the only advice Jones can give to speed human progress is to improve the "libidinal" basis of human nature.

As a specific example of the consequences of the failure of psychoanalysts to recognize the emergence of new products under new conditions, we might refer back to Jones's account of the appeal of revolutionary leaders during critical times. It will be remembered that leaders arise in critical situations, according to Jones, because the latent sense of guilt all human beings have is "stirred by any great misfortune or privation." [*206*] Without seeing the full implications of what it means for a human being to be "stirred by any great misfortune or privation," Jones tells us

that revolutionary leaders have homosexual tendencies which result in a paranoid defense, and as a consequence they have no
compunctions against violence (which for them is the murder of
the father).

We reach thus the conclusion that a successful revolutionary must
be more than a little mad. [35, 200]

By identifying himself with the leader, substituting the concept
of society for the image of the parent, the individual who takes
part in a revolution is explained. While it may, to be sure, be true
that certain leaders during critical times such as Hitler, Roehm,
and Goering had homosexual tendencies, it would seem to be
stretching the argument beyond the breaking point to account for
the leadership of such men as Washington, Jefferson, Lincoln,
Lenin, Stalin, or Franklin Roosevelt on similar grounds. As
J. B. S. Haldane has said:

Hitler may well be a neurotic. But it is only in particular circumstances that a great people chooses a neurotic of this kind as its leader.
[28, 15]

There seems little doubt that, if Hitler and his satellites had never
been born, under these same circumstances other leaders would
have arisen in Germany who may or may not have been free of
homosexual suspicions.

*Failure to recognize full implications of an individual's place-
ment in a culture.* We repeat again that social norms—institutional controls, symbols of authority, social values—are all first
external to the individual in any culture. *Among these norms*
are the ethical codes of society or of a group which do seem in
most cultures to be transmitted by the parents. In reviewing the
learning process in social situations, Murphy, Murphy, and Newcomb describe the situation as follows:

On the whole, most values seem to be "taken" and used by the
child because of a positive response to those whose values come within
his ken. The process by which many values are transmitted from one
generation to the next is largely a process, we believe, involving relatively little coercion, relatively little Freudian repression. It is more
of the character of the "Look, see!" pattern. The world is so full of a

number of things both lovely and hateful that, unless the child's interests are in gross conflict with the adult, the parent has relatively little trouble in enabling the child to see why one game is fun for three-year-olds and another is dangerous for three-year-olds. Even without benefit of identification, which, of course, plays its powerful part in forming values, the parent helps the child to structure the world in terms of his own values simply by pointing out the palpable and inherent goods and bads. [41, *238 f.*]

As we have mentioned, Piaget's studies unequivocally show that in the first stage of morality the child accepts as good or bad, as fair or unfair, the types of behavior so judged by his parents or by other adults who constitute his immediate social world (code of heteronomy). But there is for the individual no psychological difference either in the genesis of or the function of "moral" codes which psychoanalysts separate out as the "superego" and other norms of behavior the individual learns. The emerging developing ego is in large part composed of *all* these interiorized social values.

The important question, the question psychoanalysts have not squarely faced, is the question of *what* norms *are* interiorized by a given individual in a society. For it should be clear that by no means *all* persons in a given "society" are exposed to the *same* standards, values, or norms, except, perhaps, in extremely primitive and small societies. And, even if exposed to the same norms, individuals acquire ego-attitudes only in relation to certain reference or membership groups. As Sapir has pointed out:

> The culture so carefully described in our ethnological and sociological monographs are not, and cannot be, the truly objective entities they claim to be. No matter how accurate their individual itemization, their integrations into suggested structures are uniformly fallacious and unreal. [50, *411*]

The psychologist, then, who speaks glibly of a "culture" or "society" is speaking of an abstraction.

> The term "society" is itself a cultural construct which is employed by individuals who stand in significant relations to each other in order to help them in the interpretation of certain aspects of their behavior. The true locus of culture is in the interactions of specific individuals

and, on the subjective side, in the world of meanings which each one of these individuals may unconsciously abstract for himself from his participation in these interactions. Every individual is, then, in a very real sense, a representative of at least one sub-culture which may be abstracted from the generalized culture of the group of which he is a member. Frequently, if not typically, he is a representative of more than one sub-culture, and the degree to which the socialized behavior of any given individual can be identified with or abstracted from the typical or generalized culture of a single group varies enormously from person to person. [49, *235 f.*]

This warning of Sapir's becomes increasingly important when the psychologist is concerned with the study of individuals who live in complex societies, characterized by definite class, status, racial, or interest group relationships. If we are to understand the full force of the social environment on the psychological makeup of the individual, we must analyze *precisely* the interconnections between the individual and the social stimuli he is confronted with. And we must furthermore constantly bear in mind that the social environment is seldom, if ever, completely static, that it is, especially these days, in a process of flux and change, due to the impact of new technological developments, new discoveries, and new inventions.

When psychoanalysts use the concept of "culture" they seem to equate it either with intrapersonal (such as familial, parent–child relationships) or with broad "cultural patterns" transmitted to the child through the family. There is a general neglect of different class, status, racial, or group relationships which have their own characteristic standards or norms. As a consequence of this failure to give sufficient emphasis to an individual's identification with a certain class, status, or group, there follows the failure to recognize the important fact that individuals can and do seek to satisfy their own egos through the preservation of or the enhancement of a larger class, status, or group interest. And this implies that individuals can be and are conscious of their class, status, or group affiliation and identification, that this consciousness of oneself as a part of a larger social unit can be and is a relative matter, a consciousness of identification or belongingness that will vary in different situations and develop according to different conditions.

The relative degree to which different groups of people are conscious of their group belongingness is given little attention by psychoanalysts who, if they recognize group or class problems at all, generally assume that members of a group behave unconsciously and rather automatically as such.

In a penetrating analysis of the cultural orientations of Fromm and Horney, Green has pointed out that "no individual participates in the total cultural complex totally." [27, 534]

> Complex cultures do not lend themselves easily to the explaining of behavior in general-cultural terms. Since individuals interact within a small segment of a differentiated society and are inculcated with the specialized values of their various segments as well as with the general-cultural values, extreme caution is required in the use of such a concept as "modern man." [27, 536]

We can illustrate the use of "culture" in a relatively abstract sense with reference to the formulations of Fromm and Horney who, as we have seen, compared to the bulk of psychoanalysts, are distinguished for their attempt to put psychoanalytic theory in a cultural framework. Fromm, for example, speaks of the "social character" of a people in a society and equates this with majority characteristics. [26, 283] In discussing education as a mechanism for transmitting the social character of society, he points out that the family "may be considered to be the psychological agent of society." [287] But he does not give due emphasis to the enormously different types of family relationships found in our society and the widely differing values that may be transmitted by different families, as, for example, the values transmitted to a child in the family of a Wall Street banker contrasted to those transmitted in the family of a Pittsburgh steel worker or an Alabama Negro sharecropper. Another example of the tremendous variations overlooked within our own culture by Fromm is reflected in his statement that "all normal persons today have about the same impulse to work" [282]—surely a questionable thesis if one compares, for example, the motivation of a highly educated and competent young engineer with a career ahead of him and a young man whose education stopped after the first year of high school, who has no special skills, mediocre abilities, and who is looking for any kind of job that will enable him to make ends meet. And as Green indicates, this "impulse to work" posited by Fromm may be expected to undergo radical changes "in a period of contracting capitalism, with increasing emphasis upon consumption outlets and state-guaranteed economic security rather than upon expanding production, saving, and individual responsibility." [27, 536] Speaking of modern man's freedoms, Fromm says:

> He has become free from the external bonds that would prevent him from doing and thinking as he sees fit. He would be free to act according to his own will, if he knew what he wanted, thought, and felt. But he does not know. [26, 255]

This statement, too, appears unrealistic when one glances, for example, at newspaper accounts of industrial strife where both labor and management seem very definitely to know what they want or when one reads in the same newspaper of efforts to create legislation to prevent job discrimination for reasons of racial background.

Horney sees basic anxiety as a driving force that leads to a craving for affection and for power on the part of the individual and says that "craving for affection may be restricted to certain groups of persons, perhaps to one with which there are interests in common, such as a political or religious group." [29, 118] It seems to us that Horney has the cart before the horse, except in the cases of certain isolated individuals. The evidence we have reviewed in earlier chapters indicates that the values, standards, or norms of a group which become interiorized in the individual as his loyalty structure are not generally due to a basic anxiety underlying a craving for affection which is then simply attached to a group because of common interests, but, rather, that these loyalty structures develop, are learned because of an individual's placement in the social context due to the accident of birth, the role he has as employer or employed, the type of work he is engaged in or some other circumstances that define his social role.

We should perhaps in passing also mention the abstract use Kardiner makes of culture. The basic personality structure in any society is, he holds, derived from influences of primary institutions and is dependent on rather identical influences. For example, Kardiner says that "good maternal care is a feature of our culture." [37, 20] Deviations from this supposed common cultural feature are passed off as atypical or accidental. Although Kardiner does notice that "in studying basic personality structure in our culture, new differentiations must be made not only for sex and age, but especially for status," [38] this important confession does not force any modification of Kardiner's concept of the ego or basic personality structure. Status differences, no matter how great, are rationalized as different manifestations of the same basic personality structure:

> A king and a commoner may be on opposite sides of a certain situation with regard to subsistence or prestige. But the roles of both are merely different facets of the same ego structure . . . both are reacting from different polarities to the same ego situation. [36, 132]

That Kardiner's formulation is both inadequate and invalid is seen particularly clearly in his discussion of "Plainville," a modern community in the United States. He notes that "the heterogeneity of our culture becomes a troublesome question wherever we discover that within the same range of basic personality structure differences in character become involved with serious intra-social tensions and clashes of interest." [37, 339] But, he continues, "the heterogeneity of our culture in no way invalidates the attempt to establish the general characteristics of Western man." [339] Kardiner minimizes these troublesome questions and dismisses the problems raised through cultural diversity by creating "characterological types." [345]

Because the psychoanalytic formulations fail to take into full account the implications of social stratification they also fail, as Francis Bartlett has forcefully pointed out, to take into account the fact that individuals within our society can and do develop allegiances to social values that are themselves conflicting and contradictory and that individuals can and do become sensitive to contradictions between established social values and everyday life experiences. Bartlett illustrates his point with the following schematic example:

Imagine that toward the end of the depression an auto worker gets a job as foreman in a plant. He identifies himself with his men, works side by side with them from time to time, knows some of them socially and treats them as equals. At the same time, he has a new authority over them, must order them to do what the employer requires and can fire them if they refuse. He begins to find that the exertion of his authority in the employer's interests threatens his friendships. And his identification with the interests of his men threatens his ambition to get ahead and might cost him his job. Here is a simple case of the contradictions inherent in a middle-class position. It is an unstable situation. The foremen have not yet organized their own union, and a fraternal bond with the U.A.W. has not been established. Our foreman may in time begin to develop the feeling that the other men are not his equals, partly because he attributes his advancement to his own superiority and partly because the men, whose interests are no longer identical with his, may behave in what seems to him a most unreasonable manner. His relations to the men are impaired. While still regarding himself as one of the gang, he develops feelings of contempt and tendencies to disparage them. He still wants them to like him, but he no longer does like them, at least as formerly, as equals. His friendliness becomes more and more a cloak for exerting his authority. He thinks that a pat on the back and a smile make up for real injuries. At the same time, he becomes hesitant about exerting his authority or administering rebukes. He conceals his disparaging tendencies, his instability, and his ambition behind a façade of irreproachability and imperturbable calm. He may even refrain from reasonable and necessary criticism, only to burst out with tangential criticism which may then have an irrational quality. With the further impairment of his relations to the men and his failure to get ahead with the employer, he develops an increasing need for affection which he seeks from one woman or another.

At this point, our imaginary individual is hardly distinguishable from a neurotic personality. An analyst might well be able to ferret out his neurotic trends; his striving for power, his need for affection, his disparaging tendencies and his perfectionism. He would probably attribute these trends to a "basic anxiety." If so, is it not clear that he has substituted a convenient abstraction for a concrete analysis of the primary conflicts and the social situation underlying them? This hypothetical illustration shows how necessary it is to understand the relation between the conflicts which appear in a neurosis and the contradictions which inhere in the practical everyday life of our society. [5, *220 f.*]

That Bartlett's example is not wholly imaginary, is suggested by the findings reported on p. 144 that foremen in the United States tended to identify themselves with management in spite of earlier allegiances to the workers. Fromm has noted (particularly in his 1936 study of authority and the family [25]) that, the greater the contradictions of society become, the less chance will there be for an individual to develop a strong and well-integrated ego. But for Fromm it is the inherent human striving for justice and truth that resolves these contradictions and discrepancies arising from conflicts between objective conditions and old norms. He does not recognize that sooner or later new norms arise and are accepted by the individual as an apparent resolution of the contradiction or conflict.

Neglect of situational determination. Our last two criticisms of psychoanalysis—its failure to recognize that new standards, new codes of behavior, or new norms can and do emerge in certain social situations and its failure to see the full implications of social stratification and the often contradictory and conflicting role the individual is in because of this stratification—add up to the more general criticism that psychoanalytic concepts are unrealistic, inadequate, and invalid, partly because of their neglect of the effect which external situations have on the individual and on the precise relationships between the individual and his external social world. In pointing out the dangers of the analogy of the unconscious as a storehouse, Koffka stresses the fact that whatever the contents of the unconscious may be that are functioning at the moment, these are constantly being transformed, put together in new patterns, according to the situation presented:

> Things do not simply fall into those places into which they are being thrown, they arrange themselves in coming and during their time of storage according to the many ways in which they belong together. And they do more; they influence each other, form groups of various sizes and kinds, *always trying to meet the exigencies of the moment.* [38, 66, italics ours]

While this criticism is especially true of orthodox psychoanalysts, it still holds for those who have tried to reformulate orthodox concepts with reference to cultural variables. In terms of therapy this means that the way to "solve" social problems and the personal problems of the neurotic is to change those external conditions that give rise to contradictory values or that create wide discrepancies between actual experience and established norms. Haldane has suggested that this would not be a much more staggering task than that of psychoanalyzing everybody, for, he calculates, in England alone 50,000 psychoanalysts would be necessary to keep even the people in that small country relatively free from neuroses. [28, 15] It might be noted in passing that the efforts of responsible experts to prevent wars, depressions, and other major social catastrophes all lie, one way or the other, in the direction of removing what they believe are the conditions that give rise to situations which cause these catastrophes. On the personal side, it is obvious that a neurosis due to sexual maladjustment is not nearly so likely to arise in the case of a pretty girl who attracts men as in the case of a homely girl whom men avoid; that a young man who is economically secure enough either to marry or to have girl friends is not nearly so likely to get tangled up with problems of sex as is a young man similarly motivated biologically but who cannot afford the normal sexual outlets of our society. Wortis [55] has pointed out that many modern women may suffer from the conflict between their desire for business or professional success and their interest in conforming to orthodox patterns of femininity.[3]

SUMMARY

Psychoanalysis at the present time has a tremendous vogue. This is due to the fact that its method is dramatic and alluring as well as to the fact that psychoanalysts do have the courage to tackle those personal problems and to explain those social phenomena

[3] One does not have to imagine instances of individuals who are caught in the net of circumstances that constitute their own relationships to their social world. For example, Professor Edwin G. Boring of Harvard University has written an account of his own psychoanalysis, of the personal dilemma he faced and of the emotional entanglements he hoped his psychoanalysis would resolve. [8]

brought about in our present age of rapid social change. If psychoanalysis were concerned only with individual therapy, we would not need to consider it in social psychology. But psychoanalysts do deal with problems that fall within the social psychologist's domain, and psychoanalysis must, therefore, be closely examined.

For the social psychologist, Freud's great contribution was that he saw clearly that social demands of one's surroundings, on the one hand, and instinctual impulses, on the other, created conflicts in the individual and that no sharp distinction could therefore be made between individual and social psychology. On the basis of Freud's theories, he and his followers have attempted to account for a variety of social phenomena—groups are held together by their libidinal constitutions, by the substitution of a common object for ego-ideal; adjustment is viewed as the incorporation of parental images into the mental apparatus; war is viewed as an infantile regression; revolution is seen as an outlet for an inherent sense of guilt, revolutionary leadership being motivated by a paranoid mechanism which is a defense against homosexual tendencies; Fascism is accounted for as the unconscious indulgence of frustrated persons, largely of the lower middle class, who substitute a leader for the parental symbol to compensate for the weakness of their own infantilism; anti-Semitism is a projection of id impulses, and so on.

Freud's own formulation of the ego developing out of the unorganized id and of the superego as a precipitate of an inevitable Oedipus complex has been modified by later analysts who point out that Freud failed to recognize the facts of cultural variations, that the Oedipus complex, for example, is not universal but develops only under a particular set of cultural conditions as Malinowski demonstrated. They hold that Freud posited as instinctually closed systems certain psychological mechanisms that can be more accurately conceived as cultural products derived from a restricted middle class capitalist economy.

Although certain of these analysts, such as Fromm and Horney, have made considerable advance over their more orthodox colleagues in recognizing the general facts of social determination, they have yet by no means emancipated themselves from Freudian concepts which are for them still the basis of explanation even though their genesis in the individual is viewed as culturally derived. Hence criticisms of psychoanalysis as a scientifically valid and adequate formulation hold for them as well.

Scientific procedure demands that concepts must ultimately be capable of naturalistic explanation, that the validity of theories must be demonstrable, and that the rule of scientific parsimony is violated when a whole host of concepts is created without some basis in fact. On these grounds, psychoanalysis does not meet the test of scientific method. This is reflected in the frequently bitter and prolonged disputes that rage among psychoanalysts themselves, disputes which clear-cut verifiable empirical evidence should be able to settle.

Specifically, psychoanalysis is open to three major criticisms from the point of view of systematic social psychology. First, it employs simple, sovereign, and abstract explanatory principles of motivation which enable it to account for the most diversified and contrasting phenomena merely by juggling its concepts around. Freud has his universal Oedipus complex and superego, his assumptions concerning the interrelationships of erotogenic zones, in addition to his abstract instincts; Fromm posits the need to avoid aloneness derived from the libidinal structure and is also forced to assume a universal striving for justice and truth; Horney posits a basic anxiety which lies behind the guiding principles of safety and satisfaction; many analysts speak of ego-drives as self-propelled entities.

In the second place, psychoanalysts fail to take into account the fact that new psychological products such as new ego-attitudes can and do emerge under new conditions or that frames are inevitably developed after repeated exposure to stimulus situations. Psychoanalysis completely neglects, in this regard, demonstrable facts from the psychology of perception, as well as demonstrable facts from genetic psychology, such as Piaget's findings that moral codes can and do arise spontaneously in children's social groups. There is a continuous dialectical relationship not precisely seen by psychoanalysts between the individual and his social environment, with old orientations constantly giving way to new and apparently more adequate ones, with these in turn proving unsatisfactory to meet changes brought about by events, technological developments, and the like, which affect the structure of the social environment. The social environment, as well as the individual's adjustment to it, must both be regarded as processes where changes are continually taking place, where new norms are arising on the stimulus side, new frames are emerging on the subjective side.

Finally, psychoanalysts—when they do not neglect the role of culture altogether—fail to recognize the full implications of an individual's placement in a culture, fail to see the consequences of social stratification, and thus use the word "culture" in an obscure and functionless way. A characteristic of most western societies is its stratification according to class, status, racial background, or some other group interest. It is therefore quite misleading to assume that all persons in a culture are exposed to or acquire the same standards, values, or norms. Furthermore, since the values or norms of different groups or classes within the society are frequently in conflict with each other, and since the norms of any one group by no means always conform to objective conditions, the values or norms an individual interiorizes and that become so important a part of his ego, create within him contradictory orientations (frames) which can and do give rise to personal dilemmas and maladjustments or which seem unsatisfactory to him in accounting for his own experience.

In brief, psychoanalysis by appealing to simple and sovereign principles and by failing to see the precise way in which the individual is related to and affected by his external situation fails to account realistically for man's social behavior.

REFERENCES

1. ADLER, A., *The Practice and Theory of Individual Psychology,* trans. by P. Radin, New York: Harcourt, Brace, 1925.
2. —— *Problems of Neurosis* (P. Mairet, ed.), New York: Cosmopolitan, copyright 1930.
3. ALEXANDER, F., Development of the ego-psychology, in *Psycho-analysis Today: Its Scope and Function* (S. Lorand, ed.), New York: International Universities Press, copyright 1944.
4. —— *Our Age of Unreason,* Philadelphia: Lippincott, copyright 1942.
5. BARTLETT, F., Recent trends in psycho-analysis, *Science & Society,* 1945, **9,** 214–31.

6. BARTLETT, F. C., *Remembering: A Study in Experimental and Social Psychology*, Cambridge (England): Univ. Press, copyright 1932.
7. BOEHM, F., The history of the Oedipus complex, *Intern. J. Psycho-analysis*, 1931, **12**, 431–51.
8. BORING, E. G., Was this analysis a success?, *J. Abnorm. & Soc. Psychol.*, 1940, **35**, 3–16.
9. BYCHOWSKI, G., On relations between the ego and the super-ego, *Psychoanalytic Rev.*, 1943, **30**, 313–24.
10. FENICHEL, O., Frühe Entwicklungstadien der Ichs, *Imago*, 1937, **23**, 243–69.
11. —— Ego-disturbances and their treatment, *Intern. J. Psycho-analysis*, 1938, **19**, 416–38.
12. —— The drive to amass wealth, *Psychoanalytic Quart.*, 1938, **7**, 69–95.
13. —— Über Trophäe und Triumph, *Intern. Z. Psychoanalysis, Imago*, 1939, **24**, 258–80.
14. FRENKEL-BRUNSWIK, E., and R. N. SANFORD, Some personality factors in anti-semitism, *J. Psychol.*, 1945, **20**, 271–91.
15. FREUD, A., *The Ego and Mechanisms of Defence*, London: Hogarth, 1937.
16. FREUD, S., Formulations regarding the two principles in mental functioning (1911), *Collected Papers*, vol. **4**, 1925.
17. —— Instincts and their vicissitudes (1915), *Collected Papers*, vol. **4**, 1925.
18. —— *Group Psychology and the Analysis of the Ego*, London: Intern. Psycho-analytical Press, 1922.
19. —— *Beyond the Pleasure Principle*, London: Intern. Psycho-analytical Press, 1922.
20. —— Negation, *Intern. J. Psycho-analysis*, 1925, **6**, 367–71.
21. —— *The Ego and the Id*, London: Hogarth, copyright 1927.
22. FROMM, E., Die Entwicklung des Chrustusdogmas: eine psychoanalysische Studie zur sozialpsychologischen Funktion der Religion, *Imago*, 1930, **16**, 305–73.
23. —— Über Methode und Aufgabe einer analytischen Sozialpsychologie, *Z. Sozialforschung*, 1932, **1**, 28–54.
24. —— Die psychoanalytische Charakterologie und ihre Bedeutung für die Sozialpsychologie, *Z. Sozialforschung*, 1932, **1**, 253–77.
25. —— Theoretische Entwürfe über Autorität und Familie: Sozialpsychologischer Teil, in *Studien über Autorität und Familie* (M. Horkheimer, ed.), Paris: Alcan, 1936, 77–135.
26. —— *Escape from Freedom*, New York: Rinehart, copyright 1941, reprinted by permission of the publishers.
27. GREEN, A. W., Sociological analysis of Horney and Fromm, *Am. J. Sociol.*, 1946, **51**, 533–40.
28. HALDANE, J. B. S., Psychology, a Marxist Survey, *Dialectics*, 1938 (?), **7**, 1–15.
29. HORNEY, K., *The Neurotic Personality of Our Time*, New York: Norton, 1937.
30. —— *New Ways in Psychoanalysis*, New York: Norton, 1939.
31. —— *Our Inner Conflicts*, New York: Norton, 1945.
32. JONES, E., Mother-right and the sexual ignorance of savages, *Intern. J. Psycho-analysis*, 1925, **6**, 109–30.
33. —— The origin and structure of the super-ego, *Intern. J. Psycho-analysis*, 1926, **7**, 303–11.
34. —— The psychology of Quislingism, *Intern. J. Psycho-analysis*, 1941, **22**, 1–6.

35. JONES, E., Evolution and Revolution, *Intern. J. Psycho-analysis*, 1941, **22**, 193–208.

36. KARDINER, A., *The Individual and His Society*, New York: Columbia Univ., copyright 1939.

37. —— *The Psychological Frontiers of Society*, New York: Columbia Univ., copyright 1945.

38. KOFFKA, K., On the structure of the unconscious, in *The Unconscious: A Symposium* (E. S. Dummer, ed.), New York: Knopf, copyright 1927, 43–68.

39. LOEBLOWITZ-LENNARD, H., A psychoanalytic contribution to the problem of anti-semitism, *Psychometric Rev.*, 1945, **32**, 359–61.

40. MALINOWSKI, B., *Sex and Repression in Savage Society*, New York: Harcourt, Brace, 1927.

41. MURPHY, G., L. B. MURPHY, and T. NEWCOMB, *Experimental Social Psychology*, New York: Harper, copyright 1937.

42. MURRAY, H. A., *et al.*, *Explorations in Personality*, New York: Oxford, 1938.

43. REICH, W., The characterological mastery of the Oedipus complex, *Intern. J. Psycho-analysis*, 1931, **12**, 452–67.

44. —— *Massenpsychologie des Faschismus: Zur Sexualoekonomie der politischen Reaction und zur proletarischen Sexualpolitik*, Copenhagen, 1933.

45. REIK, T., *A Psychologist Looks at Love*, New York: Farrar & Rinehart, 1944.

46. —— *Psychology of Sex Relations*, New York: Farrar & Rinehart, 1945.

47. RÓHEIM, G., The psychoanalytic interpretation of culture, *Intern. J. Psycho-analysis*, 1941, **22**, 147–69.

48. SAPIR, E., The unconscious patterning of behavior in society, in *The Unconscious: A Symposium* (E. S. Dummer, ed.), New York: Knopf, 1927, 114–42.

49. —— Cultural anthropology and psychiatry, *J. Abnorm. & Soc. Psychol.*, 1932, **27**, 229–42.

50. —— The emergence of the concept of personality in a study of cultures, *J. Soc. Psychol.*, 1934, **5**, 408–15.

51. SCHUMAN, F. L., *The Nazi Dictatorship*, New York: Knopf, 1936, 2d ed.

52. SEARS, R. R., *Survey of Objective Studies of Psychoanalytic Concepts*, New York: Soc. Science Research Council, 1943.

53. SPERBER, M., Schulen und Sekten: sozioanalytische Bemerkungen zur Situation der Pathopsychologie, *Zentbl. f. Psychotherap.*, 1932, **5**, 579–93.

54. WAELDER, R., *Psychological Aspects of War and Peace*, Geneva Research Centre, Geneva Studies, 1939.

55. WORTIS, J., Freudianism and the psychoanalytic tradition, *Am. J. Psychiatry*, 1945, **101**, 814–20.

NAME INDEX

(Italicized numbers are reference pages)

SUBJECT INDEX

516

DUE DATE

~~JUL 01 2001~~			
DEC 2003			
			Printed in USA